AF292338

An Illustrated History of Snapshot Photography

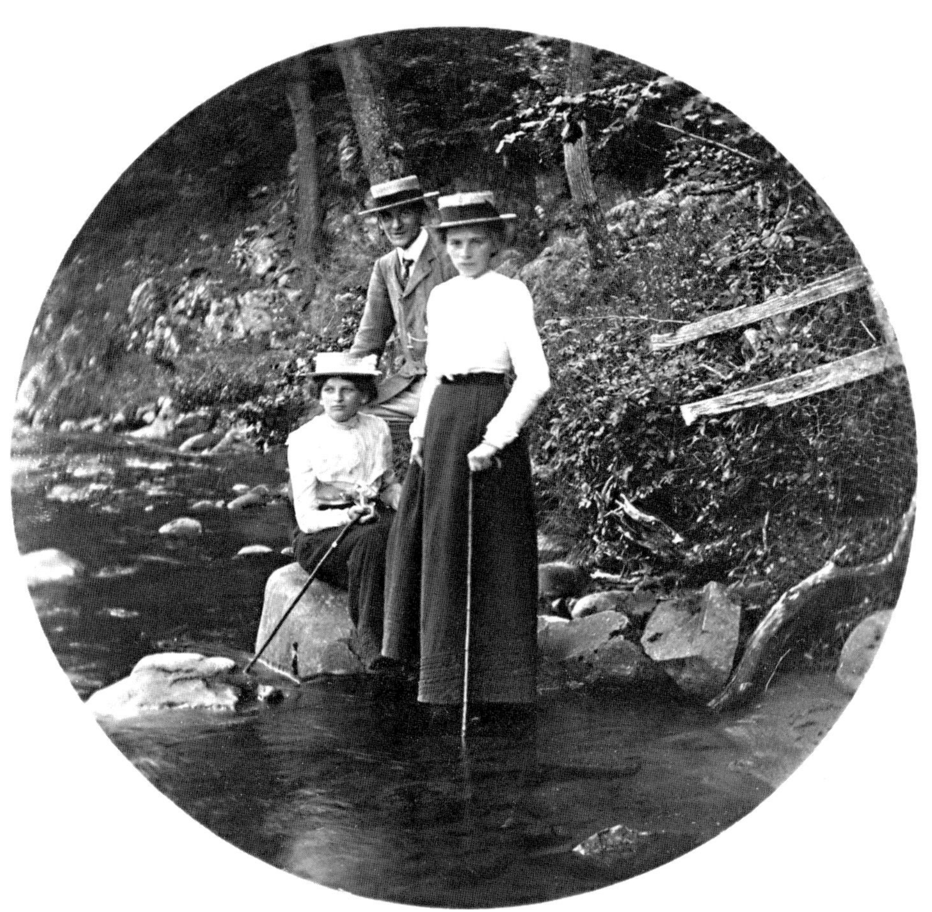

A circular snapshot from around 1889, taken with a No.2 Kodak camera.

An Illustrated History of Snapshot Photography

From a Victorian Craze
to the Digital Age

John Wade

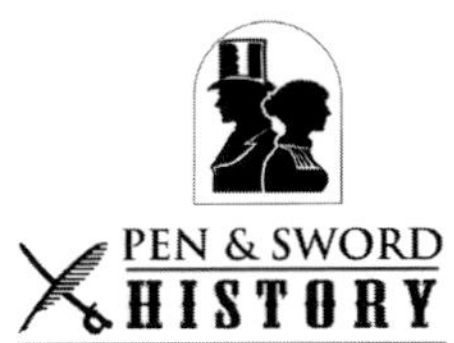

First published in Great Britain in 2024 by
Pen & Sword History
An imprint of Pen & Sword Books Limited
Yorkshire – Philadelphia

ISBN 978 1 39907 915 0

A CIP catalogue record for this book is
available from the British Library

Typeset by Mac Style
Printed in the UK by CPI Group (UK) Ltd, Croydon, CR0 4YY.

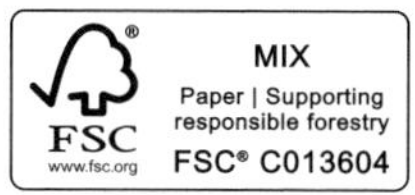

Pen & Sword Books Limited incorporates the imprints of After
the Battle, Atlas, Archaeology, Aviation, Discovery, Family History,
Fiction, History, Maritime, Military, Military Classics, Politics,
Select, Transport, True Crime, Air World, Frontline Publishing, Leo
Cooper, Remember When, Seaforth Publishing, The Praetorian Press,
Wharncliffe Local History, Wharncliffe Transport, Wharncliffe True
Crime and White Owl.

For a complete list of Pen & Sword titles please contact

PEN & SWORD BOOKS LIMITED
47 Church Street, Barnsley, South Yorkshire, S70 2AS, England
E-mail: enquiries@pen-and-sword.co.uk
Website: www.pen-and-sword.co.uk
or
PEN AND SWORD BOOKS
1950 Lawrence Rd, Havertown, PA 19083, USA
E-mail: uspen-and-sword@casematepublishers.com
Website: www.penandswordbooks.com

A good snapshot stops a moment from running away.

(American short story writer Eudora Alice Welty)

I am a passionate lover of the snapshot, because of all photographic images it comes closest to the truth.

(Austrian-born photographer Lisette Model)

You press the button, we do the rest.

(Advertising slogan devised by Kodak founder George Eastman)

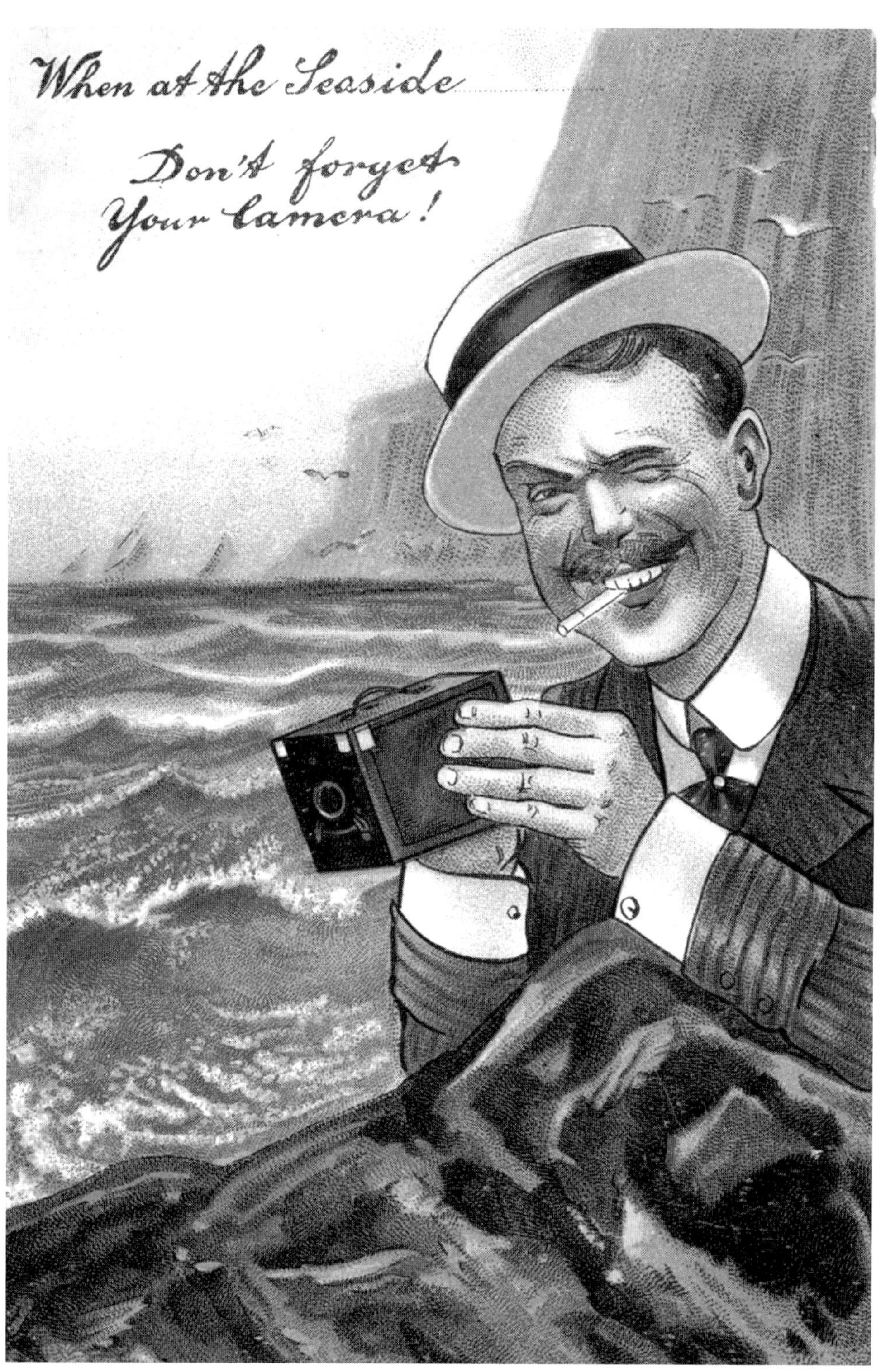

Snapshots were often associated with box cameras, and box cameras were invariably the camera of choice for holiday pictures.

Contents

Introduction

Until around the end of the nineteenth century, the word 'snapshot' had nothing to do with photography. It referred to a gunshot, fired quickly, without seriously aiming, at a fast-moving target. Then a new type of camera arrived on the market. Until then cameras had been big, heavy instruments

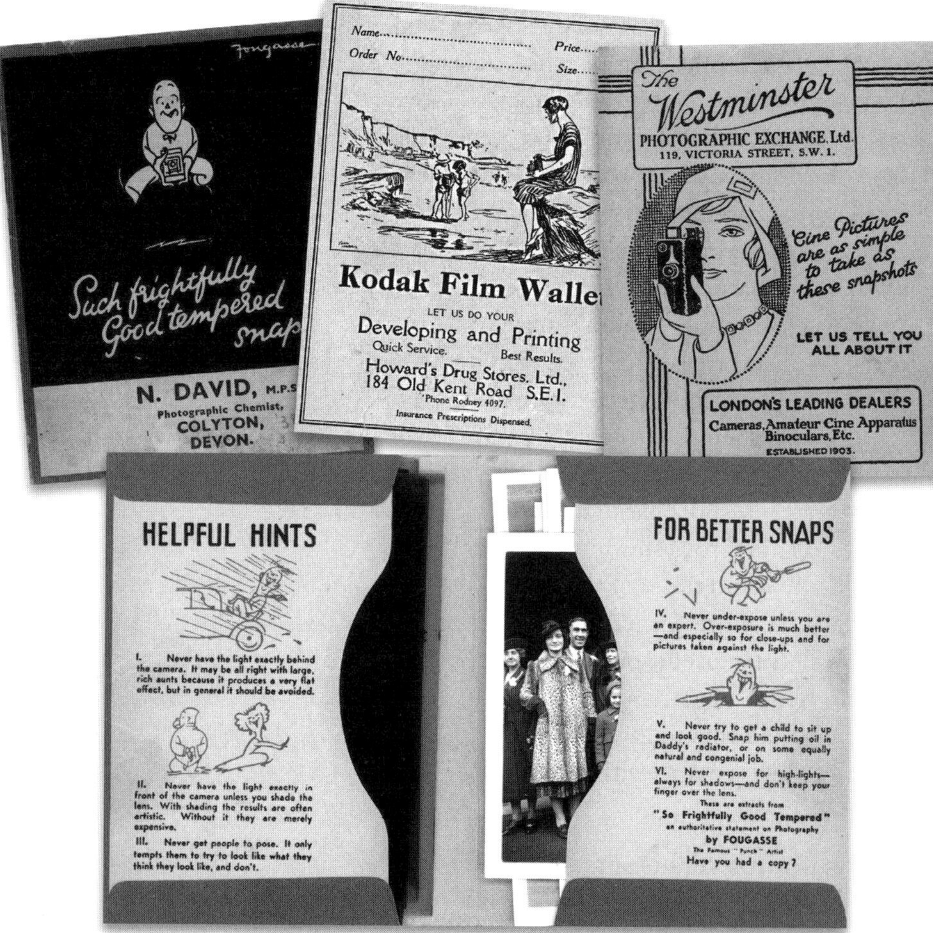

Film envelopes, in which snapshots were returned to photographers, were often decorated with helpful tips for taking better pictures, along with advertisements for the camera shop or chemist that handled the processing.

anchored to tripods, needing time and effort to set up and take a picture. Most photographers also performed the necessary developing and printing processes that required a darkroom. It meant that photographers needed to be half artist and half chemist. By sharp contrast, this new kind of camera was small and light. It could be taken anywhere and, within reason, used to shoot almost anything at a moment's notice without the need to learn a lot of frightening operating procedures. Better still, the users could leave the developing and printing to their local camera shop or, more often, chemist, where they dropped off their films and, within a few days, received their pictures back in cardboard wallets specially designed for the purpose. The inevitable word that became associated with this new type of photography was 'snapshot'.

The newfound freedom to take pictures of anything anywhere, however, was not always popular with the general public. In the early days of snapshot photography, postcards, which mostly used artists' drawings rather than photographs, often depicted snapshot photographers exercising their novel ability to use a small camera in places they couldn't, and possibly shouldn't, have done before, often as mischievous voyeurs. Favourite postcard subjects included the snapshot photographer catching people unawares, such as courting couples, or shy ladies in swimsuits emerging from bathing huts or perhaps being surprised by a sudden gust of wind that revealed more than a lady meant to show to passers-by. Even whole gangs of snapshot photographers were depicted, hiding in or leaping out from bushes and trees with their cameras at the ready to annoy others.

That aside, snapshot photography became an important part of daily life, with the snapshots themselves often going on to become equally important aspects of social history. Whether stored carefully in albums, or merely tucked away in drawers or in shoeboxes under beds and on top of wardrobes, they became destined, as numerous shutters were clicked, to tell future generations so much about the lives and times of the people both behind and in front of the cameras in a way that more formal or artistic professional photographs never could. In fact, one very useful piece of advice, printed on the inside of a cardboard wallet in which negatives and prints were returned to the photographer after processing, had this to say: 'Never get people to pose. It only tempts them to try to look like what they think they look like, and don't.'

Artistic photos versus snapshots

Imagine you are looking at a picture from a top photographer of the past – Ansel Adams maybe. He was an American landscape photographer and environmentalist renowned for producing strikingly beautiful images of the American West, in particular in and around Yosemite National Park in California.

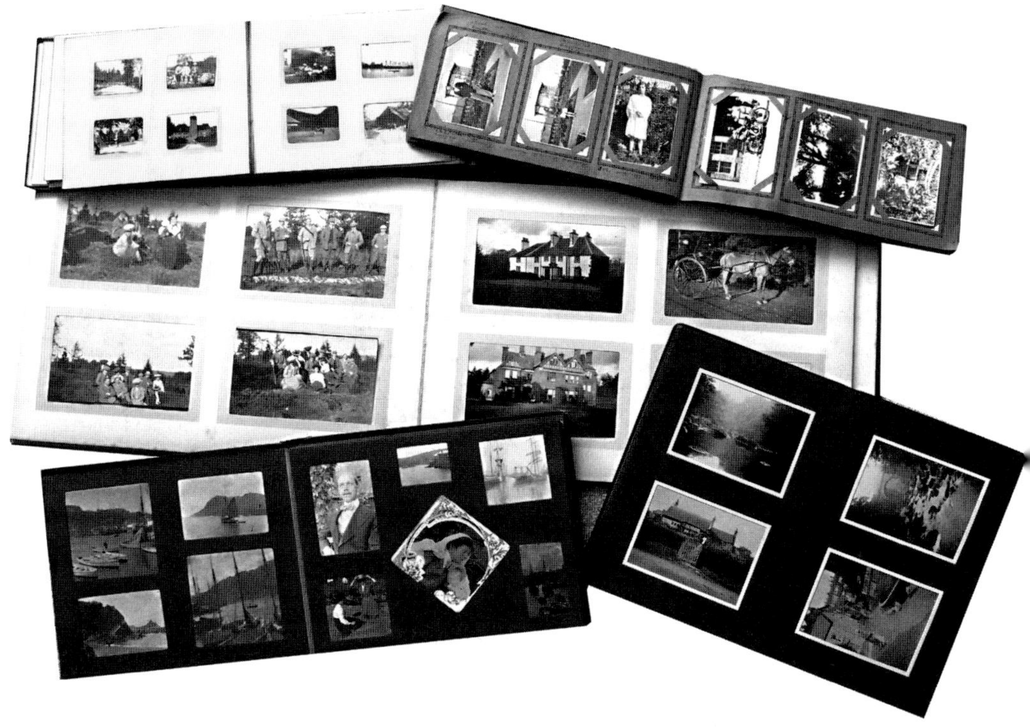

Old snapshot albums can today provide a gateway to fascinating aspects of the past.

Let's say it's his picture of Half Dome, taken in the winter of 1938 at Yosemite. The composition, light and exposure are all superb. There's no mistaking that it's a wonderful picture. But what does it tell you about the year 1938? Answer: nothing. Now look at a snapshot from the same year. It might be slightly blurred, too dark or too light, badly composed and maybe with the camera held crookedly. Nevertheless, it could help you learn what people of that time looked like, how they dressed, where they took their holidays, how they lived, the cars or other means of transport they used… and so much more. The same is true if you look at a professionally shot studio portrait of a person, and then compare it with a snapshot of another person. The professional picture might be technically perfect but seem stilted and sterile today. The snapshot will have a much more emotive sense of time and place. It's one of the many reasons why snapshots of the past are still relevant and important.

The cameras and the photographers

Snapshot cameras, by their very essence, had to be simple to use by almost anyone who had never before picked up a camera. Ideally, they needed only

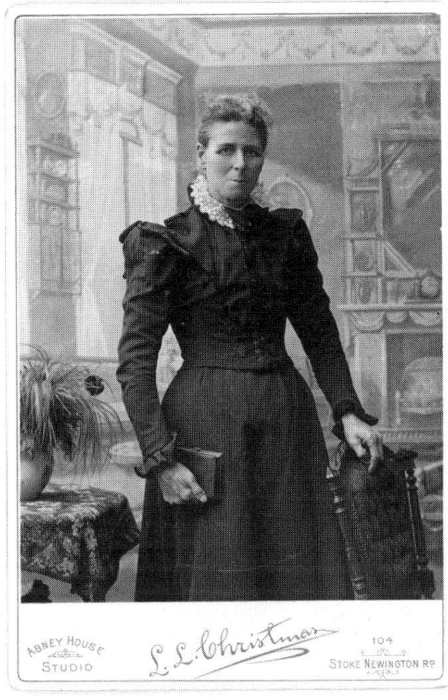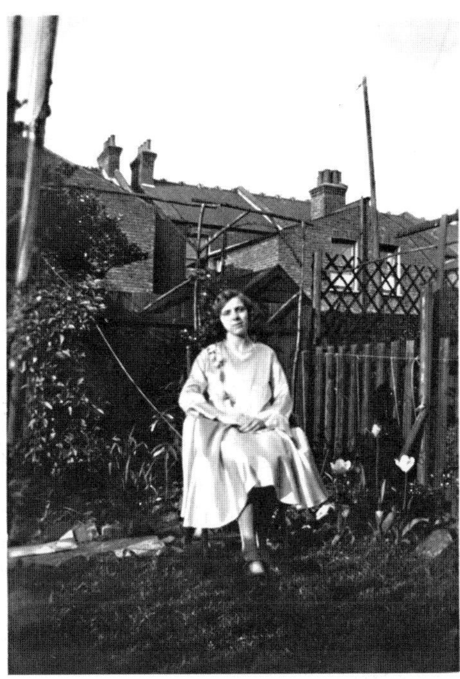

A studio portrait compared to a snapshot: the formal studio picture (left), taken *c*.1900, is technically perfect but sterile; the snapshot, taken in 1931, is far more indicative of time and place.

to be pointed in the direction of a suitable subject that could be lined up in a viewfinder before a button, or small lever, was pressed to take the picture. The only other action required was for the user to wind the film to the following position ready to make the next exposure.

Not every snapshot was taken by an inexperienced photographer, though. Professional photographers took them too. The cameras they used would have been more sophisticated and complicated than the average snapshot camera, the quality of their pictures might have been superior, but when the subjects they photographed – ordinary people either singly or in groups, for example – fell more into the realms of social history than creative masterpieces, then what they had actually produced was also a snapshot.

That said, the vast majority of snapshots were taken using simple-to-use cameras for which manufacturers found a ready market from the very earliest days of photography right up until the present digital age. The fact that snapshot cameras have proliferated in so many different types, colours, shapes and sizes is testimony to how many were bought and just how many snapshots have been taken over the years.

Identifying people and places

When happening upon old snapshots it can be fascinating trying to identify the people in them, the places where, and the years when, the pictures were taken. An old photo album that has been in the family for years can provide a wealth of possibilities, especially if the album compiler has annotated the pictures with notes about the names of the people and the locations where they were photographed. Without such notes, it comes down to detective work. Unless you're looking at your own family album, or you know someone who knows someone who knows the people in the pictures, it's all but impossible to identify who they are. The location and approximate year when the picture was taken can be a little easier.

Looking at fashions and the way people are dressed can help put an approximate year to a snapshot. Men's fashions aren't easy to pinpoint, since they mostly comprise jackets, trousers and often waistcoats, albeit in slightly different styles over the years. What is more telling is the places they choose to wear them. At the turn of the twentieth century it was not at all uncommon to see men relaxing on a beach, wearing three-piece suits, tightly tied ties and caps. Women's fashions, especially their hats, are easier to assign to specific eras. A quick search on the internet will turn up a number of illustrated websites that show fashion styles down the ages. Find one that shows women's hats, then compare the illustrations with what women are wearing in a snapshot or two, and it can provide a fairly good indication of when the picture was taken.

Places can be easier to identify than might at first be supposed, thanks to Google Images on the internet. Call this up and the first page looks like any other Google

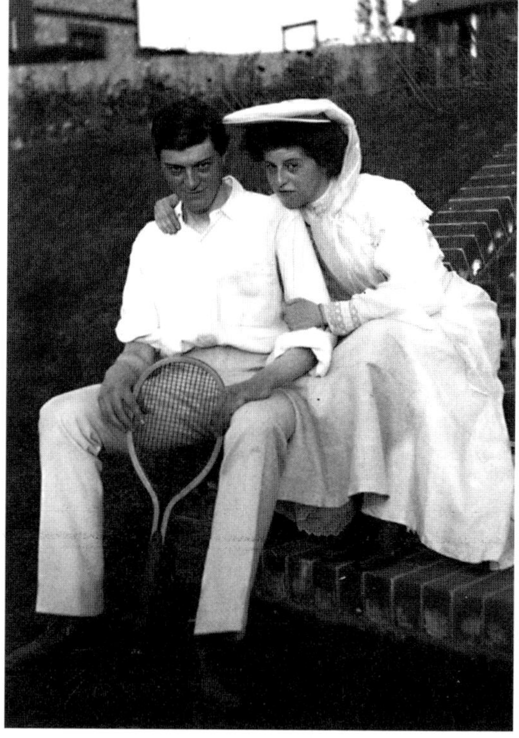

The man's fashion in this snapshot makes it almost impossible to date. The dress and hat worn by the woman, however, puts the couple straight into the Edwardian age. The picture was, in fact, taken in 1905.

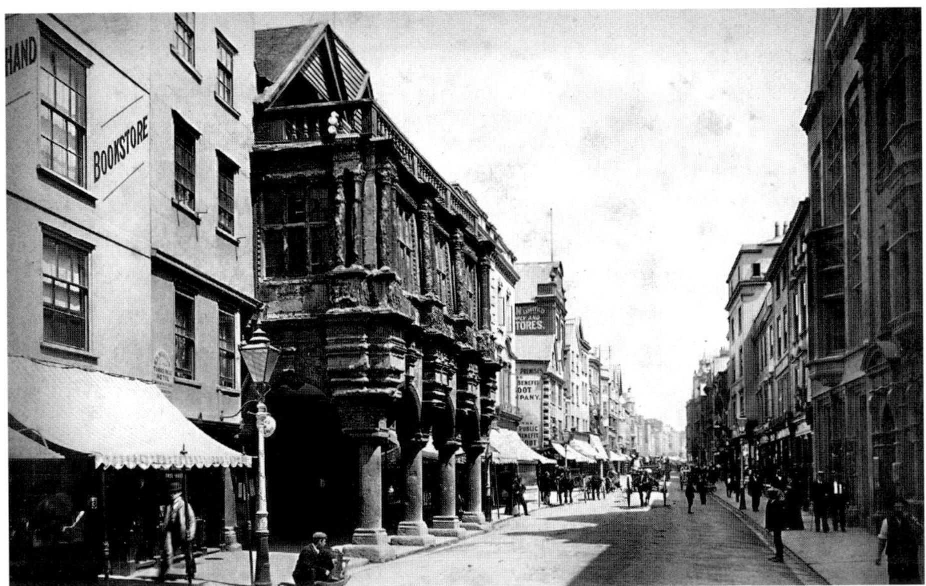

A snapshot of what would have been an ordinary and fairly unremarkable street scene more than 100 years ago can today become fascinating, especially if a way can be found to identify the location and when it was taken. Dropping a scan of this originally unknown town into Google Images identified the location as Exeter High Street, and the big building on the left as the Guildhall. But the Google picture showed trams running along the street, whereas this picture shows no sign of tramlines. A bit more Google research revealed that the first tram ran at this spot in 1905. Just discernible in the distance is a building with a sign on its wall reading *The Public Benefit Boot Company*. Google again reported that this company had branches all over the UK, but the Exeter High Street one opened in 1897. So the picture has now been identified as having been taken close to the Guildhall in Exeter High Street between 1897 and 1905.

home page, but with one exception. In the dialogue box, usually the place for the insertion of keywords for searches, there is a small camera icon. Make a scan of a snapshot then drag it onto this dialogue box and Google will search the internet for similar images, any of which might be the very location that needs to be identified. If street scenes are being investigated, an examination of the shop names and another Google search might turn up when that particular shop or branch opened and closed. Put all of this together and it's not impossible to pinpoint the location of a snapshot to within only a few years of when it was taken.

A few technicalities

It is anticipated that this book will be read by two different types of reader: camera collectors, who want to learn something of the untold history of snapshot cameras; and a general readership, interested more in the social history aspect of snapshot photography. The former group will already have a technical knowledge of how a camera operates; the latter needs to be aware of a few basics to better understand the workings of some of the cameras described throughout the book, and how snapshot cameras were capable of good results with so little control over their inner workings. If you fall into this second group, here goes…

In its most basic form a camera only really needs three controls: for adjusting focus, apertures and shutter speeds. Looking at a subject from the near foreground to the far distance, the focus adjusts the area of the subject that will be rendered sharpest, with other aspects in front and behind of that area thrown out of focus. Shutter speeds, measured in fractions of a second, control the amount of time that light is allowed through the lens and onto the film. In this way, they help the photographer to record movement. Something moving fast in front of the camera needs a fast shutter speed to capture the movement so that it remains sharply defined. If the shutter speed is too slow for the speed

of the movement, then a fast-moving subject will appear as a blur. Apertures, often in the shapes of adjustable irises or sometimes little more than holes in a strip of metal, control the amount of light that is allowed through the lens. Apertures also affect what is known as depth of field. This is the amount of the subject that remains sharp in front of and behind the spot where the lens is actually focused. Small apertures give a deep depth of field; larger apertures mean a more shallow depth of field.

Correct exposure, which means orchestrating the appropriate amount of light to fall onto the film depending on whether the subject is brightly lit or otherwise, is attained by juggling the shutter speeds and apertures. So a fast-moving subject dictates a fast shutter speed, which in turn means coupling it with a wide aperture.

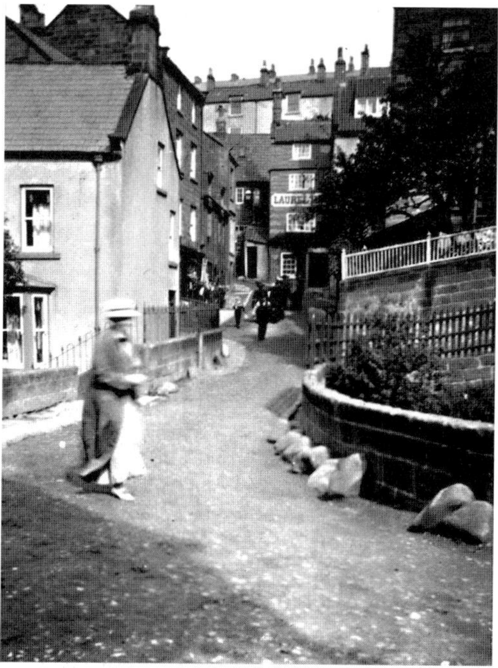

This snapshot, taken at Robin Hood's Bay on the North Yorkshire coast around the 1920s, shows one of a snapshot camera's drawbacks for the unsuspecting and inexperienced photographer. The inadequately slow shutter speed fixed by the camera means that, although most of the scene is sharp enough, the movement of the woman, as she walked left to right across the picture while it was being taken, renders her slightly blurred.

A subject that demands a deep depth of field requires a small aperture, which then dictates use of a slower shutter speed. To the uninitiated it might all sound very complicated. So how did a snapshot camera, long before the days when exposure and focus were automated, combine all these aspects into one single press of a button or lever?

First, the point at which the lens was focused was set at what is known as the hyperfocal distance. This meant that when the lens was set at a small aperture, then everything would be in focus from around 6–10ft from the camera all the way to the far distance, or infinity in photographic terms. That means the snapshot camera had to have a specific but fixed small aperture, which of course meant it also had to have a slow-to-average fixed shutter speed. When light conditions were right, these factors added up to giving an inexperienced photographer the opportunity to shoot an acceptably sharp, near-enough correctly exposed picture. All of which meant that snapshot cameras of the past were ideally used in bright sunlight, preferably with the light coming from behind the photographer to illuminate the subject in front of the camera to its best.

That's the way it was for the simplest of snapshot cameras. But side by side with these came slightly more sophisticated models that gave even the most inexperienced photographer the opportunity to play around with the controls a little. Lenses could be focused, not by distance, but by pictograms that indicated the kind of subject being photographed. These usually comprised four set distances indicated by simple diagrams of a head and shoulders portrait, a group of two people, a larger group of four or more people and mountains for the aspiring landscape photographer. Similarly, apertures might be changed according to more pictograms showing bright sunlight, obscured sun or cloud. A small range of shutter speeds might be summed up by the words 'fast', 'medium' and 'slow'.

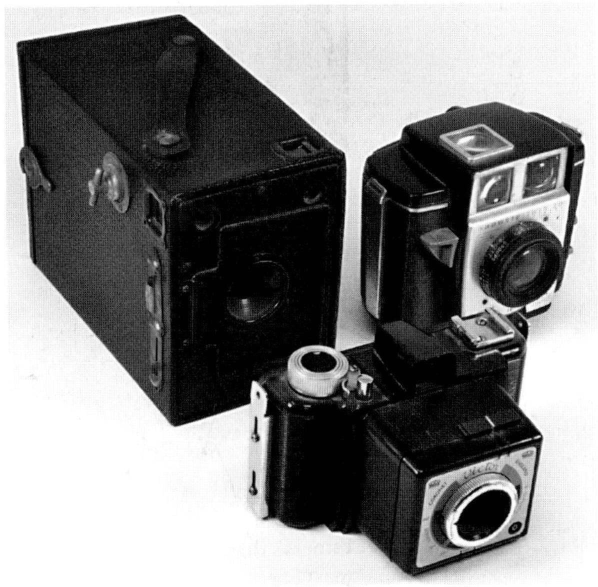

Simple cameras with the minimum of controls that needed the snapshot photographer to do little more than press a button and wind the film, represented here by an Ensign 2¼B box camera, Kodak Twin-20 and a Coronet Victor.

Early photography was carried out on rigid glass plates. Although this carried on in very simplistic terms with a few snapshot cameras, the majority used flexible film rolled onto spools, backed with lightproof paper and containing a series of numbers. Once the film was loaded into the camera, the numbers could be read through a red window on the back of the body. Winding the film after each exposure, while watching the numbers in the window, indicated the point at which the next piece of unexposed film was in position behind the lens ready for the following exposure.

The 35mm film used by more professional cameras began life as movie film and, just like film for movie cameras, it had sprocket holes on each edge to assist winding it through the camera. The film was held in small containers known as cassettes, which slotted into one side of a camera body, stretched across the opening where the picture was exposed and attached to a take-up spool on the opposite side. As many as thirty-six exposures could be made on one film. At the end of each roll, the film was rewound into the cassette. All of which was a little complicated for less experienced snapshot photographers, as were the controls of most 35mm cameras when they first appeared. Eventually, 35mm film began to be used in simpler cameras. This meant a new versatility and the chance to shoot more exposures to a roll became available to snapshot photographers.

Whichever type of film was used, apart from some specialised processes, the procedure was much the same. The film that had been through the camera was developed to make a negative, and this was then printed, either same size or slightly enlarged, to make the final positive print.

A note about measurements

Today, the metric system of measuring in meters, centimetres and millimetres has largely taken over from the old imperial measurements that used yards, feet and inches. However, in the early days of photography, the imperial system was used more extensively than the metric system for things like plate or film sizes, while the metric system was used alongside imperial measurements when describing many lenses. For this reason, the following pages contain a mixture of metric and imperial measurement references. Straight descriptions of camera dimensions are quoted in modern-day metric terms. But where equipment was originally made and defined by imperial measurements, the original classifications have been retained for historical accuracy.

The joy of snaps

Snapshot photography is, and always has been, the purest form of picture taking. It has never involved the elaborate setting up of a subject in the way associated with professional photography. A studio portrait, for example, might start with the way a subject chooses how he or she is dressed for the picture; it will dictate the way they pose for the camera; it involves the use of lighting for usually flattering, or sometimes for a more dramatic, effect. The camera angle, the lens used, maybe the addition of a filter, all contribute to a kind of falsity to show the subject in the way he or she wants to be seen, or the photographer wishes to portray them, rather than in the way they really are. Similarly, away

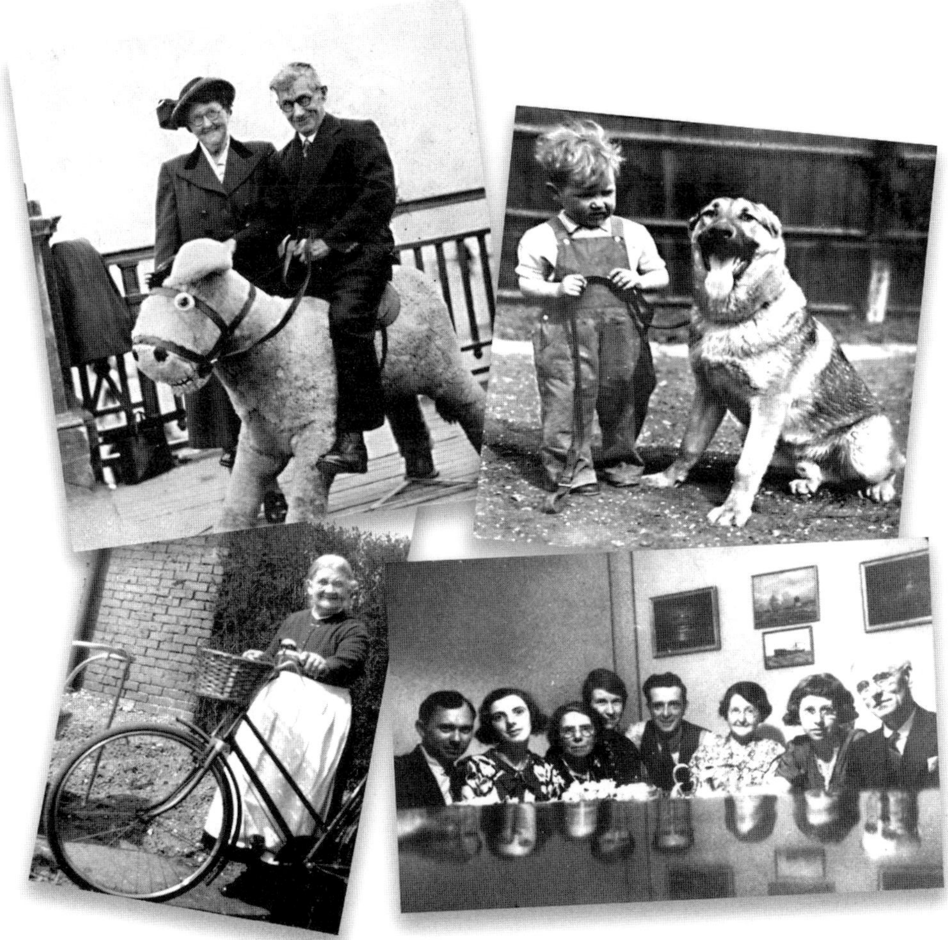

Snapshots don't have to be works of art. They just need to be reminiscent of certain times, places and people. Eventually and inevitably, they become evocative slices of social history.

from the studio, the landscape photographer will select exactly the right time of day when light falls on the subject to give the best effect; the camera angle will be chosen to make the most of certain areas and make them conform to traditional picture composition; the use of different lenses will either open up the landscape to a wider view than can be seen with the human eye, or home in on a distant aspect of the picture and bring it much closer to the camera than would be normally observed.

Whoever said the camera never lies had not thought through the process of photography very well. The camera lies all the time. It makes people look unlike the way they really are, it makes landscapes appear different to the way they appear to the naked eye. The camera takes three-dimensional subjects and turns them into two-dimensional pictures. In the early days, it turned colour into black and white, or even brown and white.

No one is decrying any of the techniques used by professional or even advanced amateur photographers if they result in artistic pictures to hang on a wall, to look at, to admire and be inspired by. That's what good photography is all about. But although the pictures produced in this way might be works of art, there is far more truth in a casually taken snapshot, be it of a person, a landscape view, or any other subject quickly captured without too much thought by the photographer.

It's why snapshots of the past can tell us so much about the age in which they were taken. And it's why snapshots and, yes, even selfies taken with modern camera phones, are worth keeping to tell people in years to come about the way we live today.

Chapter 1
The First Snapshot Camera

It isn't always easy to pinpoint exactly when any trend began. But with snapshot photography there is a definite starting point. The year was 1888, and the camera was called the Kodak, the first time that name had been used.

The man behind the camera and what was to become an iconic name was George Eastman, American entrepreneur, keen photographer and founder of the Eastman Dry Plate and Film Company. His mission had always been to make the perceived complications of photography easier for everyone. Until then, photographic exposures had been made on glass plates for use only one at a time. Early plates had to be prepared prior to exposure, used in the camera while still wet and developed immediately after. Eastman was a pioneer in making dry plates that could be bought in advance, used at any reasonable time after

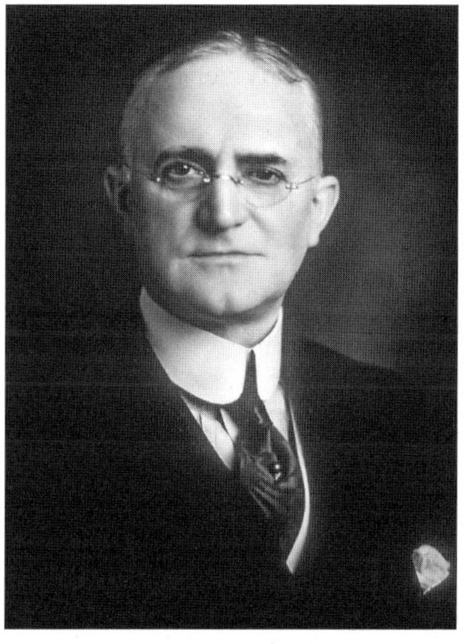

The father of snapshot photography: George Eastman, the American entrepreneur and keen photographer responsible for the first Kodak camera and a company name destined to become famous worldwide.

purchase and developed much later. Hence the name of his company.

But it was when Eastman turned his attention to making a camera that used flexible film in place of rigid plates that he produced not only a revolutionary camera, but also a name destined to become the start of the huge Kodak empire. Using the Kodak camera could not have been simpler. It was a small box-shaped model with a minimum of controls needed to operate it. Eastman's publicity said it all:

Anybody who can wind a watch can use a Kodak Camera. The Kodak is the smallest, lightest and simplest of all cameras – for the ten operations necessary with most Cameras of this class, we have ONLY THREE SIMPLE MOVEMENTS. No focusing. No finder required.

Those three controls were a string to tension the shutter, a button to release it, and a key to wind the film. The camera was purchased ready-loaded with enough film for 100 exposures. When they had all been shot, the camera and film were returned to the Eastman works for developing and printing. The camera was reloaded with a new film and returned to the photographer, ready to go for the next 100 shots. Prints, mounted and burnished, together with the negatives, arrived a little later. The slogan with which the Kodak was so often associated summed it up perfectly: 'You Press the Button, We Do the Rest.'

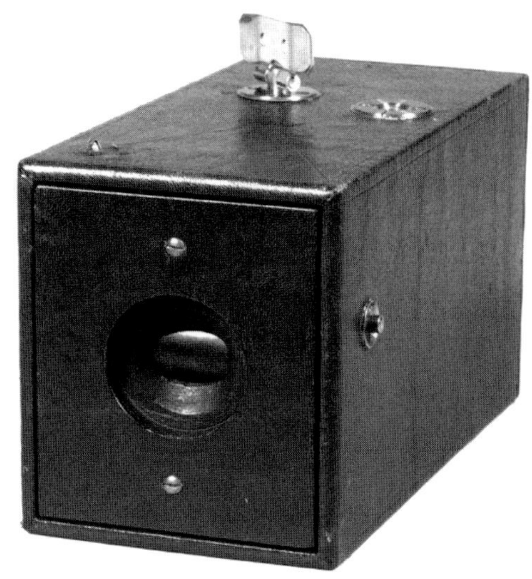

The No.1 Kodak, introduced in 1888.

Snapshot photography for the masses had arrived, and the media of the time was fast to appreciate it. *Scientific American* magazine commented:

We believe this system has never before been placed on such an extensive commercial scale as is now commenced, and it promises to make the art of photography well-nigh universal.

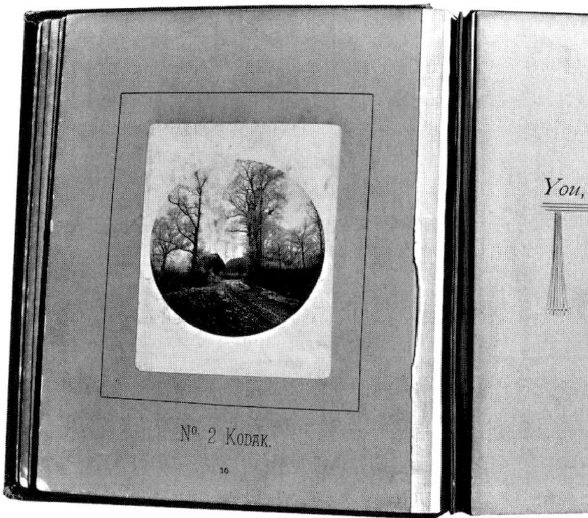

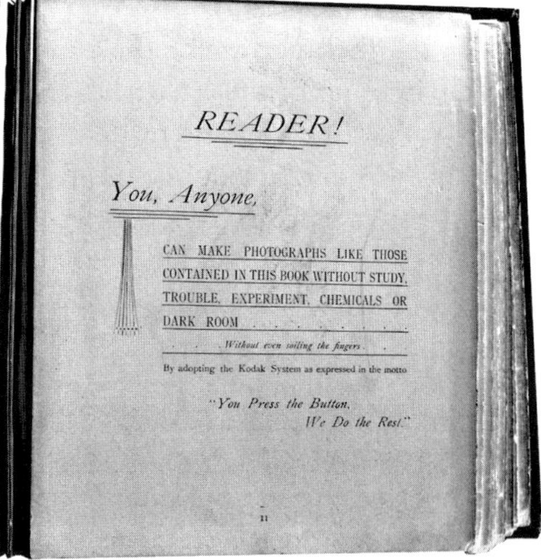

Pages from one of the now extremely rare dealer catalogues designed to show customers details of the different models.

A special catalogue was produced for camera dealers to show prospective customers. Inside each were details of all the early cameras, their specifications, prices and actual original photographs from the different models mounted on the stiff cardboard pages. In the year following its launch, sales of the Kodak were estimated at 13,000, and by 1892, advertisements claimed 90,000 had been sold worldwide.

A new breed of photographer

With the launch of this new kind of camera came a new breed of photographer. They knew nothing of how the camera worked: the way pulling the string on the side rotated a cylinder with the lens inside against a spring; how pressing the shutter button released the spring allowing the cylinder to rotate, making the exposure as a gap in the cylinder passed the lens; and the fact that the speed of the shutter, the aperture of the lens and the focusing of the lens were all fixed. They didn't even mind that there was no viewfinder. In its place, on the first cameras, a piece of card, supplied for the purpose and printed with a V-shape of lines, was placed on top of the body to give a crude guide for aiming the camera in roughly the right direction. On the reverse of the card, the numbers 1 to 100 were printed for the photographer to mark off as each

George Eastman, shown with a No.2 Kodak, and shot using a similar camera, aboard the SS *Gallia*, en route to England in 1890.

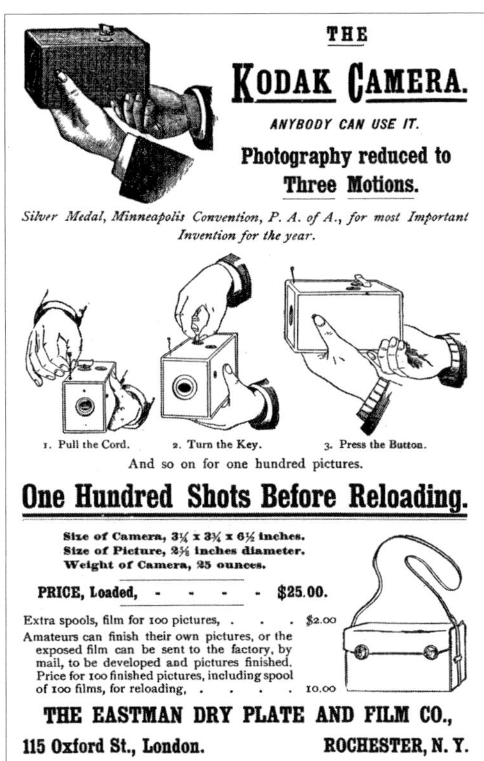

How the first Kodak was advertised, demonstrating the camera's simplicity of use.

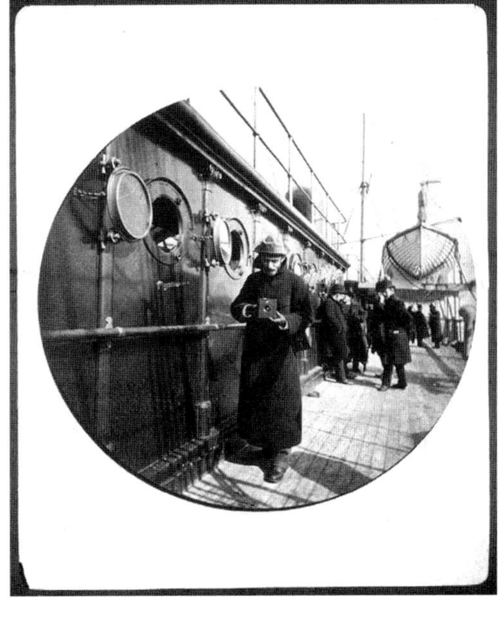

picture was taken. On later cameras, the V-lines were etched into the leatherwork on the top of the body. The complicated shutter mechanism was also soon simplified.

That the resulting pictures were circular in shape and a mere 2½ inches in diameter didn't bother this new breed of snapshot photographer either. All they knew was that it was suddenly possible to simply take pictures with a camera whose workings didn't blind them with science. And so, with a new kind of photographer out and about, a new kind of photograph was born.

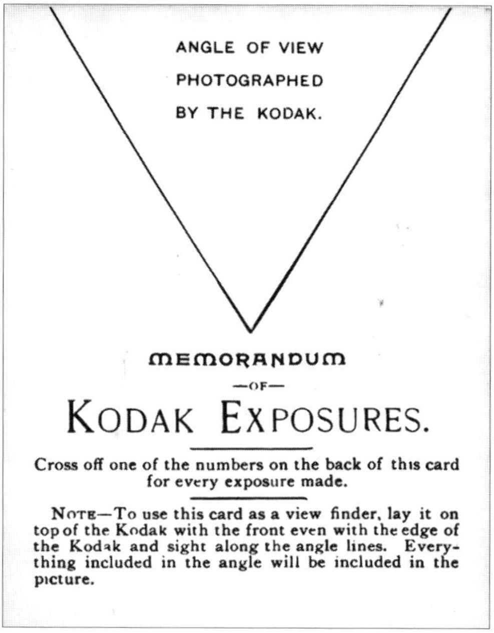

Portraits, for example, had hitherto been formal affairs with subjects sitting or standing in photographic studios adopting static poses and serious, unsmiling expressions. But now, with an easy-to-use snapshot camera, people pictures became more casual, shot away from the studio, in the home, in the garden, or in the street, with subjects going about their daily lives, sometimes even candidly without the subjects' awareness.

As outdoor photography became so much easier, snapshot cameras were taken for the first time on holidays and on days out. Until then, the serious landscape photographer would set up his large format camera on a tripod, study the way light fell on different parts of the scene, carefully measure and set the exposure, arranging picture composition on a ground-glass screen at the back of the camera as he crouched under a cloth hood to keep light off the screen. Only when the composition, lighting and exposure were deemed to be just right would he press the shutter release to take the picture. Beside him, the snapshot photographer would stroll up to the scene with his small box-shaped Kodak in his hands and, without too much thought, simply point it in what seemed to be about the right direction, pull the string and press the button on the side. His picture might not have had the finesse of the professional or even the keen amateur photographer's work, but it would provide a memory of the time and place that might otherwise have been forgotten.

Because Eastman was an American and the Kodak was first sold in America (price $25), that was where it at first achieved popularity. During New York's

This picture, taken with the first Kodak, illustrates how the camera bred a new type of photographer and photograph. Previous to the introduction of snapshot photography, children like these were unlikely to have had their pictures taken at all, such was the expense of employing a more professional photographer. Even if their parents had been able to afford such a luxury, the children would not have been shot in this way. They would more likely to have been ushered into a photographic studio, dressed formally in their best clothes, their poses stiff and stilted, their expressions maybe apprehensive or nervous. But here, shot casually in the street where they were used to playing together, the children are relaxed and depicted in a far more natural way. And what of the lady with the long dress and parasol almost out of the picture entirely and approaching from the right? Was she meant to be there? Had it not been for the circular masking of the picture, the photographer might have expected to have seen more of her. Or maybe, she wasn't even noticed

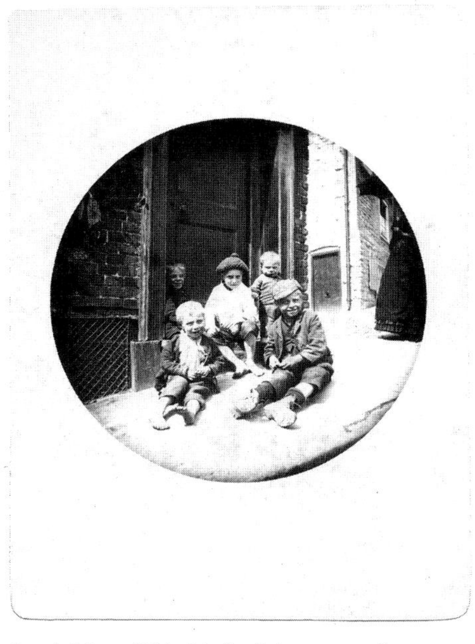

approaching as the camera was concentrated more on the children. This kind of almost careless approach would never have been countenanced from a professional photographer. Yet it's the casual look of the picture that sums up the essence, and the charm, of snapshot photography.

A scene like this would never have been documented in this way had it not been for the advent of the snapshot camera. Once again, shot with the first Kodak, and despite being taken from a British edition of the Kodak dealer catalogue, the location is apparently overseas, judging by the buildings and the way the people are dressed. The camera's viewpoint is high, certainly above the height of the average horse seen partly in the foreground. Most likely, then, the photographer was in a vehicle of some kind being pulled, at least in part, by this very horse. It would appear that the photographer had been driving along the road when he or she came upon this crowd. But why were all these people congregating at this spot? They all have their backs to the camera, so they are plainly looking at something. There doesn't seem to be any unruly behaviour, so it's unlikely to have been a demonstration of some kind. Maybe they were all gathered at this spot to await the arrival of someone important? We'll never know. A more professional photographer would not have thought about taking a picture like this, a subject which has

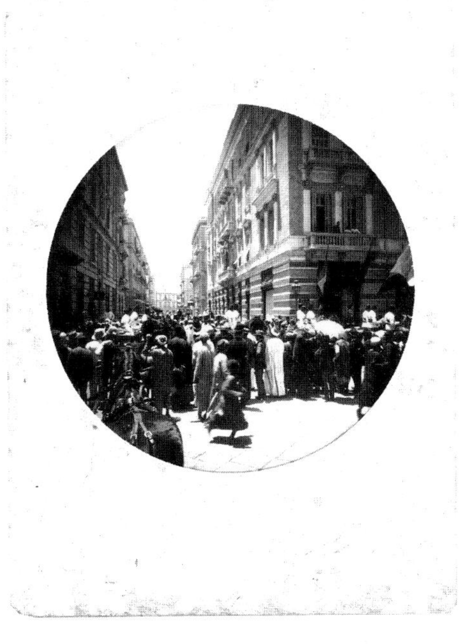

no real composition or meaning. But seeing it today, thanks to the fast thinking of a snapshot photographer of the past, it captures an otherwise lost moment in time.

centennial celebrations in 1889, snapshot photographers were responsible for around 900 Kodaks being mailed to the Eastman works in a single week. Most users received their prints back within ten days, a slightly delayed time because of the influx of so many cameras, but also because the printing process, which involved the use of natural light, was slowed down due to dull weather conditions at the time.

The Kodak name

Over the years, there has been speculation about where the word *Kodak* came from. Some reckoned it was an acronym for something that no one seems to remember. Others were of the opinion that it was the sound the shutter made – 'ko-*dak*'. Neither was true. Here's how Eastman, speaking in 1920, explained the word:

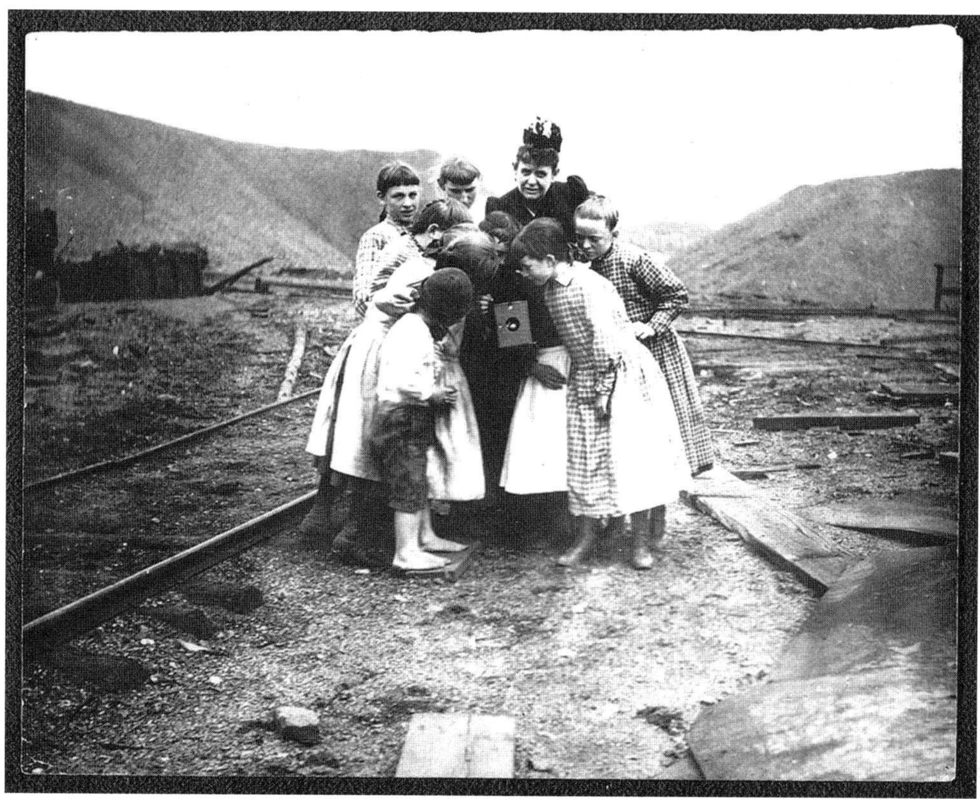

The first Kodak cameras created interest wherever they went. This picture, taken *c.*1890, shows photographer Frances Benjamin Johnston, surrounded by children fascinated by her Kodak camera, which was given to her by George Eastman, a close friend of her family. Johnston went on to be probably America's first successful female photographer.

The letter K had been a favourite with me – it seems a strong, incisive sort of letter. It became a question of trying out a great number of combinations of letters that made words starting and ending with K.

Later, he wrote:

This is not a foreign name or word. It was constructed by me to serve a definite purpose. It has the following merits as a trademark. It is short. It is not capable of mispronunciation. It does not resemble anything in the art and cannot be associated with anything else in the art.

Bigger and better

One of the very few criticisms aimed at the Kodak was the shape and size of picture it produced. The reason for the unusual circular shape was that although simple lenses of the time were capable of producing sharp results in the centre of the picture, the resolution of the lens, and therefore the quality of the picture, fell off towards the edges. That lack of edge quality, then, was disguised by placing a circular mask in the camera and only recording the centre of the subject. The 2½-inch diameter was also rather small. Eastman was quick to address both these problems and soon sharpshot photographers had better cameras with the addition of a few more basic controls to consider.

In August 1889, three new cameras with a new type of film to take larger and better pictures were announced, at which point the original Kodak became known as the No.1. The picture from the No.2 Kodak was still circular, but now with a diameter of 3½ inches, with 100 shots to a roll of film. The lens remained as a fixed focus type, but three apertures were added if the snapshot photographer had by then gained the experience needed to be a little more creative.

The No.3 Kodak offered the first rectangular picture of 3¼ × 4¼ inches, two viewfinders for

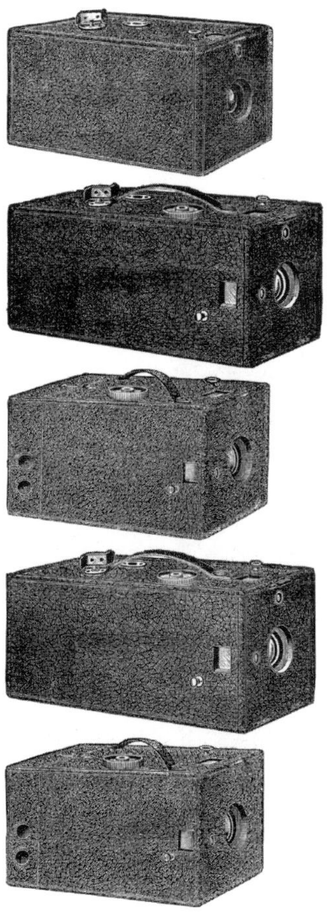

The cameras that followed the No.1 Kodak, top to bottom: No.2, No.3, No.3 Junior, No.4, and No.4 Junior.

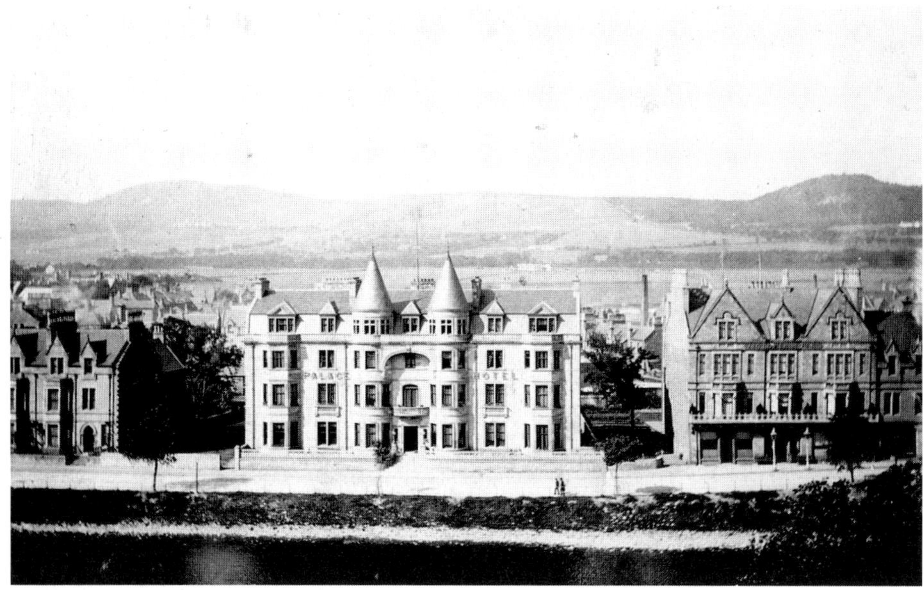

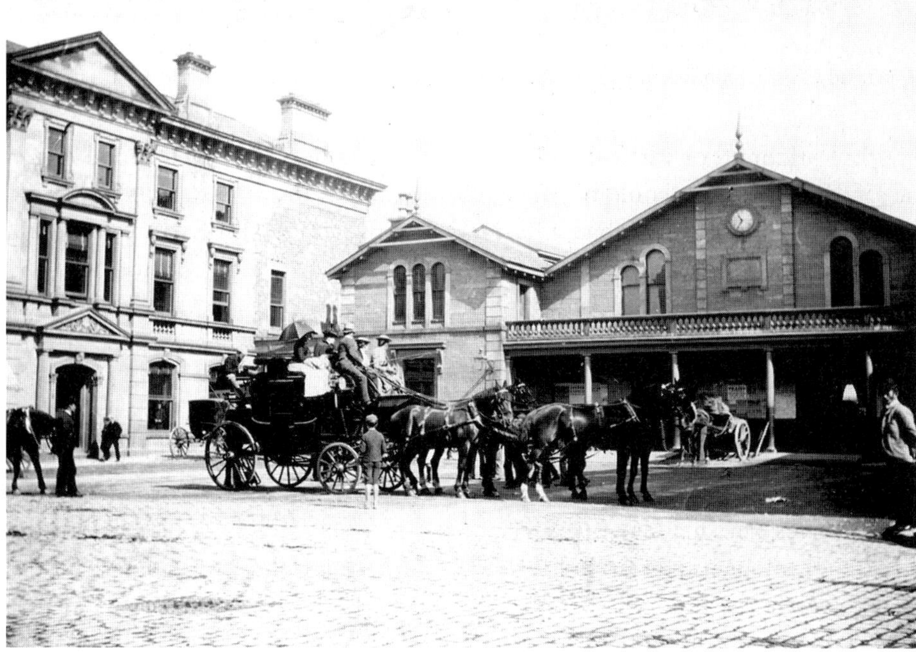

It is interesting to look at snapshots taken more than a century ago to see how little, or how much, has changed in 100 years or more. Both these pictures were taken at Inverness in Scotland. The top picture shows the Inverness Palace Hotel. Since the No.3 Kodak that was used to take the picture was launched in 1889, the picture must have been taken very soon after the hotel's opening in 1890. It has changed very little today. The picture below shows Inverness railway station, this time taken with a No.3 Kodak Junior, probably around 1890. Today, the building looks very different indeed, as does the mode of transport used by passengers on their way to the station.

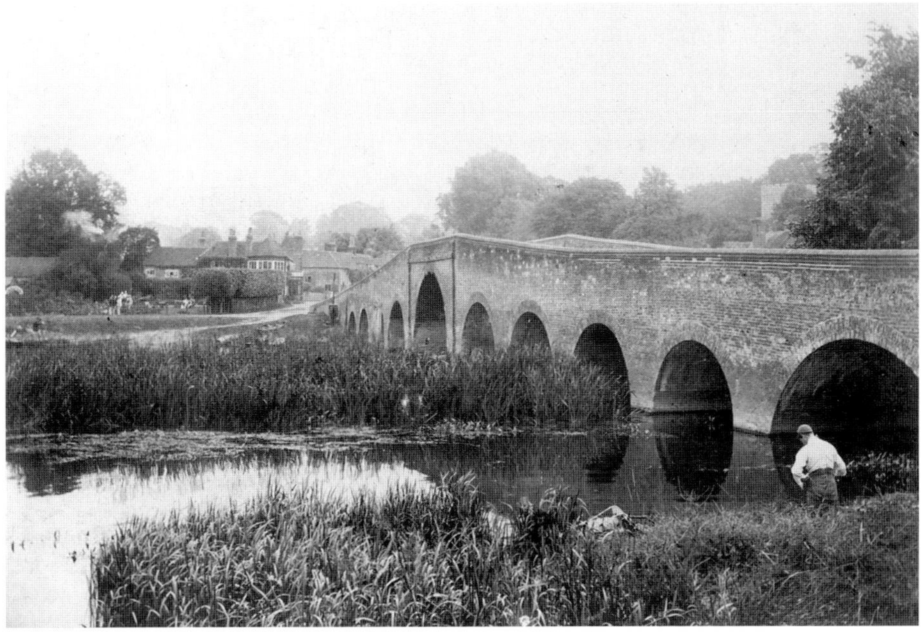

Sonning Bridge, which spans the river Thames in Berkshire, pictured with a No.4 Kodak *c.*1900. The bridge is still standing today.

taking horizontal or vertical pictures and two bushes to which a tripod might be attached. The lens could be focused for the first time, rotating apertures were available, and the shutter had adjustable speeds. It took 100 pictures to a roll, but was sold alongside the No.3 Kodak Junior, for only sixty pictures.

The No.4 Kodak was the largest of them all, producing pictures of 4×5 inches, with twin viewfinders, two tripod bushes, rotating stops, adjustable speeds and rack and pinion focusing. It shot 100 pictures to a roll and was sold alongside the No.4 Junior Kodak, which produced forty-eight exposures.

It was claimed that every camera, prior to being sold, was carefully tested by an expert operator before it was finally loaded with film. Then, between one and six negatives were made with each camera, the focus adjusted and the definition examined under a magnifying glass. Every lens that did not come up to the company's high standard was rejected. The Eastman company claimed that they kept on file the final test negative of every camera sold, knowing exactly what each lens was capable of before offering it to a customer.

The Kodak name and brand obviously went on to greater things. But it was that little box camera launched in 1888 and which remained in production until 1892 that introduced the joys of photography to so many who might never otherwise have ever thought of owning or using a camera. It was, in short, responsible for the birth of snapshot photography.

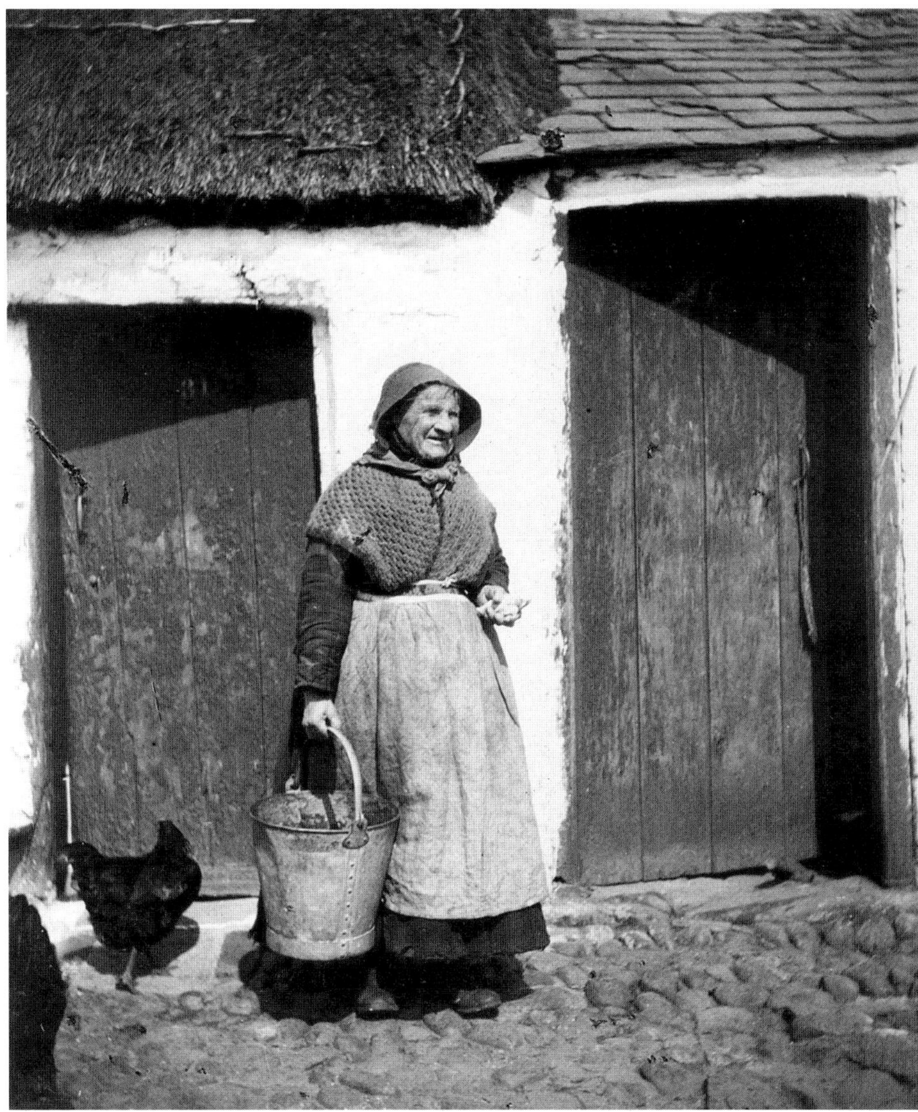

So often it's the people in a snapshot that make it special. A landscape is a landscape and one taken 100 years ago might not look very different from the same location taken today. But put a person in the picture and it tells so much more about a way of life that is now long gone. This picture was taken with a No.4 Kodak Junior.

Chapter 2
What Came Next

When George Eastman introduced the Kodak, there were those among the established camera manufacturers who saw it only as a passing fad. They had to think again when they realised how popular this new type of photography was becoming for photographing friends, family, holidays, events, or anything of a more personal nature than had hitherto been possible or unlikely to have been recorded for posterity.

Before snapshot cameras could progress, however, their owners were required to learn one more procedure. Cameras couldn't continue to be sold ready-loaded with film and reloaded by the processor when the film was developed. They needed to be sold separately from their film and their owners had to learn how to load the film – sometimes in these early days referred to as a cartridge – into the camera. The operation required the camera to be opened, a roll of film to be inserted on one side, then pulled across the back of the camera and attached to a spindle that was coupled to the film winding knob or key. This led to a new type of film, backed by lightproof paper with numbers printed on it. As this was wound through the camera after each exposure the numbers were read through a small red window in the camera back, which told the user when to stop winding between exposures and when all the pictures had been taken. The window was red because early film was insensitive to red light and so would not be damaged by light entering the window.

Film loading was a simple enough procedure that most snapshot photographers quickly learned. Those that couldn't understand how to do it, or couldn't be bothered, took their cameras to the nearest photo dealer, or more likely chemist shop,

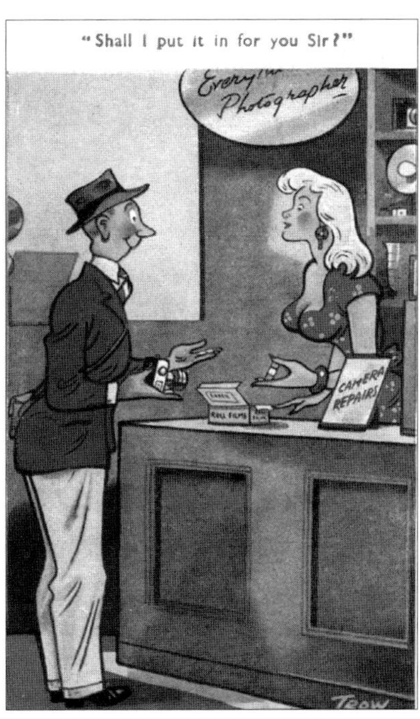

Saucy seaside postcards poked fun at snapshot photographers who couldn't load their own films.

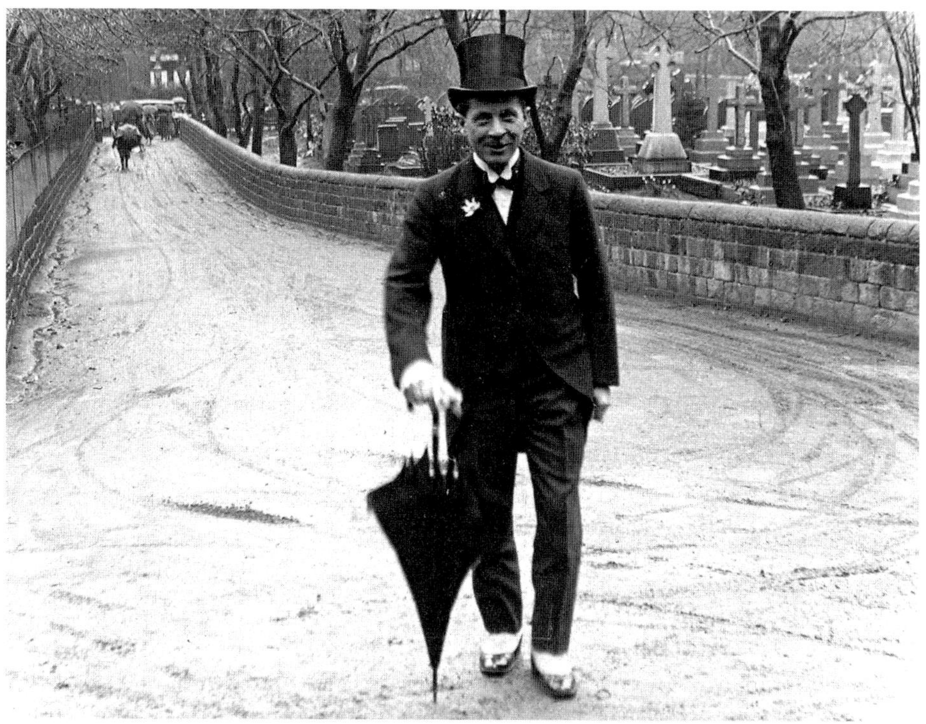

Snapshots like this can be amusing to look at today, but who knows what lies behind the picture? The location, reminiscent and evocative of the final scene from the film noir *The Third Man* seems to be a road beside or through a cemetery. Does the man's top hat indicate that maybe he was an undertaker? Or was he one of the mourners? If so, did mourners wear top hats then? So what is he doing standing here all alone with his unfurled umbrella? And, if the cemetery location has anything to do with his presence at this spot, why does he look so jolly? Mysteries that can never be solved today are what make snapshots like this so appealing more than a century after they might have been taken.

and asked the person behind the counter to load them. Then, when the film was finished, they would return and ask the shop assistant to remove it, develop it and reload the camera.

Once cameras began to be made this way and their owners had accepted this new way of working, the field was open for rivals to the Kodak to be made by other manufacturers keen to enter this new, and rapidly becoming lucrative, market.

The Luzo

In 1889, just one year after the Kodak was introduced in America, the first British roll film camera was launched by J. Robinson & Sons in London. Throughout its life, there were various models of the Luzo, made to take different sizes of pictures that matched the shapes and sizes of those from the Kodaks. The first Luzo used a very simple shutter powered by an elastic band, but this soon gave way to more reliable spring-operated mechanisms. The cameras were more compact than the Kodaks, due to the way the film rollers were placed either side of the lens, rather than the Kodak's method of placing them at the back of the body. The company's advertisements were keen to emphasise ease of use:

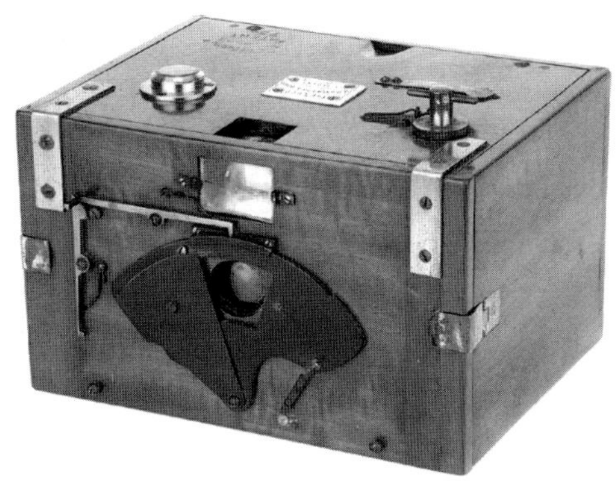

The Luzo was British and followed very shortly after the introduction of Eastman's Kodak.

A well-known fact – thousands of pounds are wasted yearly by amateurs at home and abroad endeavouring to obtain photographs with cheap and unreliable cameras. All this can be avoided and success guaranteed by securing a Luzo, the most compact, simplest and best hand camera extant.

The early cameras had single fixed shutter speeds, though later models offered a choice of different speeds. Film winding for the inexperienced snapshot photographer was simplified by holes punched in the film at regular intervals,

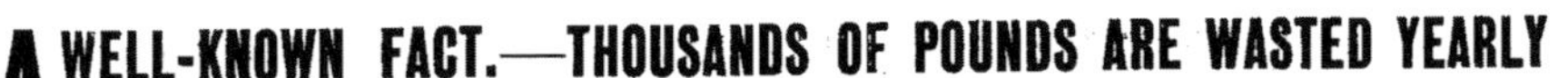

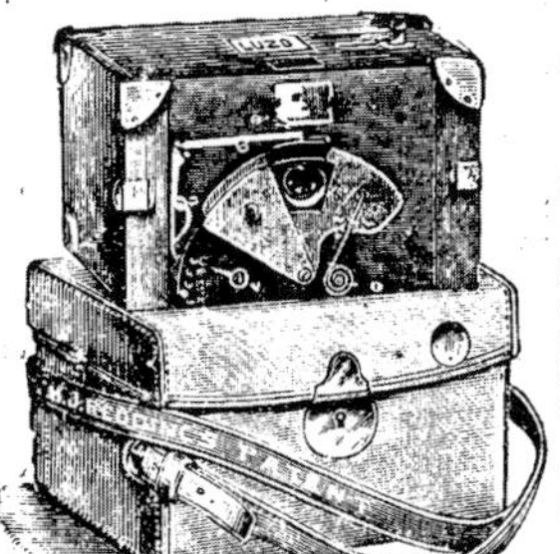

An 1899 advertisement extols the virtues of using a Luzo camera.

which actuated a 'click' as each frame was wound to its correct position. The choice of shutter speeds on later models might have confused some snapshot photographers, but that was the only control they needed to worry about. The Luzo was a very impressive-looking camera, made in polished Spanish mahogany wood with brass fittings, and in some ways that could have been its downfall with some snapshot photographers who might have thought it looked too professional. Snapshot cameras didn't just have to *be* simple to operate, they had to *look* simple to operate as well.

Kombi

The first non-Kodak camera for which Kodak agreed to make film was called the Kombi, made in 1892 by Alfred C. Kemper in America and one of the very first subminiature cameras to use roll film. The box-shaped body measured a mere 5×4×4cm and it shot twenty-five circular pictures just $1\frac{1}{8}$ inches in diameter. The camera took its name from the fact that once exposed, the film could be printed to make a positive strip, then fed back into the camera, where it was magnified by viewing it through the lens. The Kombi was made of brass, with an art nouveau design on the face. The aperture and focus were fixed and the shutter was released by a very simple spring arrangement and lever on top of the body.

Although an interesting camera in its own right, it is unlikely that many snapshot photographers would have invested in such

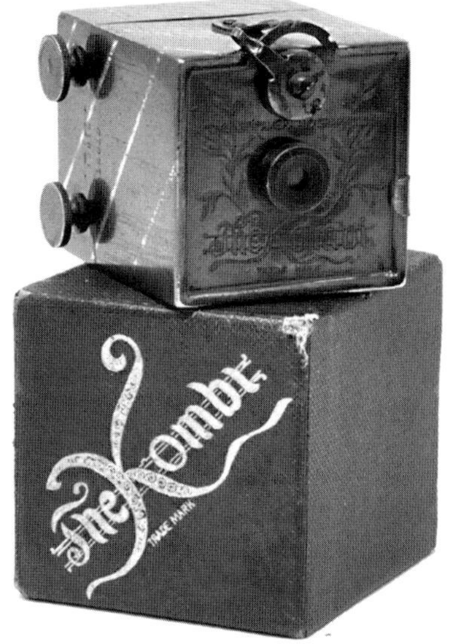

The Kombi camera, a very early subminiature snapshot camera, standing on its attractive box.

a small camera and its tiny pictures. For the kind of cameras that snapshot photographers initially took to the most there was only one name, and that name was now incorporated into the name of the company to form Eastman Kodak.

Bulls-Eye

One of the most important features of any camera that took roll film was the little red window at the back of the body though which the photographer viewed the picture numbers on the paper that backed the film. It is often thought that Kodak invented this idea, but in fact it first appeared on a camera called the No.2

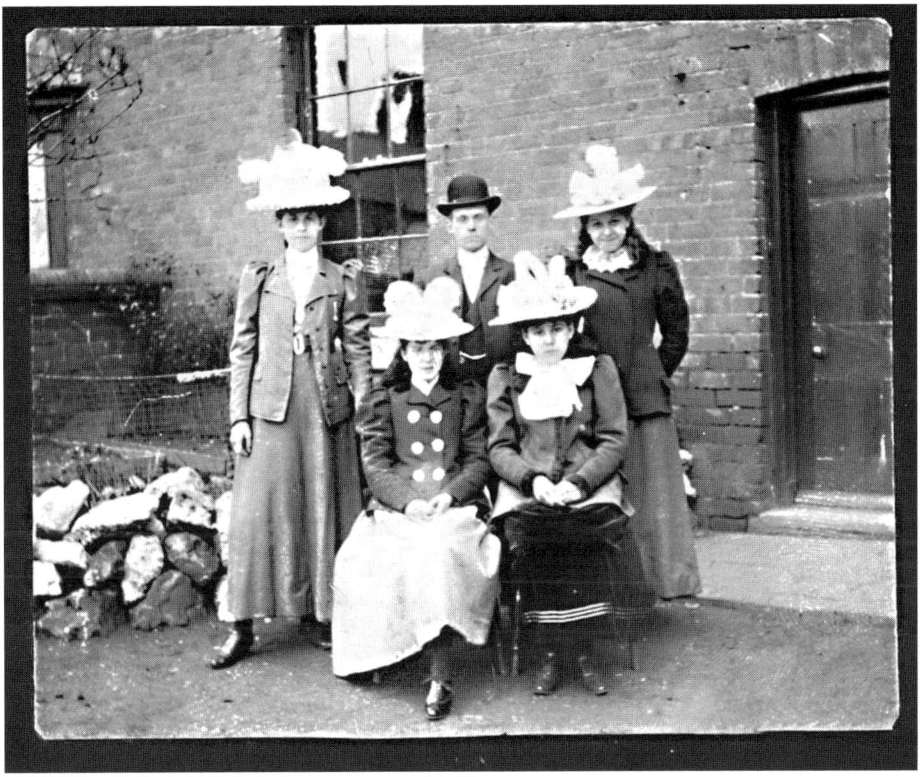

It isn't always necessary to know the history of a picture or the people it depicts to appreciate it. Maybe what we are looking at here is a brother and his four sisters, taken perhaps by their father. Judging by the women's dresses and hats, the picture would appear to be from Edwardian times, which dates it to between 1901 and 1910, perhaps even a little before, while the house in the background and its sparce garden look like a typical two-up, two-down home built in earlier Victorian times. Judging by their surroundings, the family was not rich. But here they are dressed in their Sunday best, off to where? Church? A wedding? A christening? Somewhere special, obviously. It all adds up to what makes the picture so charming.

Bulls-Eye, made in 1895 by the Boston Camera Manufacturing Company. When Eastman used a similar idea on a Kodak camera called the Bullet, he had to pay the Boston company a patent licence fee. So he bought the company, and thereafter Kodak cameras carried the red window.

Kodak went on to make Bulls-Eye cameras in a similar style to the one patented

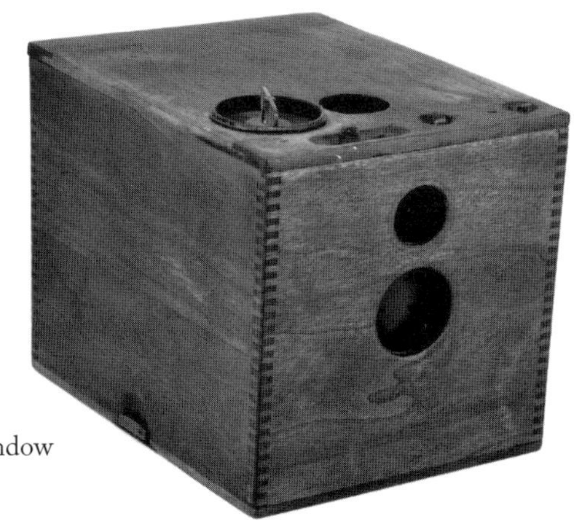

The Bulls-Eye, the first Kodak camera to use a red window on the back to view picture numbers.

by the Boston Company. The design was a simple box-type camera with the minimum of controls needed to take a 3½×3½-inch picture. Its name came from what appeared to be a second lens above the real lens on the original cameras. The second one was there to provide an image in the viewfinder on the top of the body. By 1913, when the camera ceased production, more than 250,000 had been sold.

Pocket Kodak

Back in the realms of true snapshot cameras and also in 1895, a new model arrived from Kodak, one with which snapshot photographs could readily identify because there was nothing about the look of it to frighten the inexperienced photographer.

The Pocket Kodak was little more than a small box 10×7×5cm with a single lever to release the shutter and a key on top to wind the film. A tiny viewfinder on top of the body used a mirror to reflect the scene in front

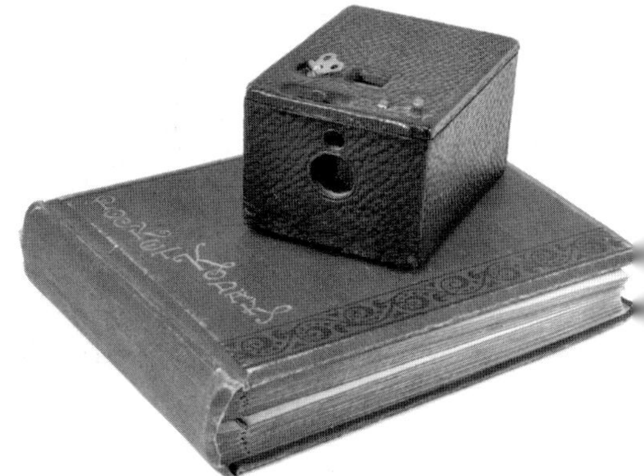

The Pocket Kodak with its own album, specially produced to store its tiny pictures.

of the camera onto a piece of ground glass in the top of the body so the photographer with good eyesight had the opportunity to preview in advance what he or she was getting on film. For a little more influence over exposures, there were two other controls courtesy of a couple of metal tabs that protruded from the top of the camera. One changed the shutter speed to something slightly faster; the other introduced a smaller aperture in front of the lens. But there's a good chance that the average snapshot photographer never used these or perhaps never even noticed they were there. The camera was supplied from the factory with one unloaded film. Specially made for the camera and designated as 102 size, this was loaded by lifting the top panel clear of the body, which brought the internal mechanisms with it, and there were brief instructions engraved on brass plates inside to instruct on how to load. A red window on the back of the body displayed the exposure numbers. It took twelve pictures to a roll of film. For the more ambitious, a single glass plate could be loaded instead of film, but this had to be inserted and removed in a darkroom.

One drawback with the camera was the size of pictures it took. A small camera must necessarily produce small negatives, and since few snapshot photographers

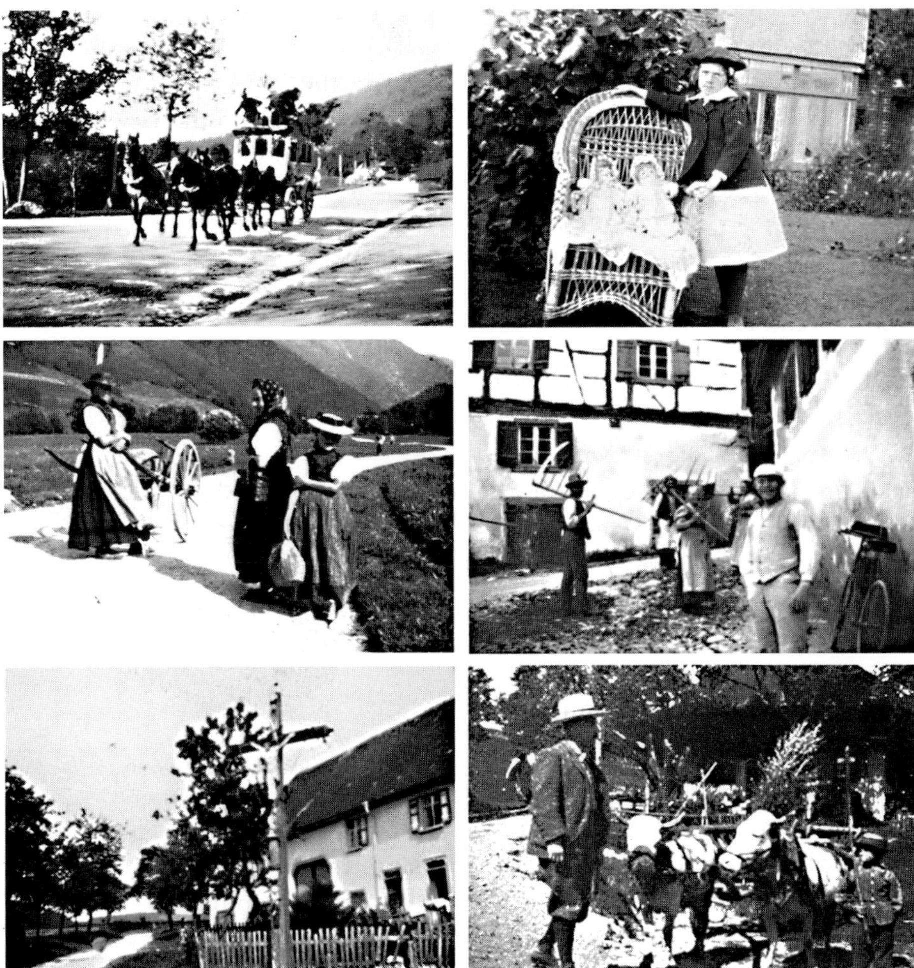

A page of six snapshots from a Pocket Kodak album show the rather haphazard way the camera's owner used the camera to record aspects of his or her life in the late 1890s.

would have had access to darkrooms and enlargers to make bigger prints from the negatives, they had to put up with pictures of only $2 \times 1\frac{1}{2}$ inches. It didn't deter determined snapshot photographers who bought albums sold by Kodak specially designed with apertures for the camera's tiny prints, probably more pictures in a single album than were likely to have been actually taken in a year.

The Pocket Kodak was made of wood with a smart leather covering and was first introduced in red or black leather versions. In 1896, a slightly improved shutter was introduced. Eastman Kodak claimed 50,000 were sold in 1895 alone and, by the time the camera was discontinued in 1900, nearly 150,000 had been sold.

Folding Pocket Kodak

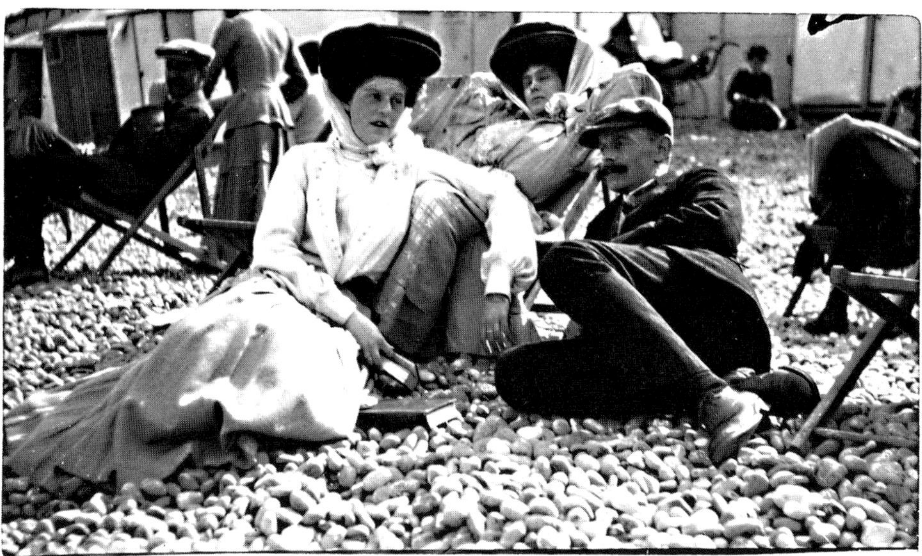

From earliest days, holidays were a popular subject for snapshot photographers. According to the album from which this picture was extracted, it was taken at Sheringham in Norfolk in 1905. Clearly, these were the days when relaxing on the beach meant women wearing long dresses and ornate hats, with men in three-piece suits, stiff collars, ties and jaunty caps. It's a pretty good bet that the women kept their hats on while the men neither removed their jackets nor loosened their ties throughout the day's frivolities.

The first Folding Pocket Kodak (left) with the newly designed No.3 that influenced the design of folding cameras for many years to come.

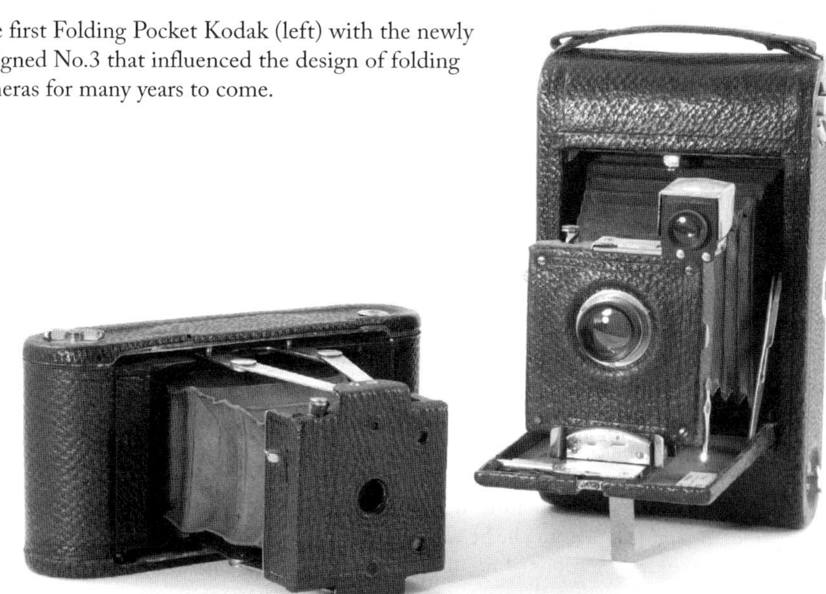

Although many snapshot photographers seemed happy with very small pictures, others craved something a little larger. Even though it was possible to make enlarged pictures from small negatives in a darkroom, the common practice among snapshot photographers was to accept contact prints, made by sandwiching the negative with the sensitive paper that became the print. Therefore, the negative size became the same size as the print that was eventually viewed. Larger negatives meant larger film, and larger film meant a larger camera, not just in the size of the back that held the film, but also in the distance between the film and the lens. This distance increased with the size of the image and, for optical reasons, could not be less than a certain specific measurement (actually what was known as the lens's focal length). The answer, if a camera was to produce larger pictures but still remain fairly portable, was to make it fold.

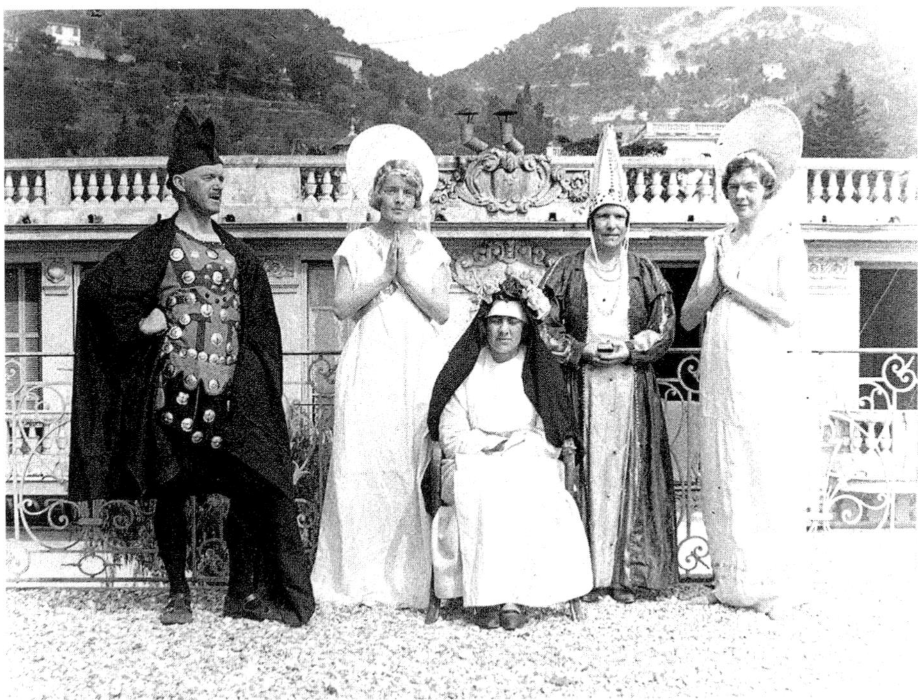

Snapshot cameras liberated people who had not before owned a camera to record their activities, pleasures and leisure time in completely new ways. A professional photographer might have coaxed this group into looking a little happier, but the more natural expressions give the picture a spontaneity as they pose at, or on the way to, what seems to be a party with a distinctly religious theme. At least, that's what might be assumed from the presence of two angels, a nun and maybe a bishop. Quite what the gentleman on the left has to do with any of this, is something of a mystery, while making the picture all the more intriguing. Often, it's possible to date when a snapshot was taken by the fashions of the time, especially clothing worn by women. But when the subjects are all in fancy dress, the chances of dating become more obscure.

When folded, the first Folding Pocket Kodak, which was introduced in 1897, measured 17×8.5×4cm, which was still small enough to slip into a fair-sized pocket. But then, tugging on the front caused the lens to spring forward on light-tight bellows supported by two struts that placed it the exact distance from the film needed for fixed focus snapshots. The camera's overall size then became 17×8.5×13cm, making it impossible to describe as pocketable. Thereafter the snapshot photographer had only a few controls to worry about: twin shutter releases for instantaneous or time exposures, the film wind key and, if needed, a metal tab that could be pulled out to offer a choice of three apertures. The camera took twelve 2¼×3¼-inch pictures on 105 size film.

The Folding Pocket Kodak went through several incarnations in its time, the most notable being the introduction of the No.3 model whose new design offered a drop-down bed and a lens compartment that pulled out on bellows along rails. This version, with similar controls to the first, was still extremely simple to use for snapshot photographers. The basic design was subsequently copied by manufacturers worldwide with specifications that added more and more technical aspects that took the cameras away from the world of snapshot photography and much more into the realms of knowledgeable amateur, and even professional, photographers.

British folding cameras too

It would be easy to assume that Kodak was the only manufacturer of snapshot cameras at this time and that America was the only place they were sold and used. Granted that Kodak was at the forefront of this new kind of photography, and many of the early models, even if they were not made by Kodak, still emanated from America. But the company and the country were by no means the only places where snapshot cameras and photographers were to be found.

In Britain, the Houghton company made Ensignette cameras from 1909 onwards. They were originally made of brass and later aluminium in a design that unfolded on four struts with extensions on each side of the lens panel used to stand the camera in a vertical position. With single speed shutters and fixed apertures, they were simple for snapshot photographers to use. The first model took pictures 1½×2¼ inches. Two other sizes were also made to take pictures 2×3 inches and 2¼×3¼ inches.

To mention just these few cameras is to touch only the tip of the iceberg. There were, of course, a great many more too numerous to mention, similar in style and made by many manufacturers around the world.

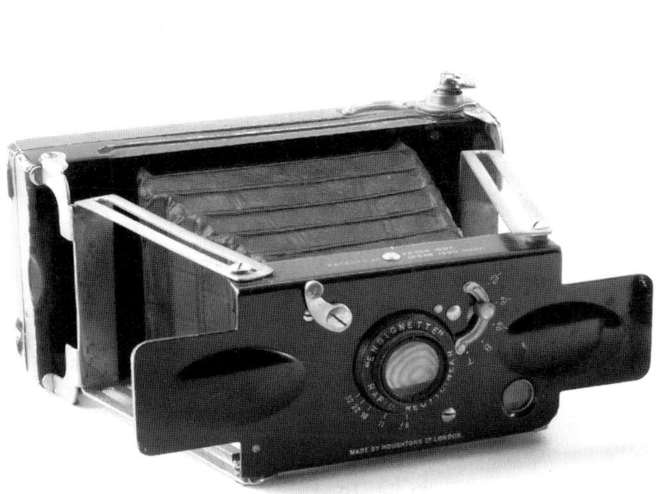
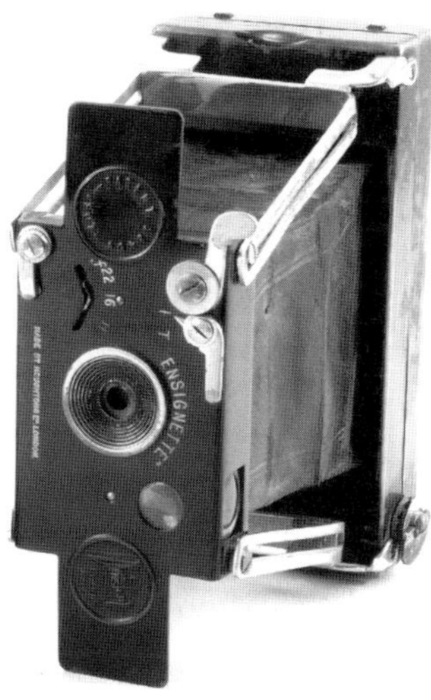

Two sizes of the Ensignette camera, made in Britain from 1909.

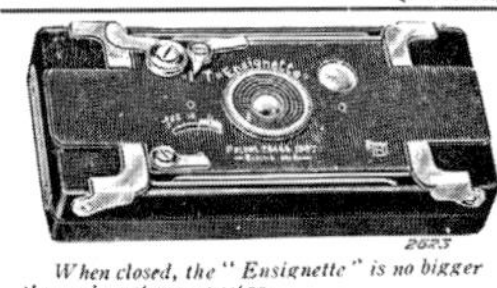

The "Ensignette."
(Patent.)

A FOLDING CAMERA FOR THE UPPER VEST POCKET.
Self-Contained. Daylight Loading.

The "Ensignette" is a Vest Pocket Camera built on a new plan, It is new in size, shape and construction. The "Ensignette" is built of metal throughout, opens smoothly and instantly, and is the ideal camera for constant use.

Attractive little pictures are produced that do not necessarily need enlarging to be interesting.

The exact size of the picture taken by the "Ensignette," $2\frac{1}{4} \times 1\frac{1}{2}$ in.

When closed the "Ensignette" measures $3\frac{7}{8} \times 1\frac{7}{8}$ in. and is only $\frac{3}{4}$ in. in thickness. It opens and locks in position for exposure by one simple movement. It is the only really small Folding Camera that is self-contained, and will go into the waistcoat pocket, and it is thinner than any camera in existence.

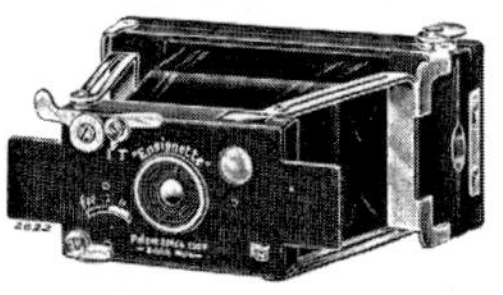

The "Ensignette" is loaded and unloaded in daylight with Special six-exposure "Ensign" Roll Films.

The "Ensignette" fixed focus printing box will automatically enlarge the pictures to the full standard size postcard $5\frac{1}{2} \times 3\frac{1}{2}$) without loss of definition. It means that you can produce full size postcard pictures with a Camera that slips into your vest pocket.

The "Ensignette" is fitted with an Achromatic Meniscus Lens with Adjustable Diaphragm openings, f/11, f/16, and f/22. It has an Everset Instantaneous Shutter, with a large and easily controlled release lever.

Time Exposures can also be given, and the Camera will stand easily on a level surface for either oblong or upright pictures.

HOUGHTONS LTD. 88 89 HIGH HOLBORN. W.C.

"The Ensignette."
(Patent.)

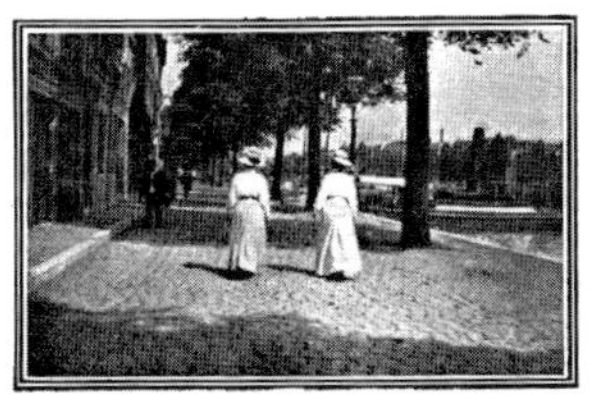

When closed, the "Ensignette" is no bigger than a box of wax-vestas.

There is a self-contained brilliant View Finder, a winding key for changing the Film, and an Indicator Window.

The system of Film changing is particularly simple, and can be mastered in a moment.

The "Ensignette" is sold in a limp Leather Pocket Case which keeps the Camera clean and free from dust, and takes up little or no room.

The "Ensignette" has a very handsome appearance, the extending struts are of nickelled phosphor bronze and all the bright parts are of the same finish.

No. 1. **"Ensignette" Camera, complete with Achromatic Menicus Lens** **30/-**

„ 1x. **"Ensignette" Camera, complete with "Ensign Anastigmat Lens f/5·6** **70/-**

"Ensignette" Ensign Film Spool (6 exposures) ... ... · ... each **10d.**

"Ensignette" Ensign Film Spool (6 exposures) ... ... per box of 3 **2/6**

"Ensignette" Printing Box. To enlarge "Ensignette" pictures by daylight to Postcard Size **5/6**

"Ensignette" Printing Frame (for 2 contact pictures) ... ... **6d.**

Developing and Printing Outfit. Complete with Book of Instructions. (For Developing Spools and making Contact Prints actual size) **5/6**

Printing Box Outfit. Complete with Book of Instructions (For Developing and Printing Enlarged Prints) **3/-**

| "Ensignette" Daylight Developing Tank **7/6** |

Spools of "Ensignette" Film can be developed, and Contact Prints made actual size, or Prints enlarged on to Postcards at the following prices :-

Developing Films ... ... per strip of 6 exposures **6d.**
Contact Prints ... ... per strip of 6 exposures **6d.**
„ „ from separate negatives ... ... per doz **1/6**
Enlarged Prints on Postcards ... ... per doz. **3/6**

The Special Six-Exposure "Ensign" Spool for the "Ensignette."

HOUGHTONS LTD. 88 89 HIGH HOLBORN. W.C.

How the Houghton company advertised the Ensignette.

The snapshot album in which this picture was found was dated as 1913. Yet the old lady, seemingly unaware of the camera as she stares out of a window, is dressed in formal attire probably retained from when she was much younger, back in the Victorian era when Charles Dickens was writing *Great Expectations*. And here personified is Miss Havisham from that novel. That aside, you can't help thinking there is a story here. Had she just returned from the funeral of someone close? Her husband maybe? The black dress, her age and morose expression seem to indicate something like that. Every picture tells a story, and snapshots tell more than most.

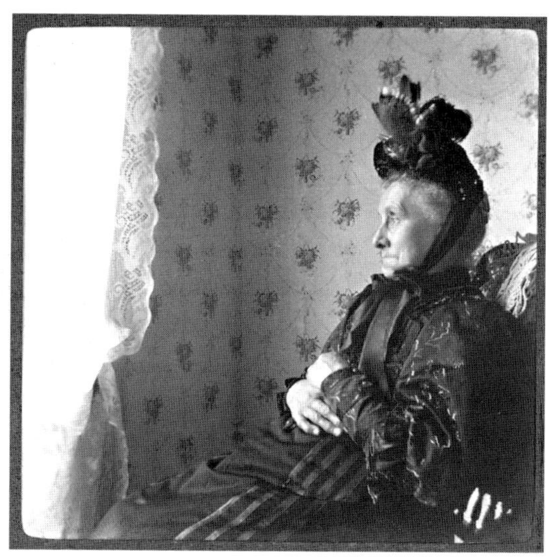

Kodak's autographic cameras

In 1914, Kodak introduced a new feature to its cameras that proved particularly useful to snapshot photographers. It first appeared that year on a folding camera called The No.1A Autographic, but went on to be incorporated into most of the company's simple folding cameras up until 1927. The feature was called an Autographic Back. It involved a hinged trapdoor in the camera back with a stylus attached to it, and was used in conjunction with special autographic film that incorporated a wax sheet between the backing paper and the film. The trapdoor was opened and the stylus used to write notes on the backing paper. Pressure from the stylus broke the wax paper in the shape of the writing and leaving the trapdoor open allowed light to fog the writing onto the rebate between frames of film. In this way, the photographer could add brief notes or picture locations to each picture.

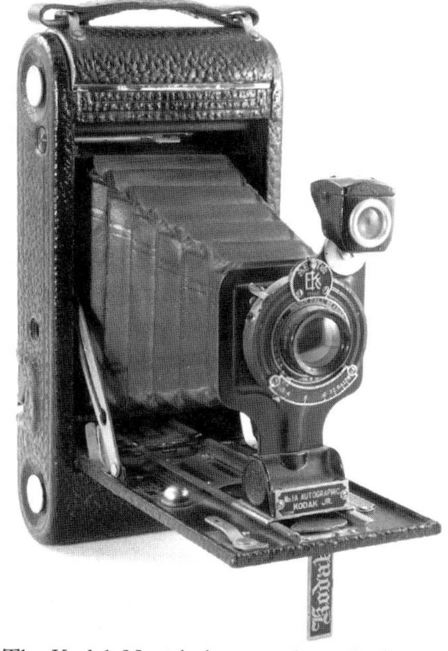

The Kodak No.1A Autographic, which introduced the unusual autographic back feature.

Specialist snapshot cameras

Alongside professional cameras of the time, snapshot models sometimes developed in unusual ways that took them away from mainstream photography.

One feature that was surprisingly seen in a snapshot camera many years before anything similar appeared elsewhere was the very first form of automatic film advancement. Every camera that used a roll of film needed to be wound after each exposure, so that a new piece of unexposed film then lay behind the lens ready for the next picture. Forgetting to wind the film and ending up with two exposures in the same picture, or forgetting that it had been wound and doing it again resulting in a blank picture were mistakes often made by the snapshot photographer. Both of these eventualities were addressed by a French camera called Le Pascal, made by Japy Frères & Compagnie as far back as 1899.

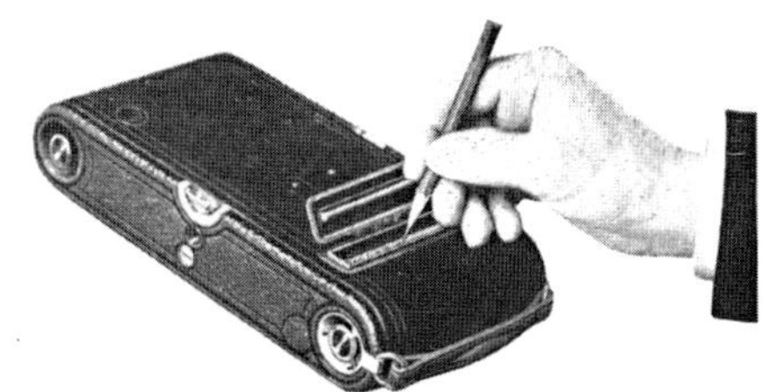

	s. d.		s. d.
No. 1 Kodak Junior ..	10 6	No. 4 F.P.K.	16 6
No. 1a Kodak Junior ..	12 6	No. 4a Folding Kodak	18 6
No. 1a (R.R. type) F.P.K.	14 6	No. 1a Special Kodak	16 6
No. 3 F.P.K.	14 6	No. 3 Special Kodak	16 6
No. 3a F.P.K.	15 6	No. 3a Special Kodak	17 6

Advertising of the time shows how the autographic back was used.

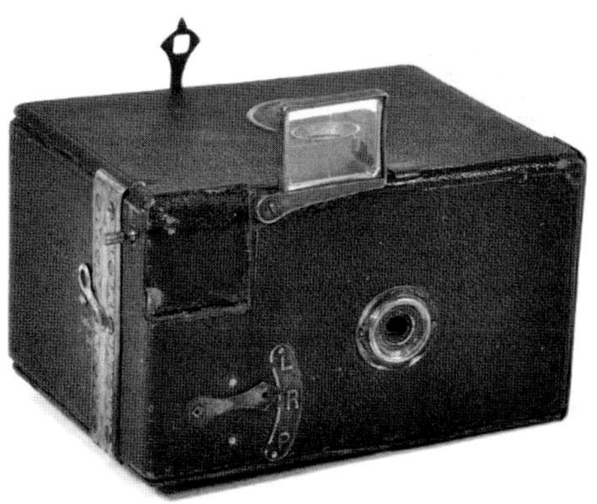
Le Pascal camera provided clockwork-driven film advance as early 1899.

Le Pascal was a simple box camera with a flip-up viewfinder and a choice of a slow or fast shutter speed, which took twelve pictures 1½×2 inches on its own specially made film. Unlike more conventional films, this did not have backing paper. Instead, the raw film was wound onto a spool with a paper leader at the front and a paper trailer at the end. Because the paper leader was lightproof and wrapped around the film, it could be loaded in daylight. With the camera back removed, the film was inserted into the

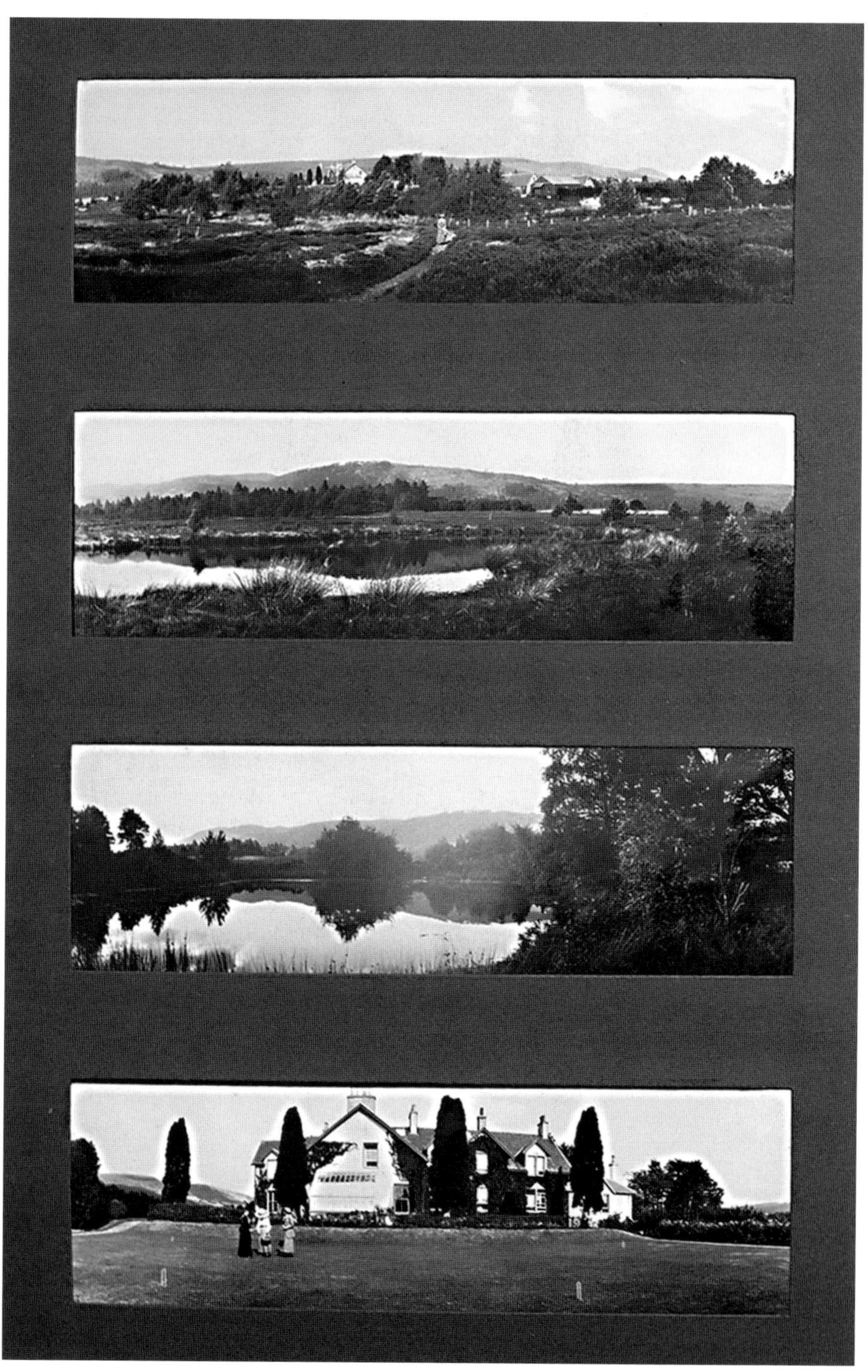

Two pages from a special album sold by Kodak for No.1 Panoram pictures.

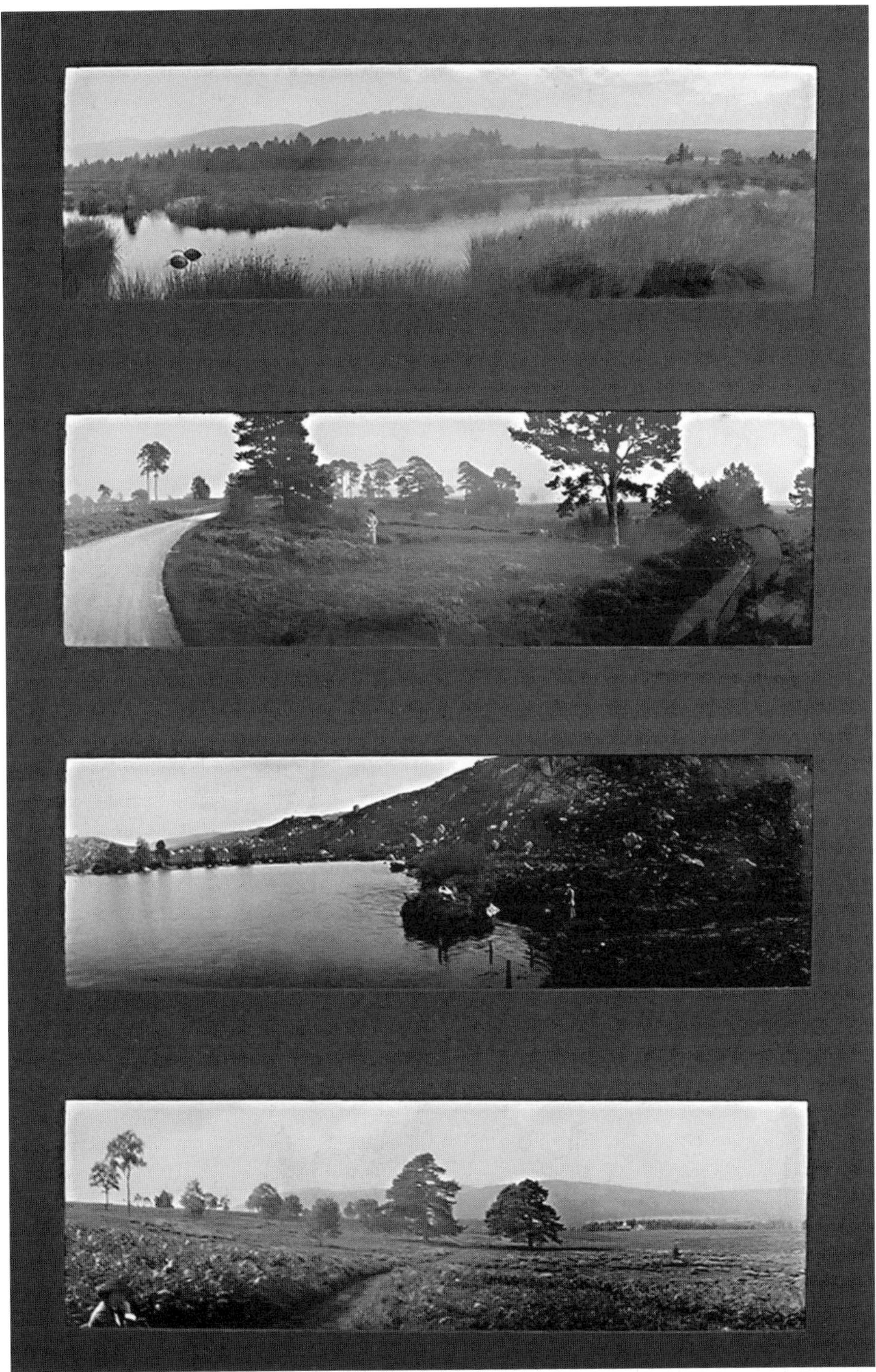

camera in the usual way, then the paper leader was pulled across and attached to a large take-up drum. The back was replaced and a small knob on the base was turned to wind the film all the way through the camera and onto the take-up drum. At the same time, this tensioned a clockwork spring and, thereafter, as each exposure was made, the clockwork automatically wound the film back onto the original spool one picture at a time.

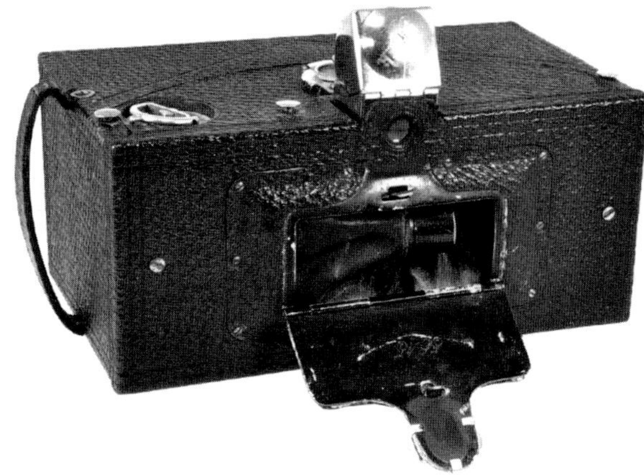

The Kodak No.1 Panoram, which took super-wide panoramic pictures on conventional film.

Panoramic cameras that took pictures much wider than normal began to appear in the early years of the twentieth century, and the Kodak Panoram No.1, introduced in 1900, was one of the first with easy-to-use controls that appealed to snapshot photographers. Its unusual design featured a lens contained at the end of a short cylinder with a slit at the opposite end. When the camera was pointed straight ahead, the lens initially pointed to one side. As the shutter was released, the lens swung from one side to the other. As it moved, the image, projected through the rear slit, was gradually built up on film, which was led around a curved arrangement inside the camera.

Before using the Panoram, the mechanism was tensioned by a lever on top of the body and released by a button to the side. The lens swung each way alternately and was covered between exposures by a flap that folded up from beneath. Also incorporated were a spirit level and a viewfinder that reflected its image onto a magnifier. The camera originally used 105 size film. It took pictures 2¼ × 7 inches wide and Kodak sold special albums with apertures in each page cut to display this unusual picture shape. Later, other larger versions of the Panoram were made to take panoramic pictures 3¼ × 10½ inches and 3½ × 12 inches.

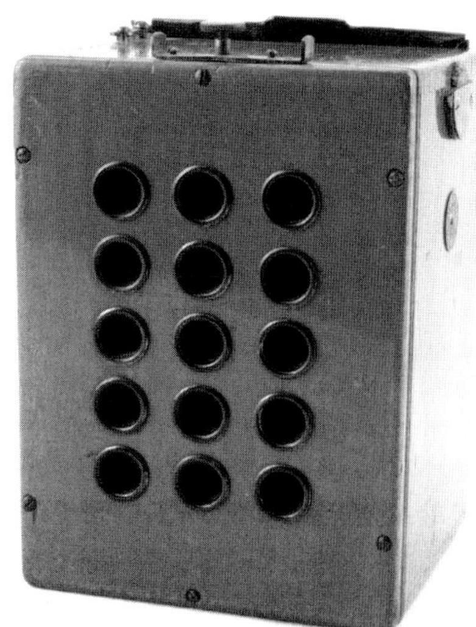

The Butcher's Royal Mail Stamp Camera with its fifteen lenses to shoot fifteen pictures at a time.

In the early 1900s there was a craze for producing ultra-small photographs that resembled stamps, and one of the best cameras for the purpose was also just about the simplest to use – which brought it firmly into the snapshot photographers' domain.

It was introduced in 1909 by the British company W. Butcher & Sons and called the Royal Mail Photo Stamp Camera. Made of mahogany, its unusual feature was the use of fifteen lenses arranged in five rows of thee. With these, it took the same number of identical portraits. A small drawback for the snapshot photographer who had grown up with rolls of film was that the camera used glass plates or cut film, one at a time in special holders that slotted into the back of the camera. The plate or film needed to be loaded into the holder in a darkroom – or, in fact, any space in a house that could be made totally dark – but once the photographer got used to it, the procedure was fairly easy.

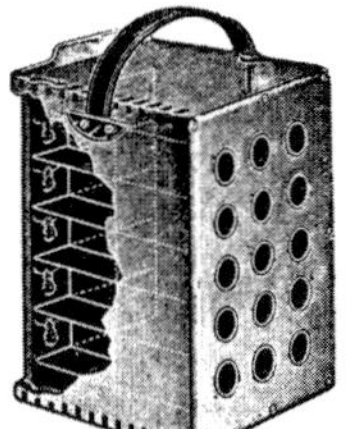

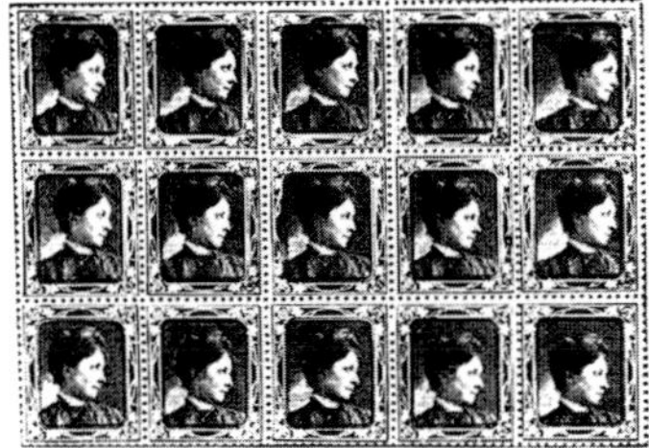

A 1910 advertisement for the Royal Mail Stamp Camera, which shows the way the fifteen pictures were all taken with a single exposure.

Making the exposure was even easier, taking only one press of a lever on top of the body and quickly releasing it. Because of this method of operation, the camera was best used standing on a firm support, or better still fitted to a tripod, for which there was provision on the base and side of the body. Each of the camera's images was about the size of a postage stamp and the Butcher company sold masks with patterns that surrounded the images at the printing stage to make the pictures look even more like stamps. Also, the photographic paper provided for making the prints was perforated to make squares into which the pictures fell, and to complete the stamp illusion, bottles of Royal Mail gum were sold to coat the back of the pictures.

The late nineteenth and early twentieth centuries saw a steep rise in popularity of stereo photography among professional and keen amateur photographers,

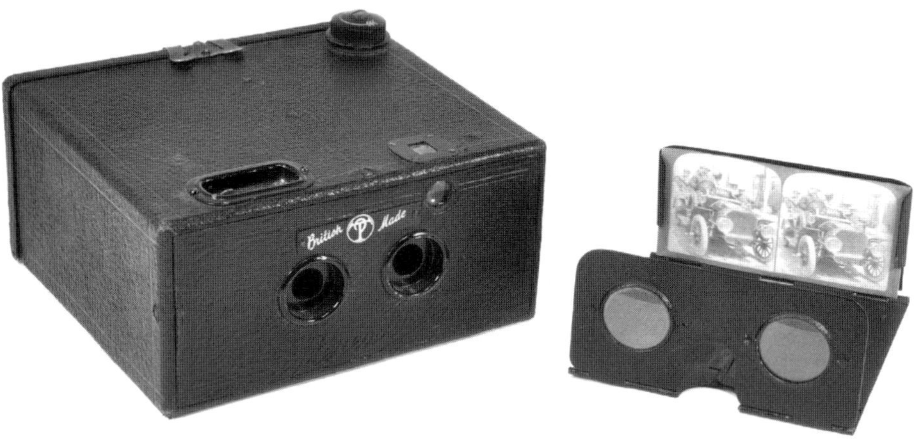

The Thornton Pickard Stereo Puck camera, pictured with its stereo viewer, with a design very similar to the No.2 Stereo Kodak.

and this also found its way into the snapshot camera market. Stereo, also known as 3D (for three-dimensional), photography needed a camera with two lenses to take two pictures from very slightly different viewpoints, in the same way as two human eyes see the world. When the pictures were viewed in a stereo viewer, so that the left eye saw only the one taken with the left lens, and the right eye saw only the one from the right lens, a single image was observed in three dimensions.

The No.2 Stereo Kodak, introduced in 1901, did this with a simple box-type camera with the required two lenses and viewfinder between them. It took two pictures 3½ × 3½ inches on 101 size film, or it could be switched to take single pictures one at a time by means of a blind that closed over one of the lenses. A similar style was used later, in 1931, for the British-made Thornton Pickard Stereo Puck camera, which was sold with its own special stereo viewer.

Then there were cameras aimed at introducing children to the joys of snapshot photography. The aptly named Little Nipper began life in 1901 as a simple camera for glass plates whose use might have been a little beyond the capabilities of some children. But by 1921, the same camera had turned into a much simpler box camera that used film and which definitely had the young market in its sights. To encourage an interest in young snapshot photographers a complete film developing and printing kit was available, to make small prints, as well as a special enlarger for making larger postcard size prints from Little Nipper negatives. Each camera also came with an invitation to join the Little Nipper Club, which entitled members to a monthly copy of the *Little Nipper Times* newsletter. Also on offer were a special album for Little Nipper prints and the Little Nipper Mount for single pictures made by the camera.

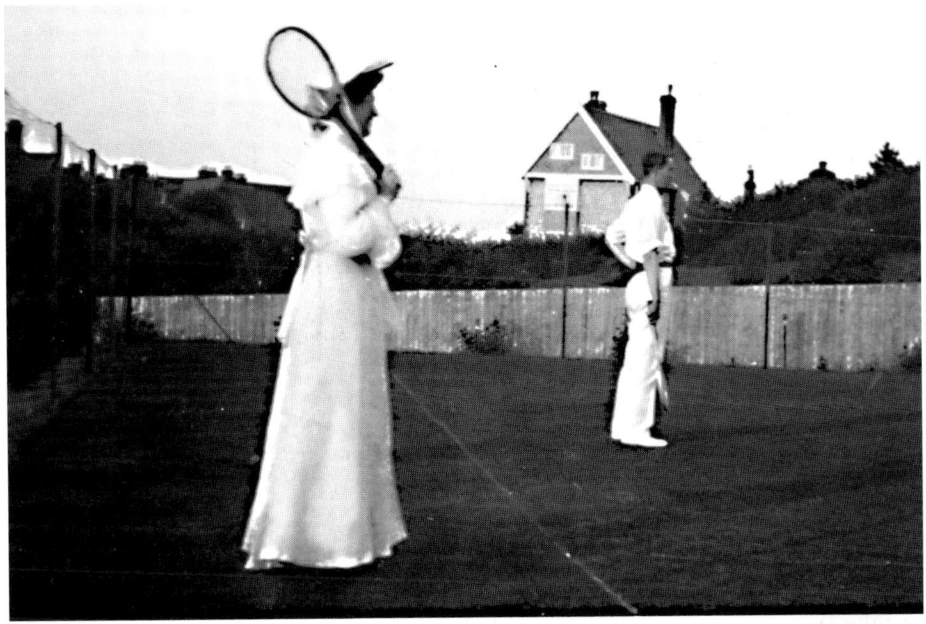

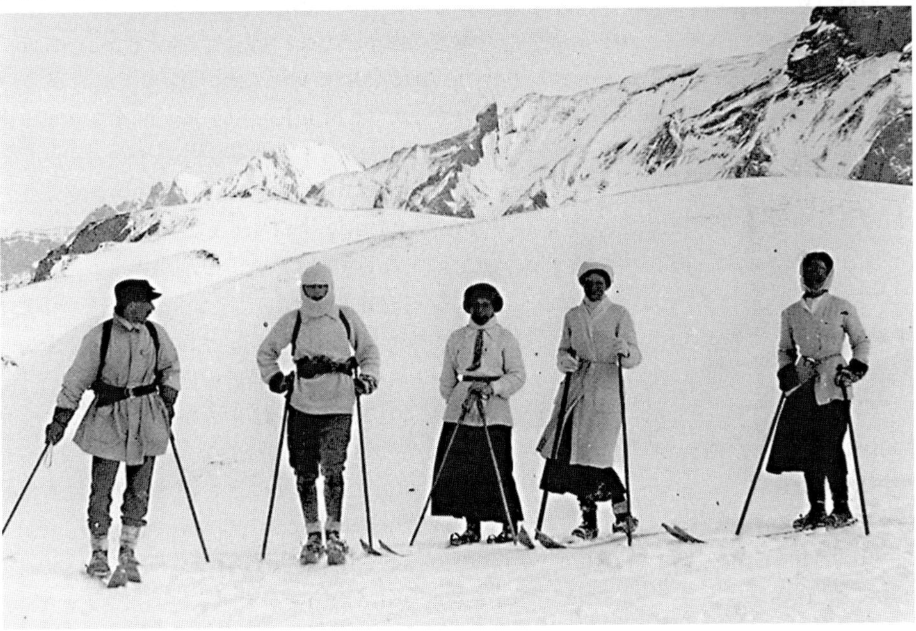

Two snapshots reveal the very different ways people approached sporting activities years ago. Here we see tennis being played by a lady in a long dress and big hat, and while the male skiers in the second picture appear to be suitably dressed, the ladies seem to think long coats and ankle-length skirts are more appropriate for a dash down the ski slopes.

By this time, Kodak had also introduced the Brownie camera, equally aimed at the younger generation. Of which, more later.

The Little Nipper, along with an advertisement for the camera, aimed at introducing youngsters to simple snapshot photography.

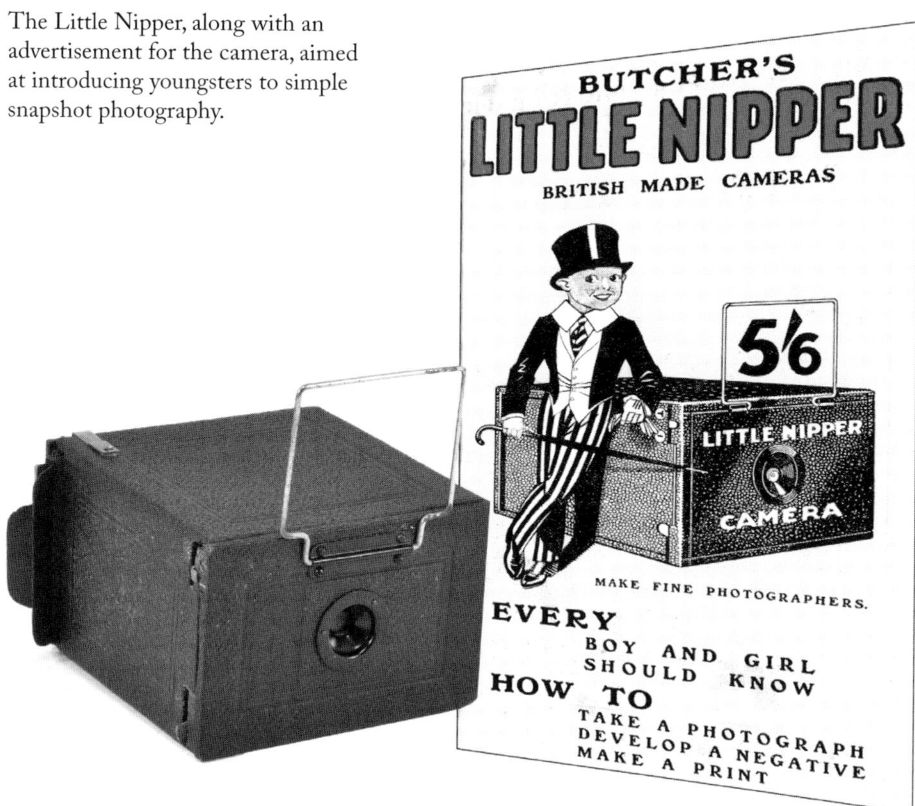

Chapter 3

Snapshots While You Wait

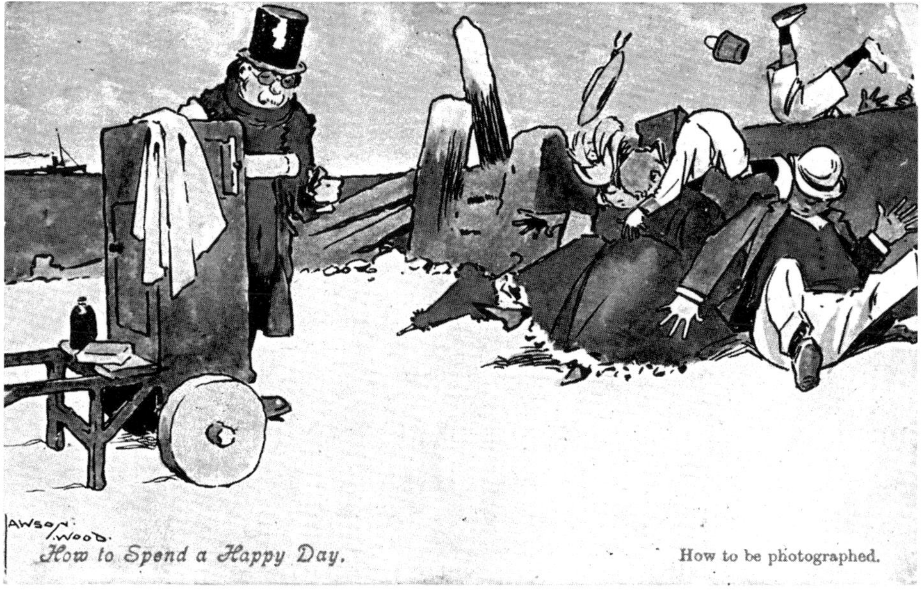

Posted in February 1909, this postcard makes fun of a while-you-wait beach photographer at work.

The premise that snapshot photography was not solely the prerogative of the inexperienced amateur, and that professionals might also take snapshots, was never more true than in the case of 'while-you-wait' photographers. This group of professionals set up their cameras in the street or at fairs, carnivals and other similar gatherings to produce photographs of passers-by, which could be shot, developed and a finished picture presented to the subject literally within minutes. If the picture didn't turn out quite as good as hoped, the photographers often touched the image up slightly using their fingers covered in pencil lead. In this way, street photographers became known as smudgers.

Many of the early while-you-wait cameras produced pictures on metal plates, backed with black lacquer. They were known as ferrotypes or, more popularly, as tintypes. Unlike more conventional cameras that produced a negative image on glass or film which then had to be printed to make a positive image on paper, the tintype produced direct positives without the need for an intermediary

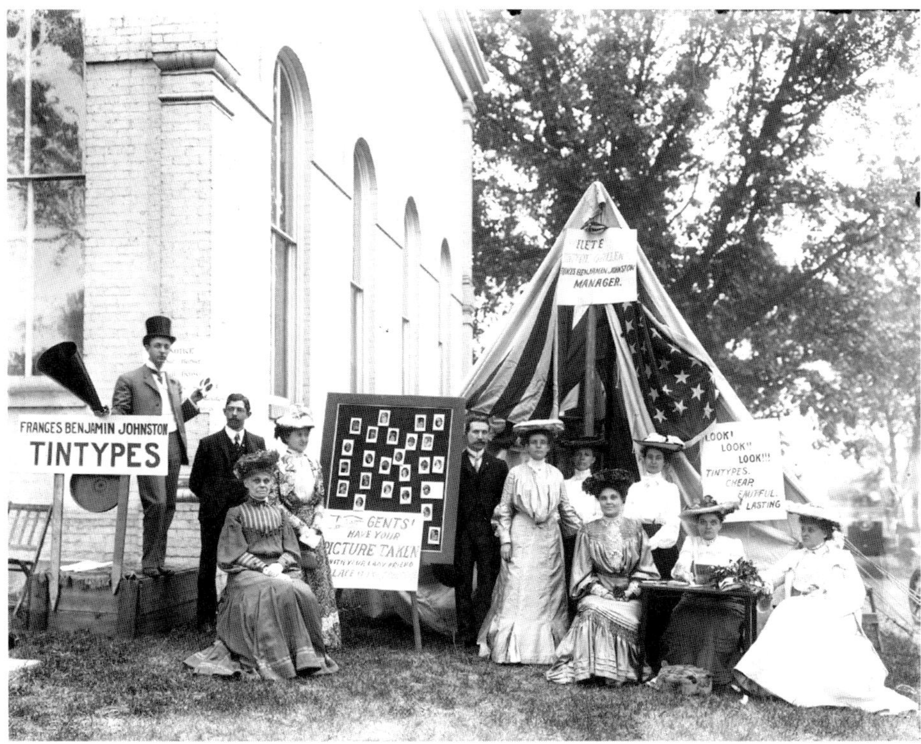

An American county fair tintype booth under the management of Frances Benjamin Johnston in 1903. The picture has more to it than first meets the eye. It was taken, not with a tintype instant picture camera, but with a professional plate camera, by Johnston herself, known for her society portraits and news pictures that included the last portrait of President William McKinley in 1901 just before his assassination and two years before this picture was taken. In fact, she was the official White House photographer throughout four presidential administrations, earning her the title of 'Photographer to the American Court'. As a public speaker and writer, Johnston also championed the rights of liberated women. Strange, then, that the notice beneath the tintype display carries the slightly misogynistic message 'Gents! Have your picture taken with your lady friend'.

negative. This helped speed up the process and get the finished picture into the hands of the subject being photographed much faster. After the exposure had been made, the tintype was dropped into a special solution, which developed the image then fixed it. The parts that were most exposed were seen as white or light grey, while the least exposed parts were translucent, allowing the black lacquer backing to show through. The result was a positive image.

The Aptus

Launched in 1913, and made by More and Co. in Liverpool, the Aptus had an extremely long life with later updated models of the camera still in use as late as the 1950s. The first models took tintype pictures. The complications of the camera's use would have been beyond the average snapshot photographer, but for the professional street photographer, they came as second nature.

The camera took the form of a large box mounted on a tripod. The shutter was incorporated into a door, which opened and closed over the lens inside. On the base of the rear of the camera, a double developing tank hung down beneath the body. The other controls consisted of a lever on the side, a rubber bulb on the end of a tube which disappeared into the body and a spindle on the base that travelled up inside the camera.

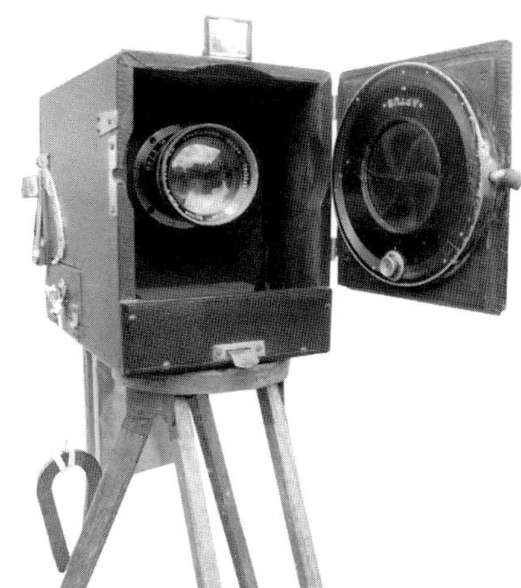

The Aptus tintype camera.

The way all those controls came together to take and develop the picture was as follows.

The tintype plates were first loaded into a magazine, which was inserted horizontally into an opening at the bottom of one side of the body. A cover was then withdrawn from the magazine so that the plates could be accessed by the mechanism inside the body. The lever on the side was turned through 90 degrees, which had the effect of lowering an arm inside the body to a place just above the magazine of plates. A rubber bed at the end of the arm was attached to the bulb outside the camera by the interconnecting rubber tube. The bulb was pressed to expel air, the spindle beneath the camera was pushed up to bring the first plate into contact with the rubber bed and the bulb was released. This had the effect of creating a vacuum and the suction caused the plate to attach itself to the rubber bed.

The outside arm was then returned to its original place, which brought the plate attached to the arm up into the right position for an exposure. Focusing was

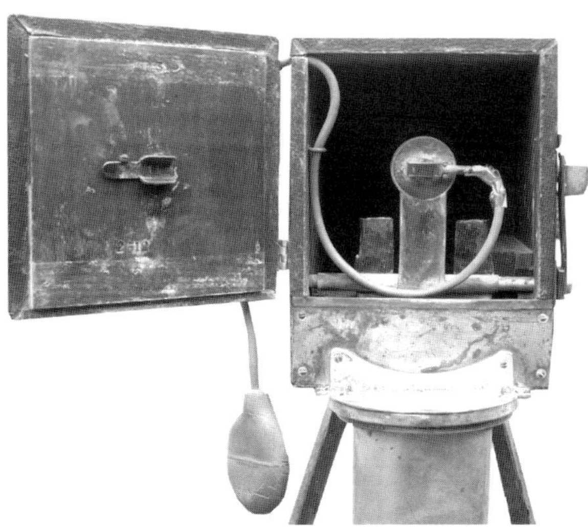

The inner workings of the Aptus.

achieved by pulling out a lever to the appropriate distance, designated as 2, 3, or 6 yards. The shutter was released, usually by means of a cable release attached to the front of the camera. The rubber bulb was then again pressed, which expelled air from the tube and the rubber bed, allowing the plate to drop down into the developing tank beneath the body. The tank contained a solution that both developed and fixed the image so that it could be viewed in normal light in about thirty seconds.

The tank was then rotated through 180 degrees. This had the effect of bringing the part containing the tintype to a position that made it easy to open a lid and remove it. Because the pictures were on metal plates, which were magnetic, they could be extracted from the tank by means of a magnet. At the same time, the action placed a second tank with more developing/fixing solution inside into position ready for the next plate to drop. The extracted plate was then washed in a bucket of water, dried and sometimes placed into a special cardboard mount, ready to be presented to the customer. In this way, the makers rather optimistically suggested that photographers could turn out at least 100 finished pictures per hour. 'Turns every minute into money,' claimed the advertising.

By 1930, the tintype plates had been replaced with black cards on which a photographic emulsion was coated. Not being made of metal, the pictures were no longer magnetic and so could not be removed from the tank with a magnet. Apart from that, the method of shooting and processing was much the same. The very similar Takuquick Ferrotype Camera, sold by the British Jonathan Fallowfield company in 1910, was similar to the Aptus in the way it was operated.

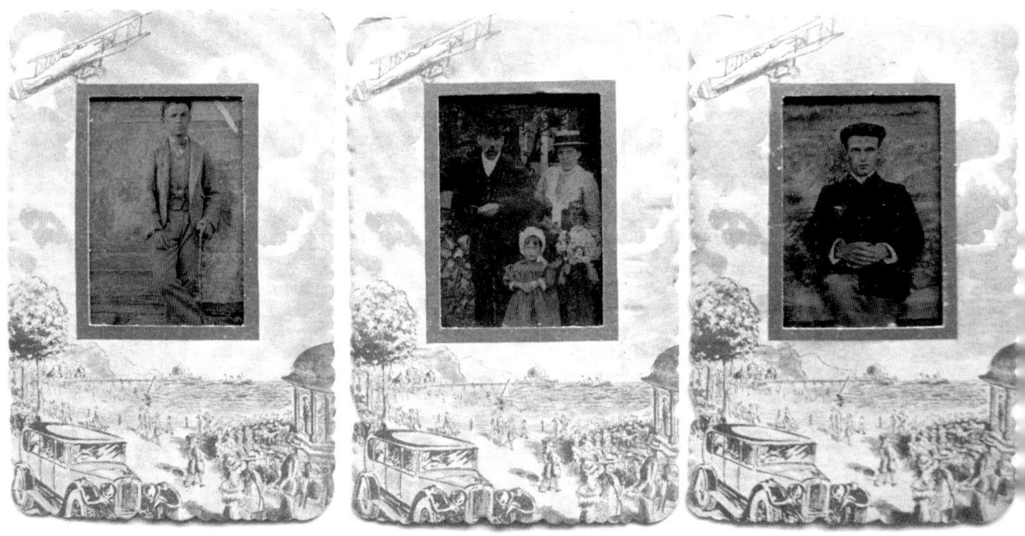

Three tintype pictures taken with the Aptus camera illustrated here and inserted in the photographer's special presentation cards, probably around 1923.

Jano While-U-Wait

A small piece of cardboard coated with a photographic emulsion was also used in the Jano While-U-Wait Camera made by a company called Janovitch, which, despite its foreign-sounding name, was actually established in London in 1929. The company began making street cameras in 1930 and continued until the 1950s.

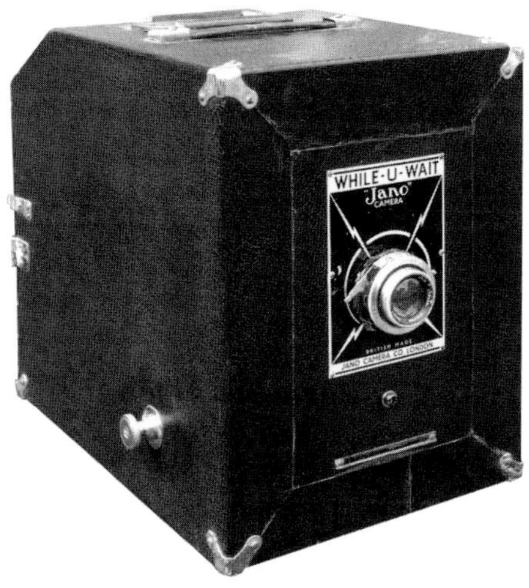

The Jano While-U-Wait camera.

The While-U-Wait camera was shaped like a large box with a lightproof elasticised sleeve covering a circular opening in the back of the body with two drawers below it. One of these drawers held a developing solution, the other a fixing solution to stabilise the photographic image after development so that it could be viewed in normal light.

With the camera back open, the picture was focused on an internal ground-glass screen. Closing the back, the operator slid an arm through the lightproof sleeve and into the inside of the body to position the picture card behind the

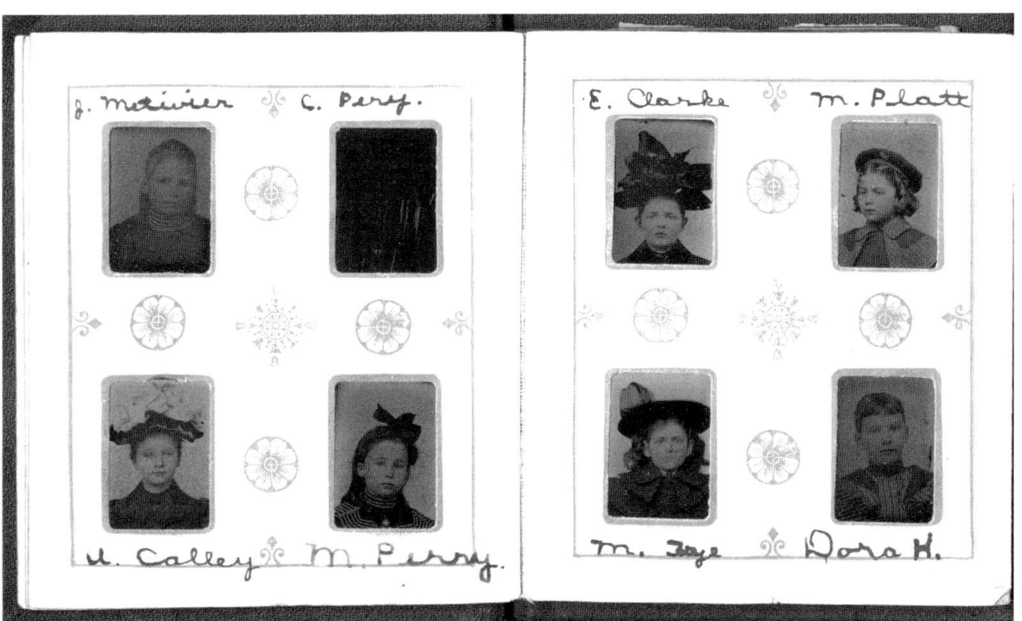

Tintypes were often displayed in family albums, like this one from *c.*1900–1905.

lens. The exposure was then made in the normal way. After exposure, the photographer once again inserted his arm into the sleeve to manipulate the card and manually drop it into the tray of developer and then fixer, while viewing development through a red window on the top of the camera. After fixing the negative image, the card was removed from the camera and placed in a cradle attached to the lens to be rephotographed, development taking place as before. Because the negative image was rephotographed as another negative, the final result was a positive picture.

Mandal-ette

The Jano While-U-Wait camera was gigantic, but a much smaller camera, using much the same way of working, was seen in the American Mandal-ette, launched in 1909. The camera shot direct positive 2½ × 3½-inch images on black-coated cardboard. The cards, sold in packs of sixteen or fifty, were loaded into the camera in daylight and were then manipulated inside the body by inserting an arm into the elasticated sleeve, similar to, but smaller than the one used on the Jano camera. After exposure, the card was dropped into a developing tank, containing a single solution of developer and fixer, attached to the base of the camera. The developed

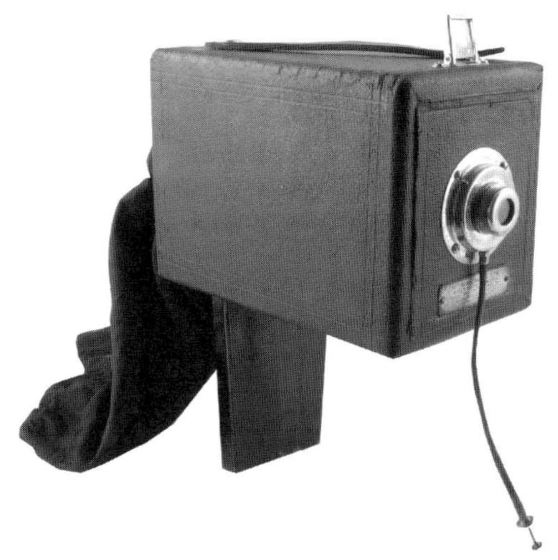

The Mandal-ette, showing the sleeve that allowed access to the inner workings of the camera body.

card could be removed in one minute and then washed for about fifteen seconds before being handed to the person who had been photographed. Advertisements placed by the Chicago Ferrotype Company, makers of the Mandel-ette, suggested that street photographers who used the camera could make a profit of eight cents per picture. Larger format pictures were available in cameras that followed the original model.

Wonder Photo Cannon

Launched in 1910, also from the Chicago Ferrotype Company, this camera took its name from its cannon-shaped body. It was a metal camera for producing

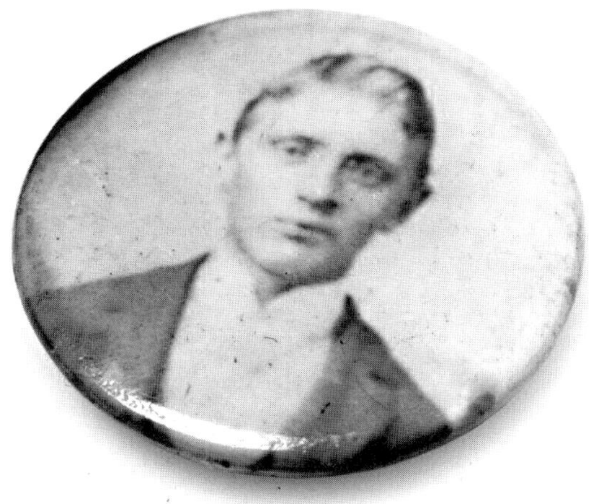

A tintype button produced by the Photo Cannon.

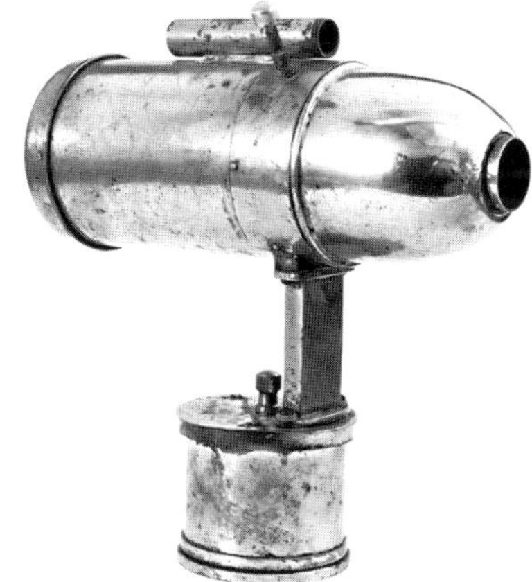

The all-metal Wonder Photo Cannon.

small, circular tintypes, 1 inch in diameter, for turning into photo badges. The tintype plates were held in a tube and, as each one was exposed, it was released to fall through a duct into a developing tank, where it was processed into a positive image. The makers claimed that the operator could make a good living shooting and processing 360 pictures an hour, which might have been a slight exaggeration.

PDQ

The acronym by which this strangely shaped camera was known stood for 'Photography Done Quickly'. The camera was launched in 1935 by the American PDQ Camera Company, formerly the Chicago Ferrotype Company. It shot

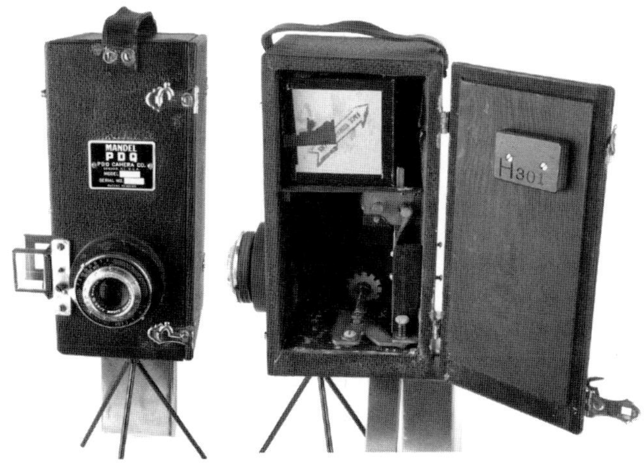

Inside and outside the PDQ.

pictures 6×9cm on rolls of what the makers called Super Speed Direct-Positive Photo Paper instead of traditional film, plates or even tintypes. The paper produced positive images when processed in the appropriate chemistry. Turning a handle on the side of the camera's body released the paper and placed it behind the lens. After exposure, the photographer pulled a knob, which activated a cutter that cut the exposed paper, allowing it to drop into the developing tank below. After a few minutes in the tank's processing solution, a positive print was produced.

Amateur cameras

The cameras mentioned so far were chiefly aimed at professional street photographers. The idea of instant – or at least very quick – pictures, in the days before Polaroid changed that particular realm, eventually filtered down to the amateur photographer market and on to the kind of photographer who took only snapshots. Here are some of those cameras…

Dandycam

As early as 1911, snapshot photographers could use this small box-type camera to produce 1-inch diameter circular tintypes within minutes of exposure. The plates were first loaded into a compartment in the side of the camera and held in place at the front by a strong spring. A lever on the side of the body was then pulled out and pressed in again to engage with the first plate and push it into position for the first exposure. The lens was in a strange place in the top left corner of the front of the camera. It was there to direct its image via an internal angled mirror up to a round viewfinder on the top of

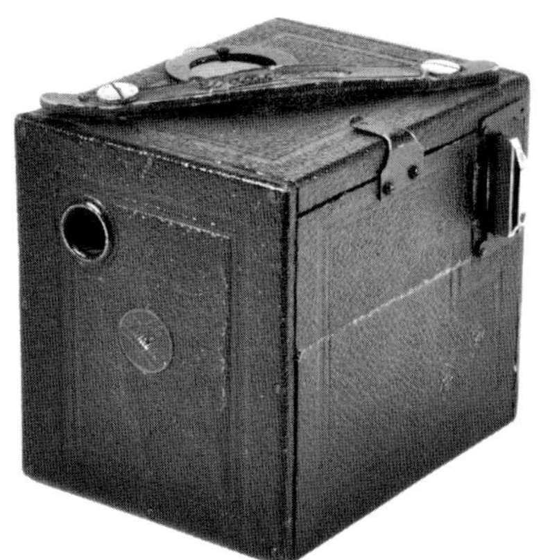

The Dandycam tintype camera.

the body. This was covered in red glass because the viewfinder looked into the body of the camera itself. The tintype plates were insensitive to red light so they were not spoiled as they would have been if normal light had seeped in through the viewfinder.

Exposure was made by turning a knob on the side of the body that lifted the mirror, allowing light to reach the plate. When the knob was released, the mirror fell back into its original position to cut off light to the plate, completing the exposure and restoring the mirror's image in the viewfinder.

After exposure, the previously used lever was pulled from the side, which released the plate behind the lens to fall into a tiny developing tank in the base of the body. When the lever was pressed in again it pushed the next plate into position for the following exposure. The tank contained a one-shot developing and fixing solution which produced a fully developed positive image in about five minutes. The images so produced were designed to be inserted into pieces of jewellery like pendants and brooches.

Photo-See
The American Photo-See Corporation made this small box camera in 1936 to shoot and develop an image in five minutes. It did so by encasing single sheets of film in light-tight sleeves. With the camera closed, the film was extracted from the sleeve by a mechanism on the back of the body, the picture was taken, and then the film was re-inserted into its sleeve. Using a similar process, the sleeve was then placed in the camera's special developing tank and processed by chemicals poured into and out of spouts on the front of the tank.

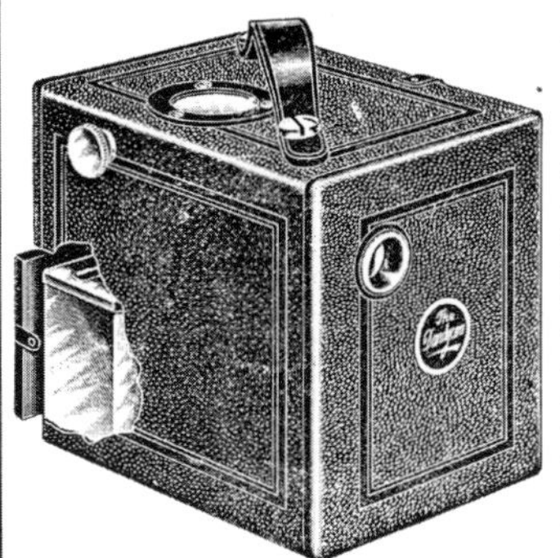
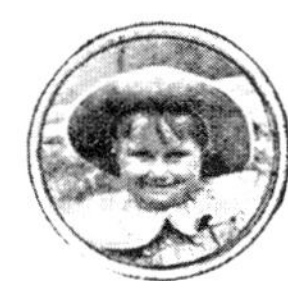
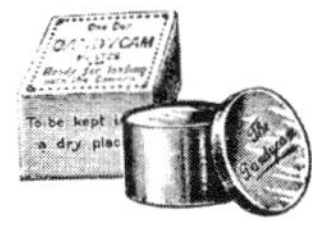

A 1912 advertisement for the Dandycam, showing the price of the camera and of the tintypes and other accessories it used.

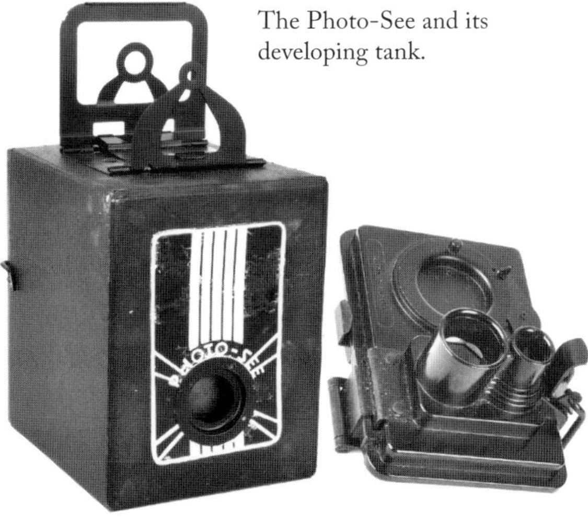
The Photo-See and its developing tank.

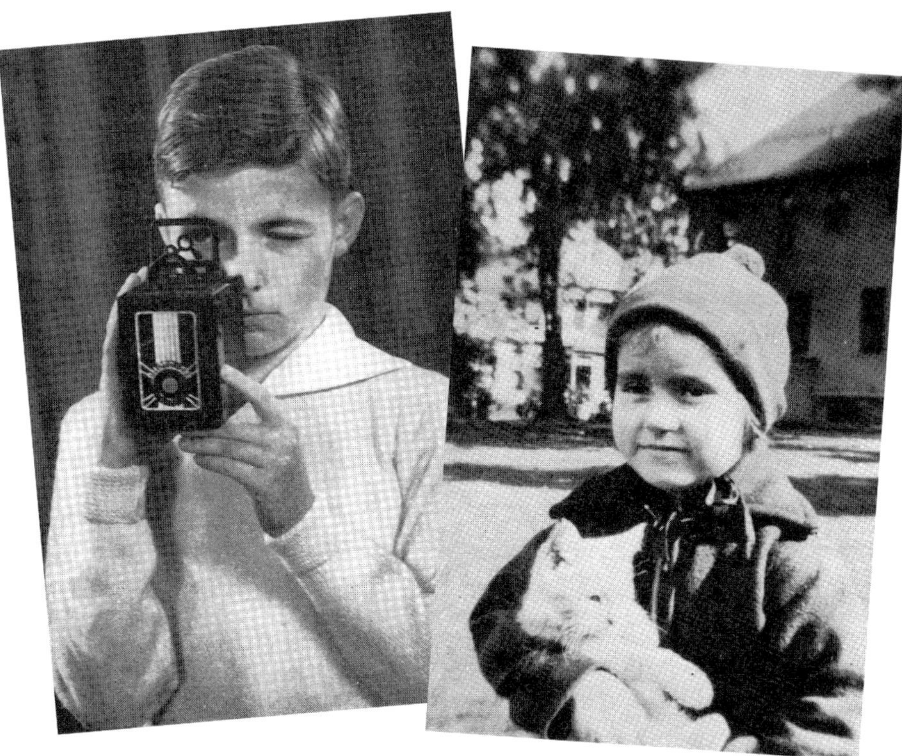

The 1936-dated instruction booklet for the Photo-See shows how simple it is for even a small boy to use, while a picture of another child inside the booklet claims it was taken by the camera.

Speed-O-Matic

The Speed-O-Matic was a Bakelite camera that took pictures on direct positive paper, sold two sheets at a time in light-tight holders. A holder was slotted into one end of the camera and a lever pulled to extract the paper and place it into position for shooting. A built-in exposure meter supplied a number that was set on a dial beneath the lens to adjust the aperture, the shutter was released and the paper pushed back into its holder.

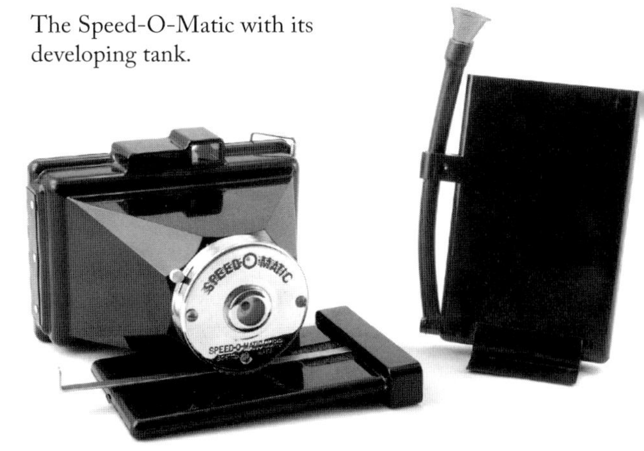

The Speed-O-Matic with its developing tank.

The holder was then fitted onto a sleeve, which

was attached to a developing tank and another lever used to pull the paper from the sleeve, into the tank. Four developing solutions were poured in and out of the tank via a tiny funnel at the end of a rubber tube, after which the sleeve was removed and the developed picture extracted.

Unfortunately for the American Speed-O-Matic Corporation that made the camera, they chose 1948 to launch it, which was the year that the first Polaroid camera also hit the market, after which the Speed-O-Matic drifted into obscurity.

Kookie

Even years after Polaroid had taken a grip on the instant picture market, at least one company attempted to have a go at producing an instant, while-you-wait picture camera. The Kookie, launched in 1968 by American Ideal Toy Company, represented snapshot photography at its best, although the camera was actually little more than a toy.

The camera stood at the top of what appeared to be a complicated pattern of pipes. Protruding from the side was an arm and a hand, holding a flashgun that accepted flashcubes. Beneath that, another arm and hand held a tray with a tin of tomato soup on it. The so-called soup can was actually a lens hood, and the lens could be better fitted with a special mirror accessory to purposely distort the images. It shot small, square direct positive images on special paper film. As each picture was taken, a cutter was operated and the paper fell into a developing tank below the body, in which a one-shot solution produced direct positive pictures. A built-in egg timer was used for measuring development times.

Chapter 4
The Rise of the Brownie

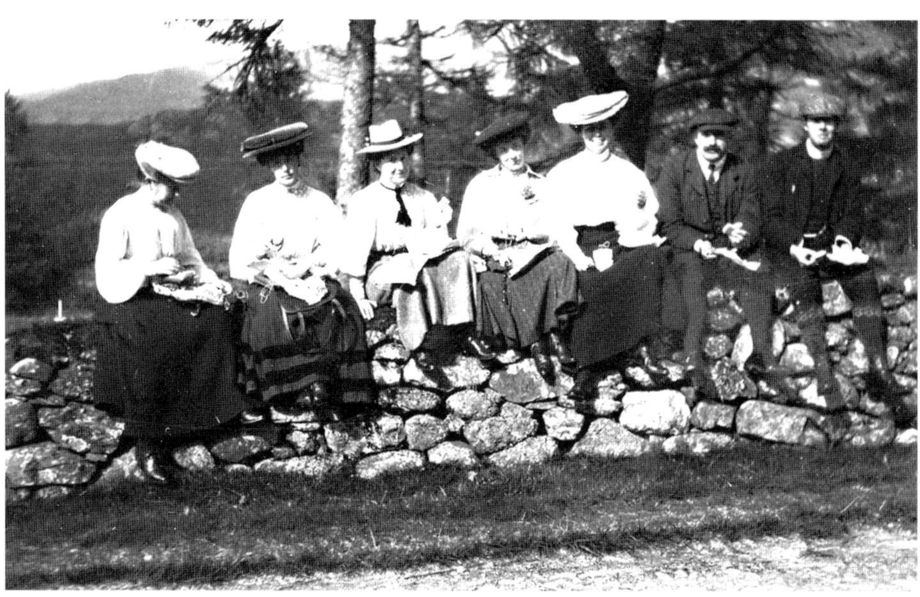

Picnics are thought to have started among the aristocracy during the eighteenth century when they were purely indoor events. By 1900, when the first Brownie appeared, ready to record people at leisure, picnics had moved to outdoors and had become a favourite way of casual eating for everyone. So here's a happy group of seven picnickers (probably eight with the photographer), one family maybe, or just a group of friends. They've come well prepared, each with his or her pack of food. Only one thing remains a mystery. Look at the height of the wall and ask yourself how they all got up there.

In the world of snapshot cameras, the Brownie was one name that stood above all others. It proved to be an iconic name which became generic so that, to most snapshot photographers, any camera that was box-shaped and easy to use was referred to as a Box Brownie, irrespective of the company that made it – rather in the way that ballpoint pens became Biros and vacuum cleaners became Hoovers. But it was Kodak that made the first Brownie and who subsequently used the name on a vast range of different types of camera, all simplified for ease of use, for best part of a century.

The first Brownie appeared in 1900. It was made of jute board and wood, covered with imitation leather, with nickel fittings, in a box shape that measured

12.5×8×8cm. The camera was designed for Kodak by Frank Brownell, the man Kodak entrepreneur George Eastman called 'the greatest camera designer that ever lived'. Because of the similarity in the name of the camera to that of the man who designed it, the assumption is often that the Brownie was named after Brownell. In fact, the Brownie name came about for much more commercial reasons. Eastman, who was a great marketeer, had already spotted a gap in the market when he introduced the Kodak to a new generation of snapshot photographers. Now he found another

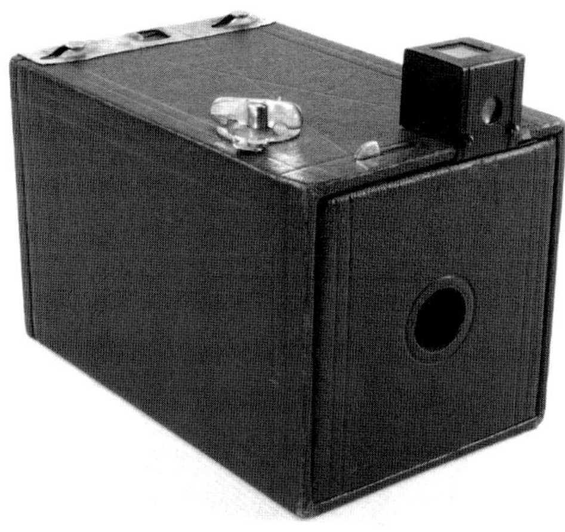

The first model of the Brownie with its extra clip-on viewfinder. The picture shows the second variation of the camera.

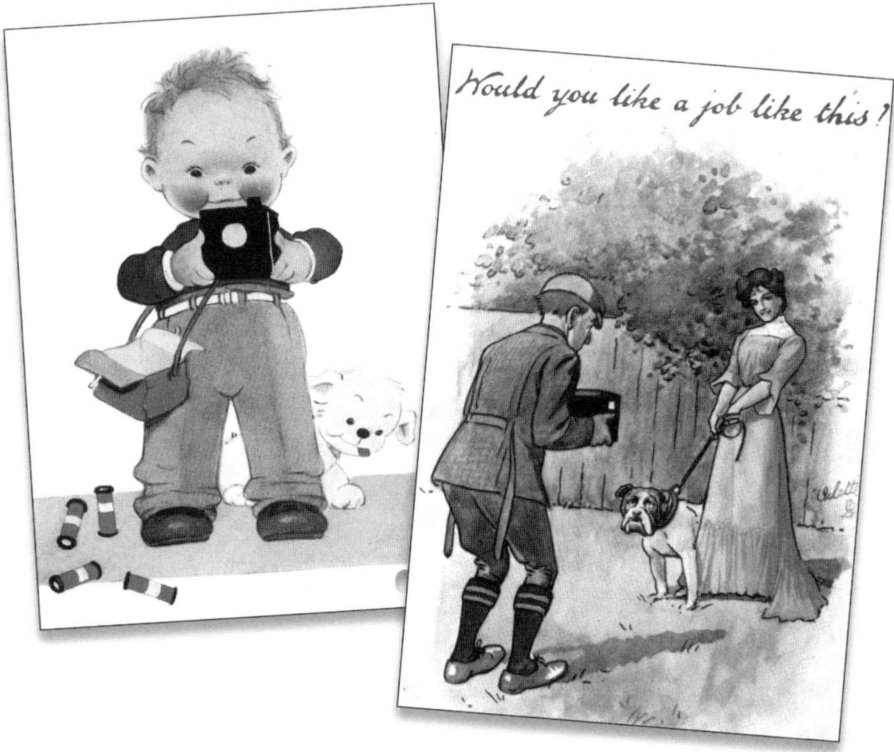

Two postcards of the time, showing how children were associated with Brownie-type box cameras right from the start, and the casual approach that snapshot photographers now began to take with their subjects.

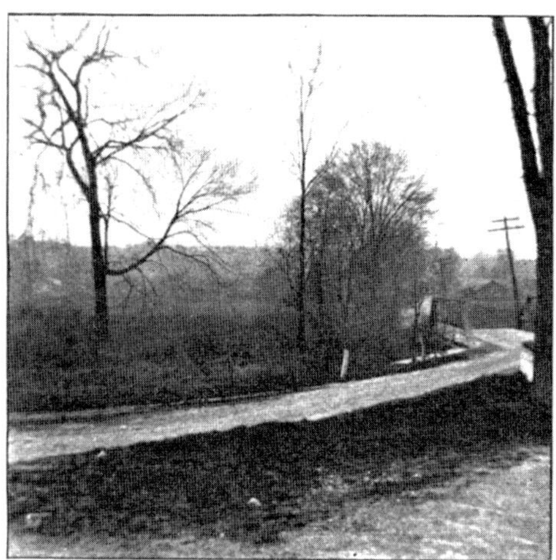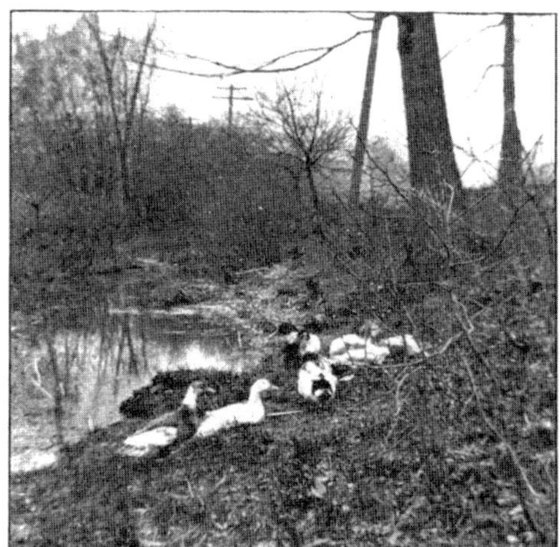

Two snapshots taken with Brownie cameras.

market gap. Brownies, at that time, were characters like elves created by Canadian author and illustrator Palmer Cox, and extremely popular with children. So Eastman chose the Brownie name for the advantage it would give him in advertising and promoting a camera whose price would make it available to children as well as their parents. A Kodak Trade Circular sent out by the company in May 1900 encouraged dealers to sell the cameras, even though their low prices meant equally low profit margins. 'Plant the Brownie acorn and the Kodak oak will grow,' they were told. In the first year of its launch, more than 100,000 cameras were sold.

Now, maybe even more than was the case with the first Kodak, Brownie owners expressed a new freedom in the pictures they took. They photographed friends, family, pets, animals, places they loved to visit. They recorded small moments in their lives as well as large and special occasions. Humour – so often lacking in older forms of photography – became a new aspect of snapshot photography. The stiff and formal poses associated with people pictures in the past became far more casual or turned into playful posturing as subjects laughed, pulled faces at the camera, or adopted weird and sometimes even naughty poses.

Using the first Brownie

The Brownie took a new film, which Kodak referred to as a cartridge, numbered 117, for six exposures, each 2¼ inches square. Advertisements of the day were keen to point out that the camera could be loaded in daylight and took the six pictures without reloading. The camera had no viewfinder. Like the original Kodak before it, the top was etched with V-shape lines as an aid to aiming it. By

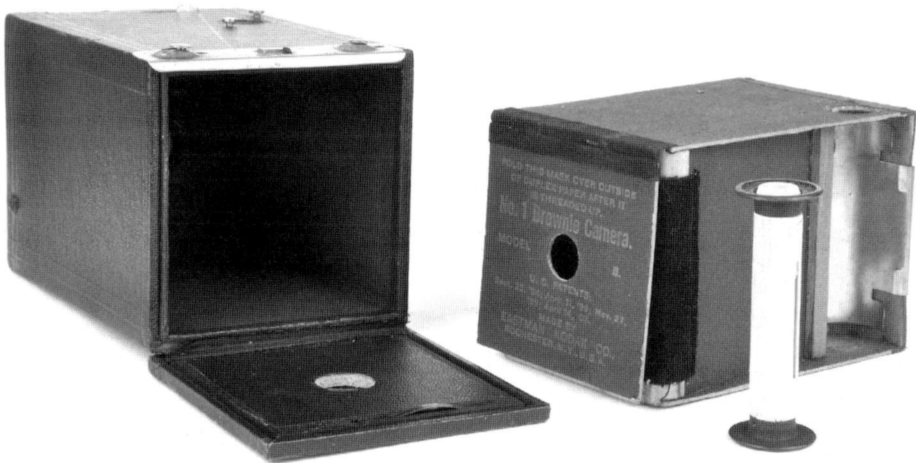

How the Brownie was loaded with film.

July 1900, however, a reflecting viewfinder was sold as an add-on that could be clipped to the front of the body. The principal controls were the shutter release and film wind knob, although it was also capable of time exposures by pulling out what Kodak called the 'time slide' from one side of the body.

With the young photographers' market in mind, Kodak made a point of explaining that the camera could be readily operated by any schoolboy or schoolgirl, though if some advertisements were to be believed, it was more likely that boys were the ones to take the pictures. In America, the camera was extensively advertised in children's magazines, where readers were invited to join the Brownie Camera Club of America. The club had a very full constitution, which, in part, stated:

> The objects of this club shall be to increase the interest of American Boys and Girls in matters pertaining to photography. Any boy or girl under six years of age now residing in the United States of America or any of its possessions or residing in Canada, shall be entitled to membership in this club if he or she is the owner of a Brownie Camera, and complies with Article IX of this constitution.

That Article IX involved filling out and signing a form confirming name, address and age, whereupon members received a certificate of membership. The first member, 13-year-old J. Franklin Putnam, joined on 22 April 1900.

The competition had two sections: one for club members who not only shot but also developed and printed their pictures, and a second for those whose pictures were commercially processed. Twenty-five prizes were awarded in each section, mostly comprising Kodak cameras. When the competition closed, Kodak produced an art brochure, containing some of the best entries, and this was sent free to all Brownie Club members who also received a special gold-coloured pin, marked 'Brownie Camera Club of America' with an engraving of two hands holding a Brownie in its centre.

Although children were a prime target for the Brownie, Kodak didn't ignore their parents. A 1901 advertisement proclaimed: 'Despite its low price and small size, the Brownie is not a toy but a thoroughly efficient instrument.' That said, marketing still treated buyers

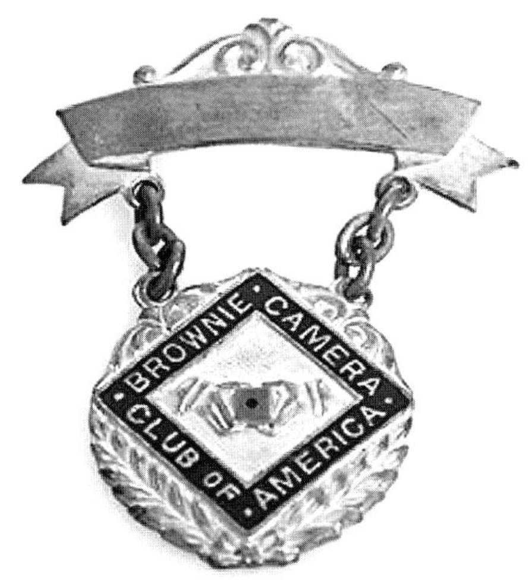

The badge proudly worn by members of the Brownie Camera Club of America.

as total novices, with the instruction book pointing out details that would have been blindingly obvious to more experienced photographers:

> The first thing for the amateur to bear in mind, is that the light which serves to impress the photographic image upon the sensitive film in a fraction of a second when it comes through the lens can destroy the film as quickly as it makes the picture. Until it has been developed and fixed, the film must never be exposed to white light (this includes gas light, lamp light etc) or it will be ruined. Throughout all the operations of loading and unloading, therefore, be extremely careful to keep the black paper wound tightly around the film to prevent the admission of light.

The instructions were equally fulsome over another six pages devoted to holding the camera steady and straight. It was recommended to shoot outside in bright sunlight.

A 1903 advertisement for the first Brownie, along with the No.2 version that was due to appear in 1901.

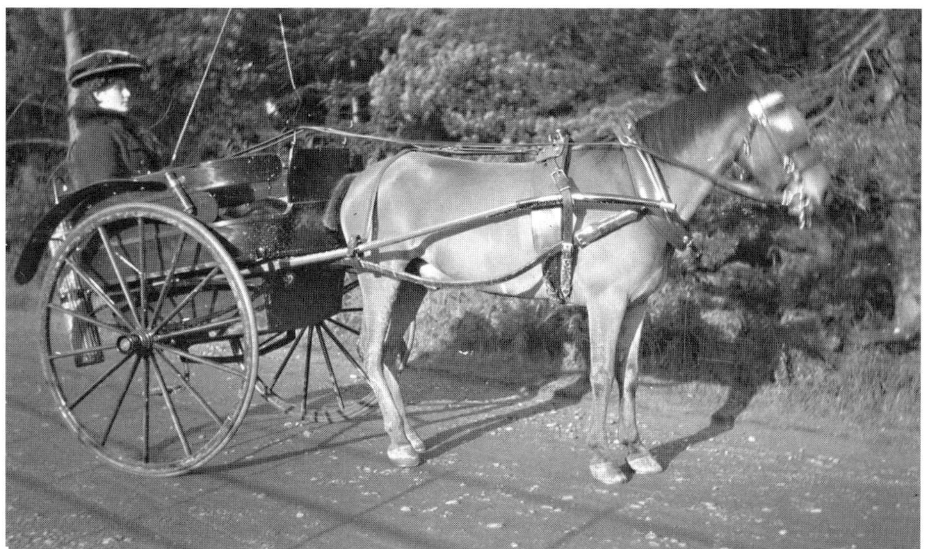

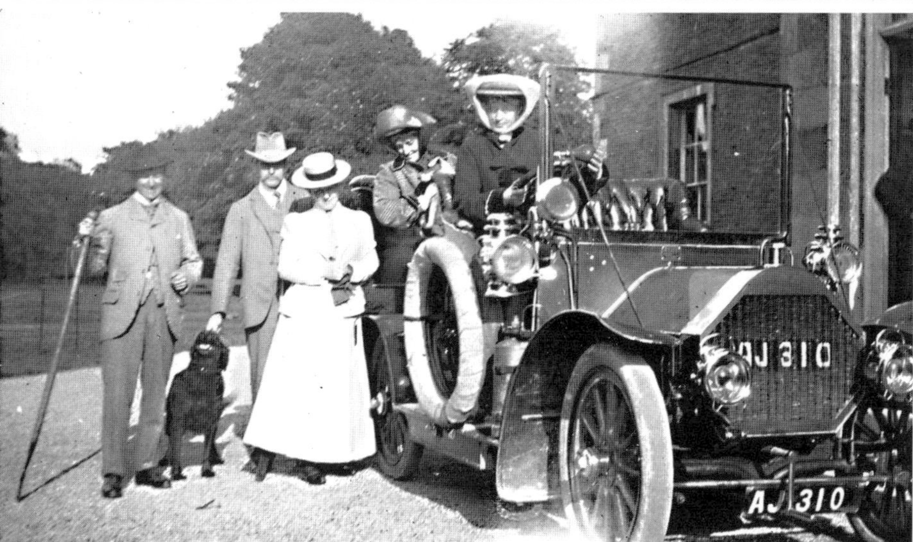

Two snapshots that give an insight into the changing modes of transport during the first decade of the twentieth century. Surprisingly perhaps, the early 1900s saw a boom in the sales of electric cars and it was only in 1908 when Henry Ford introduced his Model T petrol-driven car that enthusiasm for electric vehicles rapidly died. Meanwhile, as seen in the first picture, there were those who thought any type of vehicle that used a horse as its motive power was the only way to travel, even though it was said cities around the world where horse-drawn traffic was at its most dense, were drowning in manure. By 1912, the horse-drawn vehicle was rapidly being replaced by motorised vehicles in most major cities. Outside of towns and cities, however, during the early years of the twentieth century when this snapshot was taken, the horse still played a significant role and was a means of transport much favoured by women. The car in this second snapshot is a clue to its age, suggesting that the picture was taken sometime around 1910. It came from an album that shows the same family in front of a place identified as Rhydd Court in Worcestershire. This was a large country house that was owned, until 1915, by the aristocratic Lechmere family, before becoming a hospital during the First World War, then a school and today a care home. All of which points to the fact that the picture was taken before 1915.

Indoors, and with the help of the 'time slide', things became a bit more complicated. Detailed exposure times were suggested for numerous conditions that included white walls, more than one window; white walls, only one window; medium coloured walls, more than one window; medium coloured walls, only one window; dark coloured walls, more than one window; and dark coloured walls, only one window. Under each of these headings, four exterior weather conditions were specified: bright sun, hazy sun, cloudy bright and cloudy dull. The suggested exposures ranged from two seconds for white walls, more than one window with bright sun outside, to two minutes forty seconds for dark coloured walls in rooms with only one window and cloudy dull conditions outside.

The No.2 Brownie

In 1901, a new version of the camera was introduced. It was called the No.2 Brownie, at which point its predecessor became known as the No.1 Brownie, and continued to be produced until 1915. Although the first camera was a snapshot landmark, it was the No.2 Brownie that had more of an impact on photography in general, due to the fact it was the first camera to take 120 size roll film – the film that became the standard for professional photographers right up until the digital age.

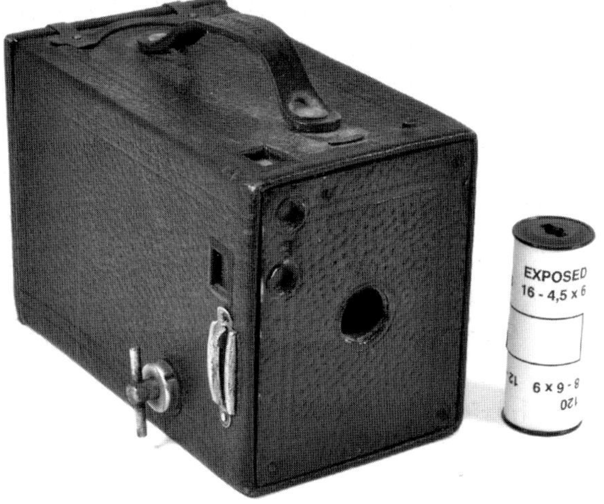

The No.2 Brownie, simple to use but important to photographic history for introducing the immensely popular 120 size film, still available even in today's digital world.

That aside, however, the No.2 Brownie was still a fairly basic box-type snapshot camera, albeit one which was a little more sophisticated than its predecessor. It took eight pictures, 2¼ × 3¼ inches on 120 size film, featured two reflecting viewfinders for vertical and horizontal pictures, and allowed a choice of three apertures on a sliding strip.

The watchword behind every Brownie was simplicity, and that extended to processing as well as the actual photography, with kits bought by some of the more ambitious snapshot photographers. A typical kit might contain a No.2 Brownie camera with all the photographic equipment and chemicals needed to develop and print the film.

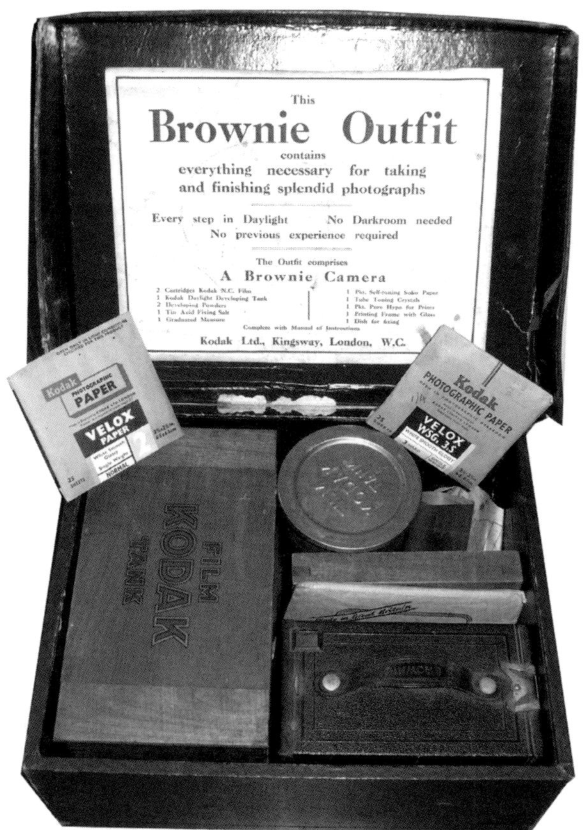

For the only slightly more ambitious, a Brownie Outfit containing the camera and everything needed to develop the film.

In the years ahead, the No.2 Brownie was also seen in the slightly larger sized 2A model, which took 116 size film, and the name went on to be used in many different forms. As well as the standard black, coloured models were made in red, green, blue and grey, plus a special version in silver, made in 1935 to commemorate the British silver jubilee of King George V and Queen Mary. In its various guises, the No.2 Brownie remained in production until the late 1950s.

Brownie variations

During the time the No.2 Brownie in its various forms was in production, Kodak came up with many other types and styles of camera that retained the Brownie name and its simplicity of use for snapshot photographers. The following five represent just a few.

Folding Brownies

Starting in 1903, Kodak made a series of Brownies in a new horizontally styled, box-shaped body with square corners. A bed folded down from the centre and the lens was pulled out along it at the end of bellows. The cameras were very attractive, with black bodies, red bellows and brass fittings. Several different sizes were made until 1915.

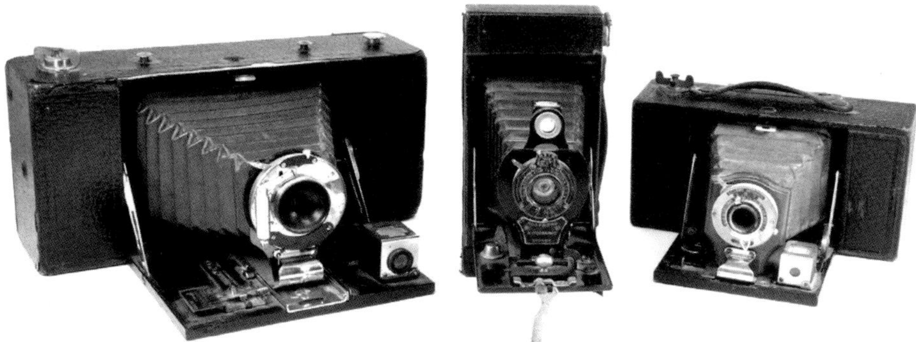

Two models of the Folding Brownie in different sizes: the No.3A (left), No.2 (right) and, between them, a No.2 Folding Autographic model.

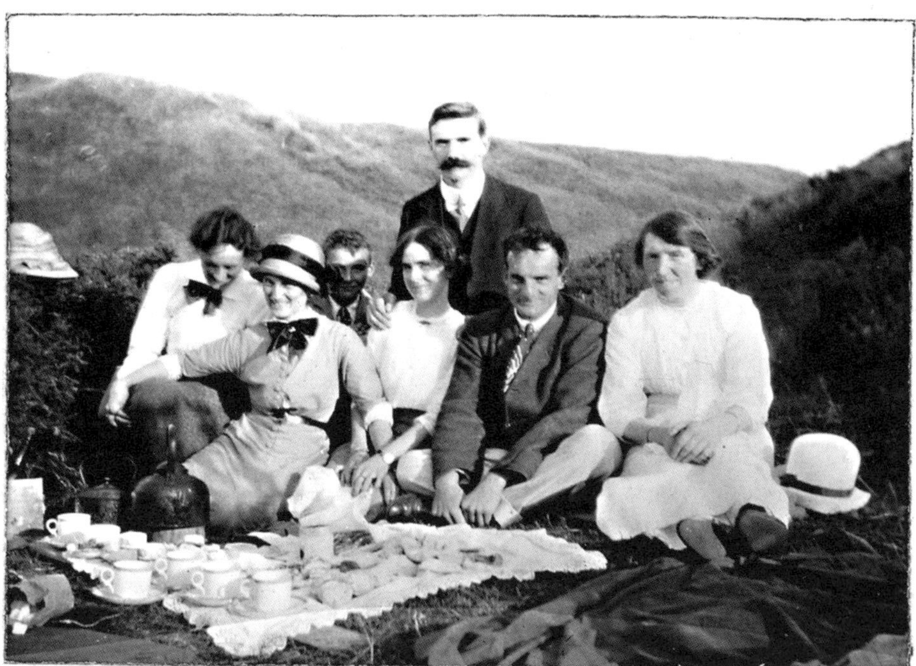

To help date a snapshot, a good clue can often be found in looking at the fashions worn by women in the picture. In this case, the hats are indicative perhaps of the 1920s and into the 1930s, by which time the Brownie had developed into a more sophisticated camera, but one which was still easy to take and use on a casual outing such as this. It was obviously a time when it was normal for a picnic to involve packing a frilly tablecloth, kettle, a Primus stove to boil it on, china cups, saucers, sugar bowl, milk jug and a selection of cakes, all most likely transported to the location by train and a good healthy walk. A snapshot of the event would have been sure to end up in the family album.

In 1915, Kodak's unusual Autographic Back feature, which allowed photographers to write on the film's backing paper and see the resulting words appear on the film, made its appearance on a new style of Brownie. Some with rounded corners, others with square corners. The bodies were used in the upright position, from which a bed, the full width of the camera, folded down for the lens to pull out on bellows. Kodak returned to their more traditional black colour for these cameras.

Beau Brownies

The 1930s was the era of Art Deco design, and the first year of that decade saw Kodak's introduction of the Beau Brownie, which made full use of the trend. The cameras, based on the No.2 and No.2a Brownies, were designed by Walter Teague, one of America's most prolific industrial designers. They were sold with faceplates that used five different two-colour combinations in a deco design: light blue and medium blue, maroon and black, brown and tan, rose and pink, and green and blue. The bodies echoed the darker of the two tones used on the faceplate. Beau Brownies were very pretty, not a word often attributed to cameras. They attracted women, who might otherwise have seen photography as much more a man's domain, into the world of snapshot photography.

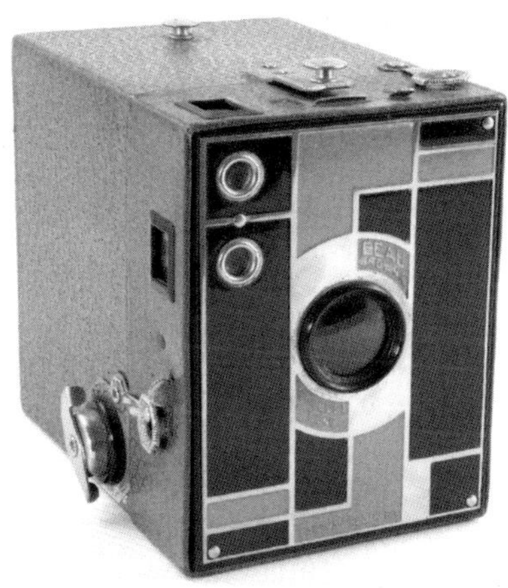

The Beau Brownie was a very stylish box camera from the art deco period.

Six-16 and Six-20 Brownies

The Art Deco fashion continued with these two sizes of box cameras that began in 1933. This time the bodies were traditionally black, but the faceplates were etched with deco designs in silver. They took 116 and 120 size film.

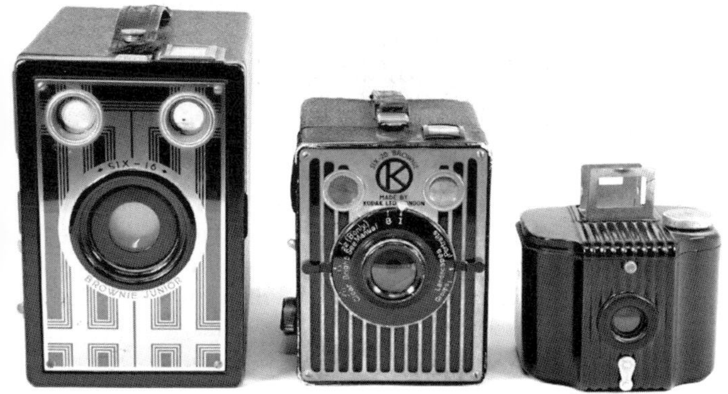

Art Deco designs on the Six-16 Brownie Junior, the Six-20 Brownie and the Bakelite-made Baby Brownie.

Baby Brownie

In 1934, Kodak introduced this completely new style of Brownie camera. It took full use of the malleability of Bakelite to produce an attractive, small, rounded body, ribbed at the front in an Art Deco style and with a wire frame viewfinder that folded up from the top of the body. The simple lever-like shutter release was situated beneath the lens. The Baby Brownie was made to take 127 size film and shot eight 6×4cm pictures to a roll.

These mentioned examples of Brownie cameras are just a small representation among an actual huge plethora of models, many of which were very similar. They were all made by Kodak up to the start of the Second World War, which began in 1939 (although America, where Kodak was very active at that time, did not participate in the war until 1941). Brownie production continued after the war with a great many new, different and sometimes surprising designs. Of which, more later.

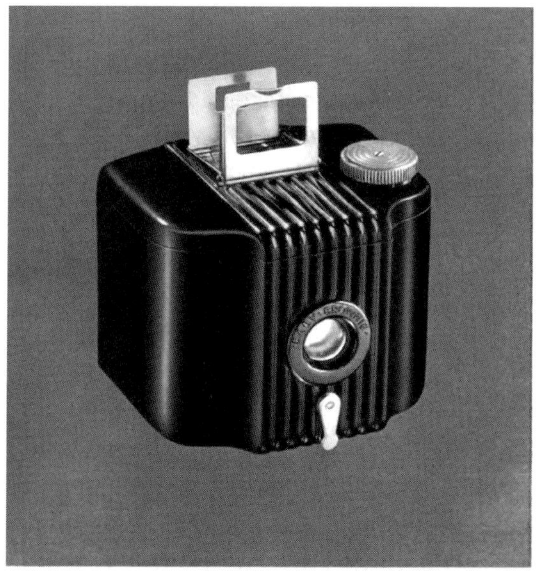

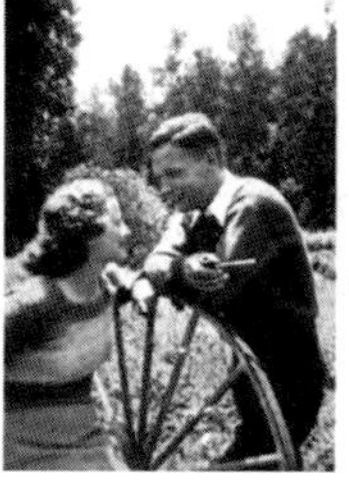
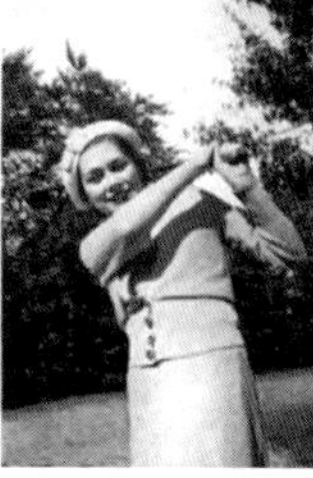

A 1935 advertisement for the Baby Brownie also shows the pictures it took.

Chapter 5

Snapshots go to War

In 1914, war broke out in Europe, with America joining forces in 1917. Many camera manufacturers at this time became involved in making non-photographic equipment for the war effort. Before long it became against the law in Britain to import photographic and other equipment made by enemy nations, severely affecting the photographic trade since so many cameras were made in Germany. The result of these restrictions was that between 1914 and 1918, when the war ended and manufacturing companies began to get back on their feet, the vast majority of cameras available to photographers were older models made before the war.

Using equipment retained from earlier times, the First World War was the first conflict to be covered extensively by professional photographers. With the men off to fight in the war and women at home busy covering their duties in factories and other work places, the joy of snapshot photography took a serious downturn. Kodak, however, pressed on regardless. Two years after war came to Europe and a year before America joined the hostilities, Kodak's annual catalogue still showed more than a dozen cameras in production, most of which could easily have been used by snapshot photographers.

In December 1914, not long after the outbreak of war, the British Army issued a General Routine Order stating that the taking of pictures by military personnel was not permitted, the sending of film through the post was prohibited and anyone contravening those rules would be arrested. Very little was done, however, to check what soldiers of all ranks were carrying in the form of snapshot cameras. Despite the difficulties and prohibitions, snapshot photographers among soldiers of all ranks continued to document the war with pictures of life in the trenches, battlefields and even the famous Christmas truce of 1914 when British and German soldiers emerged from their trenches on Christmas Day to exchange cigarettes and chocolate, to chat as best they could in their different languages and to even play football against one another. For a time the Christmas truce story was thought to be a myth. But snapshots taken by soldiers at the time proved otherwise.

An article in the June 1915 issue of *Kodakery*, a magazine produced by Kodak for its customers, headed 'The Part of the Kodak at the Front', spoke of the

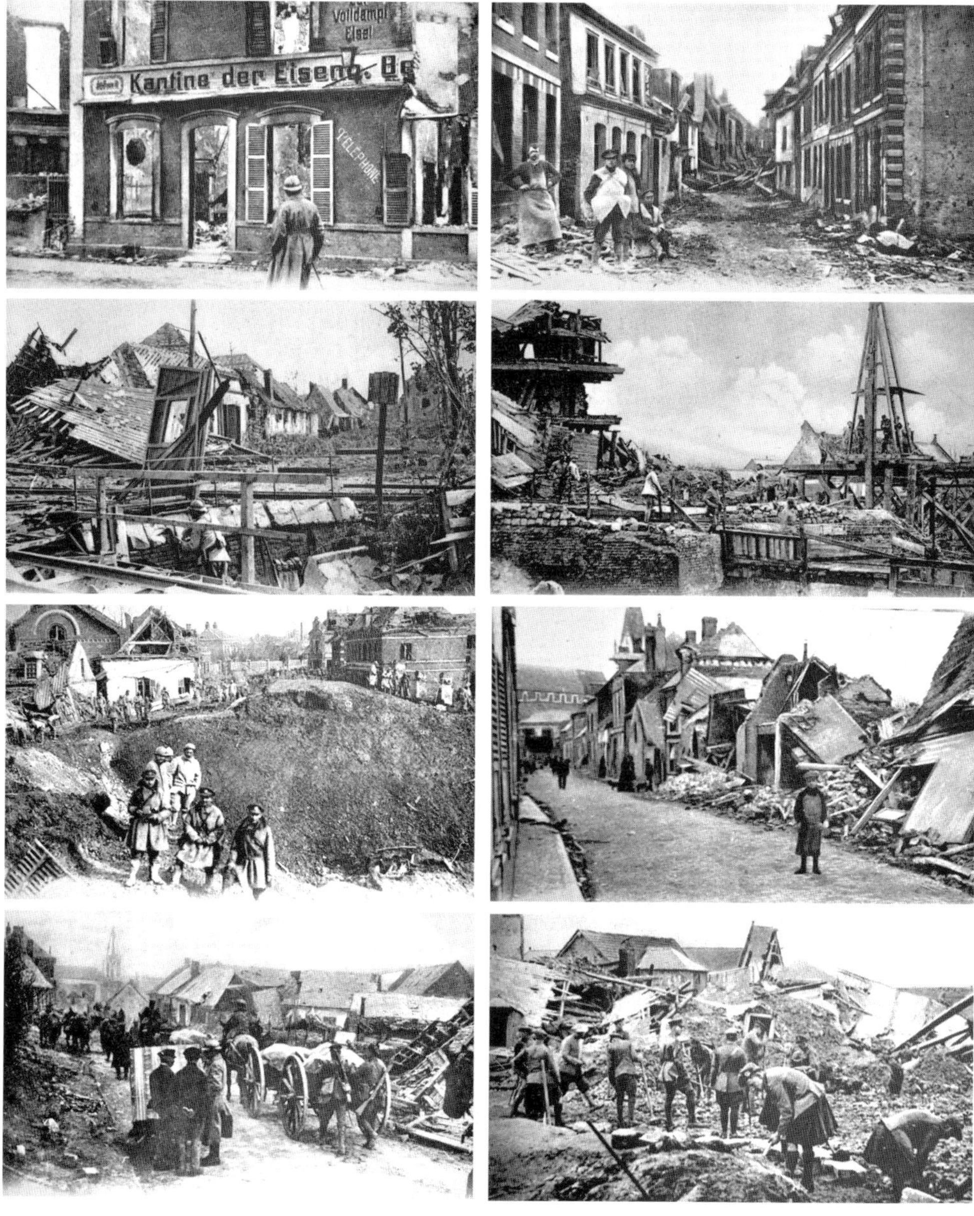

Sometimes snapshots, taken by amateur photographers, who shoot merely what they see in front of them, can get a message across with more honesty than professional photographers who take time looking for the right angle and light on a subject, the best picture composition, the posing of people within the picture etc. In this case the message, shown in the simplest of terms, is the brutal reality of war. This series of pictures was taken in Northern France, close to where the battles of the Somme took place during 1916 and 1918. Although the album from which these pictures were taken indicates that it was put together for commercial sale, the low quality of the images, and therefore the camera, indicates that they are likely to have been taken by an amateur snapshot photographer, a soldier perhaps who had illicitly taken his camera to war.

Soldiers who, against regulations, took small cameras onto the battlefield could capture moments in their daily lives that professional photographers, tasked with officially documenting the war, might have missed. Here, a British soldier photographed in the trenches is seen using a dummy on a pole to draw the enemy fire.

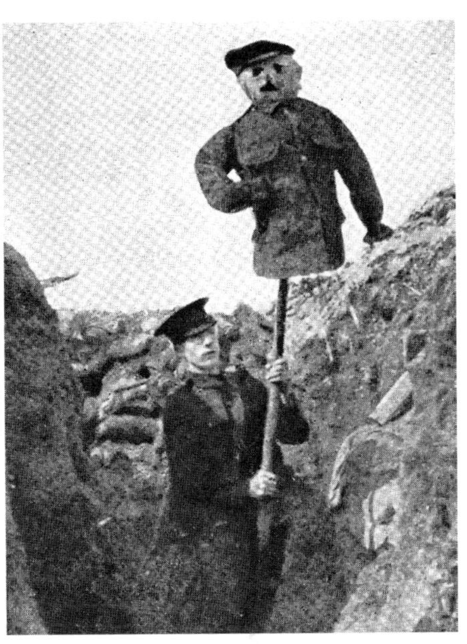

prominent place Kodak cameras were taking as historians of the war, and continued:

> Thousands of Kodaks are in the knapsacks of officers and soldiers in all the armies engaged, and when the smoke of battle has been cleared away, their tiny films will have a war story to tell – to us and to posterity – such as has never been told before.

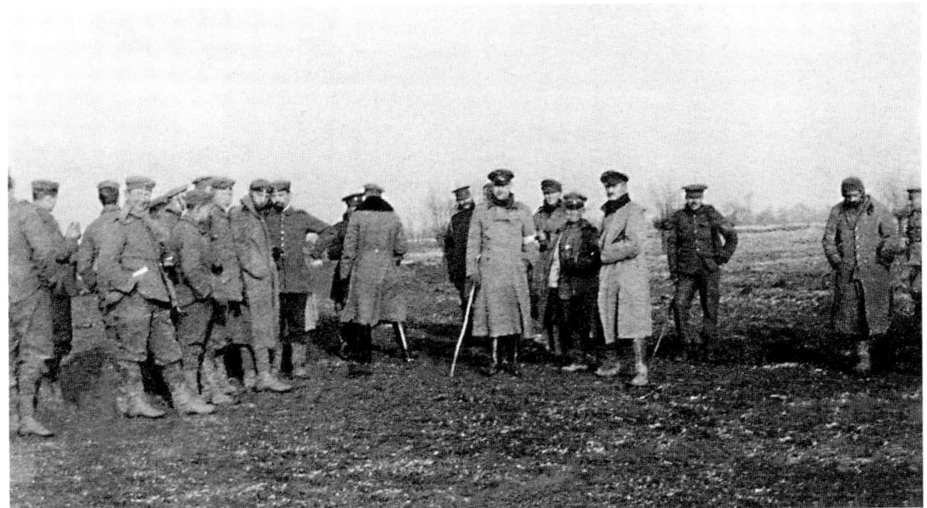

Most probably recorded by an unknown soldier with his snapshot camera, the famous Christmas Day truce, as British and German soldiers met in no man's land on 25 December 1914.

The soldier's camera

In 1912, two years before the start of the war, Kodak had produced a simple snapshot camera called the Vest Pocket Kodak, which was advertised as 'a dainty little camera for your waistcoat pocket… always with you, never in the way'. After the outbreak of war, Kodak's advertising changed to proclaim:

'Because it is so popular in the Army, this model is now generally known as The Soldier's Kodak.' Despite the fact that soldiers were theoretically forbidden to take cameras into battle, cameras like the Vest Pocket Kodak still made it through. It was small when shooting pictures and folded into even smaller dimensions when not in use, as the advertisements suggested: 'It slips easily into the tunic pocket and takes up but little more room than a cigarette case.'

The word 'vest' in the context of the camera name was the American word for what, in Britain, is more popularly known as a waistcoat. When folded, the camera measured a mere 12×6×2.5cm, a size made possible with the introduction by Kodak, at the same time as the camera, of a new small film size called 127. Tugging on small finger grips each side of the

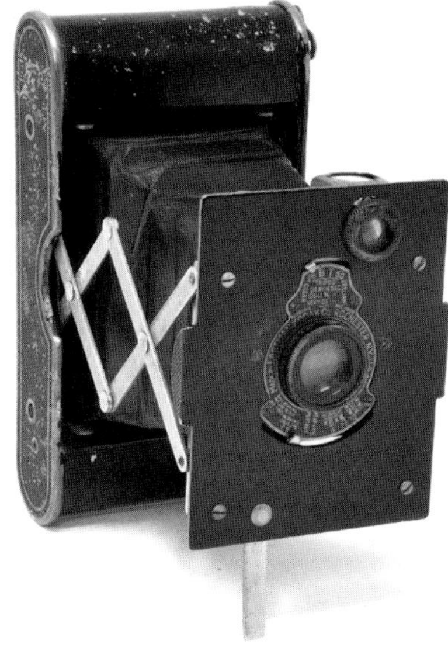

The Vest Pocket Kodak, thought to be easy for a soldier to slip into his tunic pocket.

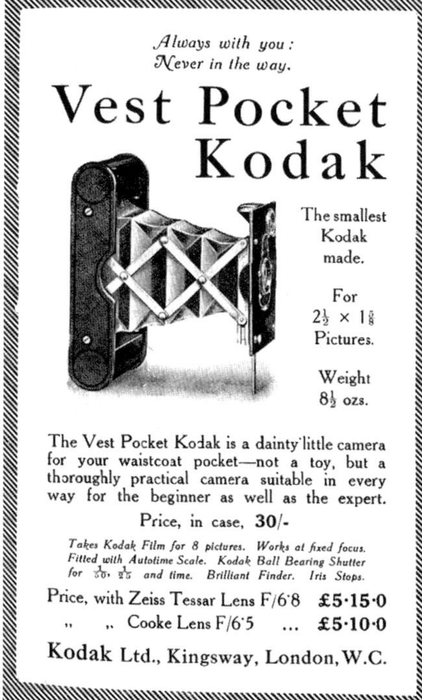

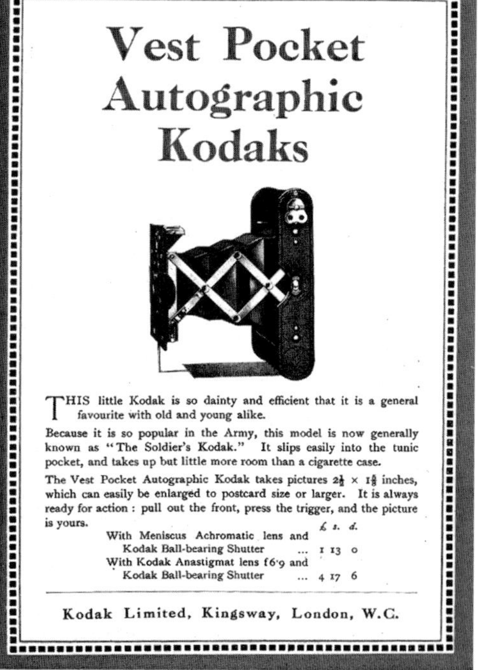

The difference between the way the Vest Pocket Kodak was advertised before and after the outbreak of war, when it was claimed to be 'The Soldier's Kodak'.

body allowed the lens panel to extend on bellows, supported by scissorlike struts, increasing the width of the body from 2.5cm to 10cm. The camera was the star of Kodak's 1912 catalogue. Here's what it had to say:

> No matter how many cameras you have, there are times when a vest pocket edition of your larger instrument will be appreciated. That's just what the Vest Pocket Kodak is – a miniature Kodak – so flat and smooth and small as to go readily into a vest pocket, so carefully made as to be capable of the highest grade of work. Quality marks the Vest Pocket Kodak in every detail. It is not made small so that we can produce a cheap camera; it is made small simply for the sake of convenience.

The camera had only two shutter speeds to worry about, and the apertures, although designated by the usual f-stops, were also described by engravings beneath the lens with reference to certain types of subject. From the smallest aperture to the largest, the descriptions ran: marine clouds snow, distant view, average view, near view, portrait, moving objects. All of which made the camera simple to use for inexperienced photographers.

Autographic backs that allowed photographers to add written notes to the film appeared on the Vest Pocket Kodak in 1915. Using this feature, soldiers who took their cameras to war could record brief information about the pictures

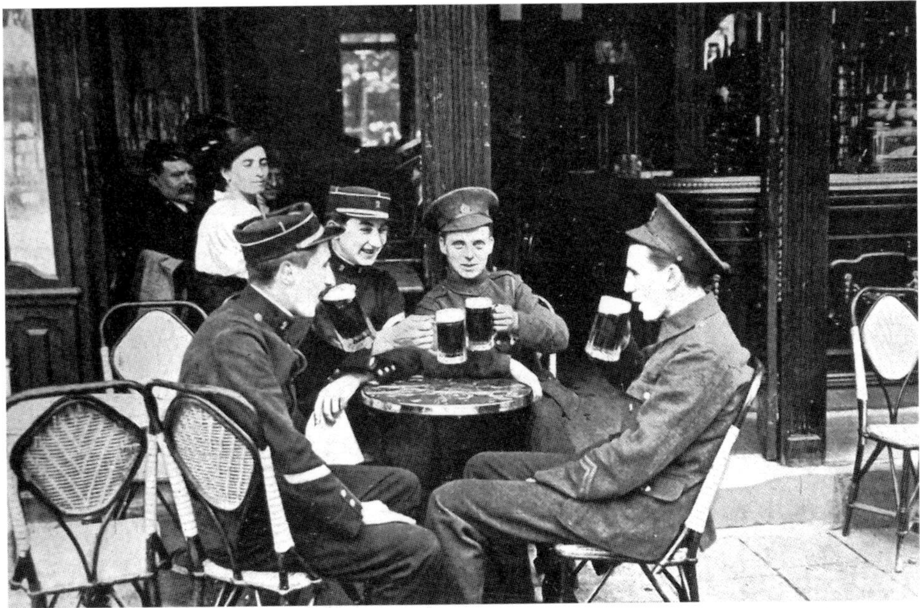

Away from the battlefront, a snapshot showing British and French soldiers drinking together in Amiens.

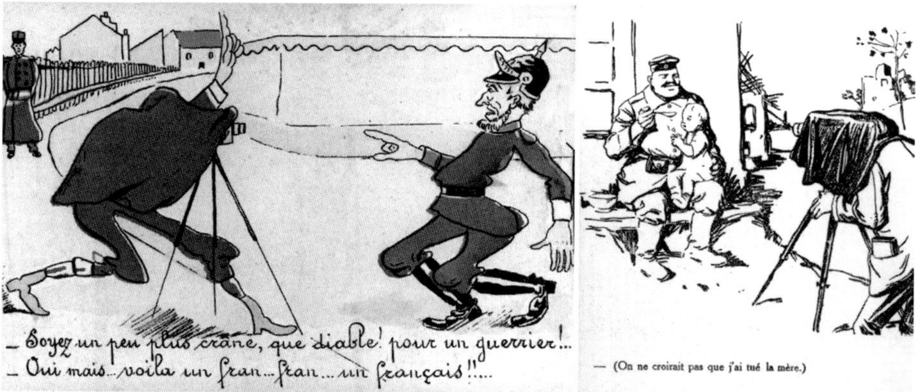

How snapshot photography was used for propaganda purposes in two First World War French postcards. In the first, the photographer is asking his subject to be brave, despite him being scared of an approaching Frenchman. In the second, rather more sinister, card the German soldier spoon-feeding a baby as he poses for the camera, is saying, 'You wouldn't believe I killed the mother.'

they took directly onto the film beside each appropriate negative. Information so recorded was usually a date and perhaps an indication of the location, although often codes were used or letters left out of place names for reasons of security.

The Vest Pocket Kodak proved to be a great success with both soldiers going to war and the families they left behind. It shot eight pictures to a roll of film, each one $2\frac{1}{2} \times 1\frac{5}{8}$ inches, and many of them found their way into family albums.

Folding Kodaks

It's probable that officers during the First World War were more likely to own cameras and less likely to be prosecuted for taking them into battle than was the case with the lower ranks. So while the enlisted men used small cameras, the better to keep them hidden, officers were likely to have used larger folding models with names like the No.1 Autographic Junior, No.1A Autographic Junior, No.2C Autographic Junior, No.3 Autographic, No.3A Autographic… and more.

The No.1A Autographic Junior is a good example of the many models. It was launched in 1914 and took the form of so many folding cameras of the time, a flat box that measured $20 \times 9 \times 3$cm, from which a bed folded down to

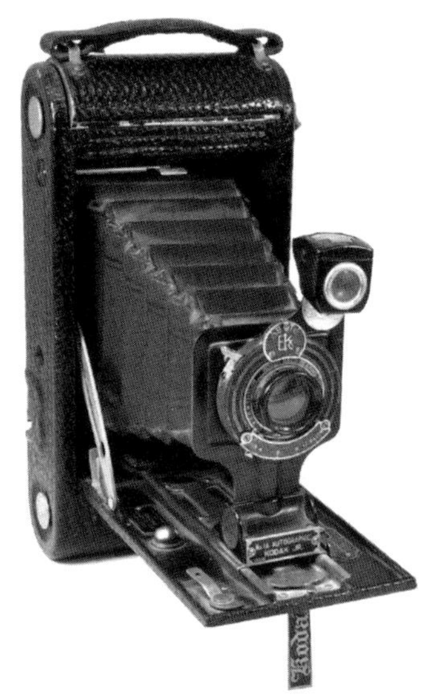

The No.1 Autographic Junior was typical of the larger folding Kodaks that officers, rather than the lower ranks, might have taken into battle.

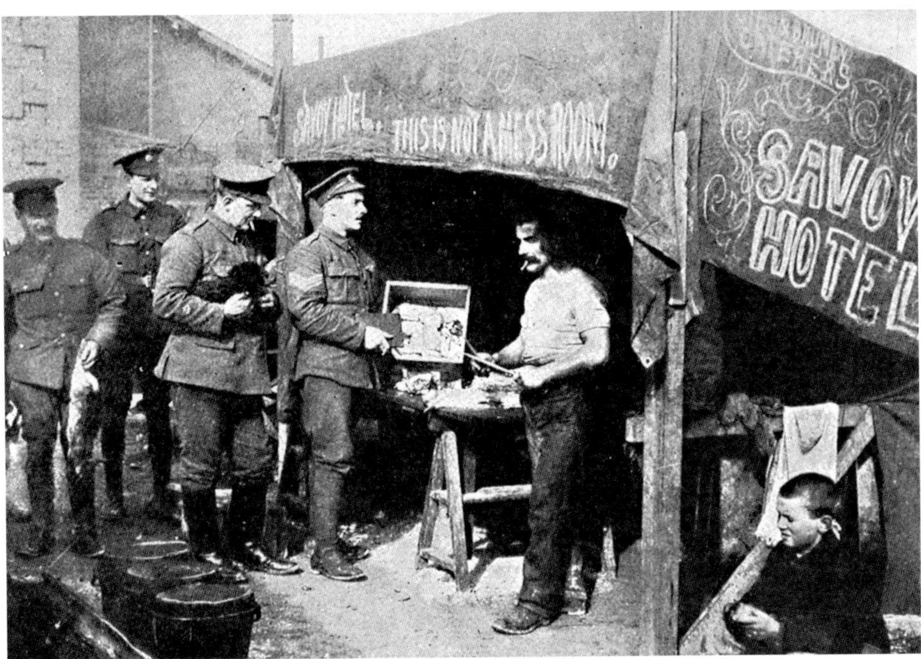

Food in the First World War trenches was something of a luxury, and when what little there was of it arrived from field kitchens, situated far from the front lines, it was invariably cold or stale. The more you look at this snapshot of a British camp kitchen in Northern France, the more you see: the name given to the camp by someone whose sense of humour has survived the hardships, the way the cook is smoking, the surprisingly young age of the small boy on the right, the soldier who appears to be carrying what might have been an adopted stray dog and the soldier at the end of the line arriving with some unidentifiable fresh meat that was probably recently killed.

allow the lens to be pulled out along rails. Focus depended on where the lens was allowed to come to rest. The few controls needed to operate the camera ensured that snapshot photographers could easily produce good results in the

right light, while its autographic feature allowed the photographer to add details of the picture in the usual way.

A few folding cameras like these did more than just take pictures. Sometimes they saved lives as well. Letters received by Kodak's offices around the world told stories of soldiers whose cameras in tunic pockets and backpacks had stopped bullets that might otherwise have killed or seriously injured them. One letter to Kodak from a First World War soldier, who sent a picture of his life-saving camera, told this story...

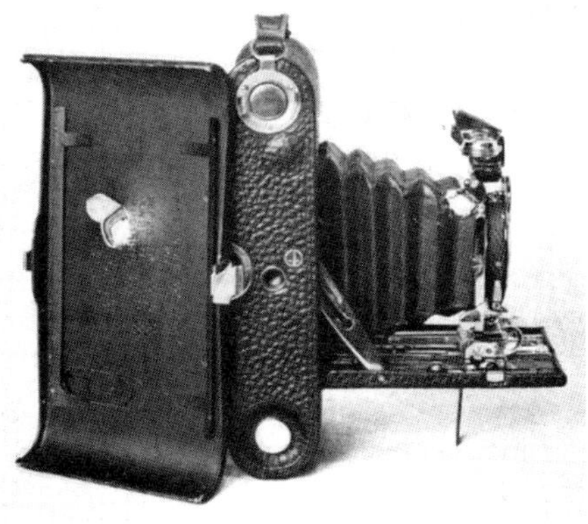

The camera that stopped a bullet and probably saved a soldier's life.

The enclosed photograph of a No.3 Folding Pocket Kodak may be of interest to you. It was carried by an Austrian officer over his shoulder in a leather case. During a battle he received a shot which passed through the back of the camera, hit against the lens ring, passed through the bellows against the shutter and remained in the body of the Kodak. When he opened his camera, the bullet fell out. He says it undoubtedly saved his life, preventing what would otherwise have been a shot in the abdomen.

The Ensignette

Not every small snapshot camera of this time was made by Kodak. The Houghton company in Britain had been very active before the First World War and the cameras they made then were still going strong well into the war years.

The Ensignette had all the conveniences of the Vest Pocket Kodak, and was actually easier to use. On the first model, the lens was fixed focus so didn't have to be adjusted for distances, the shutter had only a fixed speed, which also made it less complicated to use, and exposure was controlled by just three apertures. The camera folded to just 10×5×2cm and the lens extended on bellows supported by metal struts from 2cm to a depth of 8.5cm for shooting. There were three models of different sizes with slightly different specifications. When the first model was launched in 1909, the camera immediately became extremely successful and popular for a new breed of snapshot photographer who demanded quality results coupled with simplicity of operation. Although it is likely that many Ensignettes found their way into the pockets and kitbags of soldiers who went to war, it proved popular among the civilian population who stayed at home.

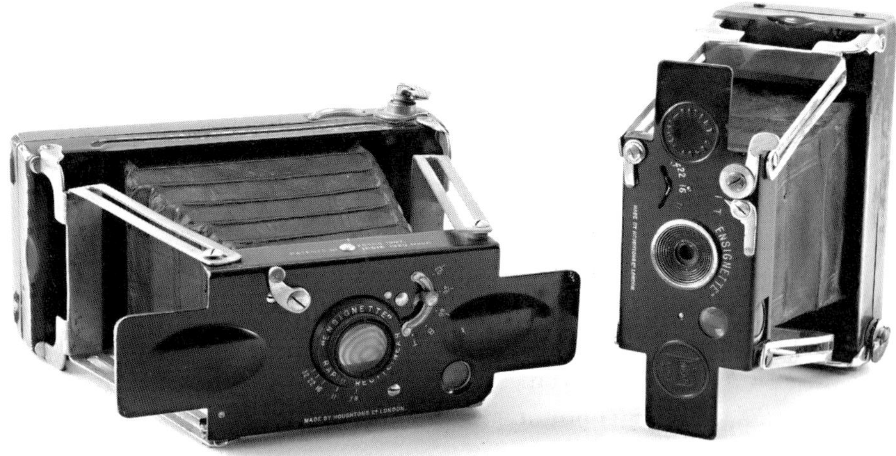

Two sizes of the British-made Ensignette camera.

A Machine Gun Camera

Calling this a snapshot camera might be stretching the genre a little. But, despite being a very strange device that handled like no other camera and would never have been owned by any civilian, when it came to its military use, its basic controls were no more complicated than those on a Brownie box camera.

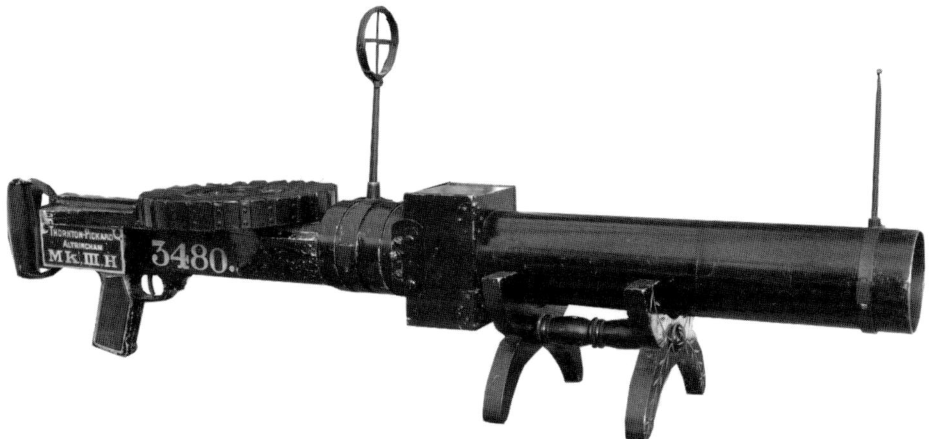

The Hythe Machine Gun Camera was not a typical snapshot model, but its absence of complicated controls would have made it familiar to any snapshot photographer.

The First World War saw fighting take to the air for the first time, and so pilots needed to be trained in air-to-air combat. It was obviously impractical to use live ammunition for the purpose for fear of actually shooting down an aircraft. So the British Government turned to English camera manufacturer Thornton Pickard, already well known for making wood and brass cameras for professional and advanced amateur photographers, to produce a very special camera. It was made in 1915 and called the Mark III Hythe Machine Gun Camera – Mark III because two experimental prototypes had gone before it went into full production; Hythe because that was the name of the place in Britain where it was built, this being the location of the Royal Flying Corps Gunnery School.

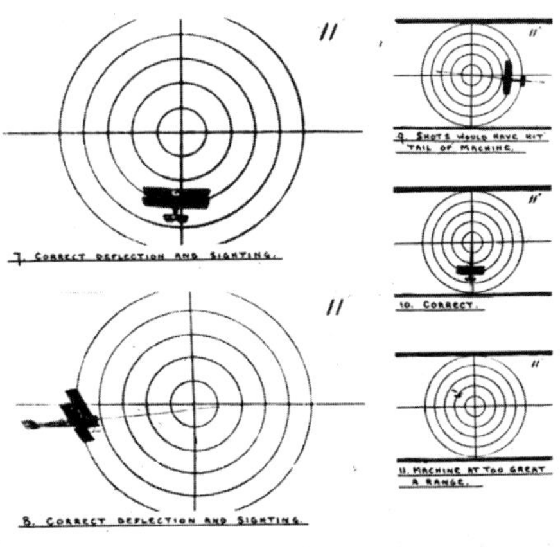

Test results from the Gun Camera showed how accurate an airman would have been using a real machine gun to shoot down an enemy aircraft.

The camera was modelled on and looked and handled exactly like a Lewis machine gun that was very popular with the British army at the time. But, as the trigger was pulled, it shot pictures on rolls of film, courtesy of a lens in the barrel. Once developed, the images indicated how accurate the airman had been in aiming the camera and, if it had been a real gun, the likelihood of him having shot down an enemy aircraft.

Meanwhile in civilian life…

Although publications like the *British Journal Photographic Almanac* continued throughout the war to publish pages of advisements for cameras, they were mainly for models made pre-war for professional and keen amateur photographers, rather than the snapshot population. New models of camera were much rarer and, although many people retained cameras made before the war, film became scarcer as time went on.

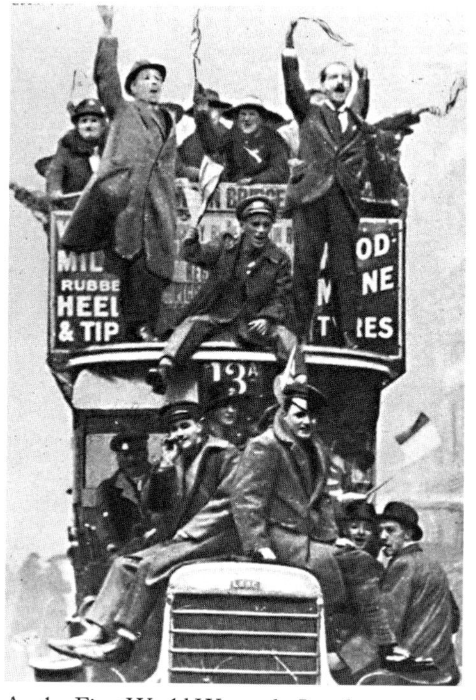

As the First World War ends, Londoners take over a bus to celebrate the armistice in November 1918.

Snapshots were taken of the effects of war, including bomb damage from German air raids. But in truth, the civilian population left behind when soldiers went off to war would have had little enthusiasm for snapshot photography. Not that photographic advertisers, aiming themselves squarely at the snapshot market, were deterred. 'Can you imagine any happier gift to our soldiers in the trenches than portraits or groups of the dear ones at home?' asked one advertisement, a sentiment shared on recruitment posters of the day. One such showed a group of jolly soldiers in what appeared to be quite a pretty little town, pipe and cigarette smoking, as they laughed joyously at some of the snapshots they had just received. The camera might have been perceived to never lie, but it was all a far cry from the realities of real life for soldiers during the First World War.

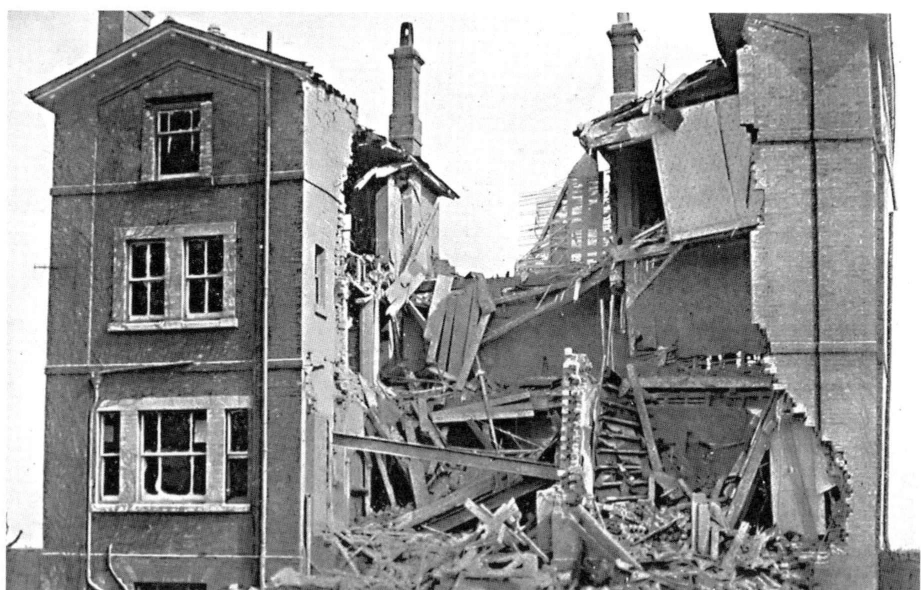

Think of German air raids on Britain and the Second World War comes immediately to mind. But aerial combat, though in its infancy, inflicted considerable damage during the First World War. It began with bombing raids on the East coast of Britain in January 1915, when bombs were dropped from gigantic airships, mostly Zeppelins. Towns that were initially bombed included Sheringham, Yarmouth and King's Lynn in Norfolk, plus Lowestoft in the north of Suffolk close to the Norfolk border. The German raids then moved south to bomb London, where the vulnerability of airships was overcome by the use of twin- and four-engine aircraft. This picture, which is likely to have been taken by an amateur snapshot photographer, shows the ruins of a house in Lowestoft that was hit by a German raid on 24 April 1916.

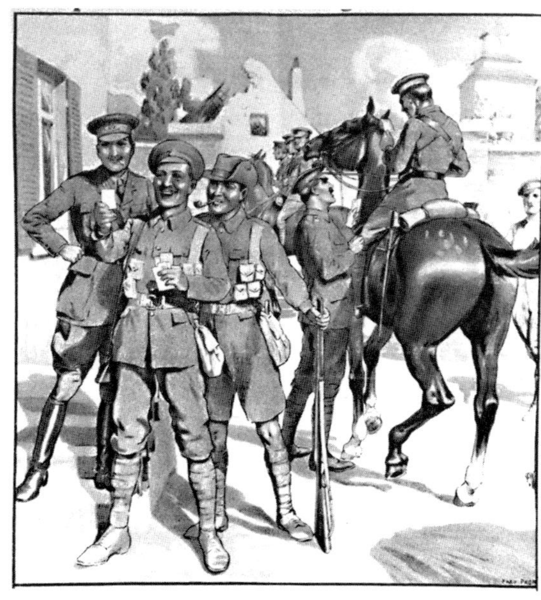

Pictured on a First World War recruitment poster: how snapshots from home purported to cheer up soldiers on the battle front.

Chapter 6
A New Snapshot Age

In the years between the end of the First World War in 1918 and the outbreak of the Second World War in 1939, camera design and manufacture went through a small revolution with the introduction of cameras whose innovative new styles would flourish and be emulated for many years to come. These cameras were essentially aimed at, and bought by, professional or keen amateur photographers, but their influences knocked on into the snapshot world.

If one type of camera epitomised snapshot photography more than any other, it must surely have been the box camera. It of course drew its name from being in the shape of a simple box, but it was equally well known for its ease of use in even the most inexperienced hands. From the 1920s onwards, new styles of snapshot camera began appearing. Some preserved the box camera shape but added more sophisticated controls and better lenses. Others retained the simplicity of box camera operation while adopting new and sometimes radical designs.

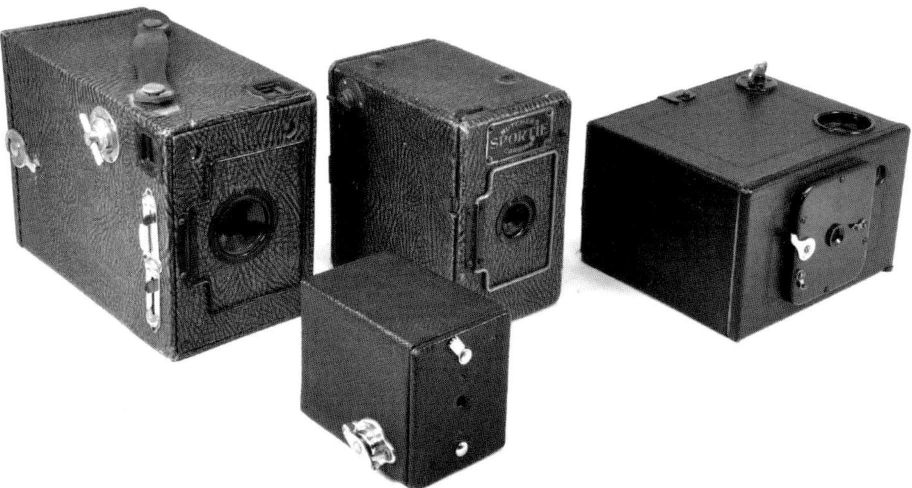

Four of the new breed of box cameras: the tiger skin Ensign 2¼B, lizard skin Butcher Sportie Carbine, the unusually designed Ernemann Film K and a tiny Kodak No.00 Cartridge Premo.

Better box cameras

After the First World War, new-look box cameras were sometimes produced by simply revamping an older model. The pre-war British Ensign 2¼B was pretty much unimposing when covered in the traditional black leatherette, but when it appeared post-war in a brown tiger print design, it became far more attractive to snapshot photographers. Likewise, the British Butcher Sportie Carbine appeared this time with an attractive green lizard skin type of covering, but still with the same basic controls that ensured it would appeal to, and could be used by, inexperienced photographers.

Kodak of course continued to make box cameras, most of which followed traditional lines with only minor difference between models. The No.00 Cartridge Premo box camera, which was on sale between 1916 and 1922, however, was an exception that might have particularly appealed to snapshot photographers purely because of its size. At a mere 7.5×6.5×5cm, this was the smallest box camera ever made by Kodak. It took what Kodak called No.35 roll film, which was actually 35mm size, generally used at that time in movie cameras and wouldn't be popularised in still cameras for several more years until the launch of the first Leica camera in 1925. Unlike conventional movie 35mm film, however, Kodak's version was backed with paper bearing the usual numbers to be read through the camera's red window on the back of the body. It shot tiny pictures 24×18mm in size. A wind knob for the film and a lever to

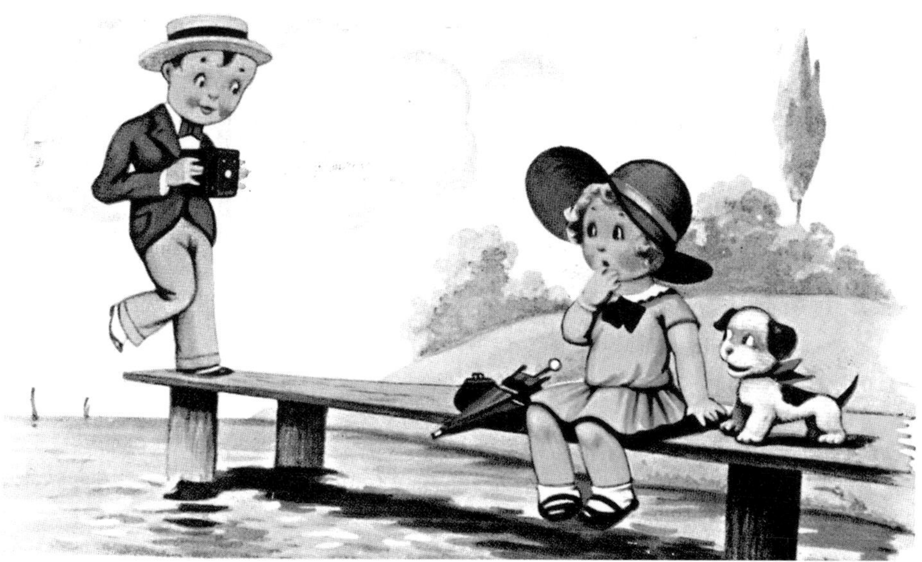

Even young children could use simple box cameras, as demonstrated by this postcard.

fire the shutter were the only controls needed to take snapshots. The camera didn't even have a viewfinder, although V-shaped lines etched onto the body's leather covering on the top and side could be used to roughly sight the subject.

In America, Ansco already had a line of box cameras produced in competition to Kodak's Brownies. While Kodak named their cameras after cartoon characters, Ansco came up with the name Buster Brown, named after another comic strip hero. Originally, the cameras were black, but in the 1920s, Ansco produced a series of Specials whose several models had dark red bodies and gold-coloured fittings.

In Germany, Zeiss Ikon, formed in 1926 by the amalgamation of four other camera manufacturing companies, revamped its series of Box-Tengor cameras in different sizes with a new modern look, brighter viewfinders and an unusual mirror in front of the lens, which slipped aside as the exposure was made. Although the Box-Tengors embraced a more professional look than most box cameras, the controls remained simple with single shutter speeds, a choice of apertures for exposure and pre-set focusing distances for the lenses.

Also in Germany, the Ernemann company, who had been making box cameras alongside more professional models for many years, offered simple snapshot models like the Film K, available in several picture sizes and unusual for situating its shutter on the outside of the front of the body, while retaining basic controls that any snapshot photographer would have understood.

Although these brief examples of cameras from Britain, America and Germany were in no way the only box cameras produced after the First World War, they give an idea of how snapshot camera manufacturers enhanced the basic box-type, while luring more people into the delights of snapshot photography.

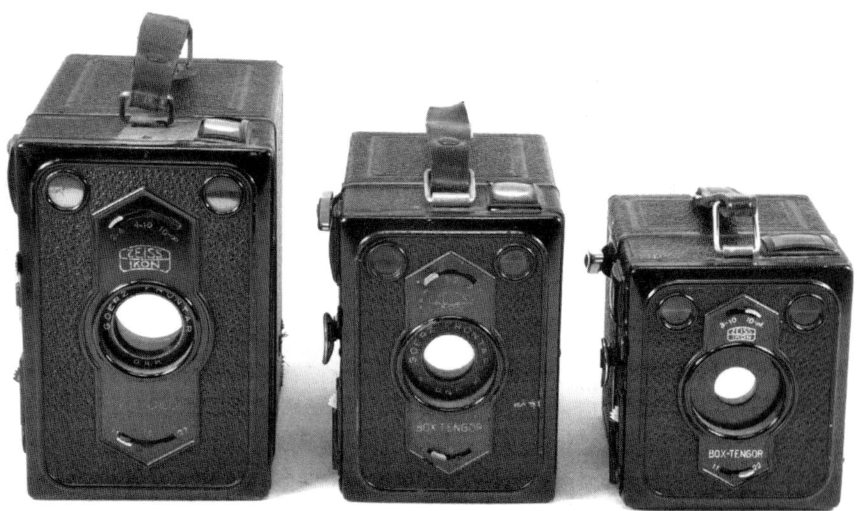

Three models of the Zeiss Ikon Box Tengor that took three different film sizes.

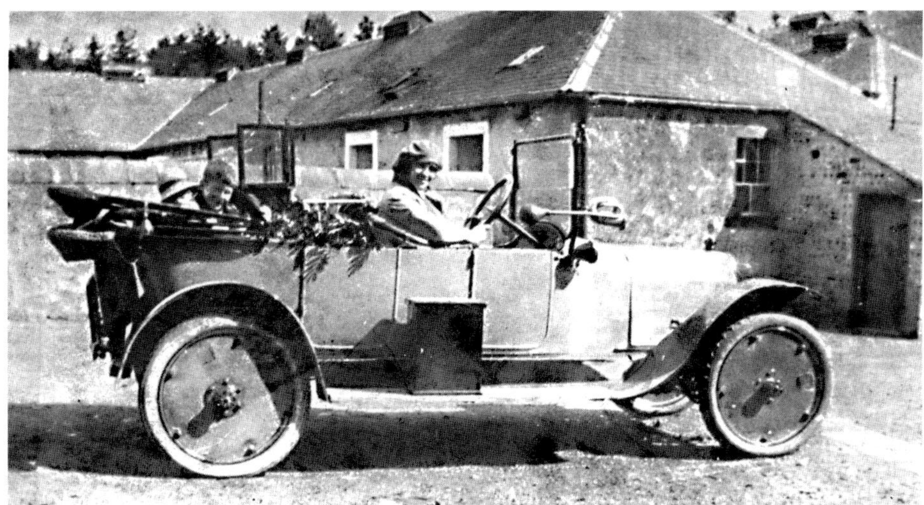

The year is 1921 and this snapshot shows two rarities in Britain at this time: a woman driver and an American car. The story behind the picture is the woman's husband who was brought up on a Scottish farm where he developed a fascination for machinery. Spending time in America as a young man, he developed a love of American cars. By the time he returned to Britain the country had become a fertile market for the American car industry. So he bought this 1914 Briscoe, married, and taught his new wife to drive. She remained a competent and enthusiastic driver for the rest of her life.

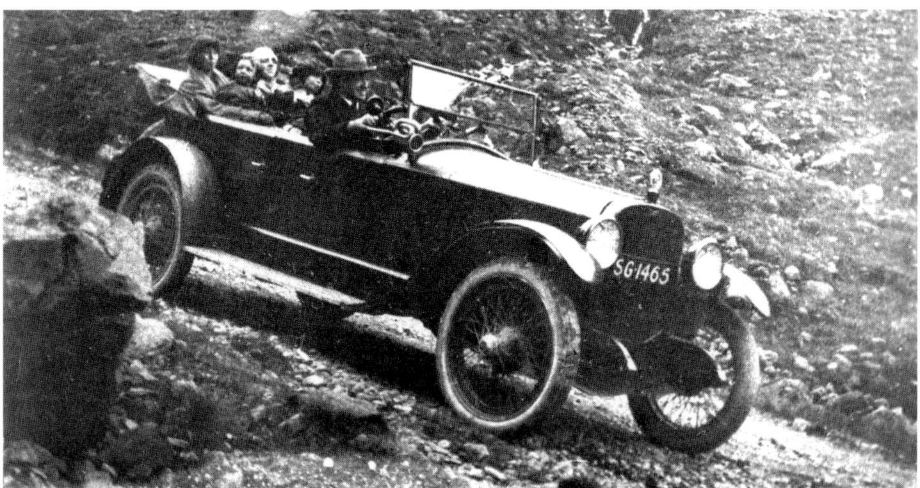

Honister Pass in Britain's Lake District is terrifyingly steep, with gradients of as much as one in three in places. Taken in 1923, this snapshot shows a grinning driver whose wicked sense of humour involved showing off his driving skills while descending the rubble road surface of the Pass at speed. The car is a 4½-litre Chandler with only rear wheel brakes. The driver's favourite trick was to turn off the car's ignition, then freewheel fast down the hill with only the help of the car's air brake, operated from the dashboard to admit air to the engine's inlet manifold, thereby increasing engine drag. Immediately after this picture was taken, the car was stopped as all the rear seat passengers got out and walked.

Taking a different look

The 1920s and 1930s were a time when some camera manufacturers strayed away from tradition to approach snapshot photography in different and unexpected ways, and the box camera was often the starting point for these new approaches. Here are two cameras aimed at snapshot photographers who might have wanted to try something a little different.

The British Coronet Camera Company was formed in 1926 and went on to produce a multitude of snapshot cameras, mostly box types. The Wonder Camera, also sold under the names Viewograph and Dinkie, was one of the company's first products and was used mainly for premium purposes, which meant it was given away free to people who collected tokens from various sources. This was a simple box camera with a fixed aperture, a fixed focus lens and a shutter that was no more than a lever operating a flap to uncover and cover the lens. The instructions recommended: 'In bright light, push lever down with right thumb and release it immediately. In medium or dull light, push lever down, count "one" and then release it.'

One thing that might have prevented snapshot photographers from getting too enthusiastic about owning a Wonder Camera was that it didn't use film. Instead, its pictures were taken on 3½×2½-inch glass plates, which were loaded singly in a darkroom and held in place only by pressure from the camera's back. The camera was sold as a kit in a box that also contained sensitised paper, chemicals and instructions for shooting, developing and printing.

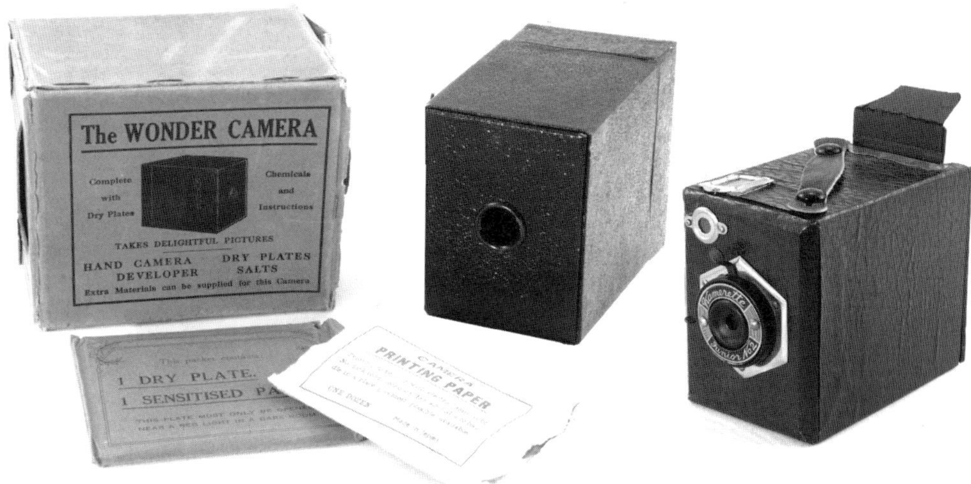

The Wonder Camera, with its box, plates and printing paper packs, with (right) a Kamerette, also known as a Yen Camera.

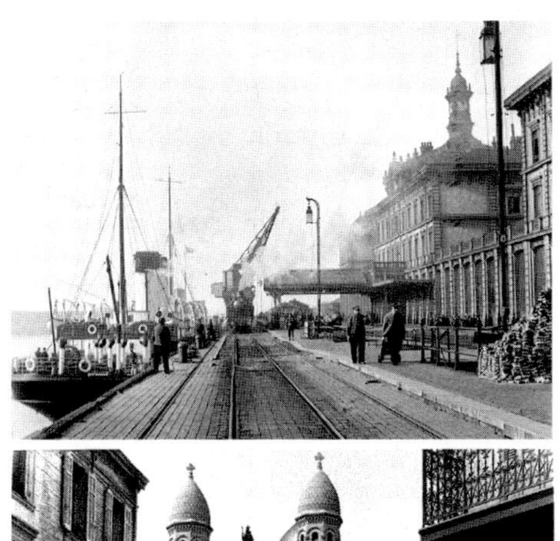
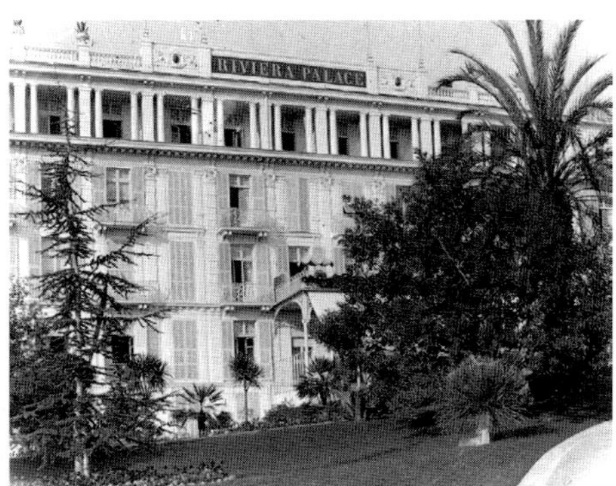
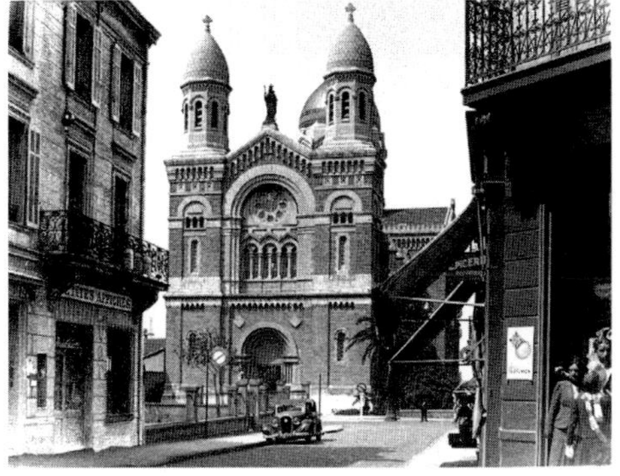
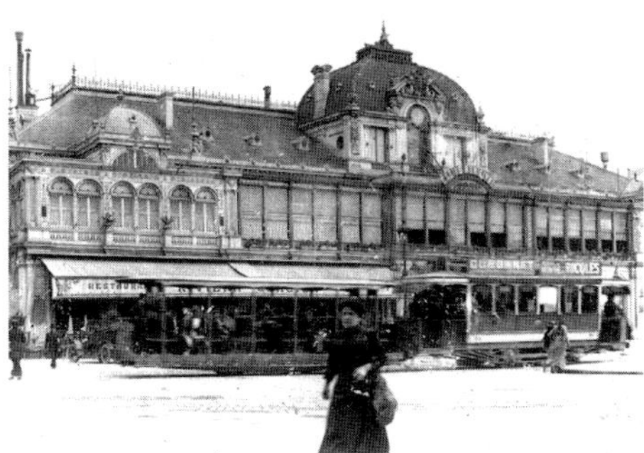
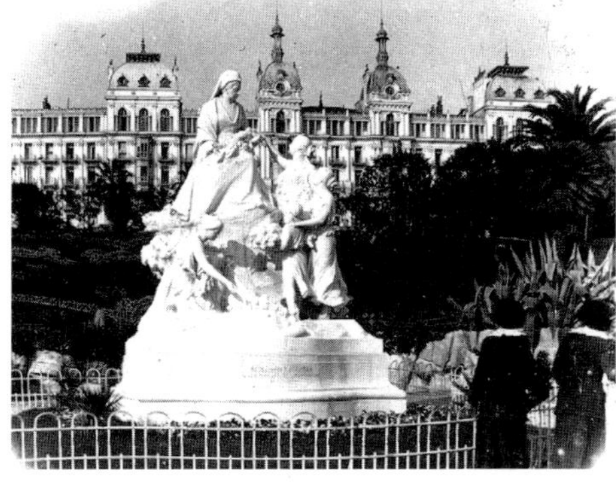
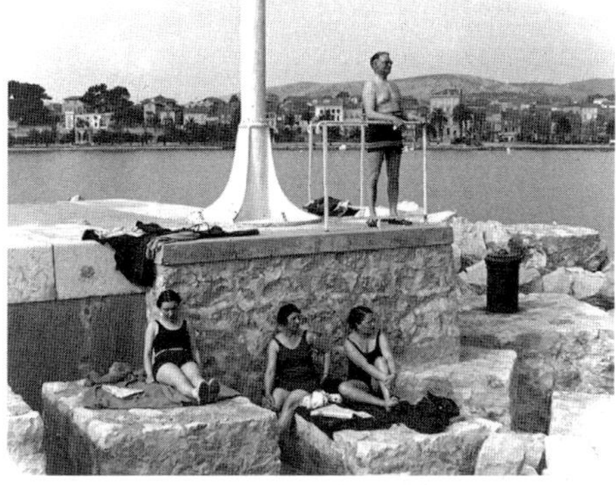

Extracting six snapshots from an old photo album makes it possible to trace aspects of a family holiday to the South of France, in what appears to be the mid- to late 1930s. The first picture shows the Gare Maritime in Calais, where passengers embarked from a cross-Channel ferry to board a train, and since the album shows no more pictures until arrival in the South, it's likely that that was how they travelled there. The Rivera Hotel, where it might be assumed they stayed, was built in the Cimiez quarter of Nice in 1889 and, in the 1930s, it was still extremely opulent. A visit to the cathedral at Saint Raphael, a little way along the coast, gives the best clue to when this holiday was taken. In the street in front of the cathedral there is a car, made in France and called the Hotchkiss, the model of which appears to be from around 1934. Also on the family's list of places to visit, and seen in the remaining pictures, are the Municipal Casino and a statue of Queen Victoria in Nice. The only clue to what the family looked like comes with the final snapshot of them sunbathing at the end of what appears to be a stone pier. All locations were identified with the help of Google Images.

The Kamerette Junior No.2 (there was no evidence to support there having been a No.1), made in 1930 by the Japanese company of the same name, was known in Japan as a yen camera, because this, and other similar models, cost just one yen. It was a small box camera, which had a viewfinder in the usual place, but with the shutter opened to its time exposure setting, the picture could also be composed on a small 4×6cm piece of ground glass in the camera back. Individual sheets of film were sold in cardboard sheathes, inserted into the camera in front of the screen. A sheet of card, which protected the film from the light, was pulled up out of the sheath, the exposure made and the card pushed back into place. Each sheet of film could then be individually developed.

Cameras like these might have seemed like a novelty at the time of their introduction, especially if received free through a voucher scheme, but they fell between two markets. The unexpected complications needed to use them, and even the necessity for a darkroom, meant they would appeal only to the snapshot photographer who was beginning to take more interest in photography and making the progression to keen amateur, by which time the meagre specifications of the cameras held scant appeal.

New shapes

While box cameras continued to proliferate, another new kind of snapshot camera began to emerge. While retaining the basic, easy-to-understand controls of the box camera, this new generation took on different and sometimes weird shapes.

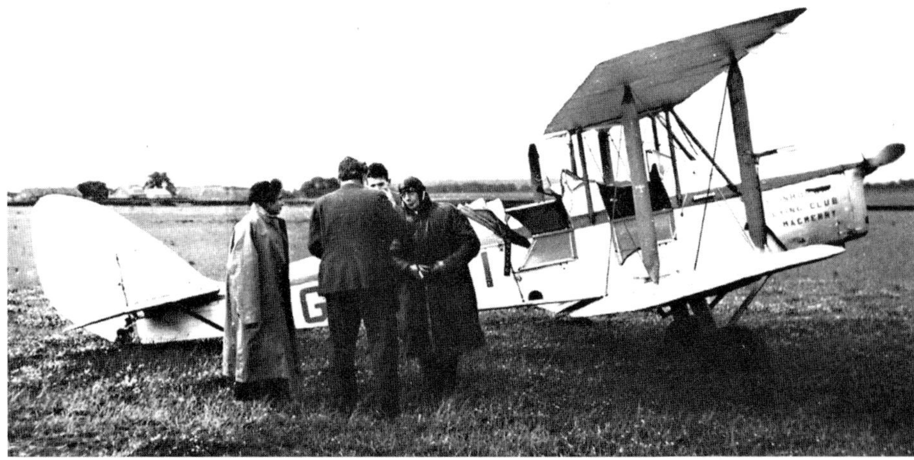

Flying lessons 1938-style. The woman on the left in the long coat is about to take her first trip in a Tiger Moth. The man with his back to the camera is her father, paying the pilot for his time. Flying remained the love of this particular woman's life and, much later, at the age of 72, she took a flight in a small, two-seater microlight aircraft.

Among the more unusual shapes, there was the Ensign Cupid that placed its lens at the end of a short protrusion from the body with a shutter primed by pulling a rod up and releasing it, before being tripped by a tiny button on the side. A large wire frame viewfinder folded up from the top. The Cupid's simplicity of operation appealed to snapshot photographers who might not have been aware that it was actually a real landmark in camera design. Most cameras had a single red window on the back, through which the film's frame numbers were read. The Cupid introduced an extra red window to the back. The numbers on the film's backing paper were wound to each of the windows in turn, thus producing sixteen exposures 4.5×6cm on 120 size roll film which was actually designed for eight exposures 6×9cm. The twin-window sixteen exposures on a roll of film system was soon adopted by many other manufacturers who built cameras that would have been too sophisticated, and too expensive to buy, for snapshot photographers.

Naturally, there were also other new styles of snapshot camera that were less groundbreaking. Among the many there was the Buster Brown, a small brown-coloured box camera with gold fittings; the Eho-Box, which at 6×6×6.5cm was a strong contender for the smallest box camera ever built; the Altissa, which was basically a box camera with an unusual eye-level viewfinder on top, in which flicking a lever to the side introduced a mirror to convert the viewfinder for waist-level use; and the unusually shaped Bilora Boy Luxus, attractively made in brown Bakelite with gold fittings.

One of the more unusual concepts came with the introduction of an American-made camera called the VP Twin. This was a small plastic camera with simple fixed controls, made to take sixteen exposures 3×4cm on 127 roll film. When the camera arrived in the UK in 1938, the Woolworth store sold it in two

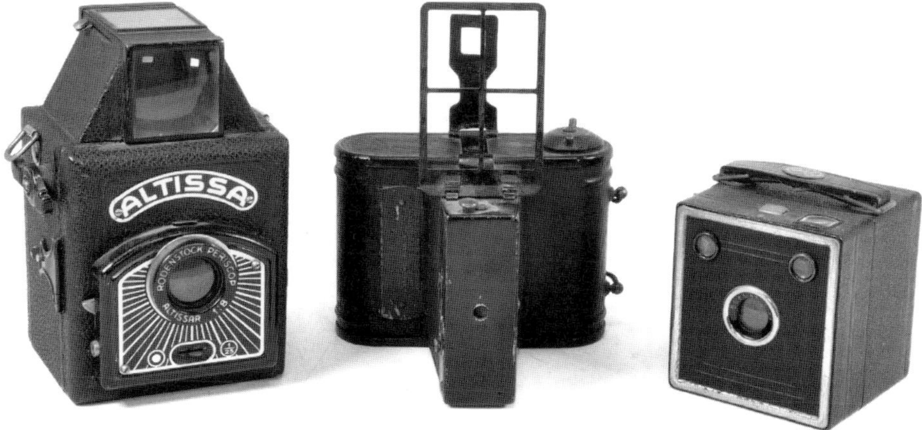

More variations on the standard box camera, left to right: Altissa, Ensign Cupid and Eho-Box.

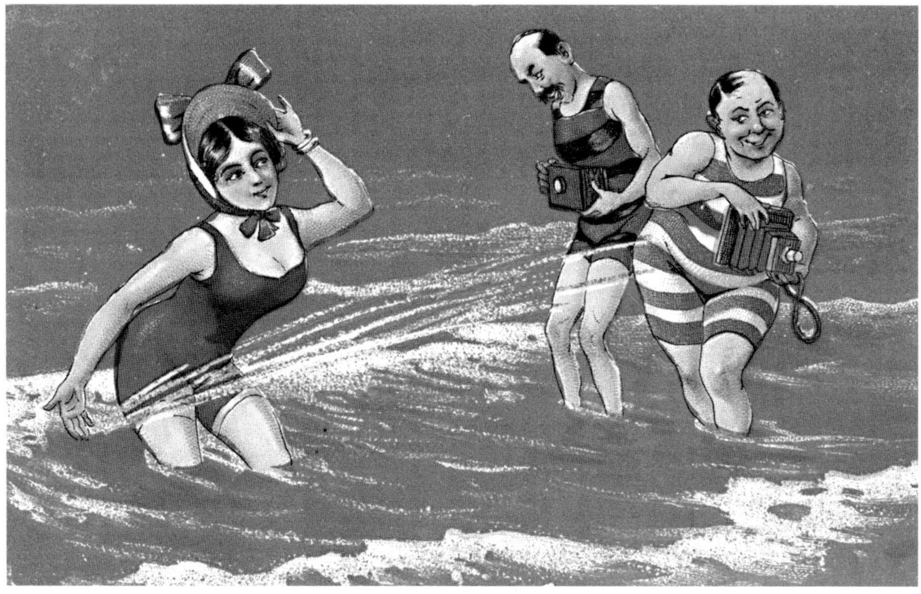

Snapshot fun in the sea, 1920s-style, on a postcard from that time.

halves to comply with its policy at that time of selling all its items at, or under, sixpence (2½p). Mostly seen in black, the camera was also sold in red, green, brown and blue.

This is only a small sample of the many new designs whose genesis lay with the box camera.

Folding snapshot cameras

Folding cameras were around long before the between-war years, but this era was one in which new kinds of folding camera began appealing to snapshot photographers who required a simplicity of controls coupled with a modern, stylish design, which often took advantage of the latest Art Deco craze for streamlined geometrically stylised patterns.

Kodak of course was at the forefront. While companies like Zeiss Ikon in Germany and Konishiroku in Japan took a look at the Vest Pocket

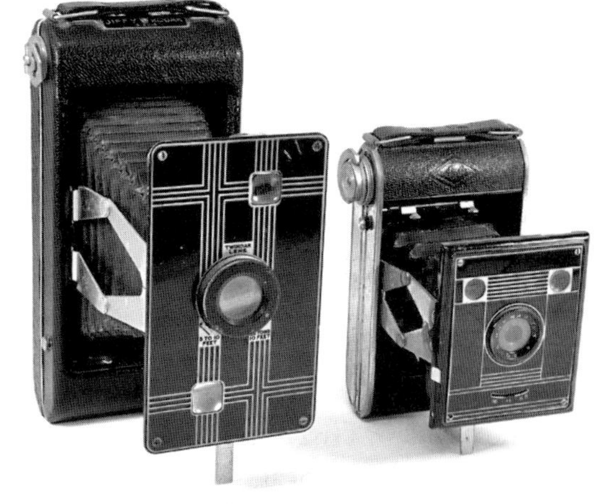

Art Deco folding cameras of the 1930s, epitomised by the Kodak Jiffy (left) and Agfa Billy-Clack.

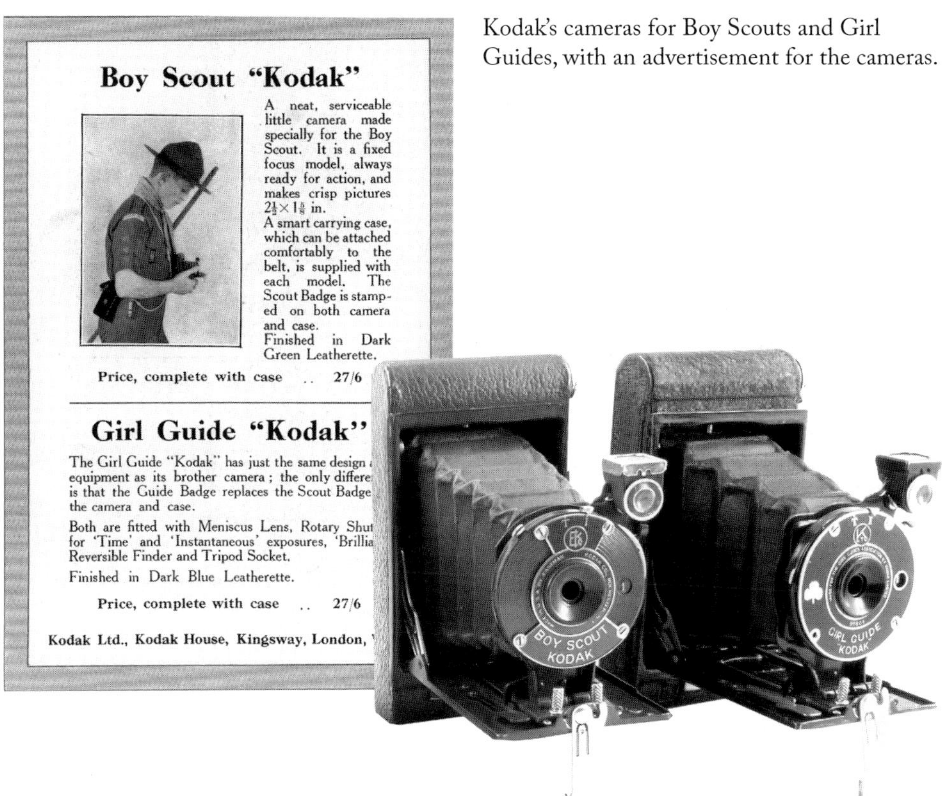

Kodak's cameras for Boy Scouts and Girl Guides, with an advertisement for the cameras.

Kodak and turned Kodak's design into something more suitable for the keen or advanced amateur photographer, Kodak stuck to its roots and revamped the same camera in 1925 to produce the Vest Pocket Kodak Model B for snapshot photographers. Small in size and made to take 127 type film, the new model resembled a miniature version of the company's larger drop-bed folding cameras complete with Kodak's Autographic Back. Several versions were made, including cameras with green or snakeskin bodies, as well as cameras for English and American Boy Scouts and Girl Guides, in green or blue and with variations of the appropriate emblem embossed on the camera bed.

The Model B was also used as the basis for a series of Rainbow Hawkeye cameras with brightly coloured bodies and bellows. In 1928, the Model B reached the peak of chic with its Vanity cameras, designed to bring more women into the world of snapshot photography and advertised as 'The Modern Camera for the Modern Girl'. The cameras were made in five colours, each with its own evocative name: Seagull (grey), Redbreast (red), Jenny Wren (brown), Cockatoo (green) and Bluebird (blue).

Few cameras better epitomised the snapshot philosophy than the Dallmeyer Snapshot camera in 1931. With a panel containing the principal controls pulled out from the main body, focusing distances were indicated as 'medium', 'near' and 'distant'; apertures were marked 'bright' and 'dull'; shutter speeds were shown as 'fast', 'slow' and 'time'.

This was an era that introduced Bakelite, the first synthetic plastic, to cameras, allowing bodies to be moulded and coloured in ways not seen before and in styles that made them particularly attractive to snapshot photographers. Bakelite was invented by Belgian chemist Leo Baekeland in 1907, but it didn't reach cameras until 1929 with the introduction of the Rajar No.6, the first Bakelite camera. This was a folding model in which the lens pulled out from the body on bellows supported by metal struts. A single shutter speed, fixed aperture and a fixed focus lens made it appealing to the snapshot photographer. The following year, Kodak introduced its first Bakelite camera and called it the No.2 Hawkette (there was no

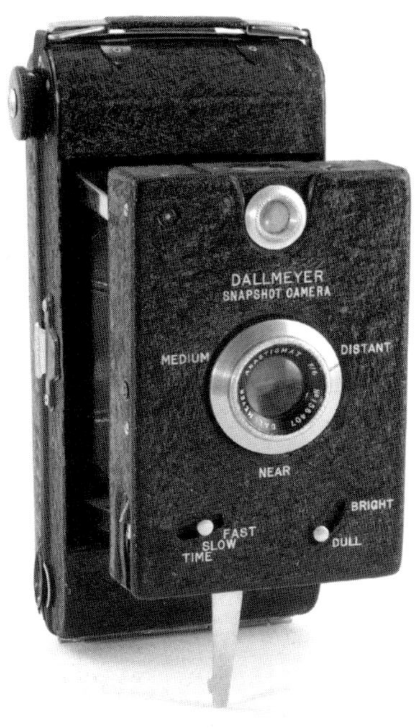

The Dallmeyer Snapshot camera made for extra simplicity of use.

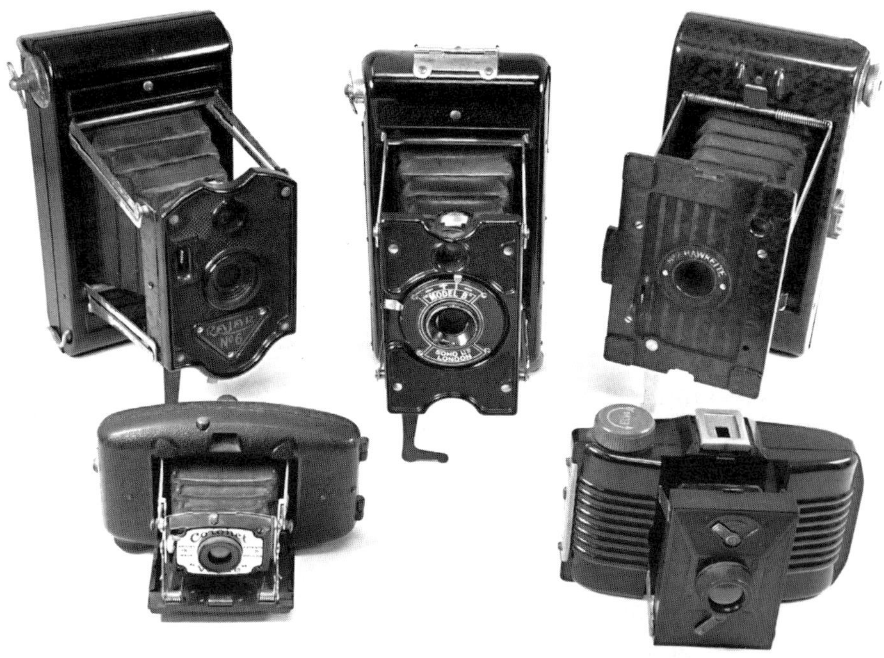

How Bakelite made a difference to camera design with models like the Rajar No.6, Kodak No.2 Hawkette, Soho Model B, Coronet Vogue and Elvo.

evidence of there having been a No.1). Like the Rajar, the Hawkette unfolded by pulling the lens panel out from the body on bellows and struts. The camera used Bakelite to its best effect, producing a body in mottled brown with smooth, rounded corners in place of the more usual square, angular corners associated with cameras up until the advent of this new kind of plastic.

Other cameras that took advantage of the versatility of Bakelite included the British-made Coronet Vogue and Soho Model B and the Italian Elvo. One Bakelite camera aimed squarely at the snapshot photographer, and very different from most others, was the Coronet Midget, advertised as the world's smallest camera. It was an upright design that took tiny 17.5mm roll film to produce six pictures 13×18mm. All the controls were fixed so it needed only to press a lever on the side to take a picture. Particularly appealing to the snapshot market was the way the camera was eventually available in a choice of six colours: black, rose, walnut, two shades of green, and blue.

Snapshot cameras of this era were often good at making complicated procedures easy to use. Purma cameras, made in Britain by R.F. Hunter, epitomised this kind of thinking by giving snapshot photographers an easy, and unusual, way of changing shutter speeds without any real knowledge of how it was being done. The Purma Special, made in 1937, used what was called a gravity shutter. The camera had three shutter speeds, changed, not by a lever, a knob or a dial, but with the way the camera was held. Holding the camera horizontally gave 1/150 second, holding it vertically one way gave 1/25 second, holding it vertically the other way gave 1/500 second. Of necessity, this required a square picture format, supplied by sixteen exposures 1¼×1¼ inches on 127 size film. The camera body was made of Bakelite with a metal interior, including a curved film plane to make up for aberrations in the simple fixed focus and aperture lens. In 1952, the camera was upgraded to produce the all-metal Purma Plus.

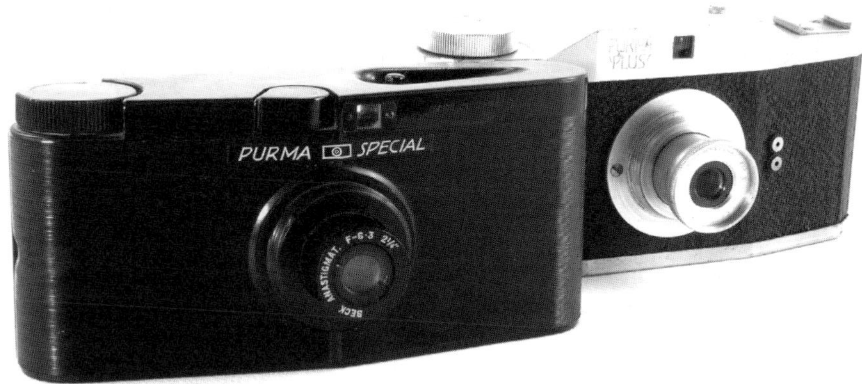

The unusual Purma Special (left) and Purma Plus.

New films

By this time, 35mm cine film was starting to become popular for use in still cameras, having been popularised by the introduction of the more professionally used Leica in 1925. Although there had been cameras to take 35mm before the Leica, this was the one that made use of this smaller-than-usual film truly viable. It was, however, way beyond the reach of snapshot photographers, because of both its price and its need for an understanding of photographic technology that few snapshot photographers were inclined to learn. When it was launched, the Leica was not without its critics. The size of negative it produced was a mere 24×36mm, miniscule compared to the average 6×9cm or 6×6cm negative produced by roll film cameras. Many claimed that a quality image could never be obtained from such a small negative, and roll film camera makers sat back and smirked, secure in the belief that the much larger negatives their cameras produced would win out in the end. The 35mm detractors soon began to change their minds. It seemed the miniature format was quite capable of producing an unexpected image quality after all. But there was another problem in the shape of the number of shots to a roll of film. Cameras using 35mm film shot as many as thirty-six exposures, and many photographers, especially snapshot photographers, simply didn't want to shoot this many pictures before having their films developed.

Out of this thinking came a new breed of roll film camera: one that shot the same, or a similar, negative size to that of a 35mm camera, but on roll film, with far fewer exposures to each roll. Many of these new cameras used film that supplied a 24×36mm image size that emulated the Leica; some offered very slightly larger images such as 30×40mm; and some turned out 24×24mm square

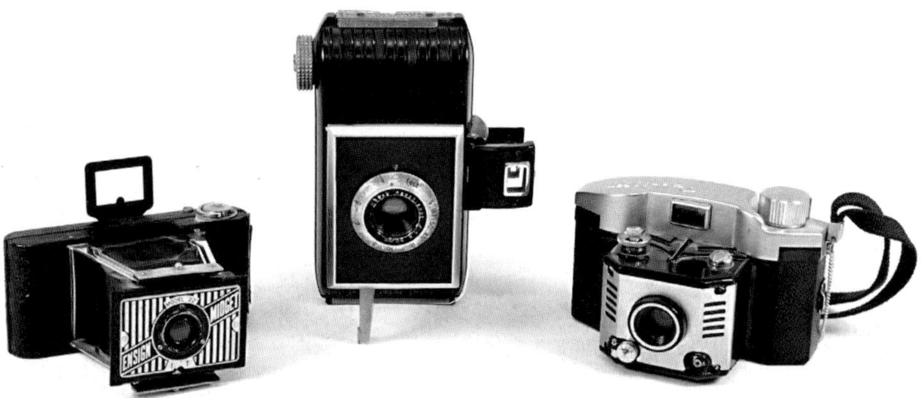

New styles of camera for smaller roll films: Ensign Midget Model 22, Kodak Bantam and Start 35 K-II.

images. The films that fed this new craze were many, and a whole range of new camera styles developed. Some were highly specified, appealing to advanced amateur and professional photographers, others fell squarely into the domain of the snapshot photographers. Starting in 1934, the British-made Ensign Midget was made in five models that covered both camps.

Each of the Midgets folded to no more than $8\times4\times1.5$cm, an ideal size for slipping into even the smallest of pockets. The lens panel extended on four struts, a wire frame viewfinder folded up from the front and a waist-level optical viewfinder folded out on an arm from behind the lens panel. All five cameras took pictures 3×4cm on E-10 film. The top of the range Model 55 was fully specified for the serious photographer, the Model 33 was slightly simplified, but the Model 22 used a fixed focus lens, fixed aperture and single shutter speed, which made it ideal for the snapshot photographer who wanted a camera small enough to slip into any pocket, but good enough to produce quality images. In the days when Britain had a monetary system that gave twelve pennies to the shilling and twenty shillings to the pound, the names of the cameras were based on their prices of 55 shillings, 33 shillings, and 22 shillings. In 1936, rippled silver versions of the Model 33 and Model 55 were produced to commemorate, in England, the silver jubilee of King George V and Queen Mary.

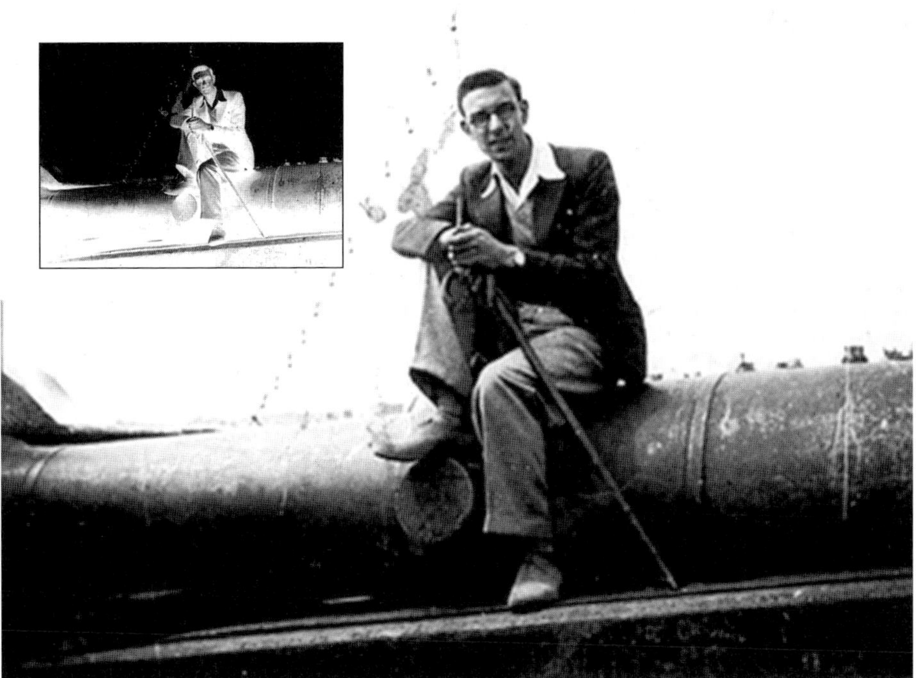

Enlarged from a tiny 3×4cm negative (inset), shot with an Ensign Midget Camera.

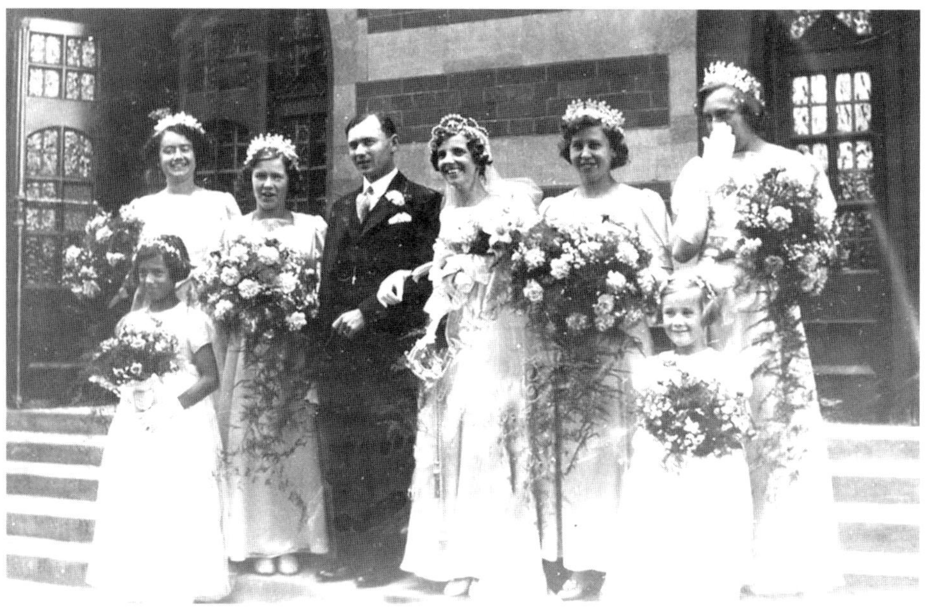

Right up until the acual outbreak of the Second Word War in September 1939, life in Britain went on as normal and it's doubtful that the people in this very typical wedding picture, taken around that time, had any inclination of what was about to happen to them. The wedding group has been posed in a style that would have been typical of the way a professional wedding photographer would have arranged his subjects. So how do we know that this was a snapshot, rather than a professional wedding picture? Quite simply, it's because no one in the picture is looking at the camera. They are all looking at the professional photographer who set up the group, while one of the bridesmaids on the right, caught by the snapshot photographer, clearly isn't ready for the picture to be taken.

The 1930s also saw a selection of cameras made first in Germany and then in Japan to take a 35mm size roll film called Bolta. While some Bolta cameras were quite sophisticated, many more were available for the keen snapshot photographer.

In 1936, Kodak launched the 828 film size, which was its own version of roll film that emulated 35mm. It was first seen in a camera called the Bantam Special, which was very well specified for use by serious photographers. Typical of Kodak's philosophy for making photography easy for all, the same film was soon seen in simplified snapshot cameras that also carried the Kodak Bantam name, while other manufacturers soon followed their lead. This was characteristic of the way Kodak worked, launching a new type of camera that took a new size of film, then allowing other manufacturers to make their own cameras to take that film, resulting in more film sales for Kodak. Nevertheless, there was one company in America who tried – and to a great extent succeeded – to match Kodak at this particular game…

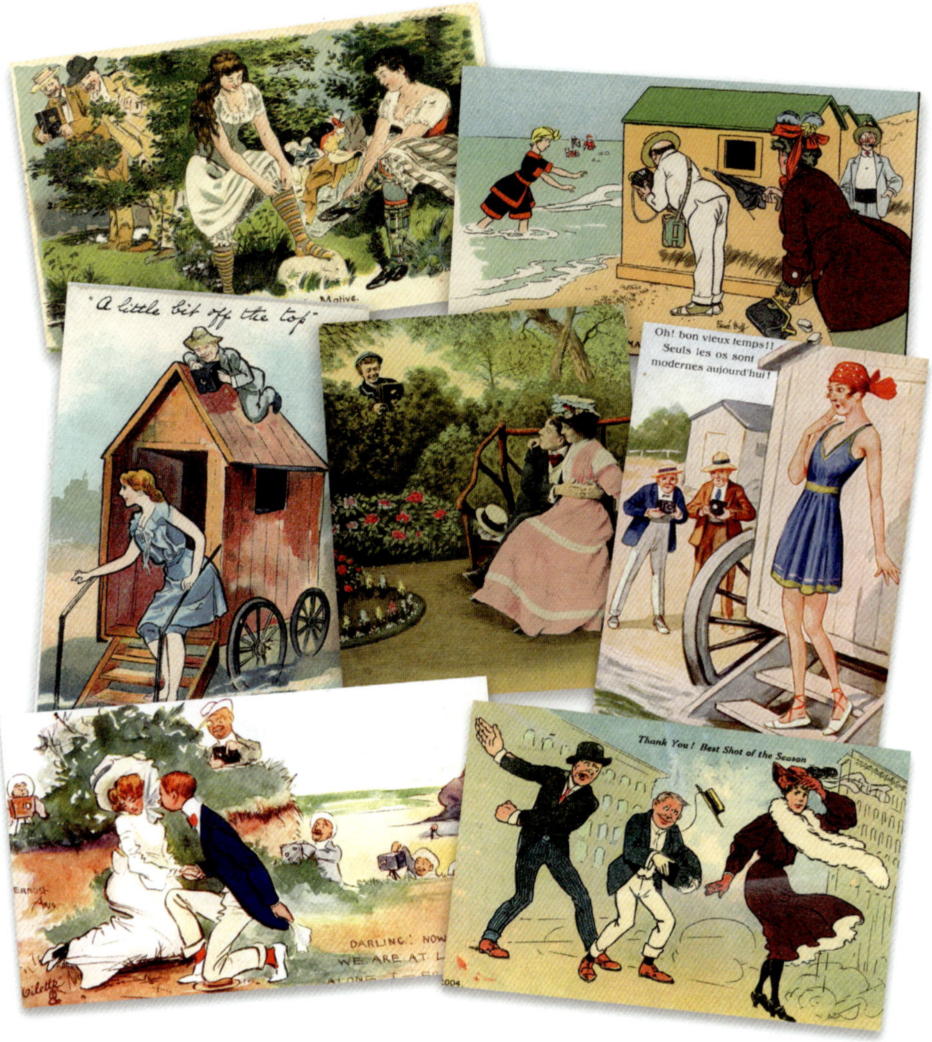

How postcards from the early days of photography depicted snapshot photographers as voyeurs.

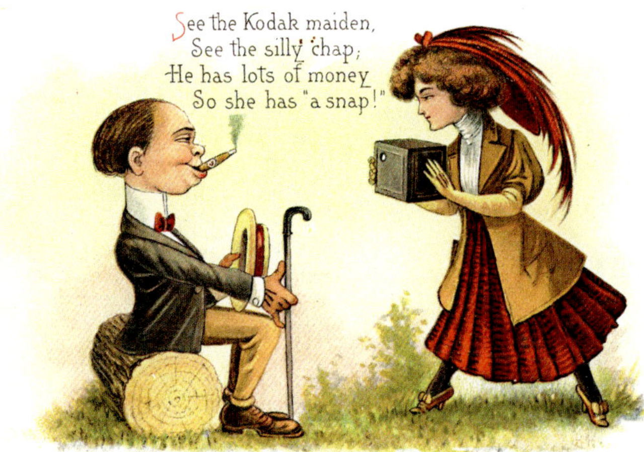

Not all postcards depicted snapshot photographers as nosy nuisances. This card, posted in 1908, shows a more whimsical approach to snapshot photography.

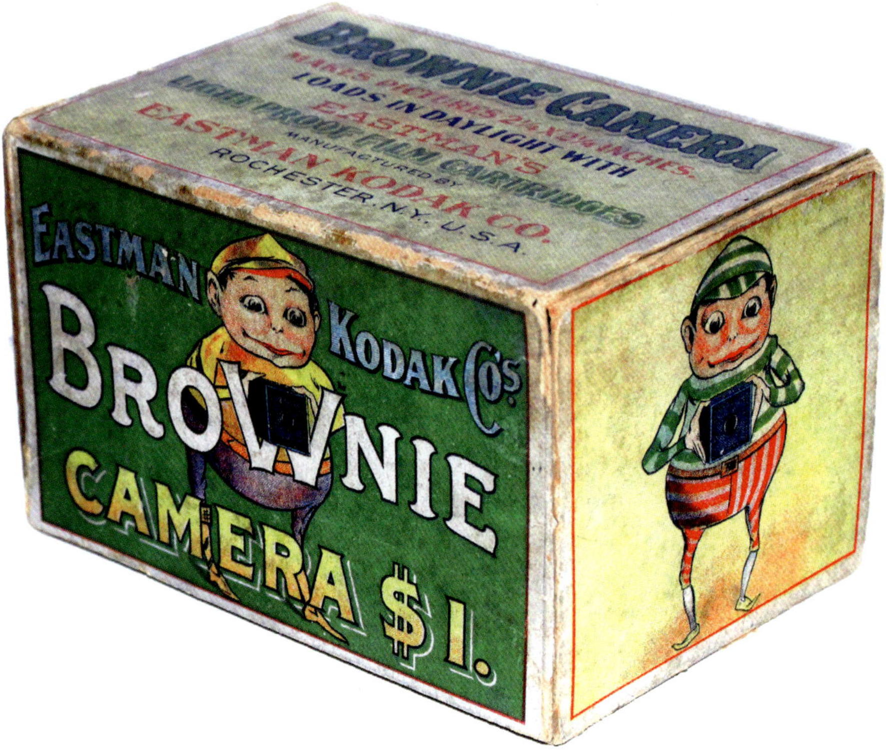

The box for the Brownie shows the elf-like characters from which the camera took its name.

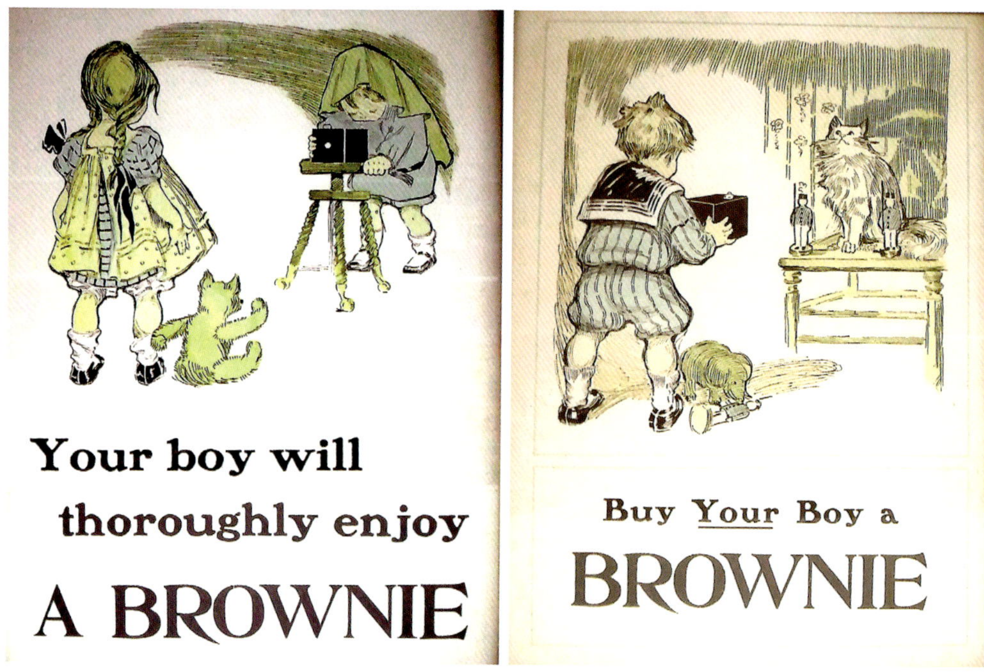

Advertising for the Brownie shows how it was aimed at children, although more at boys than girls.

Brownies

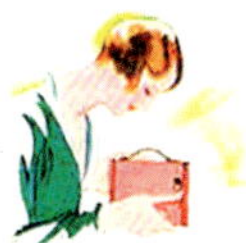

the world's most popular cameras ... now come in five attractive colors

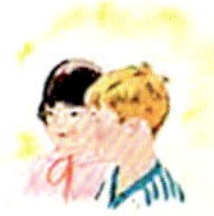

AND now the Brownie—maker of good snapshots for millions the world over—is wearing Joseph's coat.

So save up your best "Ohs" and "Ahs" of admiration. Save them for the moment when you first see these little soldiers of photography in their brilliant new uniforms. Have your appreciation all ready to stand at attention when the Kodak dealer shows you the lovely leather cases supplied to match each color.

From the smallest children to the biggest grown-ups every one capitulates to the new Brownies—they are so good to look at, so smooth and pleasant to the touch, so light and strong and compact, and such efficient picture-makers. There are five colors—each in the most approved shade. The Brownies are Models 2 and 2A, making pictures 2¼ x 3¼ and 2½ x 4¼ respectively. Put down on your list of things to be done today or to-morrow—"See the colored Brownies." Priced as low as $3. Smart cases, including handy shoulder strap, at small extra cost. Eastman Kodak Co., Rochester, New York.

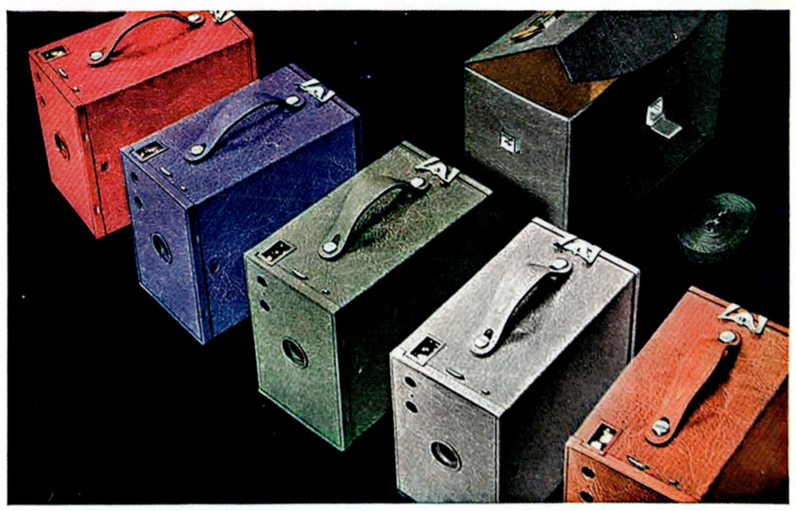

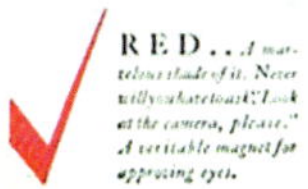
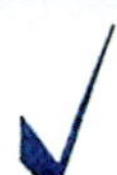
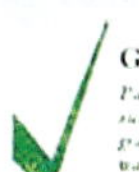

How Kodak advertised the No.2 Brownie.

Colourful Kodak Folding Brownies from 1903–1915, the No.2A (left) and No.3A.

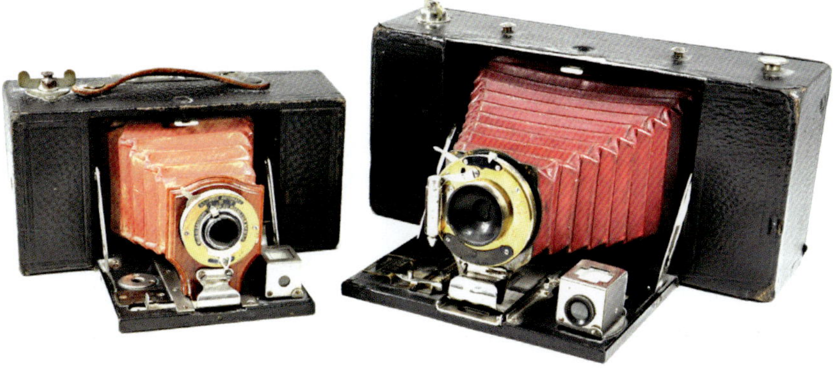

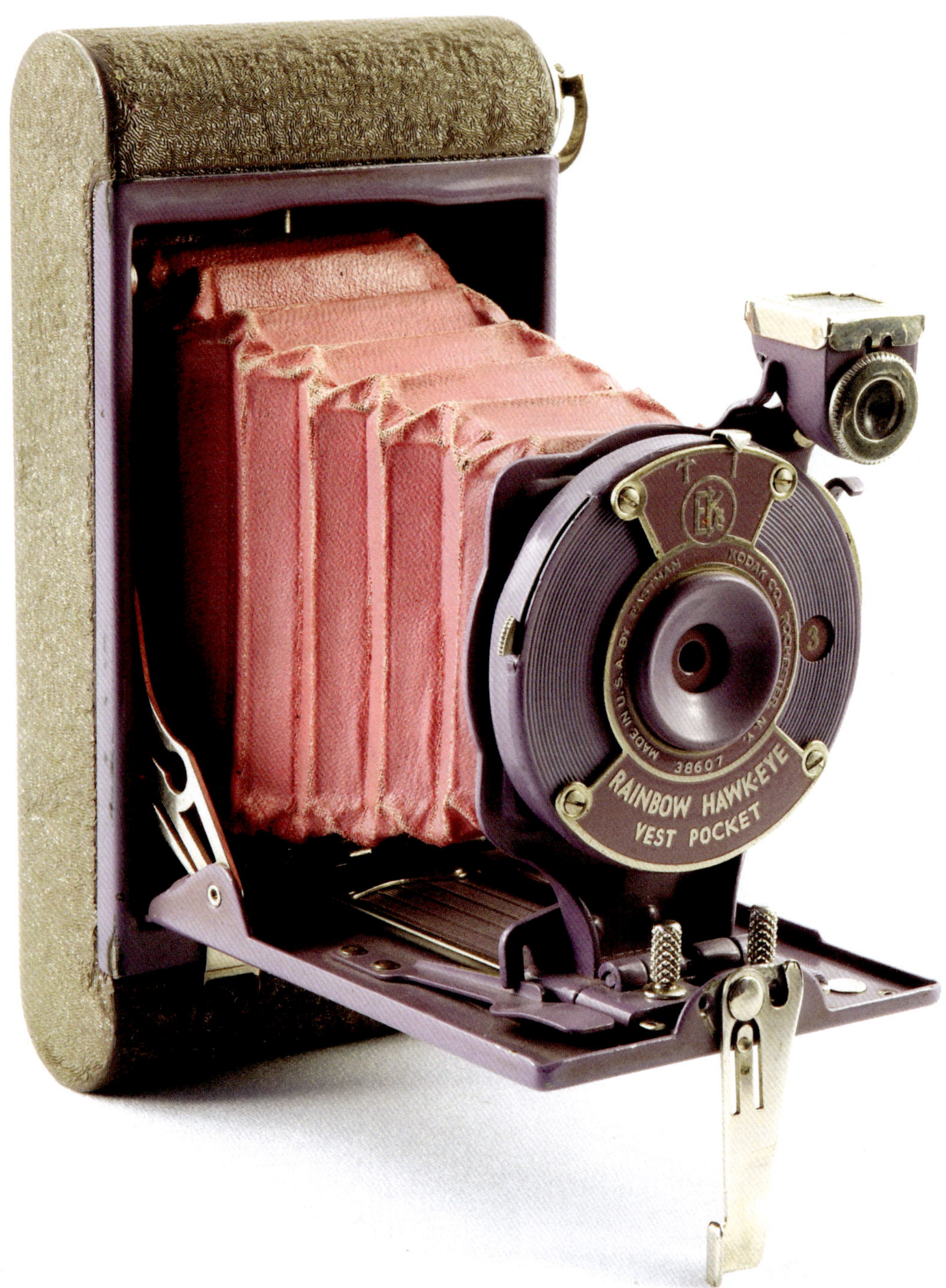

A Rainbow Hawkeye folding snapshot camera, one of a series made in different colours.

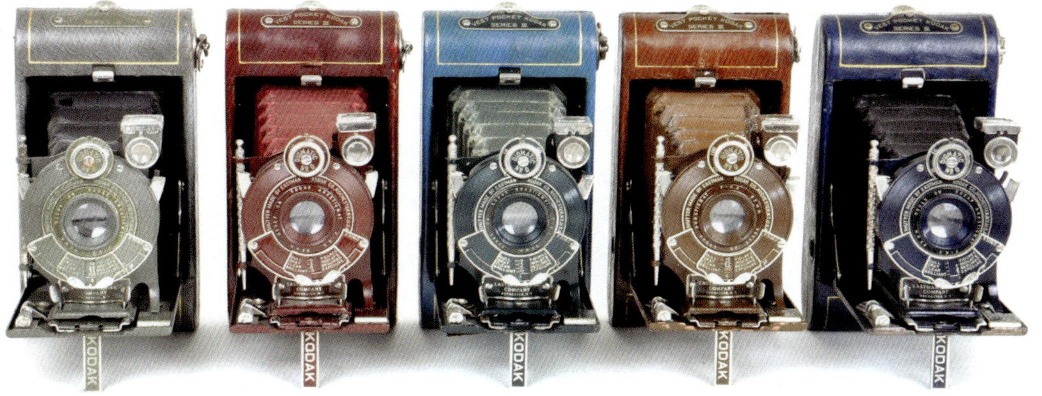

Kodak Vanity cameras in their range of five colours.

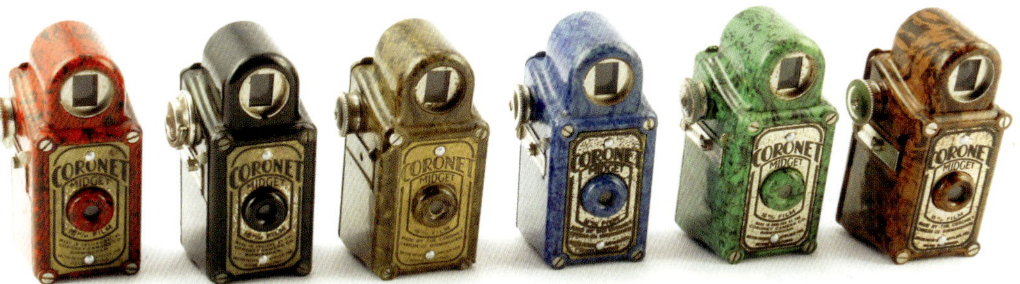

Coronet Midgets were small subminiature type cameras that came in six colours, including two shades of green.

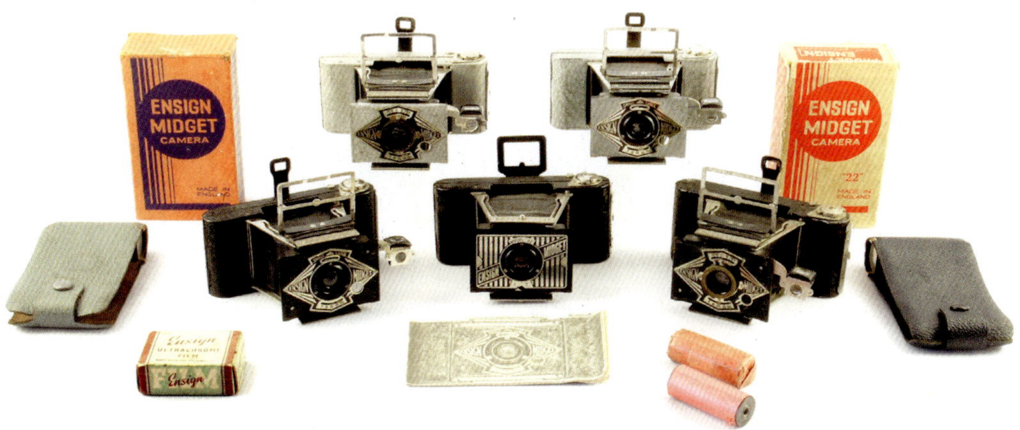

The full range of Ensign Midget cameras with boxes, film and instruction booklet.

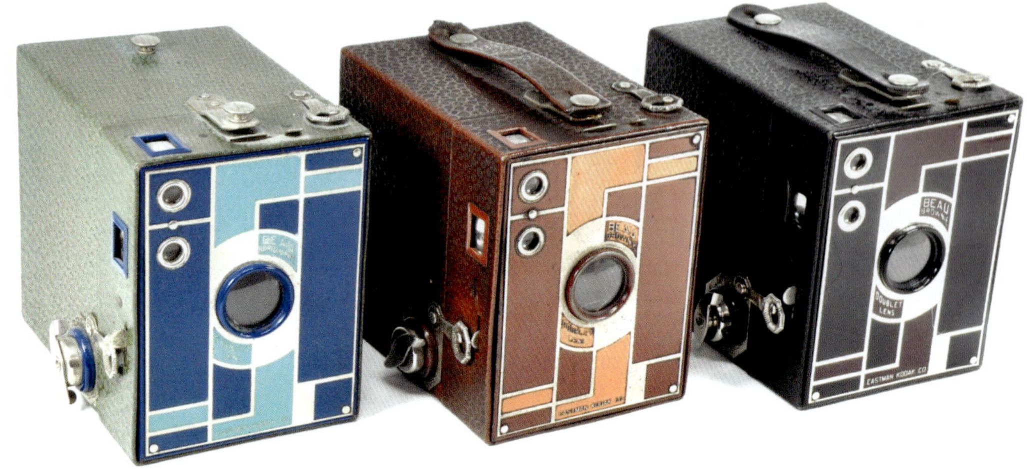

Three different coloured versions of the Beau Brownie.

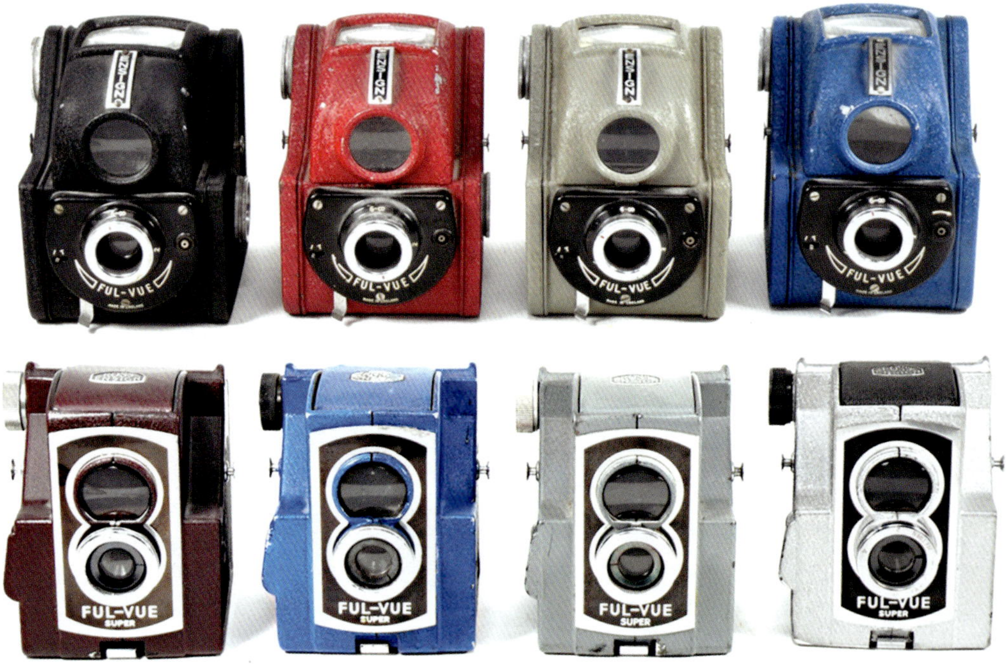

The Ensign Ful-Vue and the subsequent Ful-Vue Super were sold in different colours.

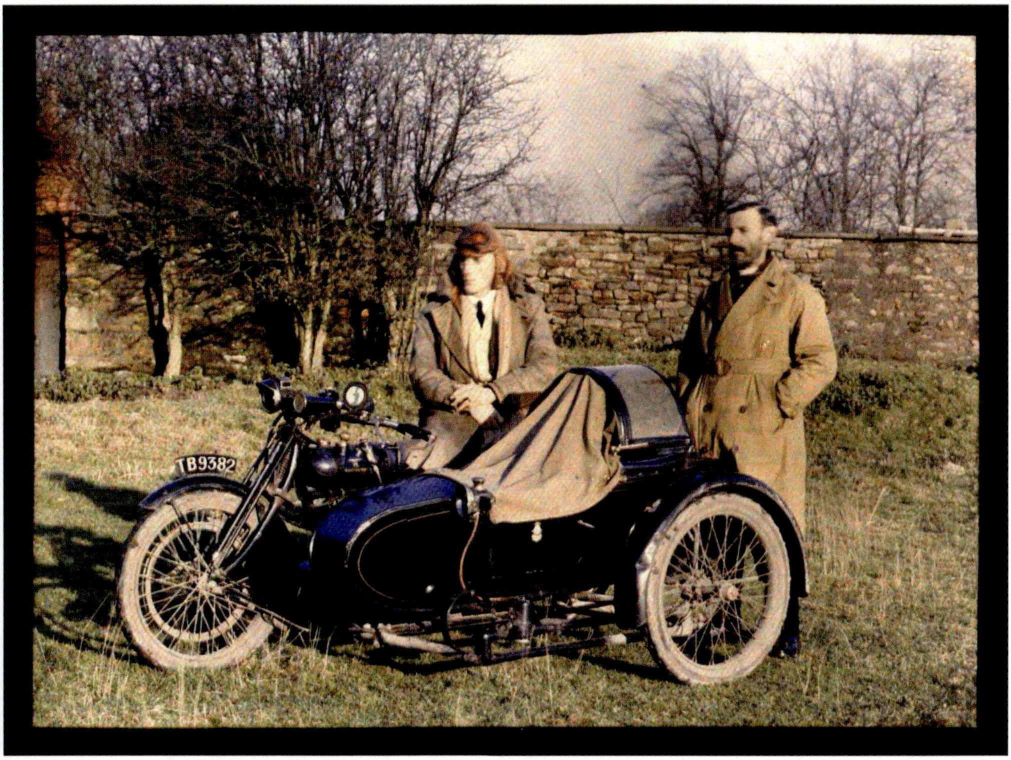

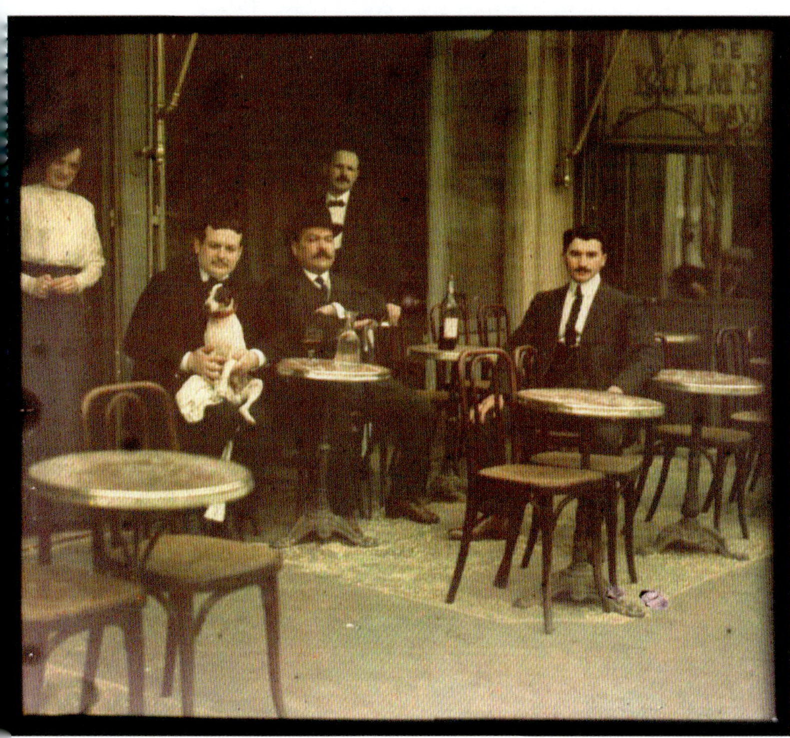

Autochromes, made on glass plates, were among the first colour processes. This example was shot in the 1920s.

A rare dioptichrome, another type of very early colour photography that produced pictures on glass plates.

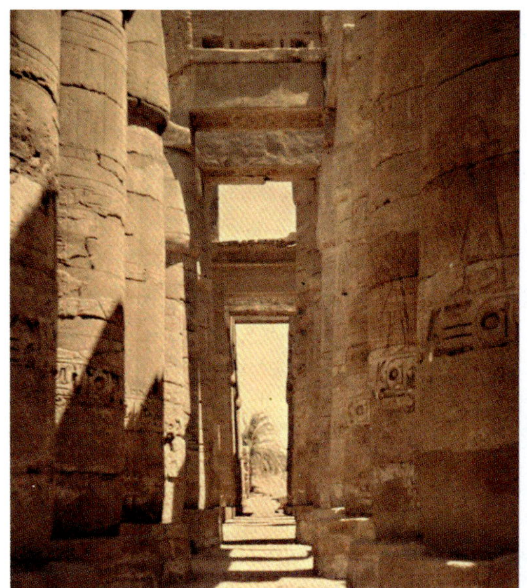
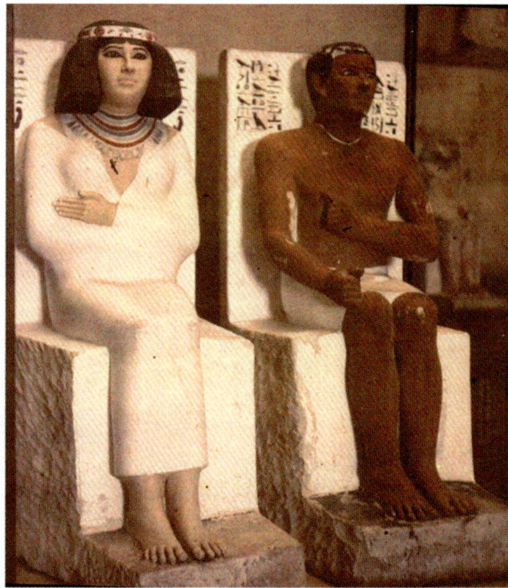
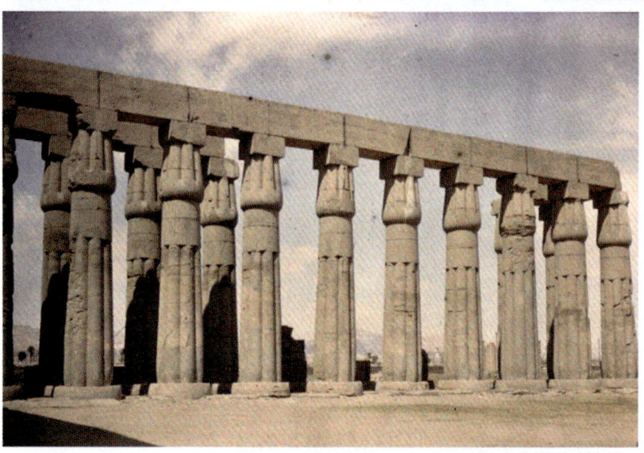
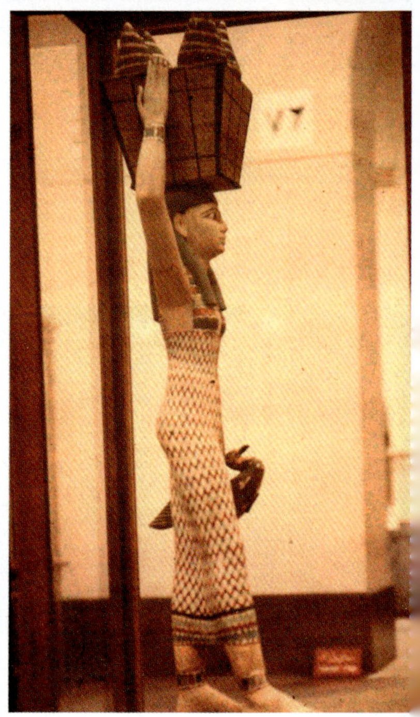
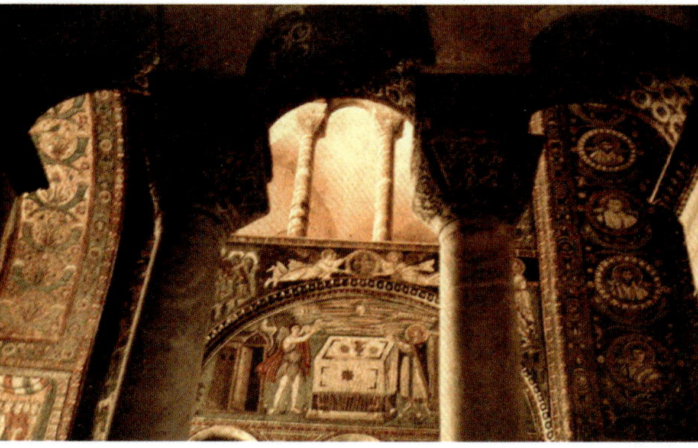

A set of pictures shot in 1934 using Filmcolor, one of the earliest colour films.

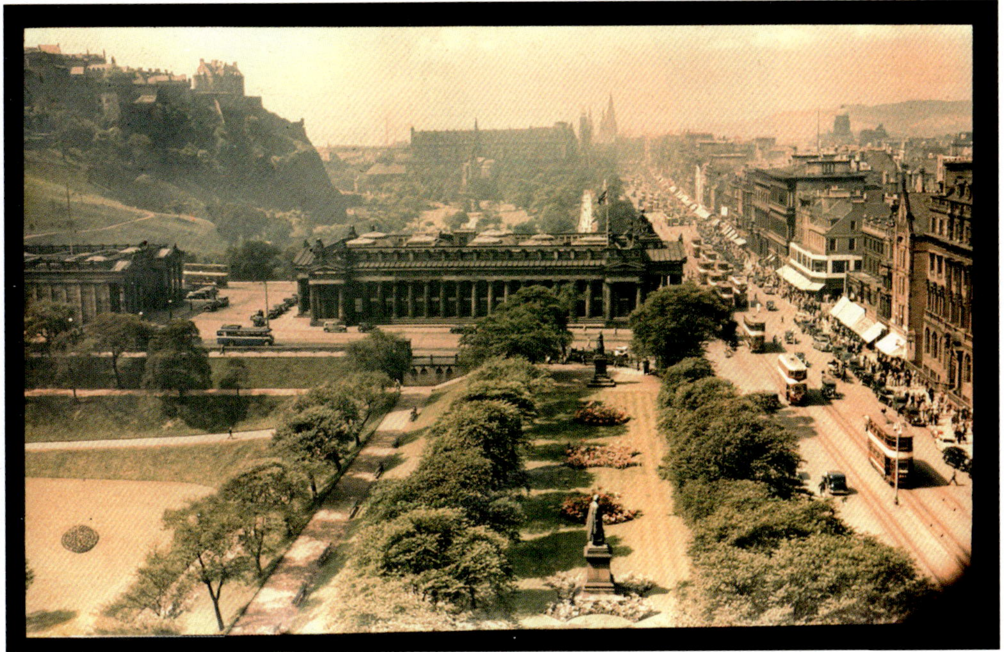

Colour photography came into its own for snapshot photographers with the introduction of Dufaycolor, used to shoot this picture of Edinburgh in 1936.

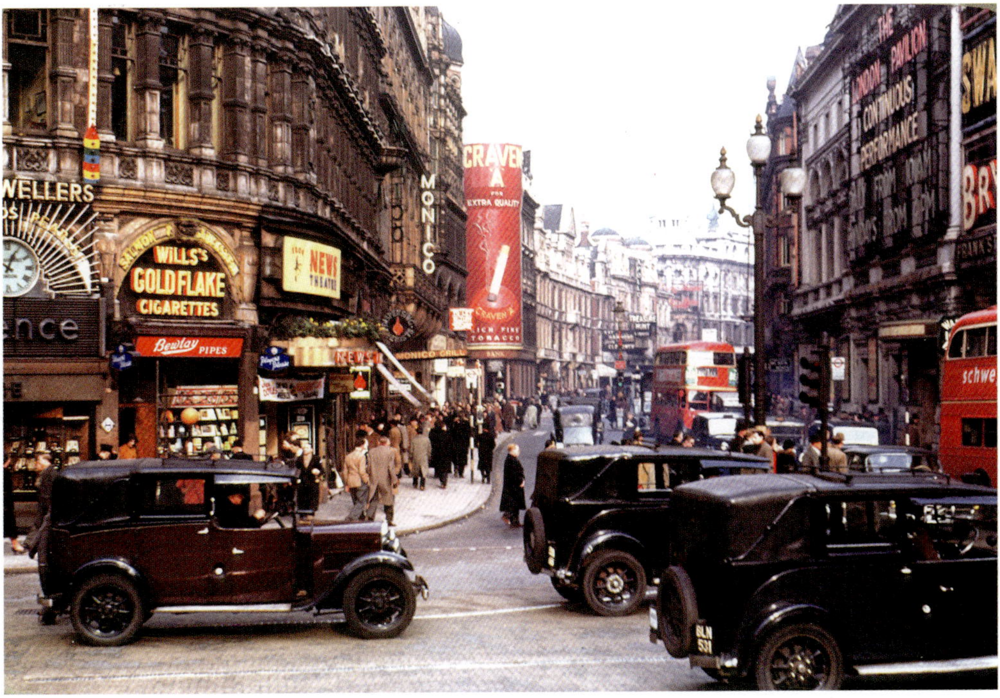

An early example of Kodachrome, taken in London in 1949, illustrates so much about the era in which it was taken.

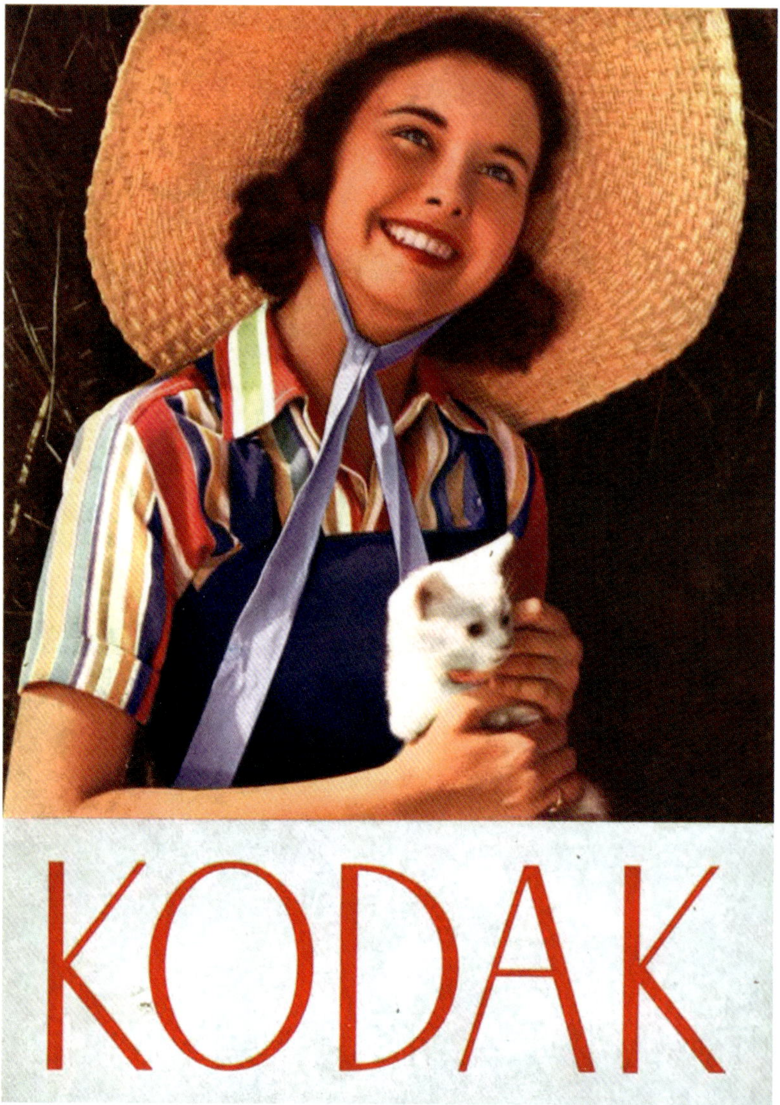

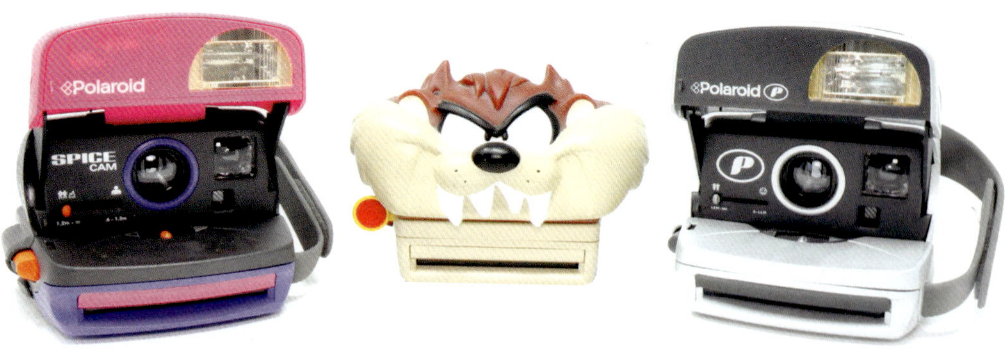

Fun cameras from the Polaroid 600 Series for snapshot photographers: the Spicecam and Tazcam, with the more upmarket P600, made in brushed silver.

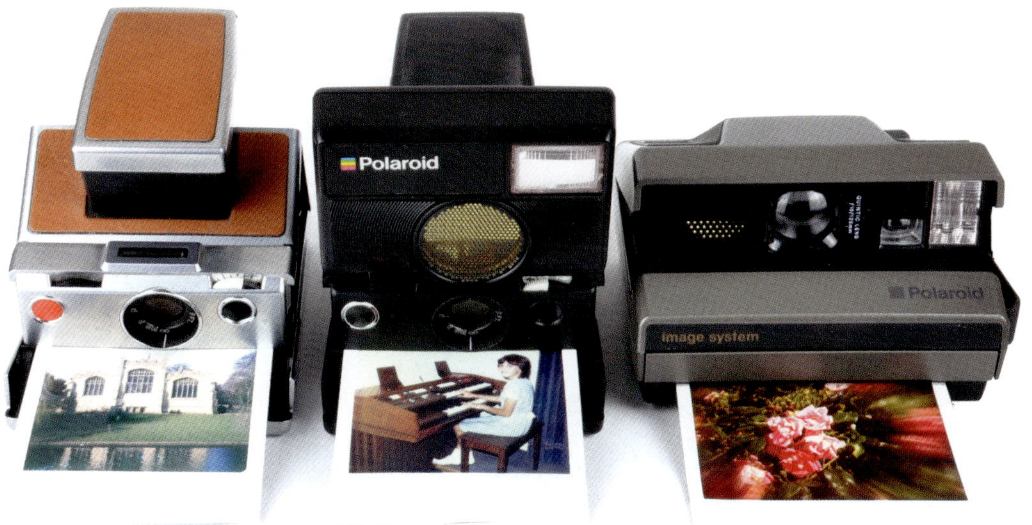

Shown with their instant pictures, the three top formats from Polaroid that were easily used by snapshot and experienced photographers alike. Left to right, cameras from the SX-70 system, 600 Series and Image/ Spectra. (The instant pictures are shown in their fully developed state, seen approximately a minute after exposure.)

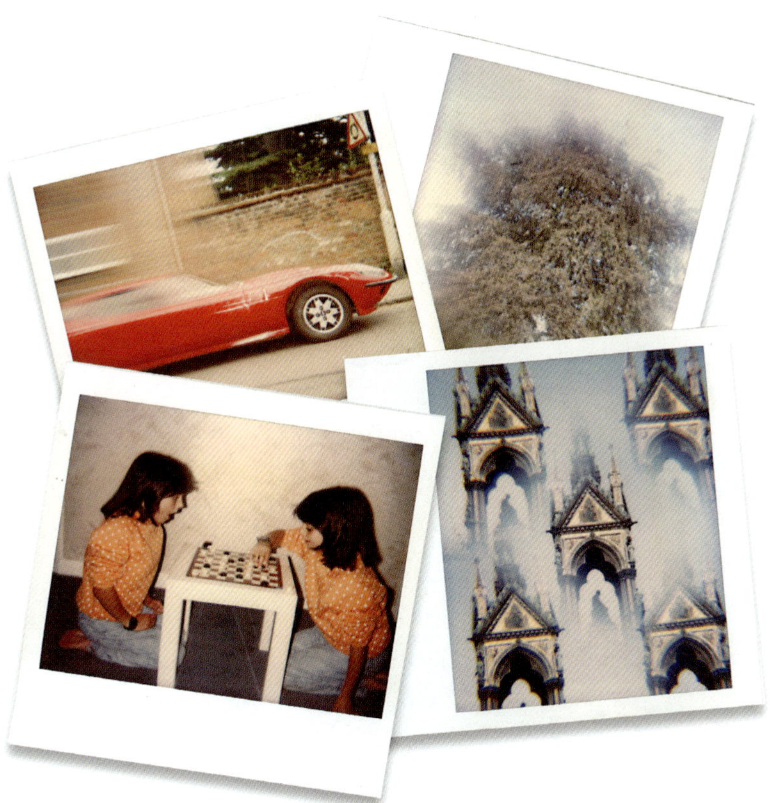

Special effect filters provided snapshot photographers with extra creativity in their Polaroid instant pictures.

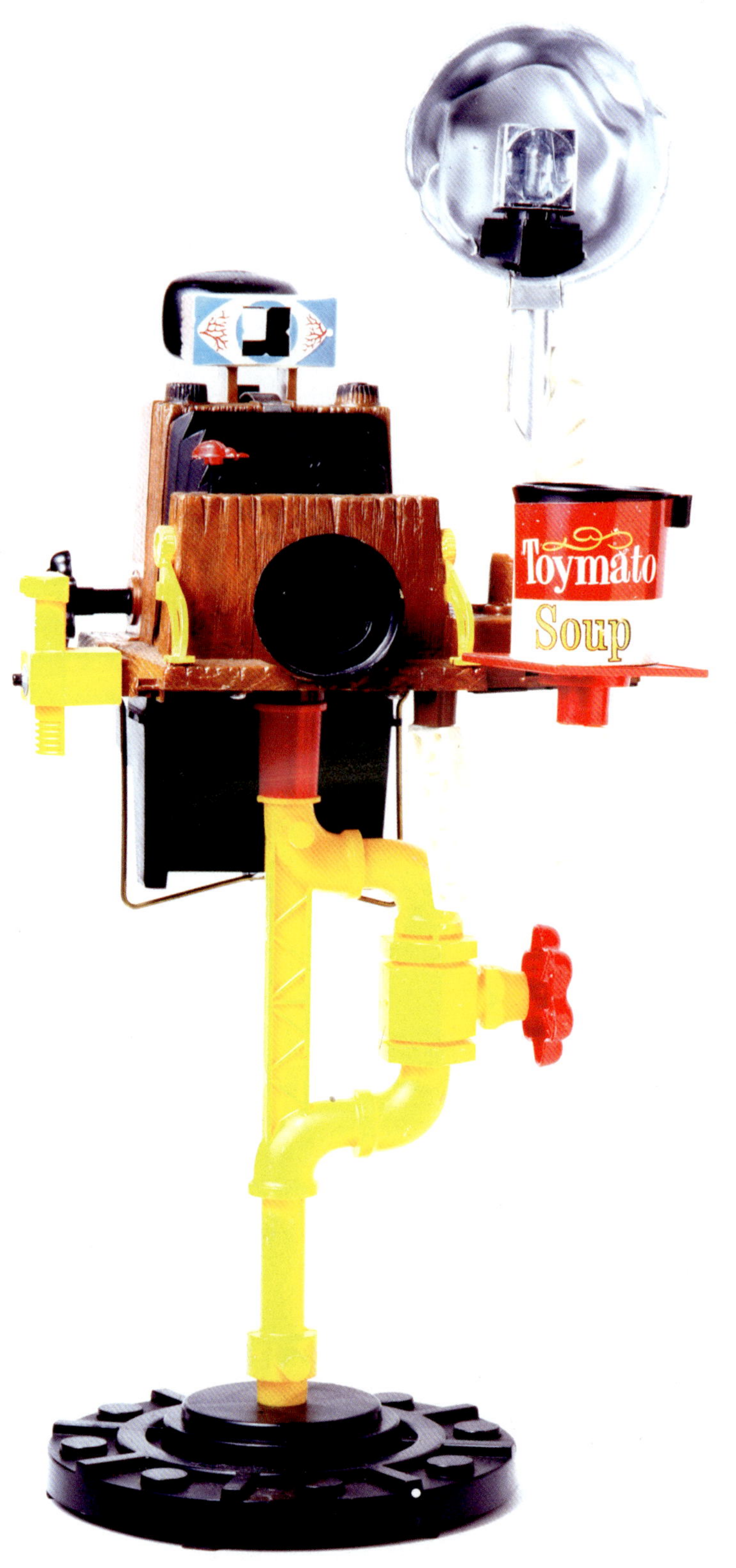

The Kookie was a strange instant picture camera made more as a toy than as a serious camera.

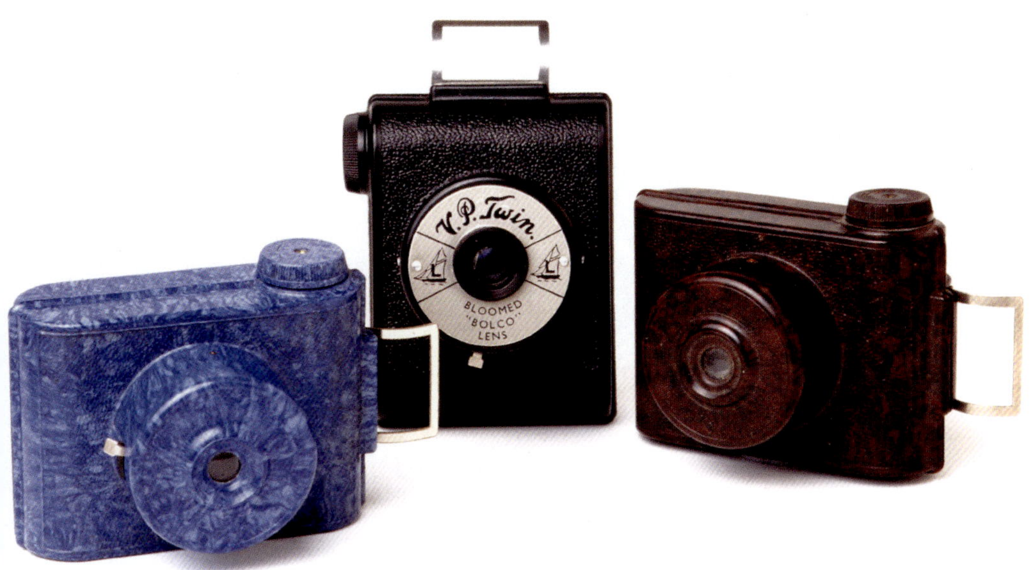

The popular VP Twin, made in black, brown and blue.

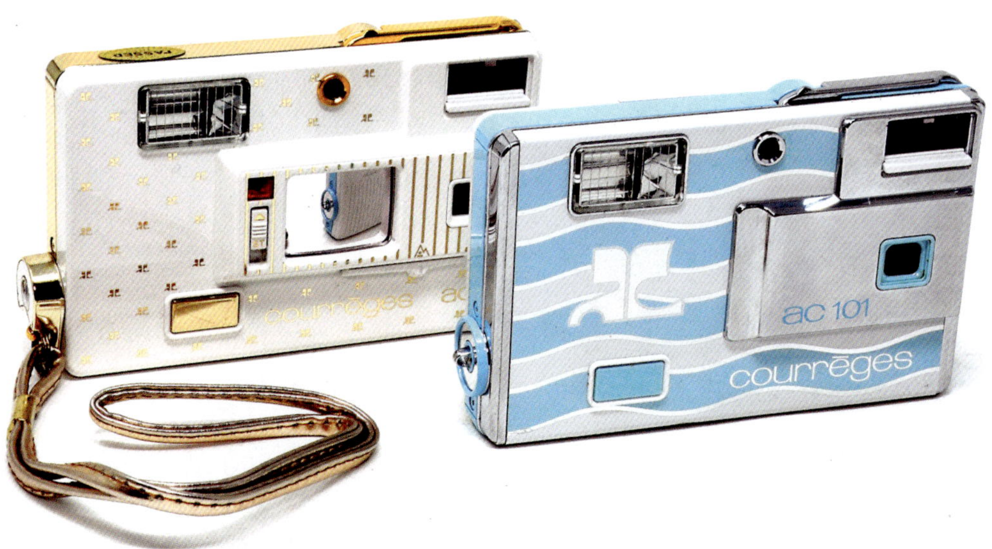

Two of the more upmarket disc cameras, adapted by Courrèges from Minolta models: the AC301 (left) and AC 101.

The Hollywood camera, an early
disposable model made by the Encore
Camera Company in America.

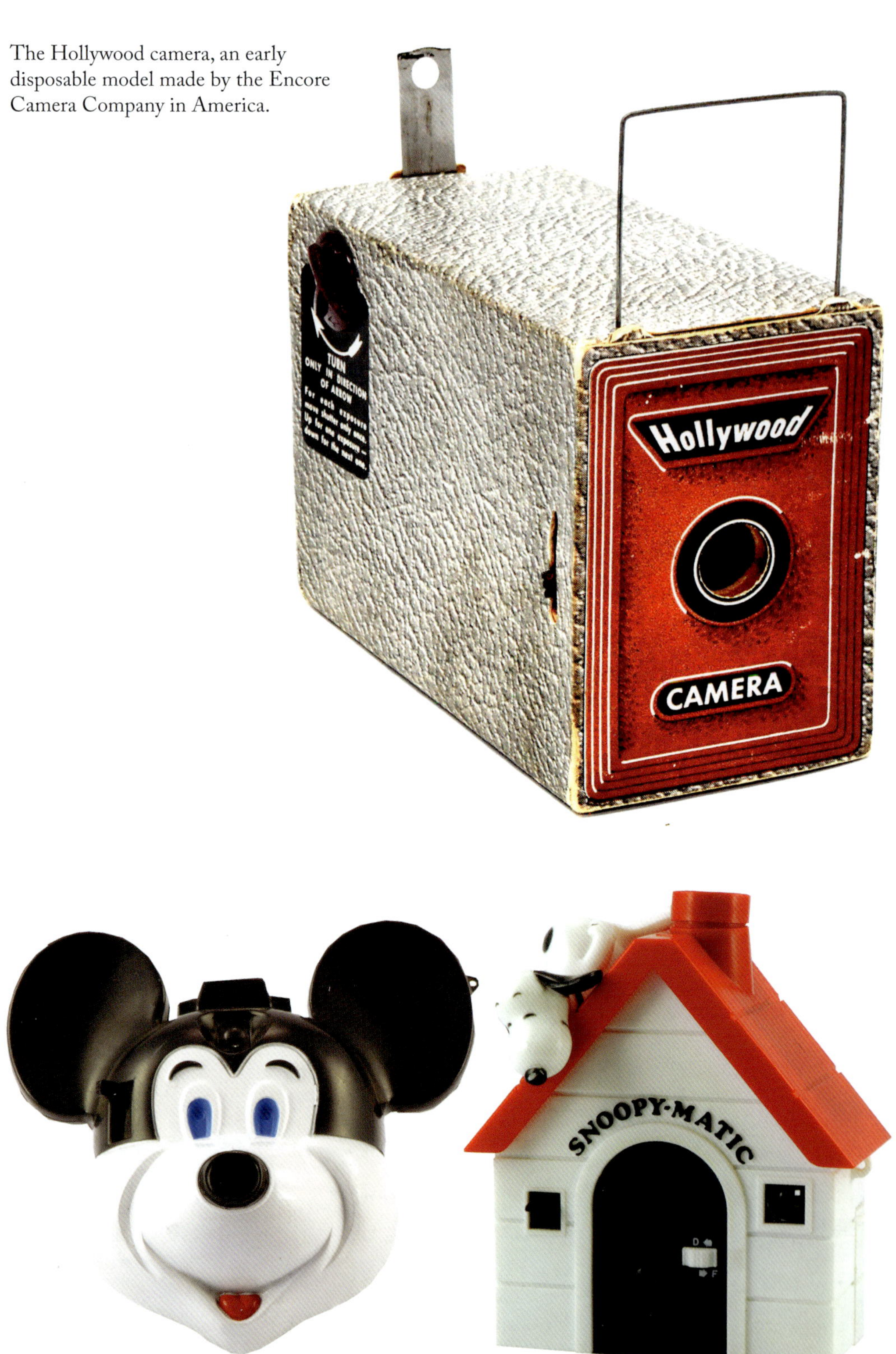

Two novelty cameras for 126 Instamatic film which were aimed at children: Mick-A-Matic (left) and
Snoopymatic.

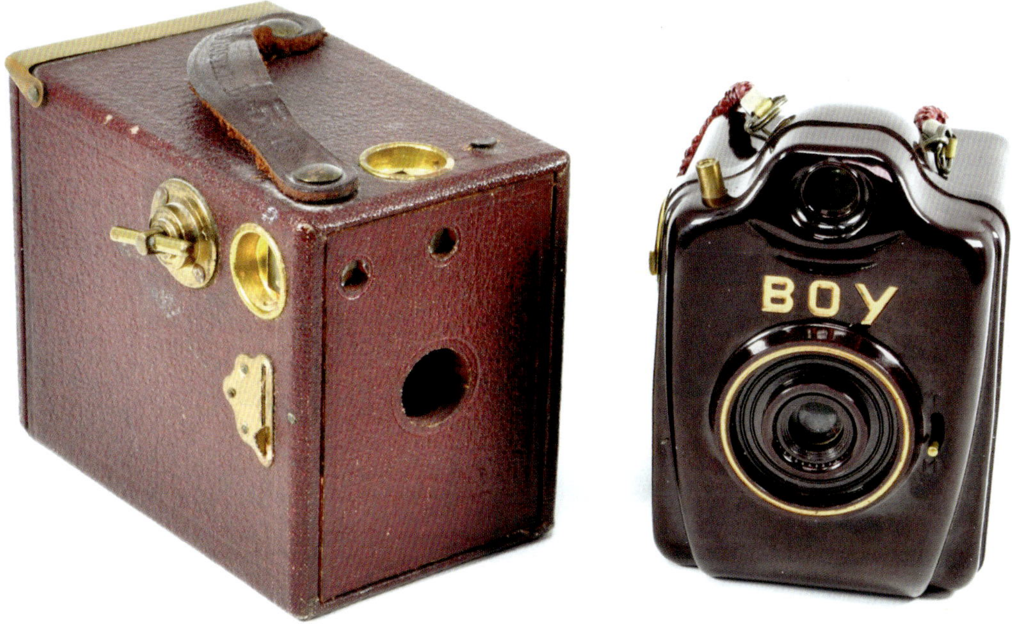

The attractive Luxus versions of the Buster Brown and Bilora Boy cameras.

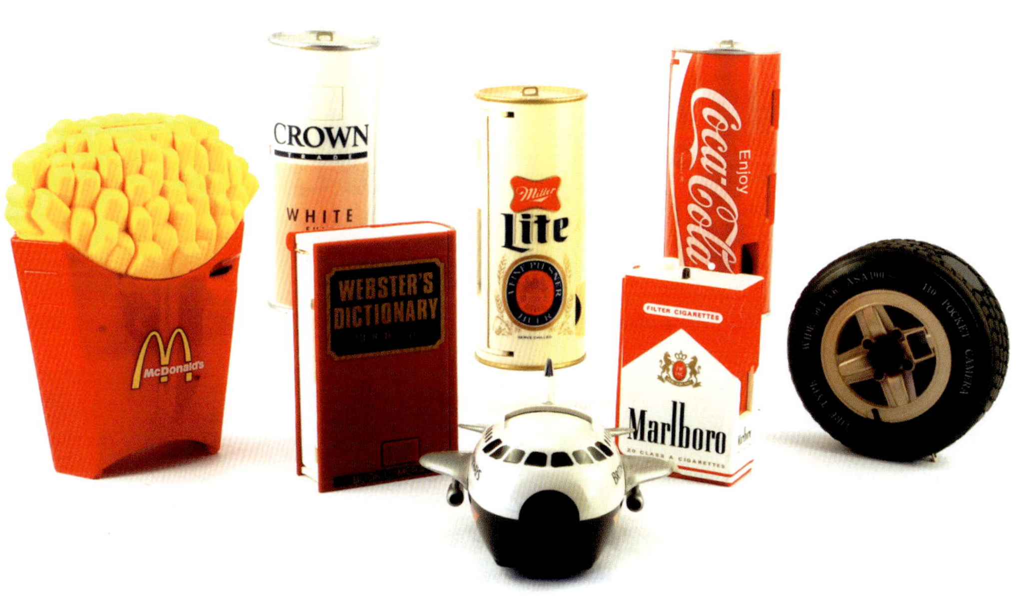

Eight novelty snapshot cameras made for 110 film.

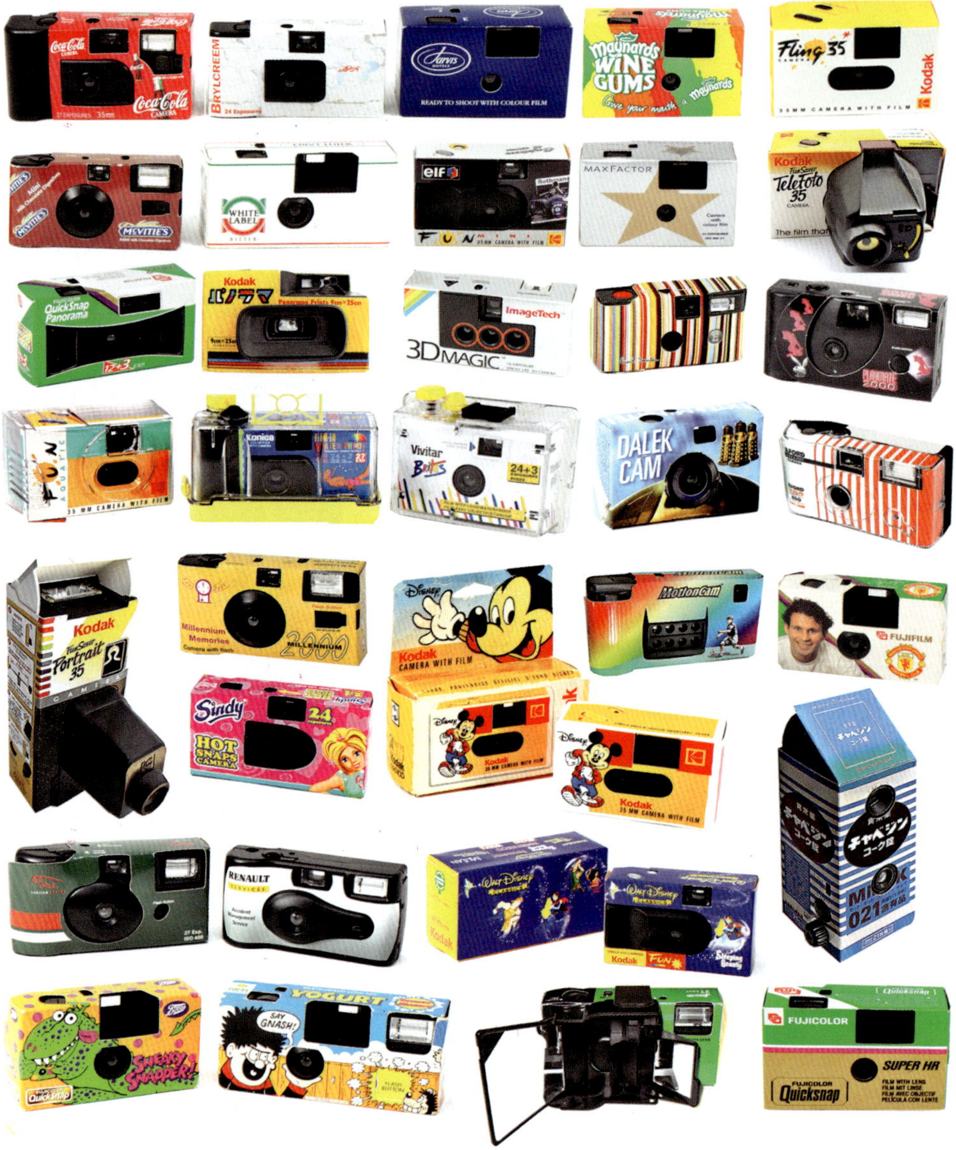

A selection of the many different types of disposable camera popular from the late 1980s and still sold today.

A super-wide snapshot taken with a disposable panoramic camera that trimmed a normal 35mm frame top and bottom.

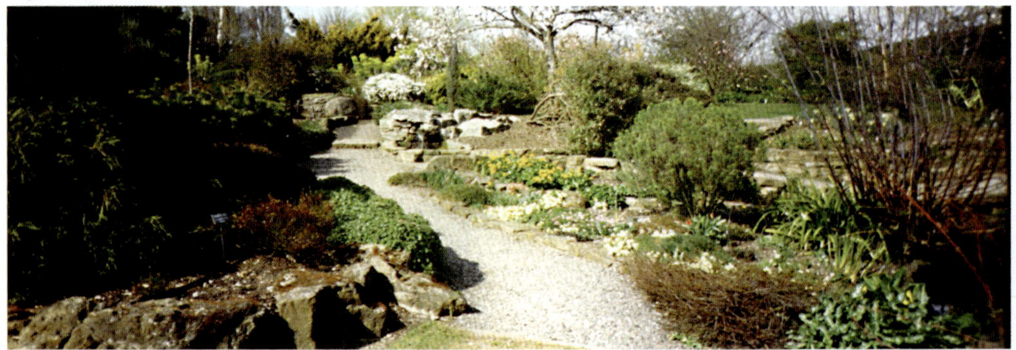

Universal Camera Corp

Kodak was the company most notable for producing simple cameras at reasonable prices for snapshot photographers. There was, however, another American manufacturer that trod a similar path, often with the intent of beating Kodak at their own game. Their cameras spanned the years from before the Second World War and later into the 1950s. The Universal Camera Corporation was formed in 1933, just as 35mm photography was beginning to arouse the interest of serious photographers.

Universal took the idea of small format pictures from 35mm, then produced low-priced snapshot-type cameras for film of a similar size, but in smaller lengths for fewer exposures and with backing paper and numbers like the larger roll films, then placed the film in a series of easy-to-use cameras aimed at attracting snapshot photographers. The company also followed another Kodak philosophy by introducing cameras that only accepted Universal's unique film sizes. In this way, snapshot photographers who bought the cameras were forced to return to Universal for their film, boosting the company's profits.

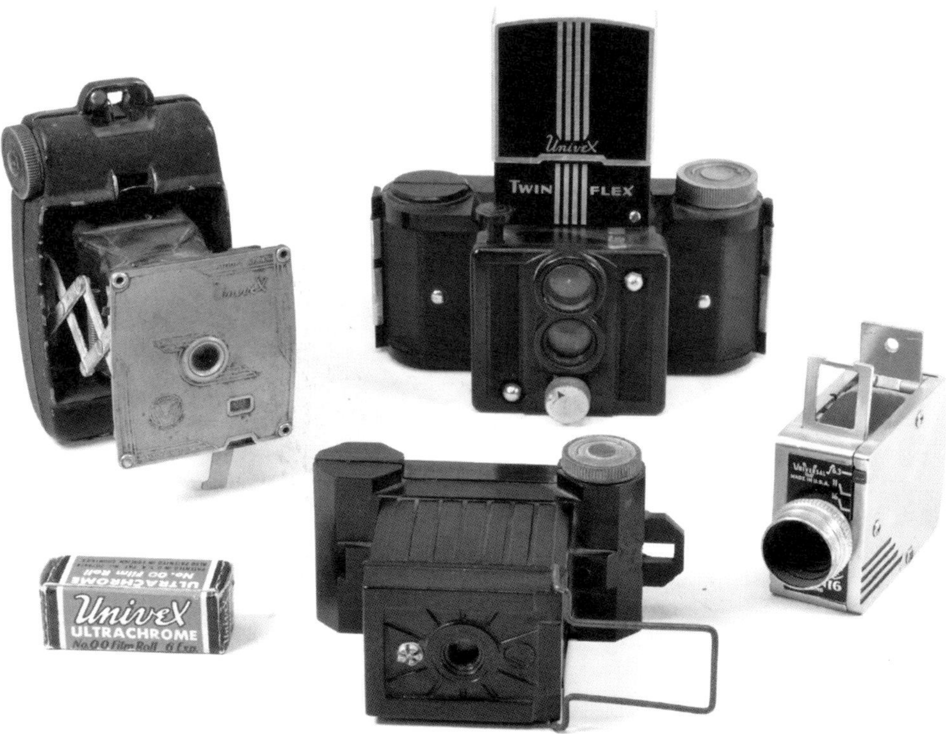

Snapshot cameras from the American Universal Camera Corporation: Univex A, Univex AF-4, Twinflex and the tiny Minute 16, with a box of Univex film.

Although the company produced a couple of cameras for more serious photographers, each bearing the Mercury name but with slightly different specifications, the vast majority of the company's cameras were aimed squarely at the snapshot market with simple, easy-to-understand controls. Here are just a few of the Universal Camera Corporation's products that followed this philosophy.

Univex A

Universal's first camera in 1933 was designed by another company called Norton Laboratories in New York, but the two companies fell out and each sold a slightly different version under its own name. In the end, the Universal version outsold the Norton camera. Many of the cameras were used as premium or giveaway items, Universal profiting from high sales of the special film that was unique to the camera.

The Univex A took six exposures on 00 size roll film with a picture size of 29×38mm, against the traditional 35mm size of 24×36mm. In the first few years of production, sales of 00 size film reputedly reached 15 million. The camera was made of plastic with a fold-up metal viewfinder frame and equipped with focus, aperture and shutter speed all fixed for simplicity. Within three years of its launch, at a price of just thirty-nine cents, Universal reported having sold 3 million cameras.

One story about the camera concerned a bank robber who dropped a Univex as he fled from a robbery. Police retrieved the camera, developed the film and, recognising a well-known robber on one of the frames, arrested him while still in possession of the stolen $10,000!

Univex AF-4

From around 1935, Universal produced a range of simple folding cameras in which the front panel pulled out from the body on scissor-like struts. Each took Universal's 00 film. The AF-4, which epitomised the range, featured a simple type of lens with fixed apertures and shutter speeds. Other cameras in the range included the AF, AF-2, AF-3 and AF-5. Apart from the last of these, which used an optical viewfinder in place of the cheaper wire frame type, it's difficult to see much difference in their specifications. More than a million were sold.

Several special versions of the AF cameras were also made for promotional purposes with the names of companies or events incorporated onto coloured faceplates. One was made as the official Girl Scout camera.

Twinflex

Although cheaply made of plastic, with only a simple lens, fixed aperture and simple shutter, the Twinflex was a true version of a more professional type of camera called a twin lens reflex. This style of camera called for two lenses, one mounted above the other. The lower lens took the picture while the top lens reflected its image into a viewfinder under a hood on the top of the body. The two lenses were focused in tandem so that the viewfinder showed the same image as the shooting lens.

The only control on the Twinflex was a knob on the front that moved the two lenses back and forth. The camera had a slightly curved film plane around which the film was led and a corresponding hump in the back of the body to allow for aberrations caused by the inexpensive lens, a cheap way of improving the picture quality. The camera used Universal's usual size 00 film.

Minute 16

In 1949, Universal entered the subminiature market with the Minute 16 (that's minute as in extra small, not as in sixty to the hour), which looked like a tiny movie camera. The lens was fixed focus, but three apertures were available,

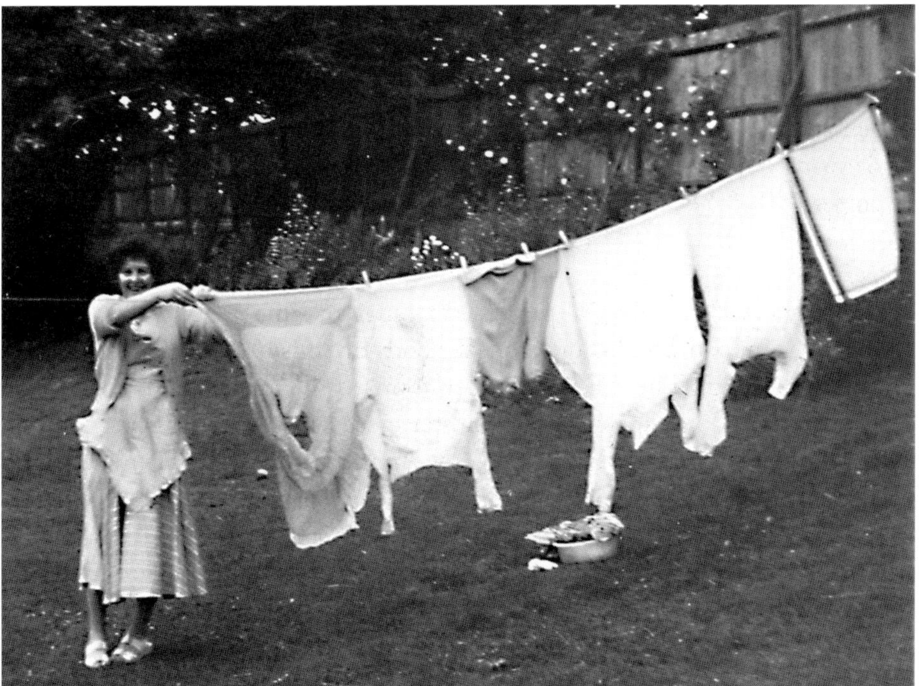

A simple snapshot which could never be considered a work of art. But it has so much to say about the time when it was taken, back in the days when, for so many households, every Monday was washday.

although the shutter offered only a single speed. The 16mm film was in a tiny cartridge and wound by a lever attached to a claw mechanism inside the body. The camera was sold with its own dedicated flashgun, which was more than three times the size of the camera. Outwardly, it appeared to be a precision-made subminiature camera, but in fact, the internal workings were cruder than first appearances suggested.

The Universal Camera Corporation invested serious money into the development of the Minute 16 at a time when 16mm looked to be the next big thing in camera design. That never happened and, because of mechanical problems and a low quality lens, the Minute 16 was a failure. It was the last camera produced by the Universal Camera Corporation, which closed for business in 1952.

Polyfoto studios

During the 1930s, an usual new type of camera, capable of taking forty-eight pictures of the same subject within a few minutes, began to be popular. The Polyfoto camera was used by professional photographers in studios rather than snapshot photographers, but the pictures it produced were a lot like snapshot portraits.

Unlike the typical photographic studio in which subjects were placed in static poses and asked not to move while the picture was being taken, people who posed in front of a Polyfoto camera were encouraged to move all they liked, while often chatting to the photographer at the same time. The result was a far more relaxed portrait than was often the case, and with forty-eight variations on the same basic pose to choose from, as Polyfoto publicity of the time put it: 'One of them must be good.'

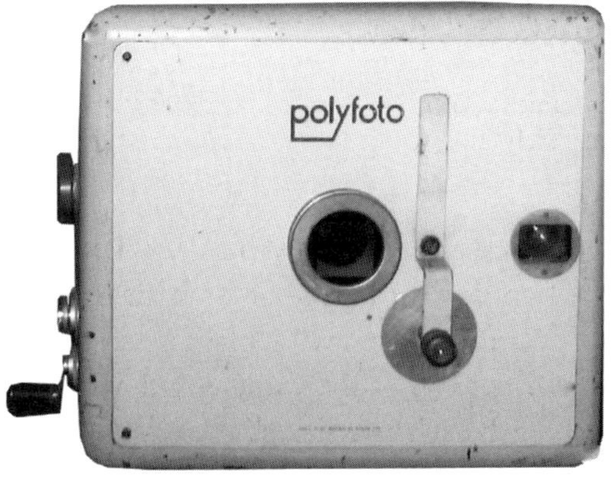

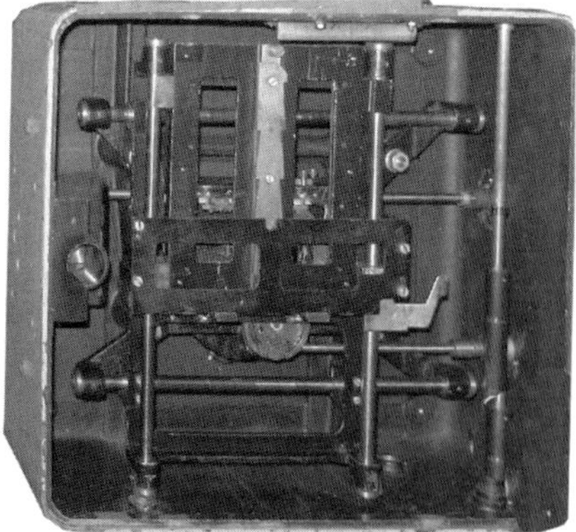

The Polyfoto camera and its ingenious inside workings.

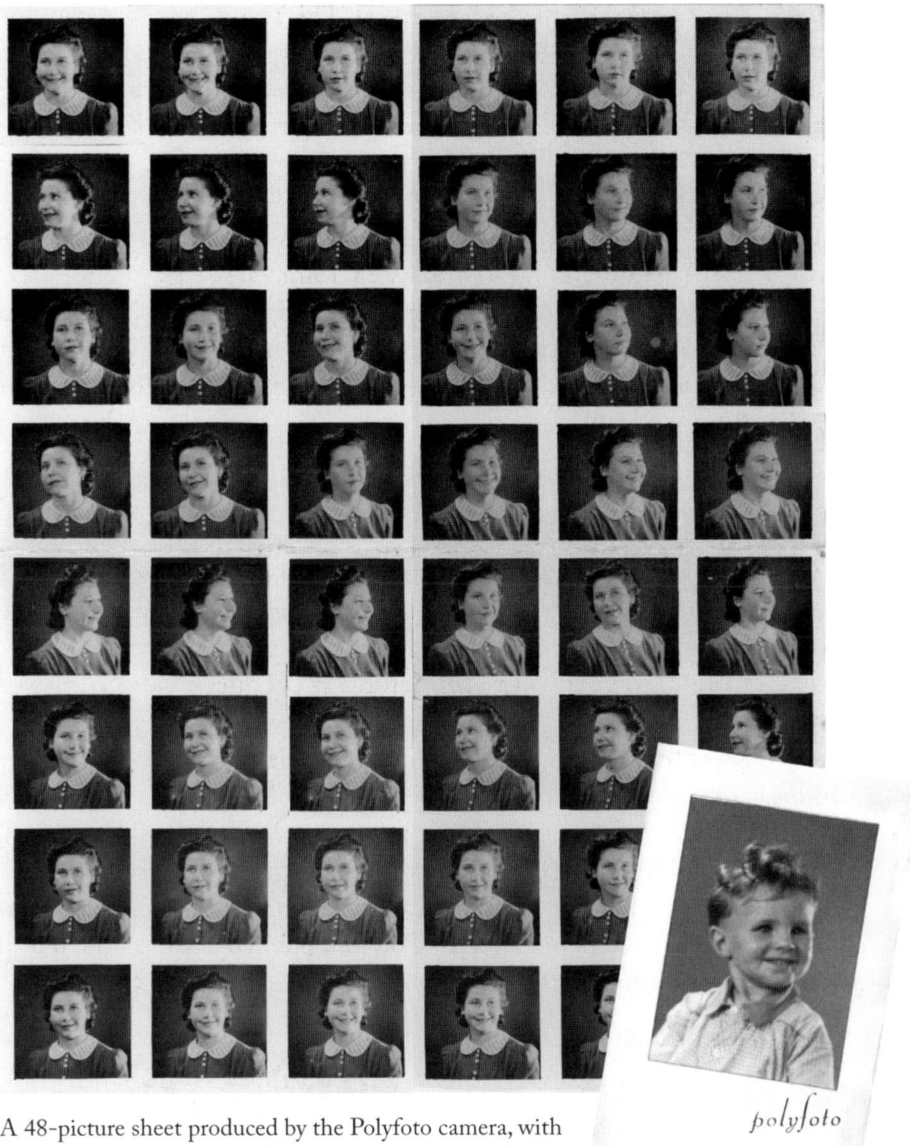

A 48-picture sheet produced by the Polyfoto camera, with
an enlargement of a single frame from another Polyfoto
shoot.

The camera looked like a large metal suitcase, measuring about $50 \times 50 \times 25$ cm
with its lens in the centre and a large handle on the side. It took glass plates
rather than film. With the subject in position in front of a plain background,
the photographer inserted the plate into the top of the camera and, when all
was ready, he began turning the handle. With each turn, the shutter was released
to take a single picture and the plate moved sideways. When six pictures had
been taken across the width of the plate, it dropped and a further six pictures

were taken as the plate moved back in the opposite direction. When the handle refused to turn any more, forty-eight pictures in eight rows of six had been taken, each showing a subtly different expression or inclination of the subject's head. Each picture measured ½ × ½ inches and they were often cut out for use in lockets and the like.

On-the-spot photography

The while-you-wait approach to snapshot photography was not unique to the years between the world wars. The use of cameras like the Aptus, discussed in

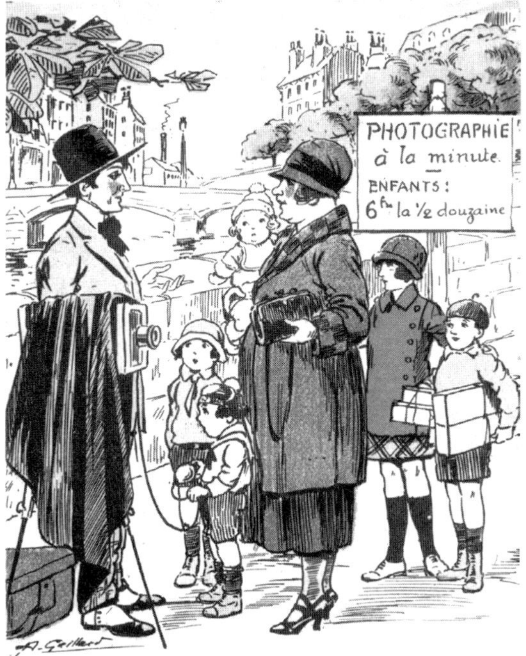

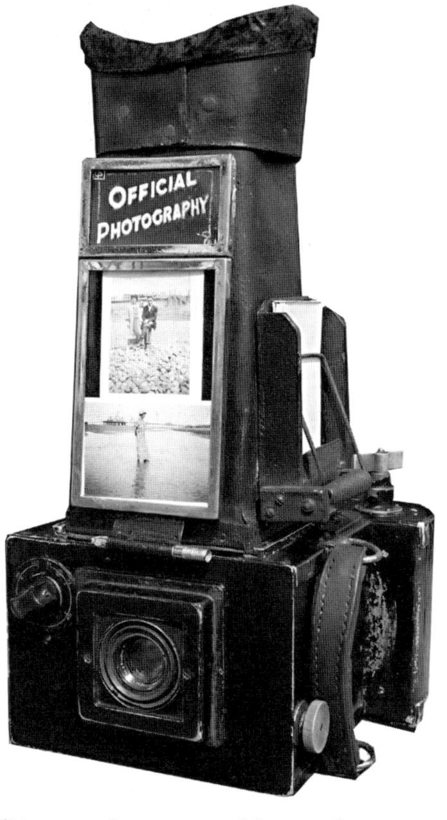

A French postcard from 1931 shows a street photographer offering half a dozen shots of children for six francs. The woman is saying she only has five children, but she is awaiting the sixth.

This unusual camera, used for seaside photography, was based on an older plate camera, a type made much earlier. It incorporated a large picture frame on the front of the lens focusing hood in which the photographer could display pictures or advertising material and even had a slot for the photographer's pencil and a spring clip to hold sales slips.

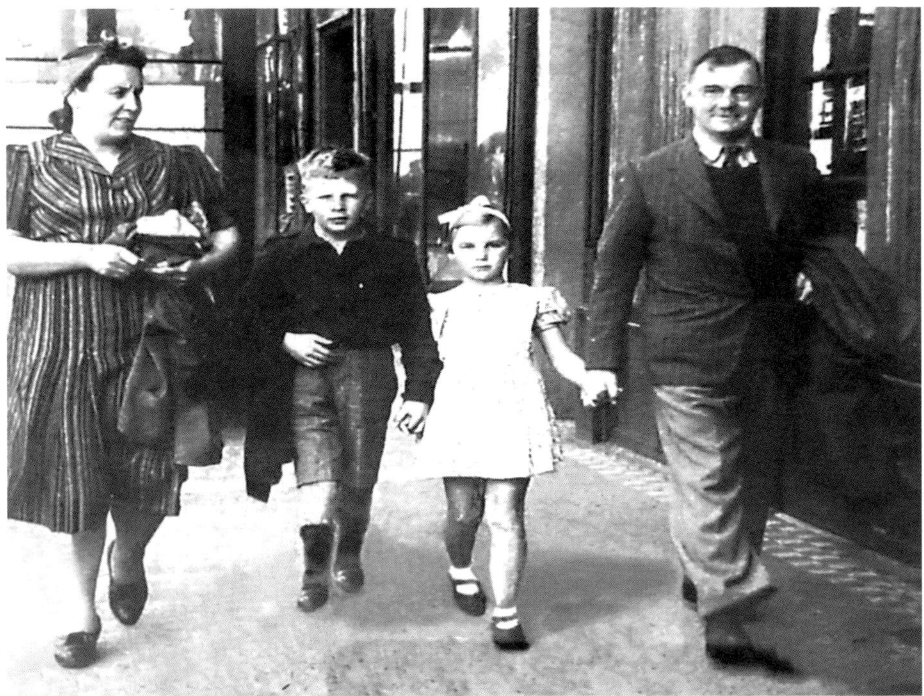

A family of four is caught by a seaside photographer in Rhyl in the late 1930s.

an earlier chapter, continued at this time, used mostly by street photographers, offering snapshot-like pictures on the spot and within minutes of exposure. Seaside photography was also prevalent, carried out by professional photographers, even though the results they produced were little more than snapshots. The photographers would roam beaches, taking pictures of holidaymakers, giving out tickets to people they photographed, inviting them to come later to places like seafront kiosks where they could see and buy the pictures taken earlier.

Photobooths

One thing that contributed to the demise of on-the-spot street photography and Polyfoto studios was the rise of interest in, and use of, photobooths. These gave anyone the opportunity to take their own snapshots of themselves simply by entering a small cubicle, sitting on a seat, placing a coin in a slot and waiting for the picture to be automatically taken. A few minutes later, a strip of four pictures would issue from the side of the machine.

Photobooths are still very popular, as digital technology has made them more sophisticated and versatile than ever before. But today's photobooths are a long way removed from the first version, known as the Photomaton and

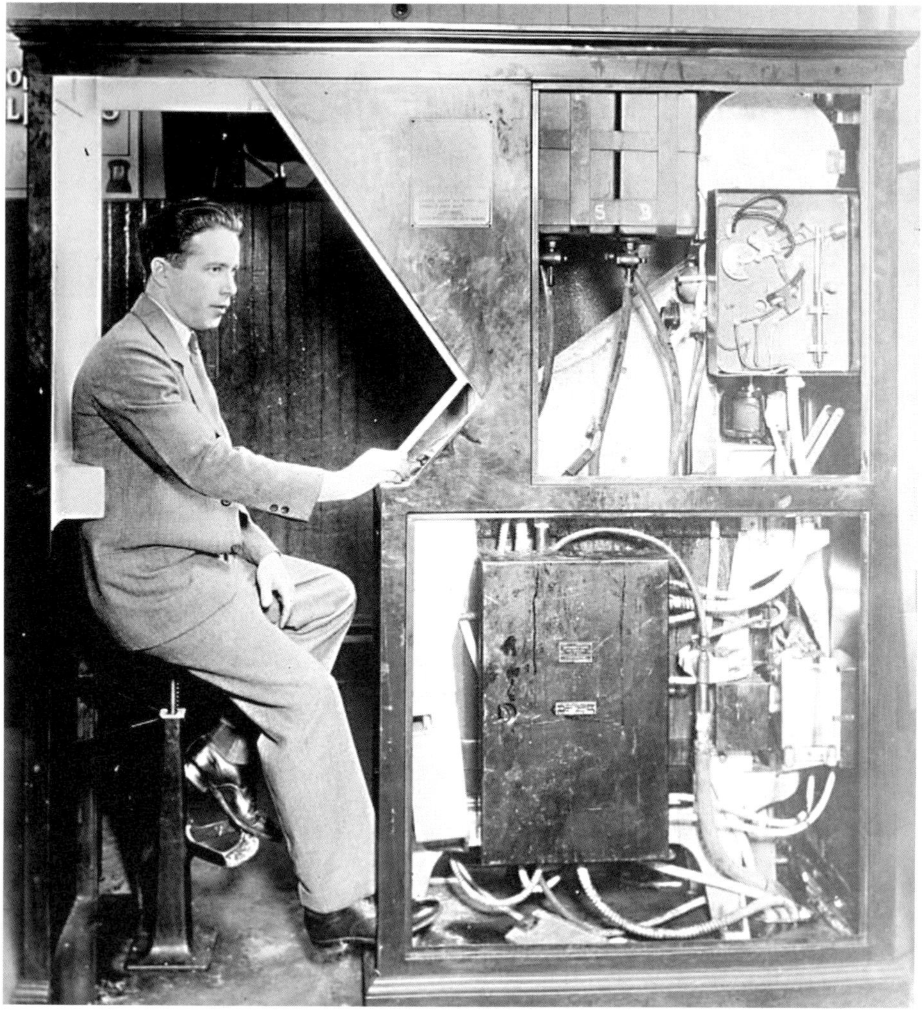

One of the first photobooths created by Anatol Josepho.

patented as far back as 1928 by photographer Anatol Josepho. Initially seen in America, these early versions of the photobooth were soon up and running on the streets of New York and at subway stations. A set of four pictures was delivered to those who sat in its rather crowded interior, developed in ten minutes and at a cost of twenty-five cents. The pictures of course were in black and white. It was the early 1970s before photobooths were capable of producing their instant snapshot-type pictures in colour. Early forms of colour photography, however, came to the more general snapshot photographer much earlier, as we shall see next…

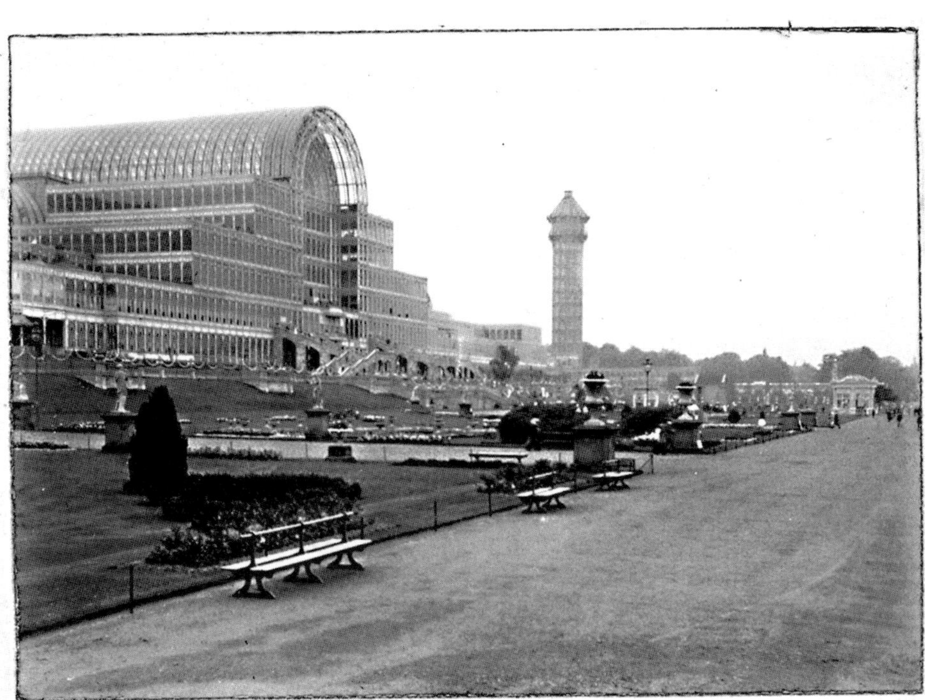

In 1851, Prince Albert, Consort to Queen Victoria, became the guiding force behind The Great Exhibition of the Works of Industry of all Nations. The exhibition was housed in the Crystal Palace, erected in Hyde Park and at that time the largest glass building in the world. When the exhibition closed in October that year, the Crystal Palace was taken apart and transported piece by piece to the top of Sydenham Hill in South London, where it was reborn in 1854 as the centre of a kind of Victorian theme park. Photographs of the Crystal Palace in is original location are extremely rare because photography was in its infancy then. There are more professional photographs of the building from later days when it was at Sydenham, but few amateur snapshot pictures are to be found. This one was obviously taken after 1854 and could not have been taken later than 1936 because that was the year the Crystal Palace burned down.

Chapter 7
Colour Comes to Snapshots

Colour photography didn't come easy to snapshot photographers. What made it difficult in the early days was the way it involved shooting the same subject three times on black and white plates through different filters. The most common method of achieving this was to use a special repeating back that fitted to the rear of a conventional plate camera. Instead of holding one photographic plate, as was the case with black and white photography, the repeating back held three plates, each behind a red, green or blue filter. As the photographer operated the shutter, three pictures were taken in quick succession, the repeating back dropping between exposures so that each of the pictures was exposed through a different

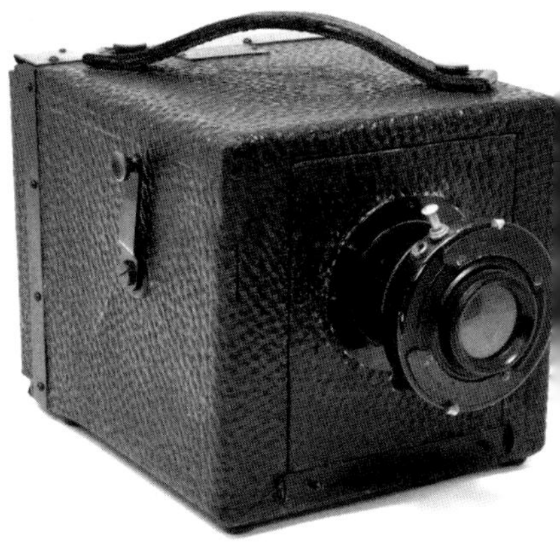

The Hess Ives Hicro, an early one-shot colour camera that simplified colour photography, taking it a few steps closer to the capabilities of snapshot photographers.

filter. Once the plates had been developed, special viewers or projectors were used to combine the three images optically, once again through their appropriate red, green or blue filter. The result was a picture perceived to be in full colour. This was the kind of procedure that was inevitably undertaken by professional or keen amateur, rather than snapshot photographers.

This complicated procedure took a step closer to the abilities of the snapshot photographer when one-shot colour cameras were introduced to use a combination of mirrors and prisms internally to deflect light from the lens in ways that allowed all three filtered pictures to be taken simultaneously. It did away with the need to use a repeating back, but operation of the special cameras that made the system work, while taking a step closer to the needs of snapshot photographers, was still too complicated for many.

Around this time, however, there was already a system in place that allowed colour pictures to be taken on a single plate. The autochrome process, invented by French brothers Auguste and Louis Lumière and first seen in 1907, involved special photographic plates onto which a pattern of minute red, green and blue particles, made of potato starch, was coated. The picture was actually black and

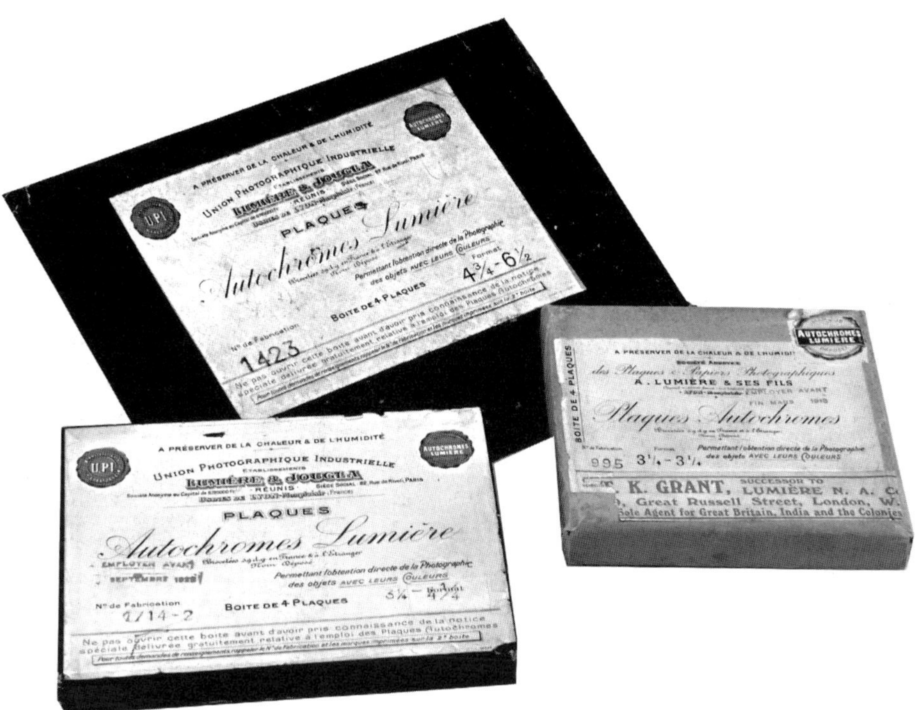

Autochrome plates, for shooting colour pictures with a single exposure, were available in all the popular sizes.

white, but when shot through the coloured particles, developed and then viewed through the particles again, a coloured picture was seen. Now, anyone could slide a single photographic plate into a camera and produce a photograph in colour without the need for filters or multiple exposures. But it still needed knowledge of plate camera operation, and exposure times were longer than normal.

Colour photography had taken a major step forward, but it was still beyond the reach of most of the snapshot fraternity. What they needed was a roll of film, rather than a glass plate, that could be loaded into any simple camera, as opposed to a far more complex one, then operated without the need for the kind of expertise more associated with professional and keen amateur photographers. That goal was reached in 1932 when the Lumière brothers transferred their autochrome process from glass plates to flexible film. Initially, it was only available as sheet film called Filmcolor, which was more likely to be used by professional photographers. But in 1934, the brothers introduced Lumicolor, which came in the form of roll film, and that would have been far more practical for use by amateur photographers and even snapshot photographers. However, despite the debut of these two colour films, colour photography for amateur and snapshot photographers didn't really take off until the arrival of a new type of English colour film in 1935.

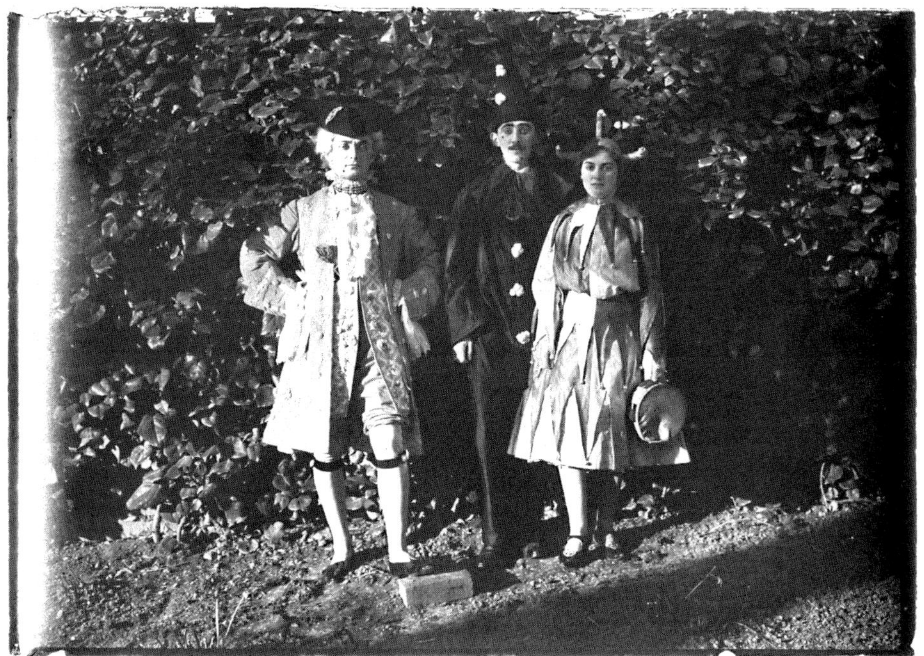

An autochrome, the original of which was in colour but illustrated here in black and white, taken
c.1910. Operation of the kind of camera required to shoot autochromes would have put this more
into the realms of the keen amateur who had better knowledge of photographic technicalities
than might have been understood by a snapshot photographer, but clearly not the skills needed
to pose people in the way a professional would. The best guess is that these three were guests at
some kind of fancy dress festivity taking place during the day rather than the evening because
the autochrome photographer would have needed the benefit of daylight to take the picture.
The quality of the costumes indicates that this was a fairly well-to-do event, and the gentleman
on the left is certainly taking his role as Lord of the Manor seriously. The clown and jester with
whom he has deigned to share the picture don't look quite so confident. All of which adds to
the charm of what in the end, despite the complications of the technique needed to take it, is
still a simple snapshot.

Dufaycolor

This new age of easy-to-use colour film began in France in 1909 with French
inventor Louis Dufay. He took the principles of the autochrome process and
improved on them by coating a glass plate with a much more regular-shaped
pattern of lines than the haphazard pattern used by autochrome's method of
scattering coloured potato starch filters at random. The coloured pictures so
produced on glass plates were called dioptichromes. Dufay went on to develop
a similar colour matrix on flexible film, aimed primarily at the cinematography
industry. However, to perfect his dream of making a viable colour film that
could be used in any still photography camera as well, he needed an input of
cash. It came from two British companies: Spicers Ltd, founded in 1796 as a

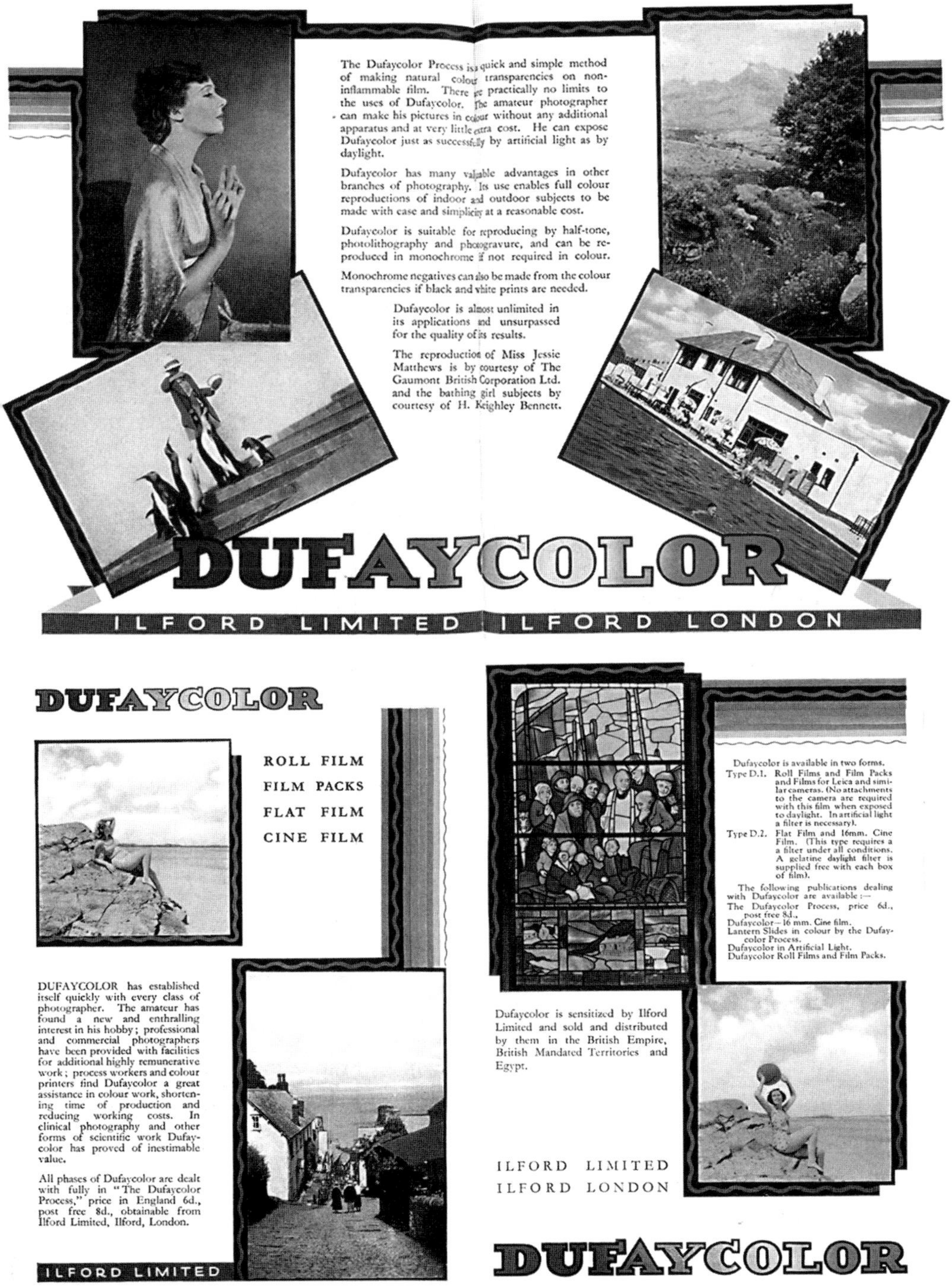

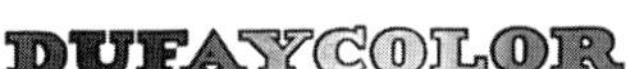
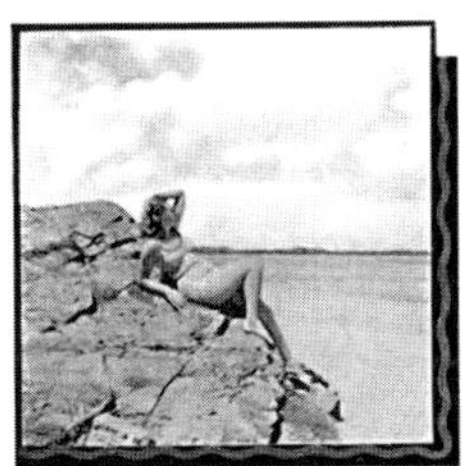
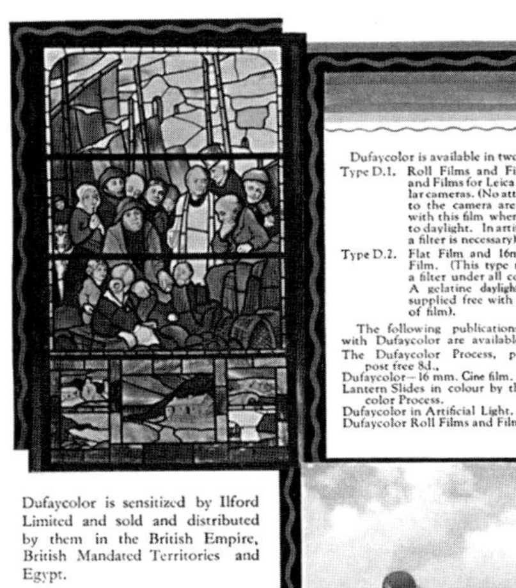

How Dufaycolor was advertised (the original in colour) in 1937.

paper mill, and Ilford Ltd, founded in 1879 to make photographic plates and, by the time of the association with Dufay, a reputable photographic plate and roll film manufacturer. Both co-operated in the development of Dufay's colour film, which became known as Dufaycolor. It was launched as a 16mm cine film in 1932 and as a still photography film in 1935. The fast-growing popularity of Dufaycolor soon far exceeded that of the French Filmcolor and Lumicolor. Now, for the first time, people who knew little about the more complicated technicalities of photography could buy rolls of film, put them in their snapshot cameras and produce pictures in colour.

Few snapshot photographers who used Dufaycolor to produce their first coloured photographs would have been aware of, or cared about, the complicated process involved in manufacturing the film. Some, who might have progressed

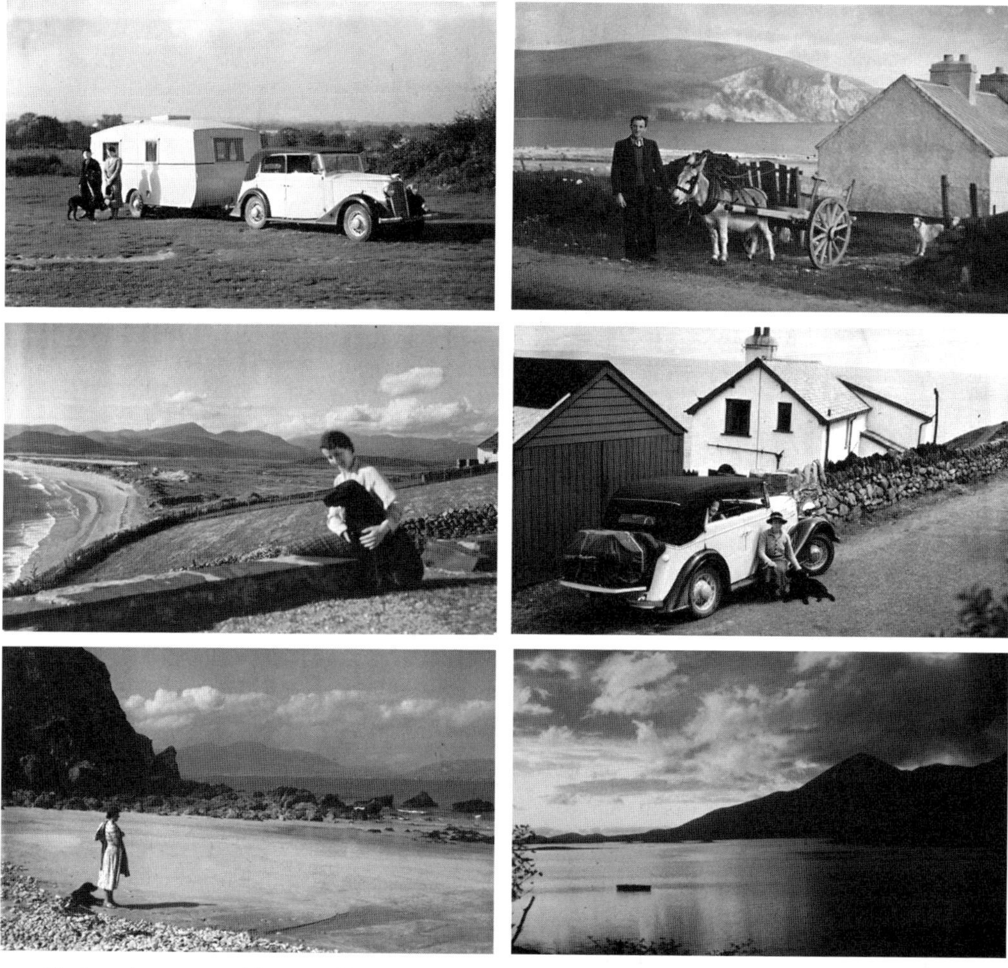

Dufaycolor pictures (illustrated here in black and white) taken on family holidays in the 1930s.

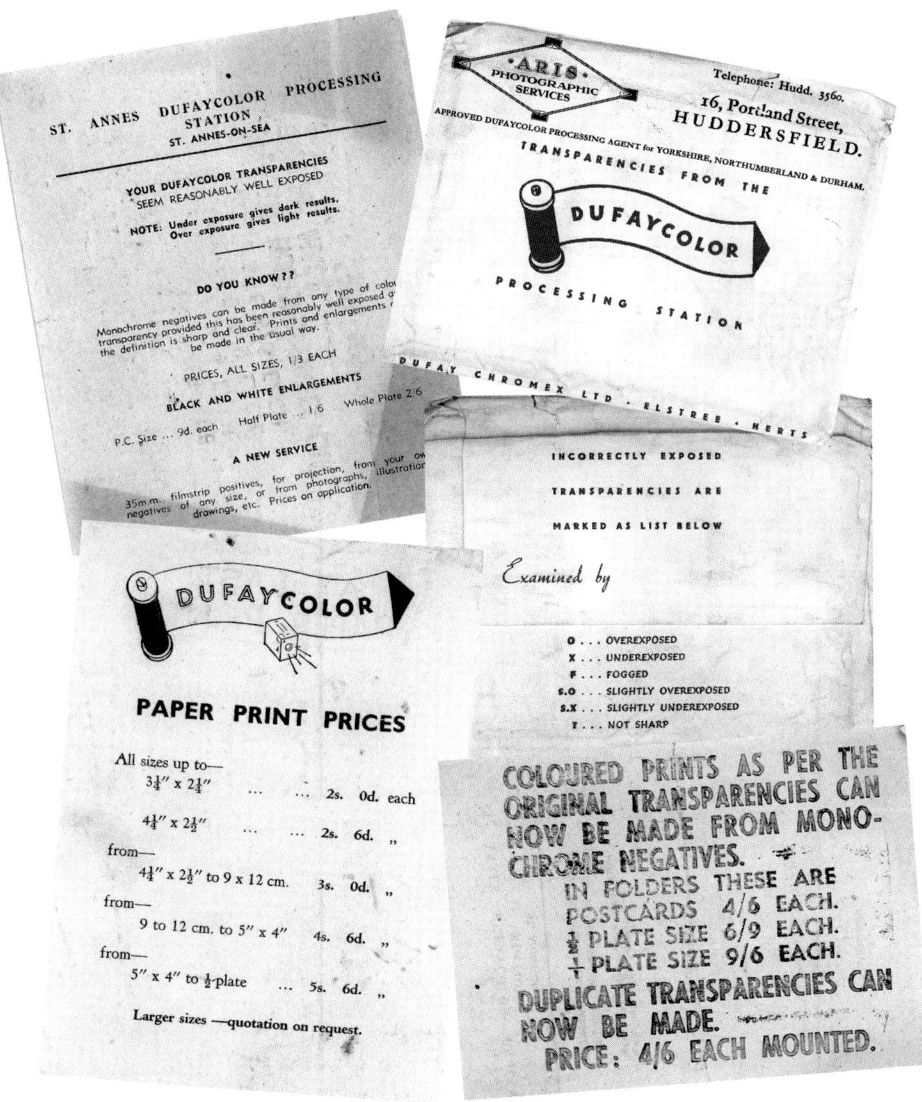

Film envelopes in which Dufaycolor was returned to photographers after processing, with information from specialist Dufaycolor processing companies about the services they offered.

to developing their own black and white films, might have been able to process the colour pictures themselves. Most, however, took advantage of the network of professional Dufaycolor processing stations that sprung up around the country, many of whom, as well as processing the films, also offered free advice to the photographers. Aris Photographic Services in Huddersfield, for example, returned the coloured pictures in envelopes whose contents had each been analysed by the processor who signed his or her name on the envelope, then explained why certain pictures might not be as good as expected. Below the signature there was a list of possible problems for the examiner to highlight as necessary: 'O = overexposed, X = underexposed, F = fogged, S.O. = slightly overexposed, S.X. = slightly underexposed, ? = not sharp.' The processing stations also offered the chance to buy duplicate Dufaycolor pictures or black and white negatives and prints made from the colour originals.

Colour prints from Dufaycolor transparencies was a service that Dufay offered in 1938. Starting in October that year, Dufay film processors began examining every transparency sent to them for processing, and those they thought suitable for making prints were marked with a gold star. Snapshot photographers were

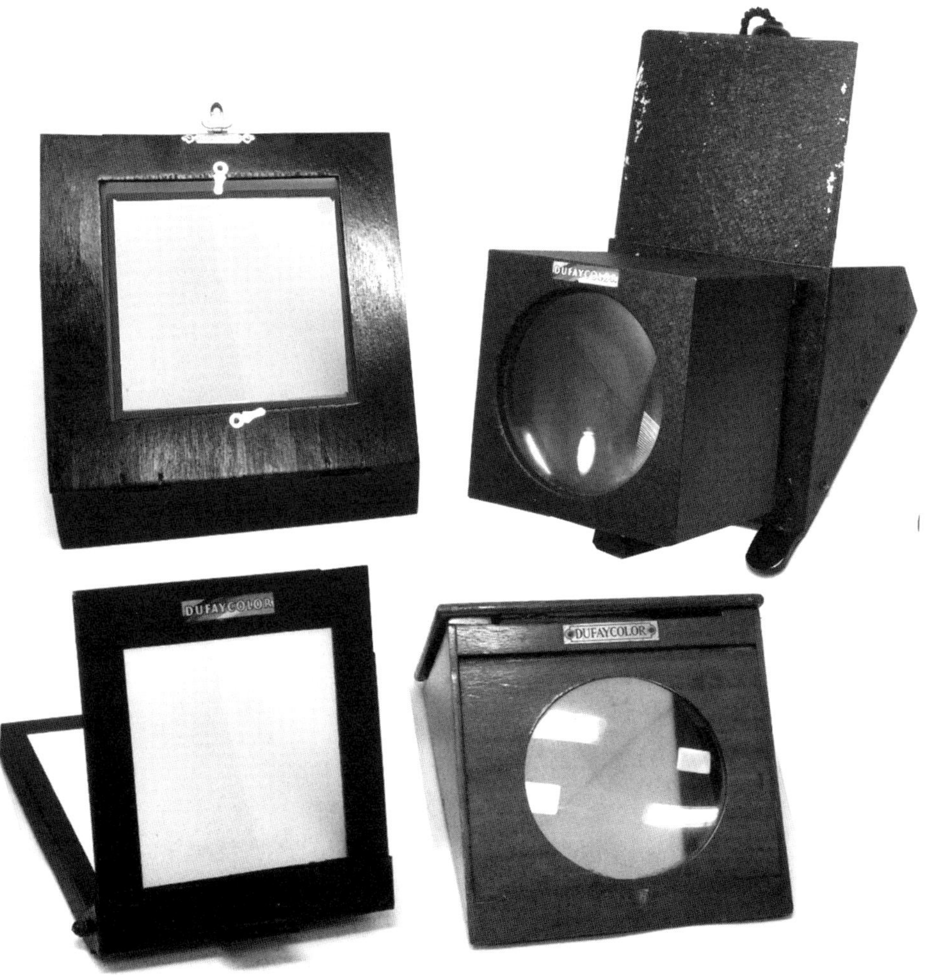

Three Dufaycolor viewers that used natural light to view the transparencies and a fourth (top right) that illuminated the pictures with a mains-powered light bulb.

then invited to hand the gold star transparencies back to their photographic dealer to request as many colour prints as they required from each transparency.

The service didn't take off in any big way, so Dufaycolor pictures remained mainly in the form of transparencies which had to be viewed by projection or by holding against a light source. The pictures were a little dense and not easily viewed in a projector, but they could be easily seen by holding them up to the light or, better still, inserting them into a special viewer purpose-made for the job. The simplest of these comprised a straightforward two-part frame that hinged open in a V-shape with a ground-glass viewing screen on the top surface and a mirror in the section below. The mirror threw light up to the screen, on which the transparency was placed for viewing. Later Dufaycolor viewers worked differently, with the transparency placed on top of the viewer, a ground-glass screen folded over it to diffuse the light and then the transparency viewed from the front of the apparatus by looking into the mirror in the base. A rarer version also incorporated a large magnifying glass through which the image was viewed, and there were versions with mains-powered light bulbs to illuminate the pictures. Dufaycolor dealers sometimes had special display cabinets combined with viewers on their counters. The upper part of each cabinet formed a display area in which the dealer might show some of the more prestigious cameras for sale, while the lower part contained a light bulb that illuminated a frosted glass screen on the sloping front. The transparency was placed against the glass and a bell push type of button on the front of the cabinet was pressed to illuminate it.

Such was the success of Dufaycolor that it was even employed to make a few cinema films in colour, and was used by Movietone News, shown weekly at cinemas, for coverage of the George V silver jubilee celebrations in 1935 and the coronation of George VI in 1937. It was all going well for Dufay – and then Kodak fought back.

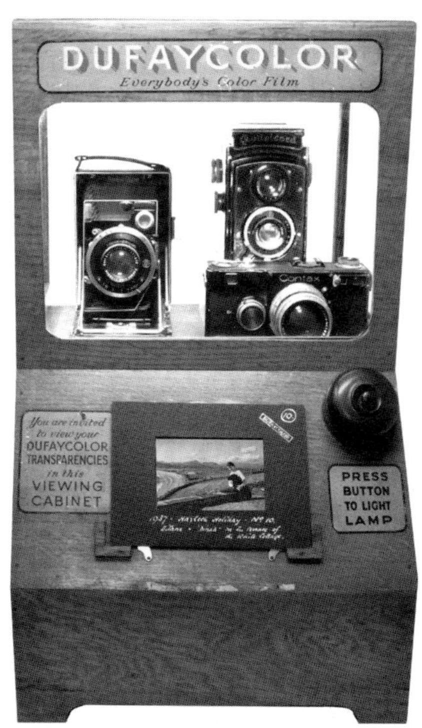

A rare Dufaycolor dealer's display cabinet. The upper section shows cameras that were sold in the 1930s when Dufaycolor was available. The lower half provided an illuminated panel for customers to view their transparencies.

Kodachrome

Renowned war photographer Robert Capa once said: 'If your pictures aren't good enough, you're not close enough.' That is a criticism that can so often be aimed at the snapshot photographer who looks through the camera's viewfinder and selectively sees only the thing or person that is being photographed without taking in the fact that the subject is actually surrounded by a lot of empty or irrelevant space. It's the reason why so many snapshots show people too small in the overall picture. So yes, a more professional photographer might have moved in closer for this picture, cutting out about a third of the empty space taken up by the lawns and concentrating more on the garden behind the people. Maybe the professional would also have had both subjects gazing towards the camera and looking a little more relaxed. But that's not what this picture is all about. It's a snapshot, a memory of a certain day, the people it involved, the way they dressed for a day out and their surroundings. It speaks about time and place in the way every good snapshot does. The picture was taken, originally in colour, in 1937 using Dufaycolor film in a camera that produced 6×9cm images, the size very popular with box camera manufacturers of the time.

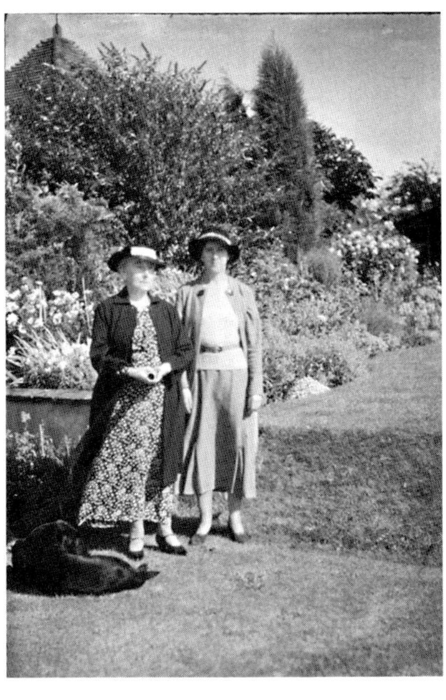

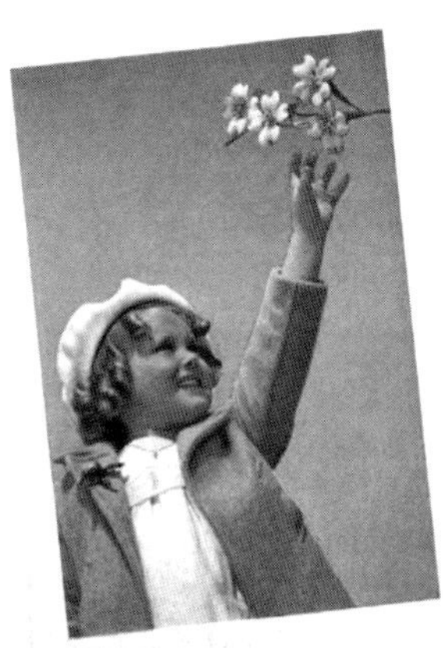

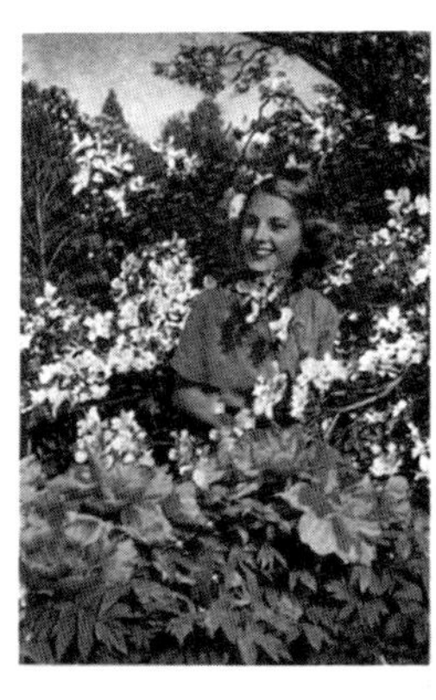

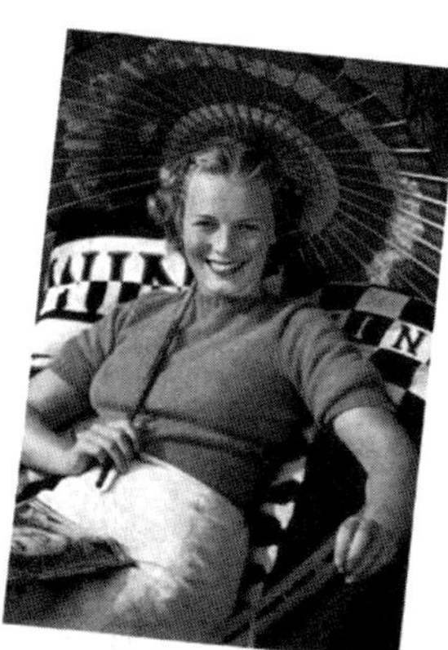

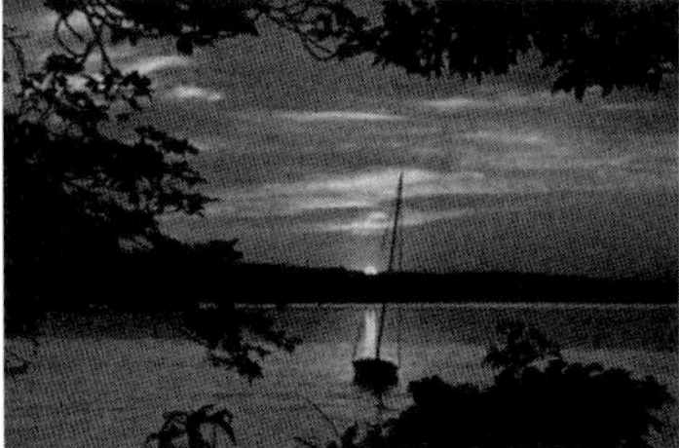

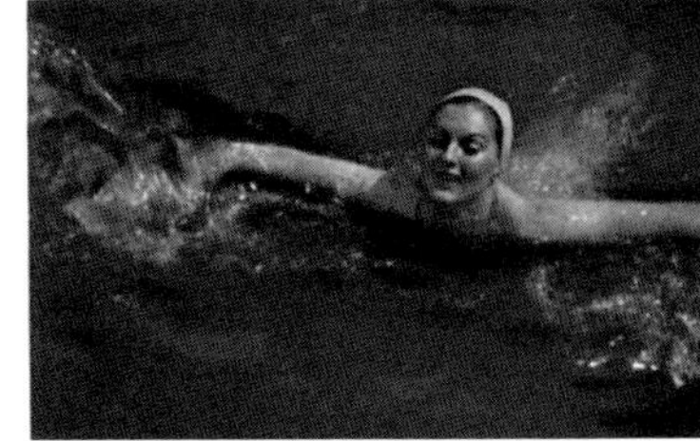

● The illustraons on these pages and on th cover are from Kodachrome orinals. Several of the Kodaks cscribed in this catalog can be ied for making Kodachrome picres in the form of transparencie which may be projected on a screen ...with strikingly beautal results by means of the Kocslide Projector. For such camer, see pages 7, 24, 25, and 29. or details about Kodachrome Fil, see page 35.

Inside Kodak's 1938 catalogue: how the company advertised its new Kodachrome film.

The two people who discovered a method of producing what would become the most popular – and, many agree, the best – colour film ever, surprisingly, were not scientists by profession. They were musicians, and they were both called Leopold. Leopold Mannes was a pianist and Leopold Godowski was a violinist. Back in the early 1920s, as graduates of Harvard, they had experimented with colour photography on glass plates, with a process patented in 1924. Fast forward to 1930, when Kodak became sufficiently impressed by the work of the two musicians to offer them full-time positions with the company and access to their research facilities. It proved to be a fruitful relationship. The result was Kodachrome, launched as a 16mm cine film in 1935, then as Standard-8 amateur cine film in May 1936, followed at last by 828 and 35mm film in September 1936.

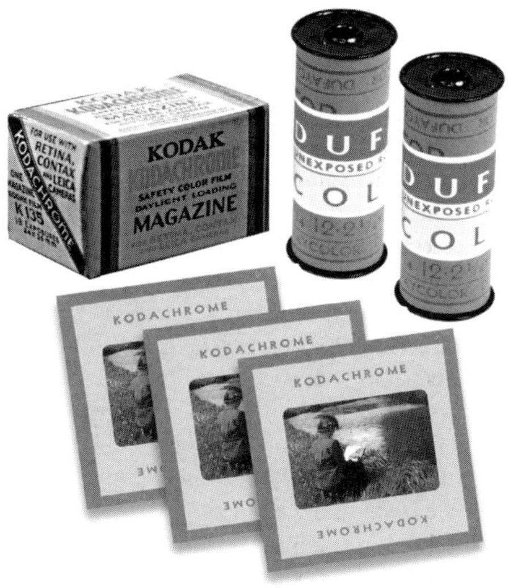

Right from the start, Kodak pushed the use of 35mm for its Kodachrome film, rather than the roll film size favoured at first by Dufay. The 35mm transparencies were returned from processing in 50×50mm size cardboard mounts ready for projection. Over the years, the mounts were produced in several different styles. The one shown here was the first.

Kodachrome produced colour pictures by a very different method to that pioneered by Dufaycolor. It was a complicated process, but put in simplistic terms it involved three photographic emulsions,

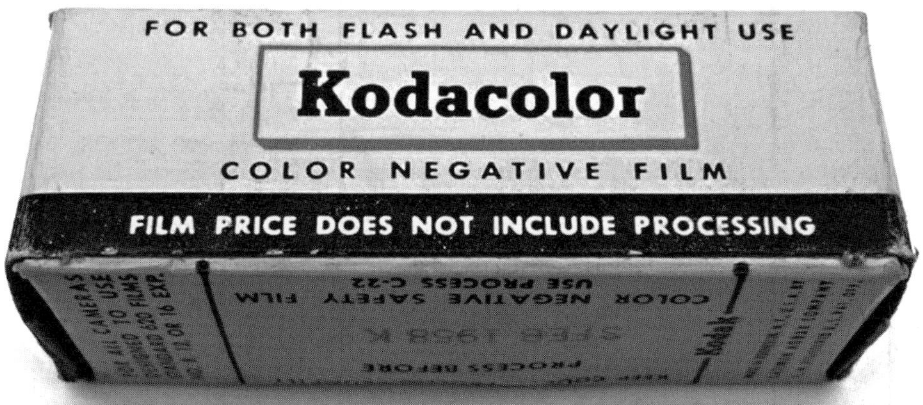

Kodacolor film, launched in 1942, led the way for snapshot photographers to produce coloured prints.

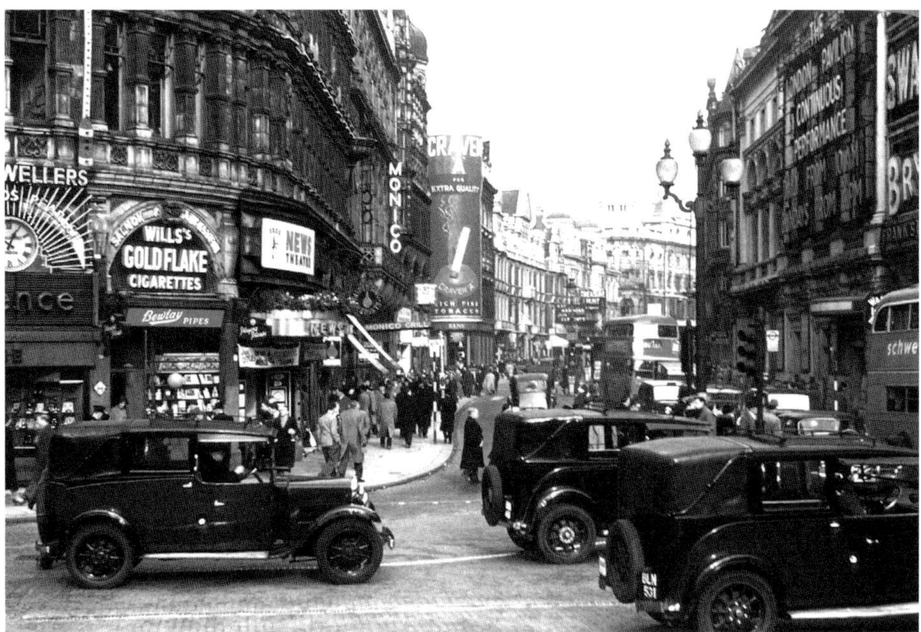

This picture, taken from Piccadilly Circus, looking along Shaftesbury Avenue in London in 1949, is little more than a straight record snapshot with no attempts at creativity. Yet it illustrates so much about the time: London getting back on its feet after the end of the Second World War, the iconic red double-decker buses of what was then London Transport's Central Area, the proliferation of taxis and the crowds, nearly all of whom are men because the women were expected to be back home rearing children, looking after the house and preparing a meal for the return of their menfolk later. The London Pavilion cinema on the right is offering continuous performances all day long, as is the much smaller News Theatre opposite, which specialises in showing newsreels and cartoons non-stop all day. The Apollo Theatre in the distance is staging a play called *Treasure Hunt*, a comedy by M.J. Farrell and John Perry, starring Jean St Clair and Milo O'Shea, with performances every night at seven o'clock and matinees on Thursdays and Saturdays at 2.30 pm. Craven A and Wills's Goldflake were clearly popular cigarettes of the day. Café Monico, whose sign is seen on the left, had already been open for seventy-two yeas on this day in 1949 and would go on to become one of London's oldest restaurant names before closing for good in 2021 after 144 years of business. What starts as a simple snapshot has so much to say about an era and, thanks to Kodachrome, it could all be seen in colour. (See colour pages for the original Kodachrome version.)

each sensitive to a different primary colour, coated onto the film base, with dyes to simulate colours of the subject added during the processing stage. This made processing Kodachrome very complicated, out of the reach of even professional photographers. For that reason, the film was sold process-paid, ready to be returned to Kodak for processing.

One thing Kodachrome shared with Dufaycolor was the way it was viewed – not as a print, but as a transparency that needed to be held up to the light, placed in a viewer or projected. Because Kodachrome transparencies were less dense than Dufaycolor types, projection was the favoured way to view the pictures.

Dufay and Kodak were not of course alone in the colour film market. There were others, most notably Agfa in Germany. There was, however, still one big disadvantage in all the colour films for snapshot photographers who were used to looking at their old black and white pictures in the form of prints that they could hand around to friends and relations. Holding their pictures up to the light, placing them in a viewer or having to set up a projector was not ideal. If colour photography was truly to become the domain of the snapshot photographer, the end result needed to be a colour print, not a transparency.

In 1942, Kodak launched a new film called Kodacolor, expressly designed to produce negatives from which prints could be made. Unfortunately, by that time, the world, including America, the home of Kodak, was embroiled in the Second World War. It was therefore the post-war years before snapshot photographers really began to explore the possibility of colour photography in preference to black and white, and a good many years more before it was fully embraced.

Chapter 8
Snapshots in the Second World War

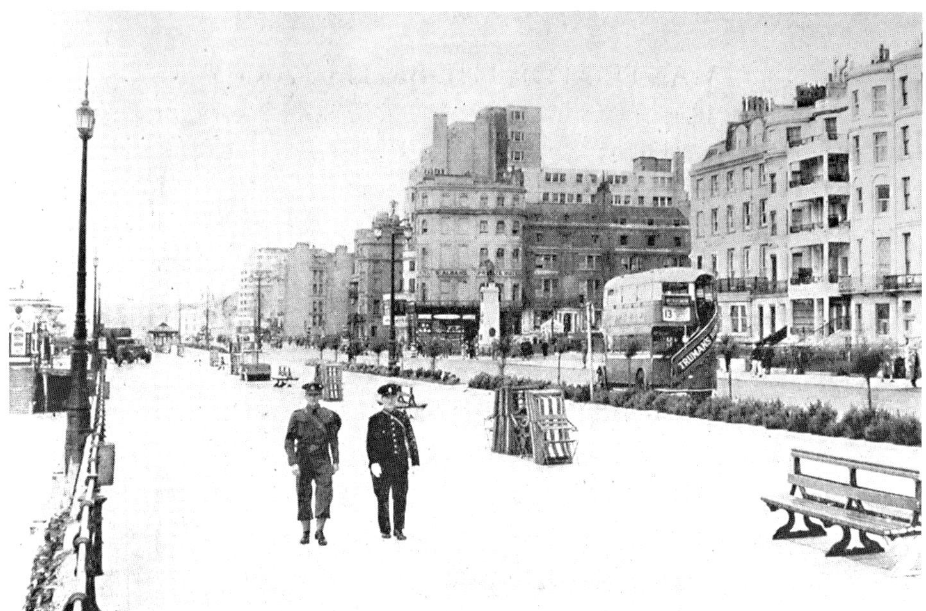

Brighton seafront in July 1940. Two soldiers walk along the otherwise empty promenade. The lack of people seems strange until you know that, during the war, the seaward side of the road was banned to civilians.

The Second World War broke out in Europe in 1939, with America joining the hostilities in 1941. During this time, manufacture of all types of camera, snapshot models included, took a downturn as many camera manufacturers turned their attentions to producing items for the war effort, while others suffered from bombing raids that damaged and in some cases totally wiped out their factories.

Not that Kodak seemed to have noticed. In America, only months before the attack on Pearl Harbor that was the major catalyst in bringing the Americans into the Second World War, Kodak's 1941 catalogue was full of the company's latest cameras and the kind of pictures they were capable of taking. Many of these cameras were aimed at the advanced or more experienced amateur, but for the snapshot photographer there were simple cameras like the Jiffy – 'box camera simplicity… folding camera style' said the description – and a range of Bantam cameras, advertised as 'small cameras that lead to big pictures'.

These aside, there were of course plenty of cameras around from the days before the outbreak of war, but in the UK at least a good proportion of them were commandeered for military use. A 1941 advertisement in *The Miniature Camera Magazine* from R.G. Lewis, one of the country's largest photographic dealers at the time, made this plea:

WANTED FOR THE BRITISH ARMY

We have been instructed to collect immediately for use by the Army, all available Super Ikontas, Models 530/16 and 532/16. If you have such a camera for disposal, please allow us to purchase it, and as the need is urgent, customers are asked to send such instruments without delay, either to Shrewsbury or to Holborn, enclosing with them a note stating the price required. We are, of course, quite willing to quote a purchase figure, either after inspection of the camera, or receipt of its description, but we are very concerned with the time factor, as these instruments must be in without delay. This is a unique opportunity to put your camera to national service. All cameras received will be passed on by us to the Army authorities without delay. Cheques in settlement will be sent by return of post.

ALSO WANTED

Miniature Equipment of all kinds. As the only firm specialising exclusively in Miniature Cameras, our prices for these are obviously the highest. We urgently require for firms engaged on National work, RAF stations, etc, Leicas and Contaxes and all telephoto and wide-angle lenses for these. Special accessories such as contameters, universal finders and copying equipment are also in great demand, and in most cases we are paying in excess of full list prices for these. In addition to Contax and Leica equipment, we wish to buy and are paying exceptional

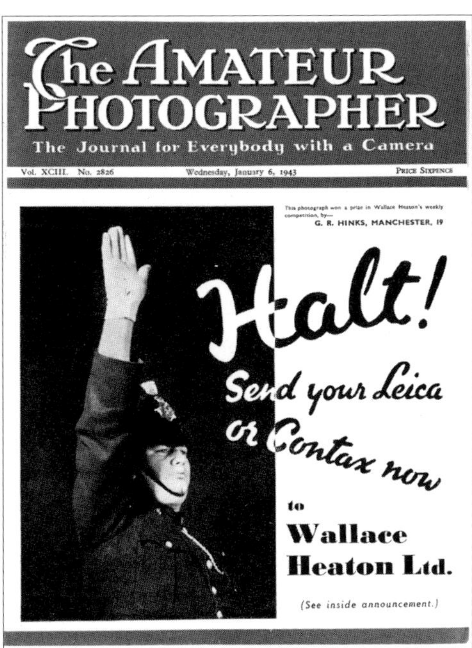

The front cover of *The Amateur Photographer* magazine for 6 January 1943 with its plea for good quality cameras needed for the war effort.

prices for Rolleiflexes, Super Ikontas, Exaktas, Makinas, Reflex Korelles and Primarflexes.

All the camera names mentioned in the advertisement were models aimed at professional and advanced amateur photographers. The snapshot cameras stayed behind. Professional cameras were used by the Army Film and Photographic Unit (AFPU), set up in Britain to record military events concerning British and Commonwealth armies, with its photographers recruited from the ranks of the British Army. So while professional war correspondents and military photographers used the best cameras to officially document the war, it was the snapshot photographers who recorded life on the home front.

The cameras they used were mostly left over from the 1930s and earlier. While more advanced photographers were taking advantage of prestigious landmark cameras introduced in the years between the two world wars with names that included Leica, Rolleiflex and Exakta (unless donated to the war effort), snapshot photographers contented themselves with box cameras and simple folding models from the likes of Kodak, Ensign and Coronet.

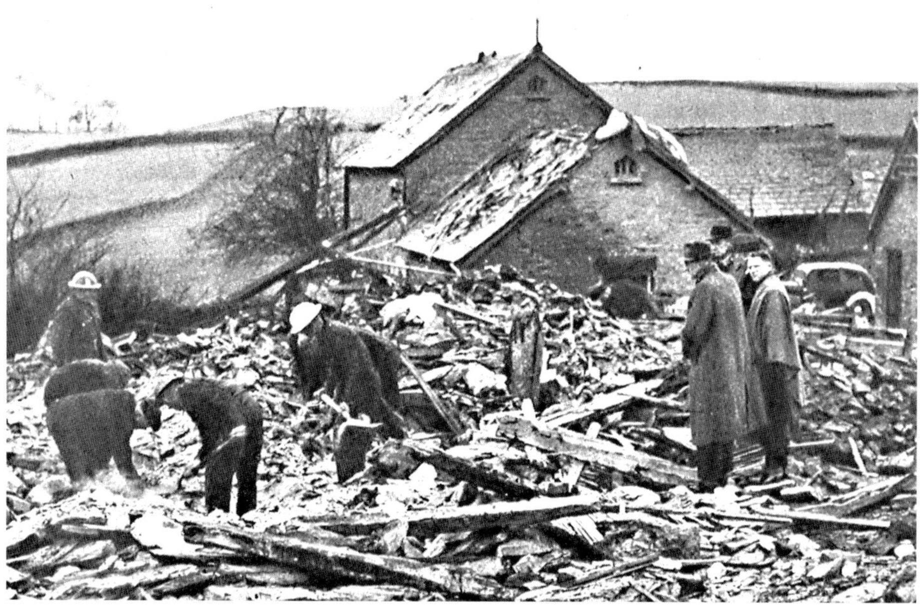

In the middle of the Westmorland countryside, a lonely farm receives a direct hit from an enemy bomb. No one is looking at, or posing for, the camera. The people busy trying to make sense of what has happened to their lives probably weren't even aware of the snapshot photographer, who was unlikely to have spent time taking pictures from different angles, looking for the best shot, the way a professional might. It's far more likely that a camera with only eight pictures to a roll of film was being used, and so why waste film on more than one picture? It's just a snapshot, but it has a strong story to tell.

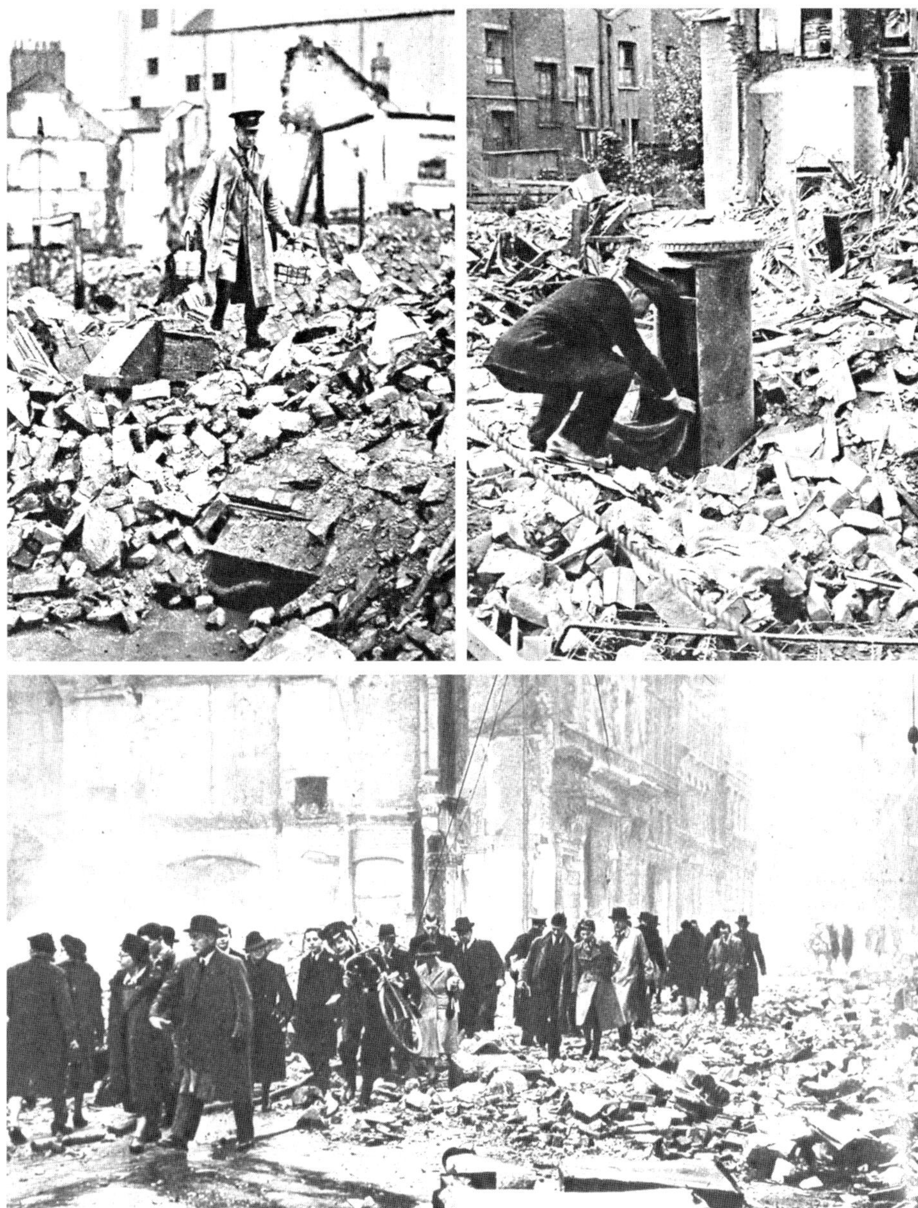

Three snapshots which show the way life went on in London during the Second World War bombing raids. A milkman picks his way across the rubble of a bombsite, a crate in each hand. One crate contains the milk he is about to deliver, the other contains empty bottles that have been left out for collection. Elsewhere, a postman collects letters from a post box that has remained standing in the midst of a ruined street. At the same time, Londoners pick their way through more ruins, one man carrying a bike where he obviously can't ride, the men in bowler and trilby hats, as they make their way to work. The amazing thing about all these scenes that have been captured so well by snapshots is how everyone is behaving so naturally, getting on with the minutiae of their daily lives, perhaps only hours after some of those lives might have been shattered for ever by a bombing raid.

Although film was in short supply much of the time, using cameras like these, snapshot photographers showed the effects of the war at home in a way that was very different from the work of professional photographers of the time. Where a professional photographer might look for drama in a subject, sometimes exaggerating the situation a little to make a more powerful statement, often taking several different angles on the same subject from which the best could later be chosen, the snapshot photographer simply pointed his or her camera,

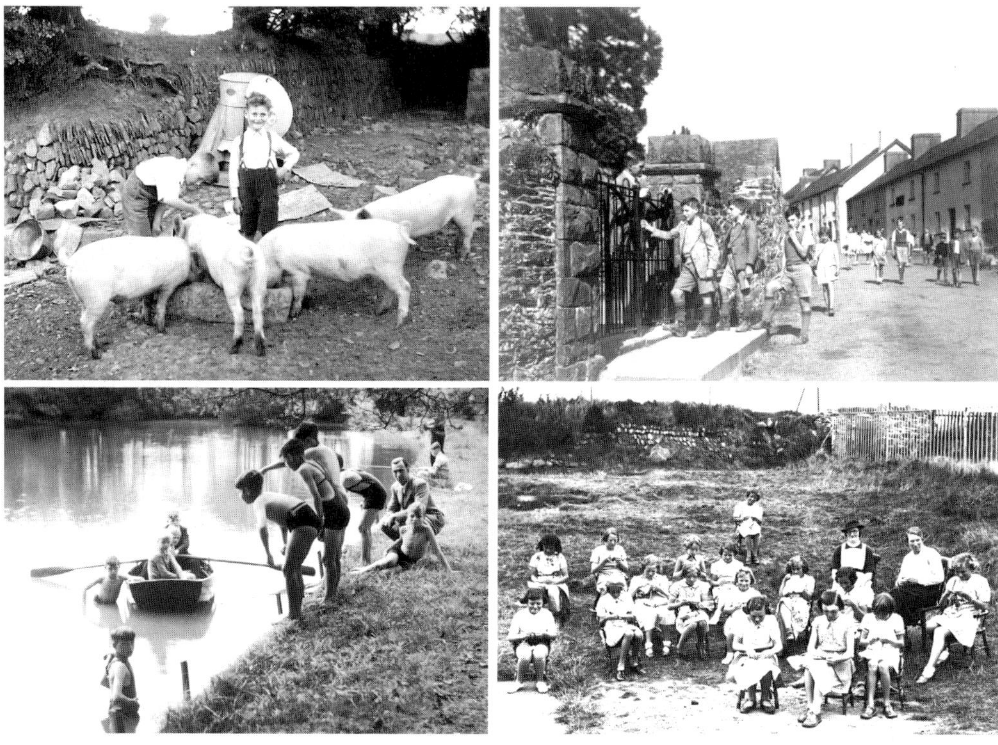

As always, it's the stories behind the pictures that make them interesting. At first sight, here are four snapshots of children, none of them doing anything remarkable: feeding pigs, walking to school, playing by a river and sitting in a field sewing. What makes each of these snapshots something special is that the children are all evacuees. In 1938, a year before the Second World War broke out, the British government had the foresight to develop Operation Pied Piper, an evacuation programme that would see children evacuated from areas of the country likely to come under attack in the event of war. By the summer of 1939, the operation was in full swing, with buses and trains being requisitioned, and on the morning of 31 August 1939, three days before war was declared, an evacuation order was given for the next day. On 1 September, with two days to go before the outbreak of war, children began to be transported out of cities and into the safety of the countryside, to stay with families who would be total strangers to them. For many, it was a time of heartbreak for both the children and the parents from whom they were separated. For others, it turned out to be something of an adventure. These four pictures show children from London schools in Streatham, Battersea, Whitechapel and Deptford working and playing in their new homes in South Wales.

clicked the shutter and showed things the way they really were. The people in the pictures were rarely posed. They were merely captured going about their daily lives in often exceptional circumstances.

The humble box camera was a particular favourite among snapshot photographers of the time, not just for its ease of use, but equally for its affordability. At a time when the average wage for a manager or clerk was only a little over £7 a week, professional cameras like the Leica cost anything between £28 and £40. For those on a tighter budget, whether civilians or soldiers who risked taking cameras to war, a simple box camera could be bought new for between 10 shillings and a little over £1.

A new snapshot market

Camera manufacturers might not have been making new models at this time, but they still had plenty of older stock to sell, and what wasn't needed for the military was soon targeted at the snapshot market, with advertisers often using military connections such as soldiers in uniform to help sell their cameras.

Alongside markets that already existed, it wasn't uncommon for advertisers to invent new markets to suit their own ends.

The Ensign Midget, for example, was made in 1934 and originally advertised as a miniature camera that could be slipped into a pocket so that photographers

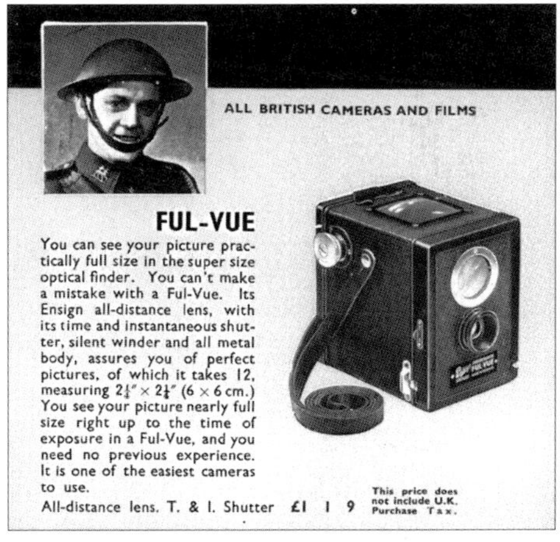

How Ensign introduced a soldier into its advertising for no apparent reason.

'need never miss anything of pictorial interest'. With the outbreak of war, subjects 'of pictorial interest' were forgotten as new advertisements aimed at snapshot photographers in the military claimed the Midget to be, 'A remarkable War-Time Camera…'

> The Midget is a camera for those who have to consider space. It is a bare half-inch longer than a packet of cigarettes, and no thicker. It goes into a tunic pocket with room to spare. It is essentially the camera for the man in camp. Just the thing to give to a fellow who is called up or to a woman in Service.

At the same time, manufacturers found ways to show prospective buyers that their cameras were equally useful to those who stayed at home, who might use them for completely new purposes…

> Some people are making war-time diaries with these Midgets, taking snaps of subjects like children going to school with their gas masks, cars bearing war-time notices, men digging for victory on allotments, or of someone pasting strips of paper on the window. All these little war-time incidents make photographs which will be treasured later on. These cameras are splendid for capturing that sort of thing. It is an idea. Keep an Ensign Midget war-time diary. The photographs will be wonderfully interesting in the years when war is a thing of the past. Buy a Midget and start now.

Production of the Ensign Midget halted in 1940 as its manufacturer, Houghton Butcher, went over to war work. On the night of 24/25 September that year, the company's premises in London's High Holborn were wiped out in a German bombing raid. Production of the Ensign Midget did not resume after the Second World War.

A soldier's snapshot album

This is a book about snapshot photography. Its intention is not to cover the way the Second World War was officially documented. So

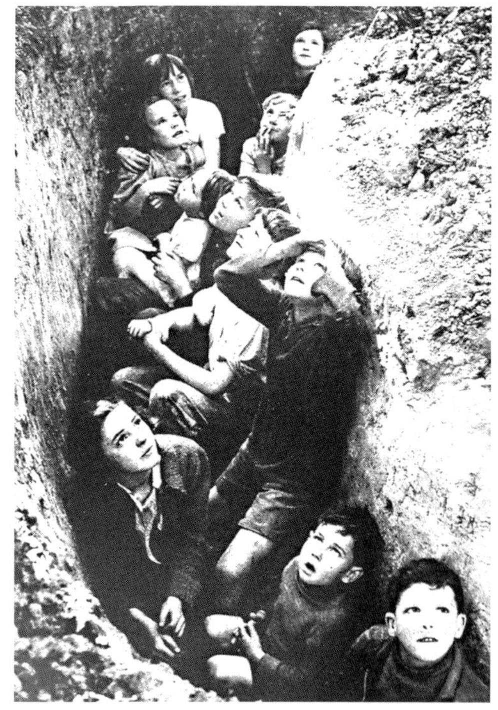

Long before the war, for a few weeks around September each year, whole families would make annual pilgrimages to the country's hop fields. Most notably, these were in Kent, where families spent their holidays on farms sleeping in huts at night and occupying their days picking hops which were used to make beer. The activity continued into and after the war years. Many saw it as a chance to earn extra cash while getting away from the towns and cities to spend time in the countryside. For the adults, it was hard work, for the children it was more of an adventure, which became intensified with the outbreak of war. Here, in September 1940, while the RAF engage with German raiders overhead, children shelter in a hop field trench.

there are no pictures on these pages showing battles or conflicts into which armed forces were thrown. That's the kind of thing that has been covered extensively in many other books, found elsewhere, dedicated to war photography and carried out mostly by professional photographers. Look instead at the snapshots taken by members of the military, away from conflict and often a long way from home, and you see a far more personal view of the world at this time, with pictures taken by men and women thrust into a world that they would never have known about had it not been for the war. It happened to people all over the world, too numerous to record in a book like this. So the concentration here is on just one place, the soldiers who found themselves there and the snapshots they took of what to them was a strange new land.

The year is 1943. The place is Sierra Leone in West Africa. A regiment of British soldiers have been uprooted from a cold British winter, crowded onto a troopship and sent south on a journey that began in the wintery rough seas of the North Atlantic and ended in the far calmer and much hotter waters off

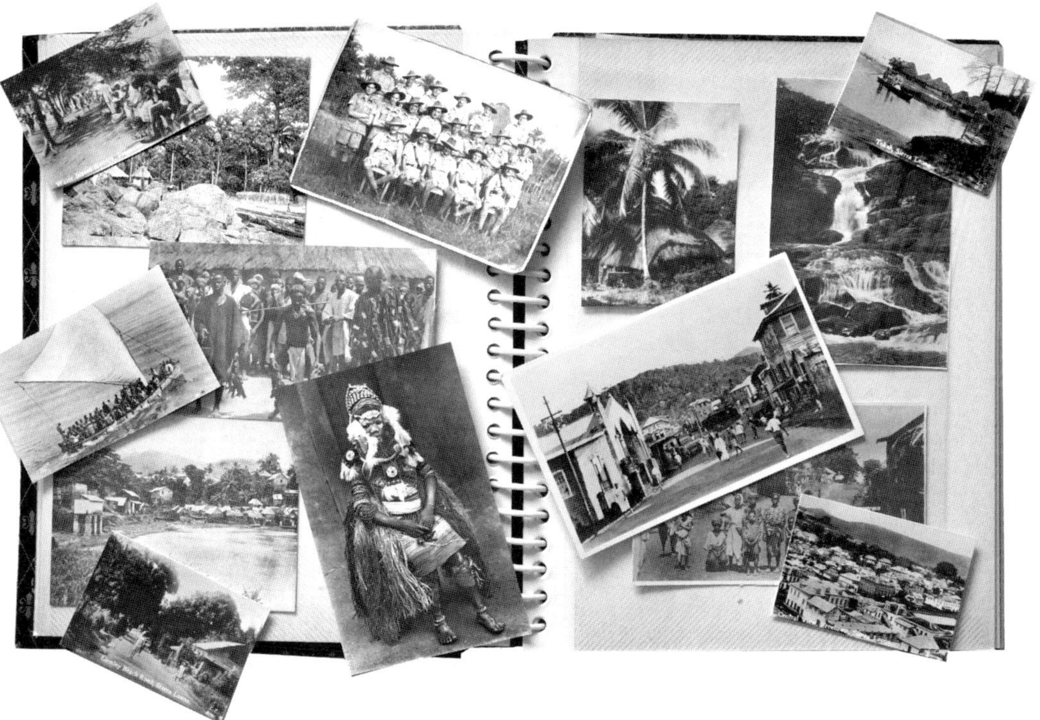

A snapshot album compiled by a soldier in West Africa during the Second World War. Some of the pictures in his album were taken by soldiers, others were postcards available for the soldiers to buy in Freetown. Mostly the pictures are black and white, but some have been hand-tinted with slightly garish colours. Together they tell the story of the life of one soldier during his few years in Sierra Leone during the Second World War.

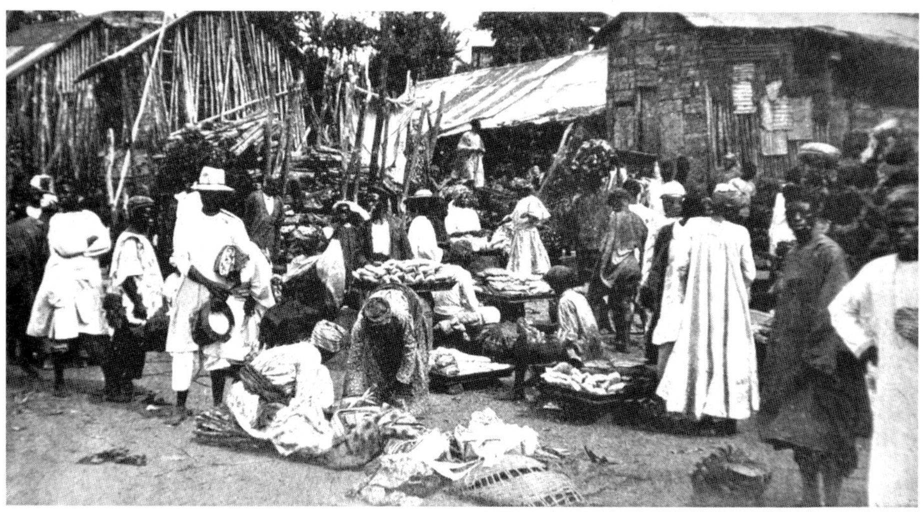

The market in Freetown, captured in a soldier's snapshot during his time there.

the African coast. They are in Freetown harbour, where the majority of the population are Creoles, descendants of slaves liberated in the British territory or rescued by the Royal Navy from slave ships, thanks to the abolition of slavery, a movement dating back to the late eighteenth century. British West Africa, being a British colony at the time, was dragged into the war when Britain declared war on Germany. The solders had arrived to help defend Freetown, a strategic base and convoy station for the Allies, while training members of the Royal West African Frontier Force.

Dressed now in the tropical gear that had been issued to them back home, the soldiers disembark from the troopship to be marched to their barracks. Everywhere they look, colourfully dressed Africans, the women topless, roam the streets, many with their goods balanced precariously on their heads, all talking and laughing out loud, while over it all hangs the pervading smell of dried fish, the local delicacy. They pass small compounds where chickens scratching for food are dyed bright colours to prevent straying or theft; an open-air market sprawling along the roadside, where long-gowned Africans sell mirrors, cigarettes, tropical fruits, nuts, prayer mats, slippers, leather curios, hippopotamus teeth and home-made soap prepared from wood ash and palm oil; an open-air kitchen where women, some sucking on tobacco pipes in their mouths, pound grain with long wooden poles, and where food is cooked over fires in large pots, while a tethered goat looks on.

Any budding photographer among the regiment must have looked at the amazing sights that surrounded him and longed to unpack the box camera or maybe a simple folding camera that he had brought from home so that he

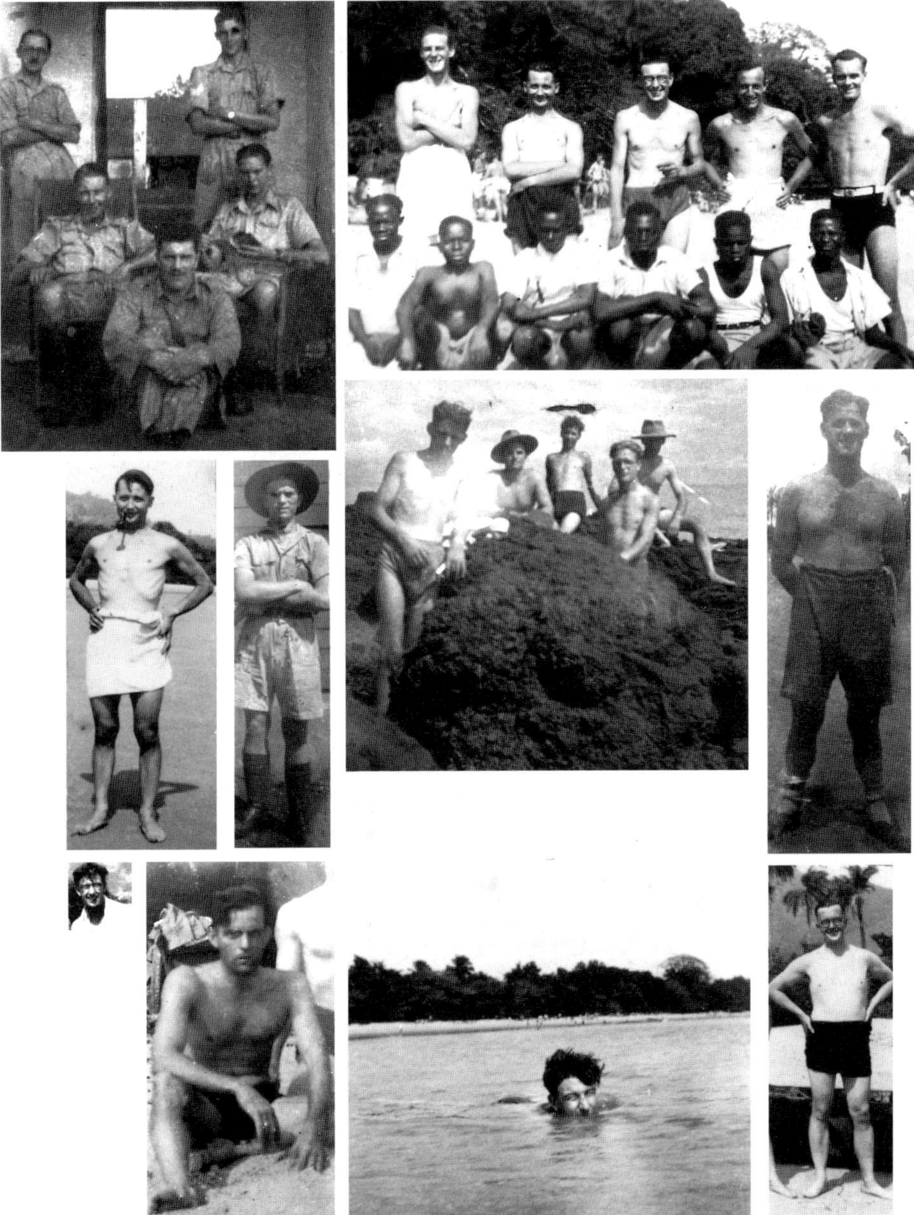

Although little more than snapshots with no real artistic merit, these snapshots taken by British soldiers of each other in West Africa during the Second World War typify their lives at that time.

could start snapping as soon as possible. He might also have foreseen a problem. The kind of snapshot cameras likely to have been packed in kitbags were the sort that only took eight pictures on a roll of film. Once the film brought from home was used, where in a place like this could someone hope to buy more?

What appears here to be a straightforward picture of a young African man becomes fascinating when you know that his name was Sorry Commara and that he was a servant boy to one of the British soldiers in West Africa during the war. There was nothing incorrect or degrading about being a servant boy, as is evidenced by what Sorry wrote on the back of this picture when his soldier 'master' was about to return to England…

My contact with some of you British personnels in the Army has really changed my views about British peoples. It has revolutionised my outlook in life, and indeed I have the sincere hope that after this chaos we may surely enter into the new reforms – new life – new freedom – democratically speaking…
Best of luck, Dear.
Sorry Commara.

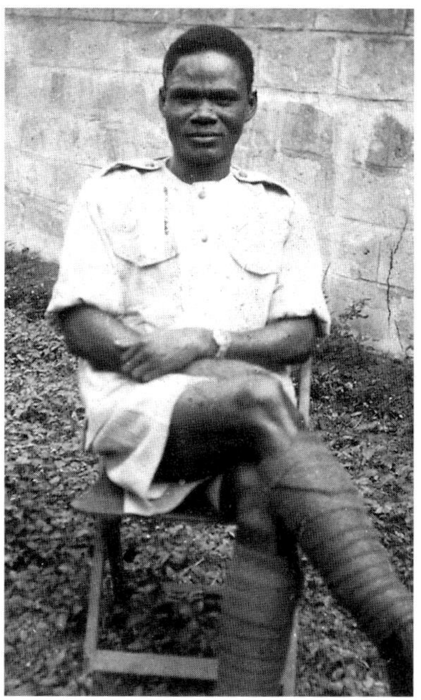

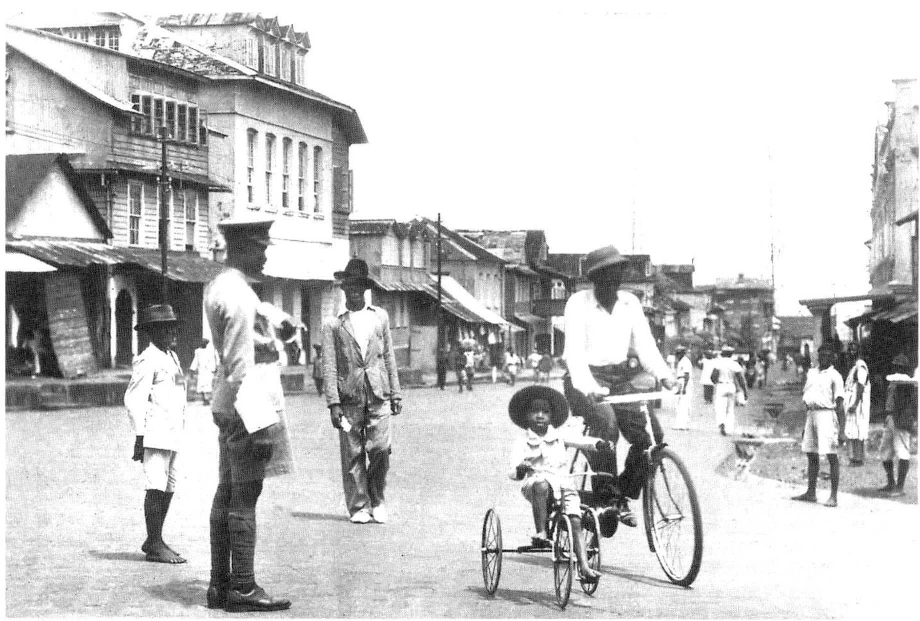

Wilberforce Street in Freetown shows more than just a view of the town. Most likely unbeknown to the photographer who took the snapshot, the picture illustrates an aspect of West Africa that was very much a part of its history, namely the riding of bicycles (or, in the case of the boy, a tricycle). The 1940s was a time when the bicycle was beginning to make a serious impression in West Africa, and soon a craze would develop for taxi-cycles. In this way, a simple snapshot has captured an important and emerging aspect of the country's culture.

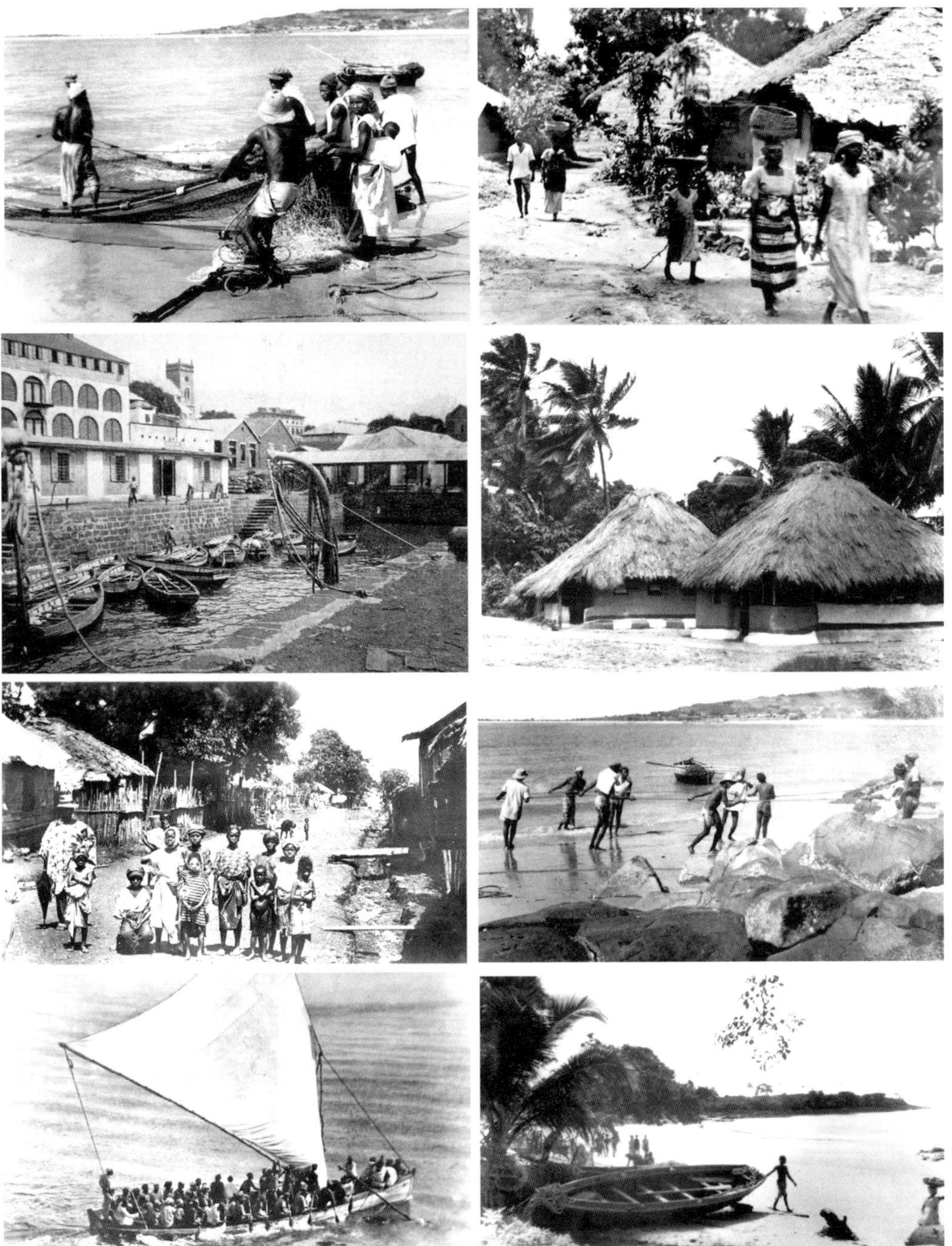

British West Africa during the Second World War, seen through the camera lens of several soldier snapshot photographers.

As for soldiers who hadn't brought cameras with them and now regretted it, was there the slightest possibility of buying one now? Strangely, the answer to both these questions was yes.

Brothers Alphonso and Arthur Lisk-Carew were photographers who ran studios out of their house and at their business premises, both in Freetown. They advertised themselves as photographers, importers of photographic materials, stationery, toys and fancy goods. The brothers shot hundreds of pictures in and around Sierra Leone, many of which were turned into postcards that were bought by the soldiers. They were available along with smaller, hand-tinted pictures, which were sold as souvenirs. The Lisk-Carew studios were also visited by the soldiers to have formal pictures taken of themselves in their tropical kit as mementos of their time abroad. And they sold film, not likely to have been at its best if stored under the harsh African sun at temperatures as high as 110 degrees Fahrenheit. But it was available and by and large, it performed adequately for snapshot-shooting soldiers.

While the pictures shown here do little to document the Second World War in the traditional sense, they do show maybe unexpected aspects of the war in a location that might have seemed unreal to professional photographers dedicated to showing the more customary realities of war. But for the soldiers who found themselves in this place at that time, a situation that would never have occurred had it not been for the outbreak of war, it was all too real, and the pictures they took have helped to preserve a moment in time. Eventually, given enough time, that is perhaps the most important aspect of snapshot photography.

Chapter 9

Instant Snapshots

Prior to 1948, snapshot photographers had a long wait between actually taking a picture and seeing the result. Most snapshot cameras used roll film that shot eight, and sometimes more, pictures to a roll. If the photographer had graduated to a simple 35mm camera, then the number of exposures to a roll of film could be as many as thirty-six. That fact alone could mean a long wait between the first and last pictures to be taken on any roll of film. When they had been taken, then the film needed to be developed and printed. Some amateur photographers might have carried out this work themselves in their own darkrooms. But for the majority of snapshot photographers it was more likely to have involved a trip to the nearest chemist, where the film would be dropped off followed by a wait of perhaps three days or maybe even a week before the processed negatives and prints were returned. American inventor Edwin Land changed all that in 1948 with the introduction of the first Polaroid camera. Now, a picture could be taken and, no more than a minute later, the finished print could be seen.

There is a story that might be apocryphal, but which is probably grounded in fact, that one day in 1943, Land was photographing his young daughter who expressed surprise that she couldn't see the photograph immediately after it had been taken. That led him to begin thinking about instant photography. Four years of research later, Land announced his process to the Optical Society of America.

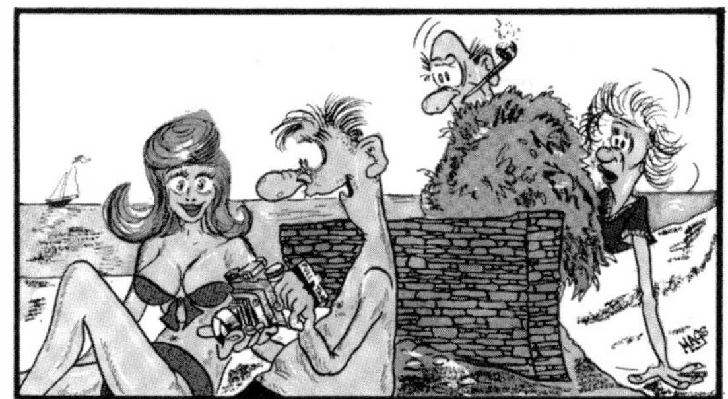

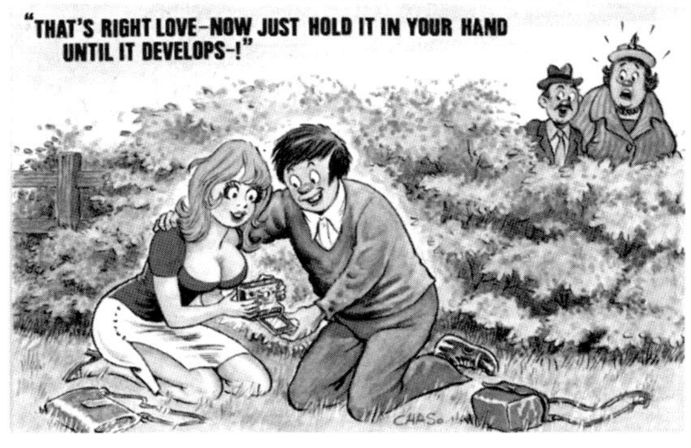

Two risqué seaside postcards derived from the popularity of instant picture cameras.

Polaroid Model 95

There had been cameras before Polaroid capable of producing pictures soon after exposure, but the Polaroid Model 95 was the first truly viable instant picture camera. It was shaped like a large version of the old-fashioned Kodak folding cameras with a bed that opened on hinges, from which the lens panel extended on bellows. The main control was a single thumbwheel set into the lens panel and numbered from one to eight. Using this thumbwheel alone had the effect of setting different combinations of shutter speeds and apertures at the same time, thus simplifying an otherwise complicated procedure for the snapshot photographer.

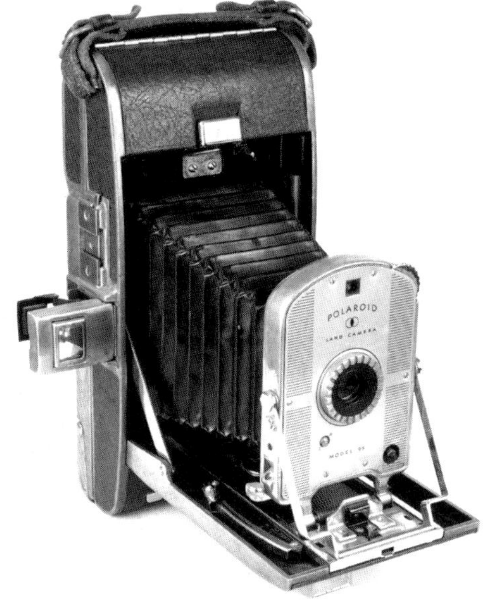

The Model 95 was Polaroid's first instant picture camera.

The camera used twin rolls of sensitised paper connected by a leader. The rolls were dropped into chambers at opposite ends of the body with the leader threaded between rollers and out of the back. One of the papers faced the lens. After exposure, the leader was pulled, causing the exposed paper negative from one spool and the sensitised printing paper from the other to come into contact. Chemical pods burst under pressure from the rollers, spreading a chemical solution between the two layers. A minute later, a positive sepia image could be removed through a door in the camera back. Later films produced the instant pictures in normal black and white.

The procedure was a little more complicated than the average snapshot photographer was accustomed to, but with a little practice, it was possible for even the least experienced photographer to produce instant pictures for the first time. Polaroid produced a great many cameras using the twin-roll film method, including models with built-in exposure meters to help make exposure setting more accurate. At the same time, some of these made operation more complicated for the inexperienced photographer. But a version of the twin-roll film idea eventually culminated in what might be considered as the ultimate snapshot camera…

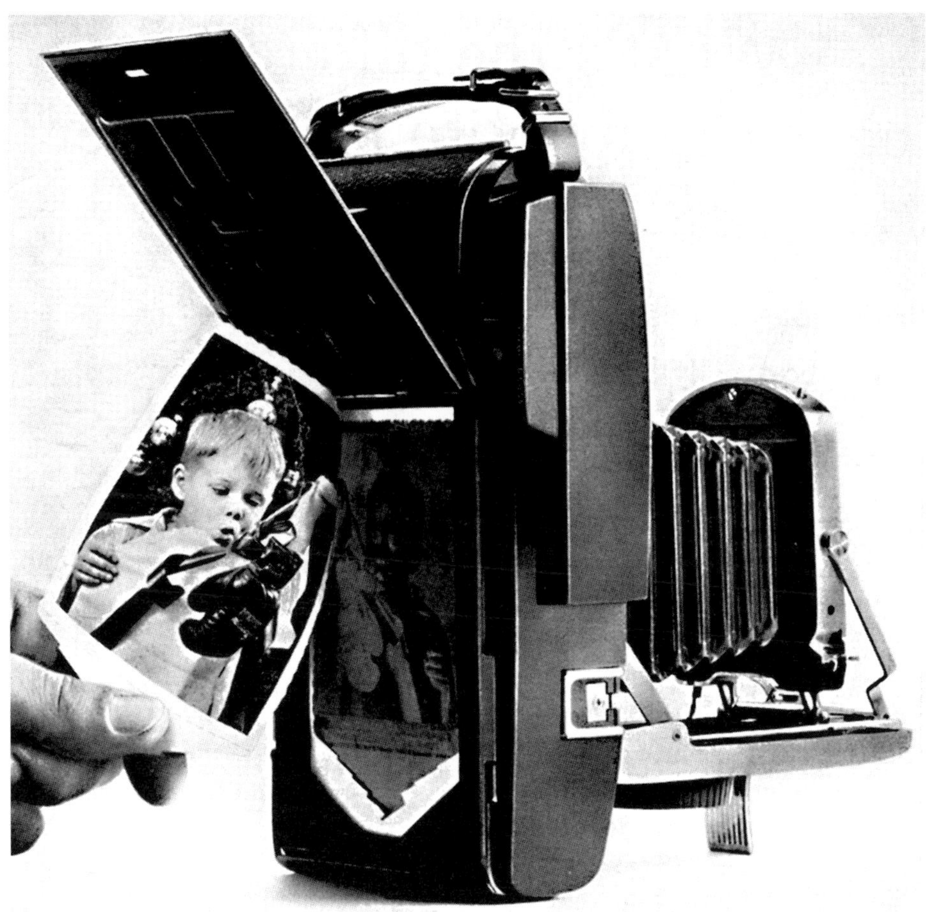

How the first instant picture cameras were advertised.

Polaroid Swinger

One of Polaroid's most successful cameras, the Swinger, launched in 1965, was also one of its simplest, and perfect for instant snapshot photography. It was made of white plastic with a large eye-level viewfinder mounted on top of the body. The photographer set the correct exposure for the prevailing light conditions

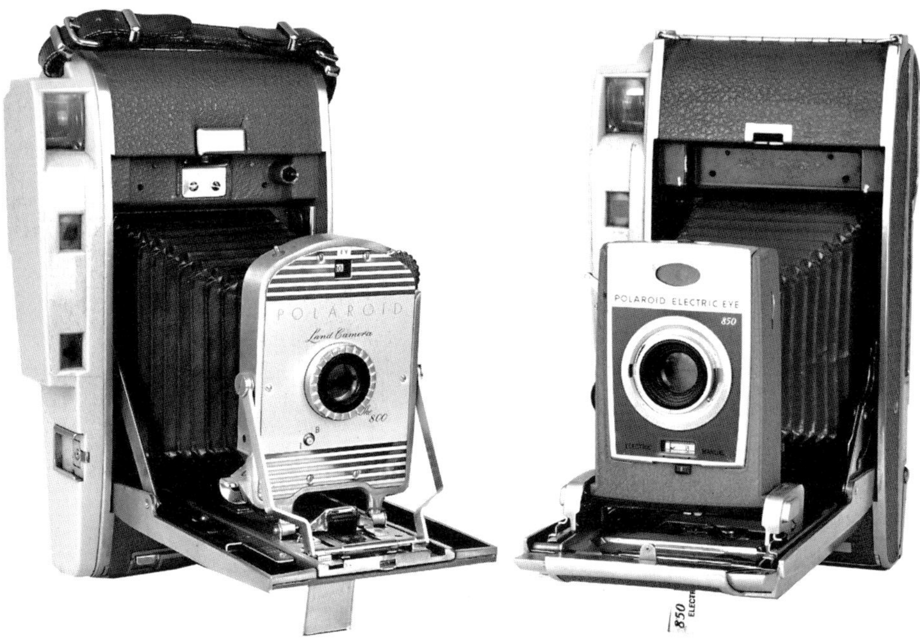

Other Polaroid cameras that used the twin-roll instant film system included the Model 800 (left) and the Electric Eye.

by twisting a red knob until the word 'yes' appeared in the viewfinder. Pressing the white tip of the same knob activated the shutter and took the picture. Next, a blue button was pressed and the film pulled from the side of the camera. It appeared as a sandwich of two pieces of paper, which were peeled apart to reveal the black and white picture. It was the first Polaroid camera in which the picture self-developed outside the camera body. When light conditions fell too low for correct exposure, flashbulbs could be inserted behind a small diffuser.

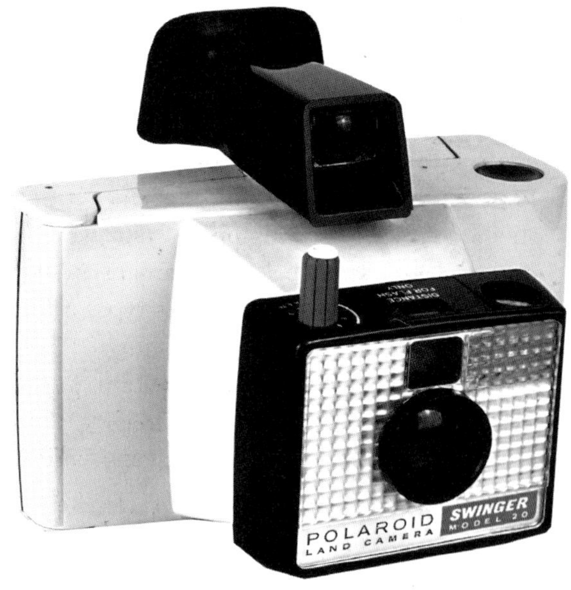

The Polaroid Swinger was one of the most successful instant picture cameras among snapshot photographers.

Automatic 100

Meanwhile in 1963, two years before the success of the Swinger, Polaroid had announced a new kind of instant film. It was sold in flat packs and became known as peel-apart. After exposure, a sandwich of two layers was pulled from the pack in the camera, activating chemical processing pods as it passed through rollers. One layer developed as a negative and transferred its image as a positive on the second layer. After sixty seconds, the two were peeled apart, and the negative discarded, leaving a positive print. The film was available for black and white prints, colour prints and even

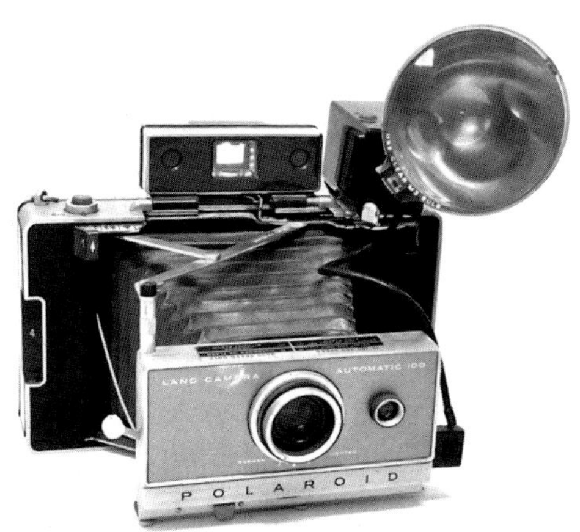

The Automatic 100 was the first of the new peel-apart film cameras.

for the production of instant black and white negatives that could be used to make conventional prints in a darkroom.

The first camera to use peel-apart film was the Automatic 100. It was also the first camera, instant or otherwise, with an electronic shutter coupled to an automatic exposure system. As the first shutter blade opened, light began to be measured through the lens, while an electromagnet held back the second blade. When sufficient light was judged for correct exposure, electric current was cut to the magnet and the second shutter blade closed. A lighten/darken control was added for fine-tuning. This meant that, although very sophisticated in its internal workings, on the surface it was a fairly easy camera to use, which should have increased its appeal to snapshot photographers. In fact, despite many different models of peel-apart cameras being made during the decade following the Automatic 100's launch, this type of film became more the prerogative of professional photographers who used it in special backs fitted to their normal film cameras, giving them an instant way to asses lighting, composition and exposure before committing an image to conventional film. Peel-apart film was also used for ID purposes and in special Polaroid cameras for taking passport pictures.

Polaroid Big Shot

One peel-apart film camera that should have appealed more to snapshot photographers than to professionals was the Big Shot, made in 1971. Specially designed for portraiture, the Big Shot had a lens whose focus distance was fixed at one metre, while a built-in rangefinder, fixed at the same setting, told the photographer when the camera was the correct distance from the subject. A flashgun was built in, with a flashbulb situated behind a diffuser to soften the light. The camera was simple to use and, in theory, gave inexperienced photographers the means to shoot correctly composed portraits, but it never achieved great success.

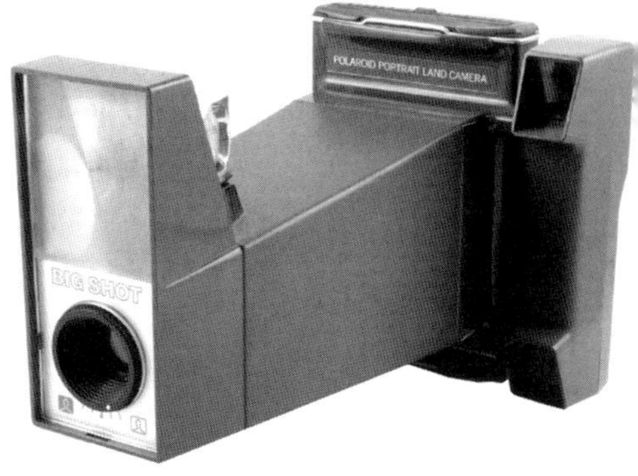

The Polaroid Big Shot made portraiture easy for inexperienced photographers.

Polaroid SX-70

In 1972, Polaroid came up with another approach to instant photography, and this one really did appeal to snapshot photographers. By this time, automation had begun to be more common in cameras. It meant that snapshot photographers, accustomed only to using cameras with the simplest of controls, could now use a new type of camera, one that had a far higher specification than the average snapshot camera, but which, thanks to inbuilt automation, was just as easy to use. The first Polaroid SX-70 camera had a metal body that folded flat before a tug on the rear of the viewfinder assembly unfolded it to a triangular shape

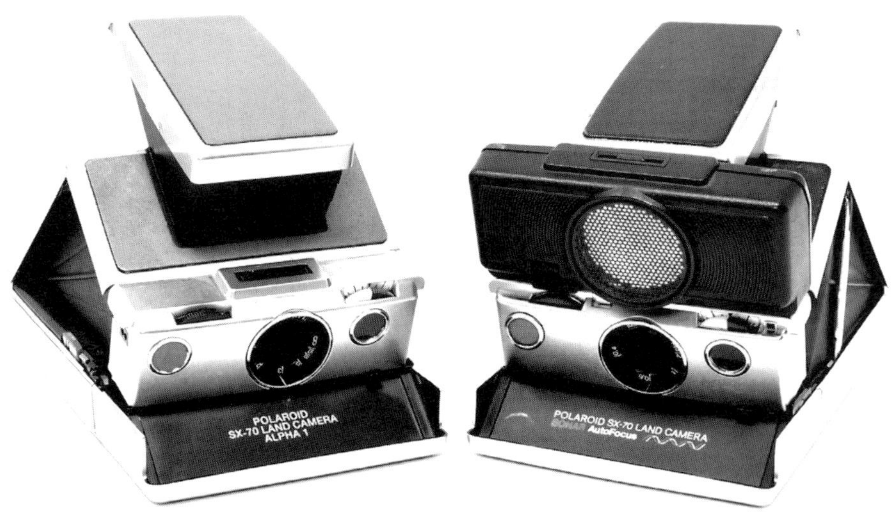

The Polaroid Alpha 1 (left) with the SX-70 Sonar Autofocus camera.

for shooting. Then, when the shutter button was pressed, a second after the exposure had been made a print was automatically ejected from the front of the camera to self-develop in normal daylight to form a full colour instant picture.

The Polaroid SX-70 was a single lens reflex, a kind of camera that most snapshot photographers would not have encountered before. Snapshot cameras used a viewfinder that,

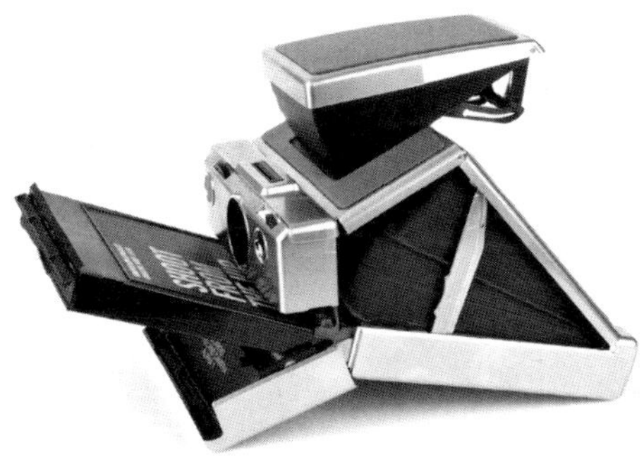

How the film pack was loaded into an SX-70 camera.

because of the way it was positioned in relation to the lens, showed a slightly different view to that which would appear in the picture being taken. A single lens reflex used a mirror to reflect the image from the lens into the viewfinder so that the photographer saw exactly what would appear on film, before the mirror moved away at the moment of exposure to allow light from the lens to reach the film. Exposure was programmed, which meant that the system automatically selected and set a suitable combination of shutter speeds and apertures for the correct exposure. Film was sold in flat packs that slotted into the front of the camera and which also incorporated a battery that drove all the electronic and mechanical functions needed to produce an instant print.

All the photographer needed to do was focus the lens with the help of a rangefinder in the viewfinder, and even that slight complication was automated in 1978 with the arrival of the SX-70 Sonar Autofocus, the world's first autofocus

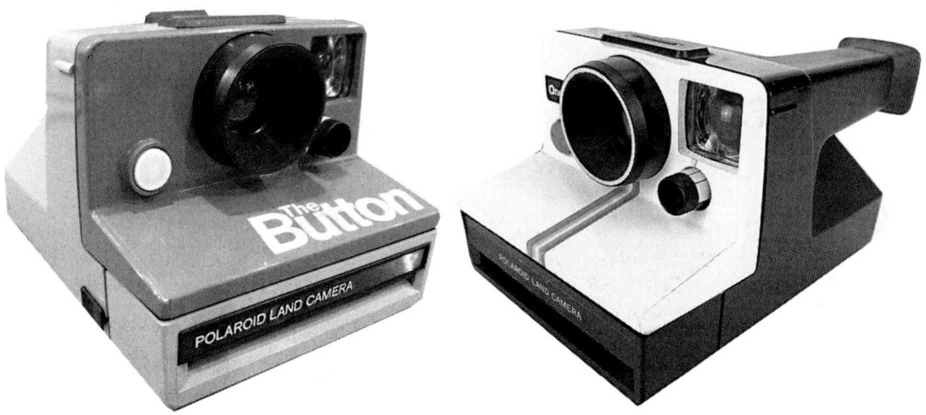

The Button (left) and One-Step cameras brought SX-70 more into the world of snapshot photographers.

single lens reflex. It worked by emitting a sonic beam that bounced off the subject to be picked up by a receptor above the camera lens. The time taken for the beam to be emitted and return told the camera where to focus the lens.

The SX-70 system also included simpler plastic-bodied, non-reflex cameras with names like The Button and The One-Step. These were a lot more like the kind of camera that a snapshot photographer would have been used to, but with the addition of Polaroid's instant colour picture that was automatically ejected from the front of the camera immediately after exposure. The picture size was 78×80mm in an 88×110mm white mount where photographers often used ballpoint pens to write details of the picture, where it was taken, the people shown, humorous captions etc.

The SX-70 cameras, in particular the simpler plastic models, introduced a whole new kind of snapshot photography. Although it had been possible to produce instant pictures with previous Polaroid models, there had never before been cameras that could be raised to the eye, a picture taken without any adjustments of controls and to then have the result in full colour in the

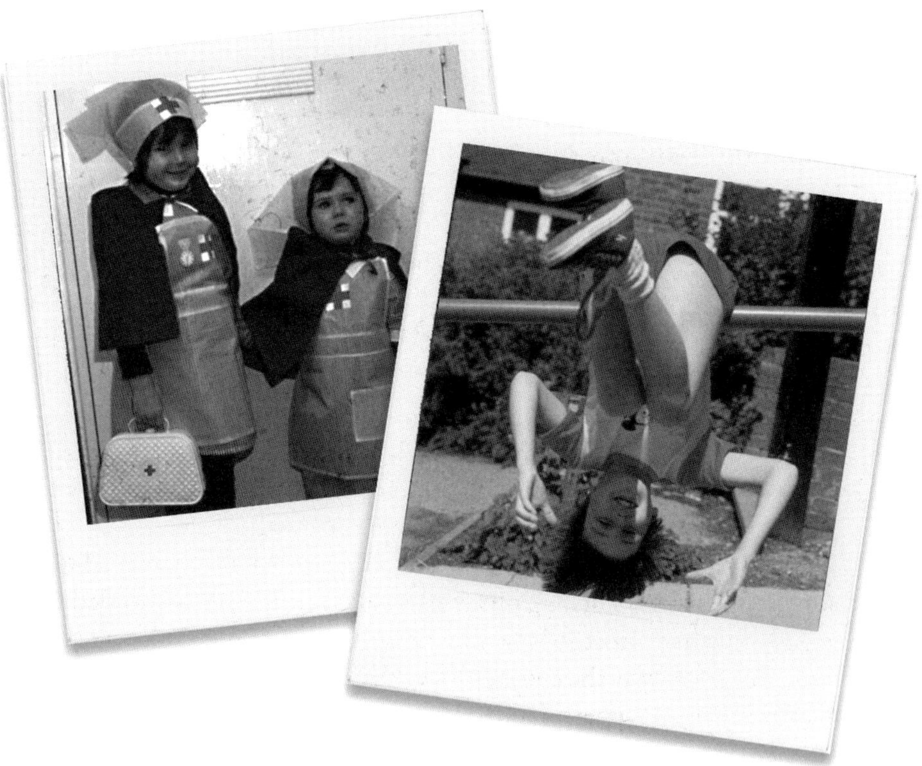

SX-70 instant prints became synonymous with spontaneity and having fun. (Original pictures in colour.)

hand a minute later. What more could a snapshot photographer need? This new type of camera bred a new kind of snapshot photographer for whom spontaneity was truly the name of the game. Polaroid cameras became synonymous with having fun. Holidays, outings, parties, whenever and wherever people got together socially, there was usually someone on hand to record it all with instant pictures of people enjoying themselves – maybe even more than usual when they could immediately see photographic evidence of just how much enjoyment was going on!

That side of instant snapshot photography continued with the launch of Polaroid's next system, whose cameras were even more snapshot orientated.

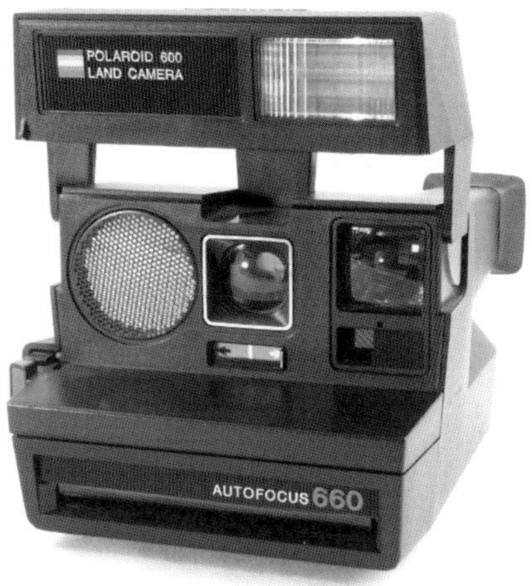

The Polaroid Autofocus 660 was one of the first to use the new 600 Series film.

600 Series

In 1981, the 600 Series introduced a new style and shape for Polaroid cameras. The battery was retained in the film pack and the instant picture was still ejected on exposure from the front of the body, but it gave more vibrant colours in a film four times faster than SX-70. The cameras were made in a series of different models, many of which were aimed squarely at the snapshot photographer. They included a talking camera; the Spicecam, made in association with the Spice Girls, a popular girl power band of the 1990s; and the Tazcam, disguised as Taz, the Tasmanian Devil cartoon character. The most stylish of the variations was the Polaroid P600, made in brushed silver with sleek, rounded lines. The cameras shot instant 78×80mm size pictures in 88×110mm white mounts, which again were often used for recording picture details.

The basic 600 Series camera took on a square, chunky shape with a built-in electronic flashgun that folded up on a bar ready for shooting, then folded down again to act as a lens protector. It was this flashgun that brought a new kind of automation that took away the complications of flash photography and simplified it for snapshot photographers. Unlike a traditional flashgun that was fitted to the camera as a separate accessory, then had to be turned on for shooting, the integrated and built-in flashgun on Polaroid 600 Series cameras was designed to fire with every shot. Outdoors, exposure was automatically adjusted to allow

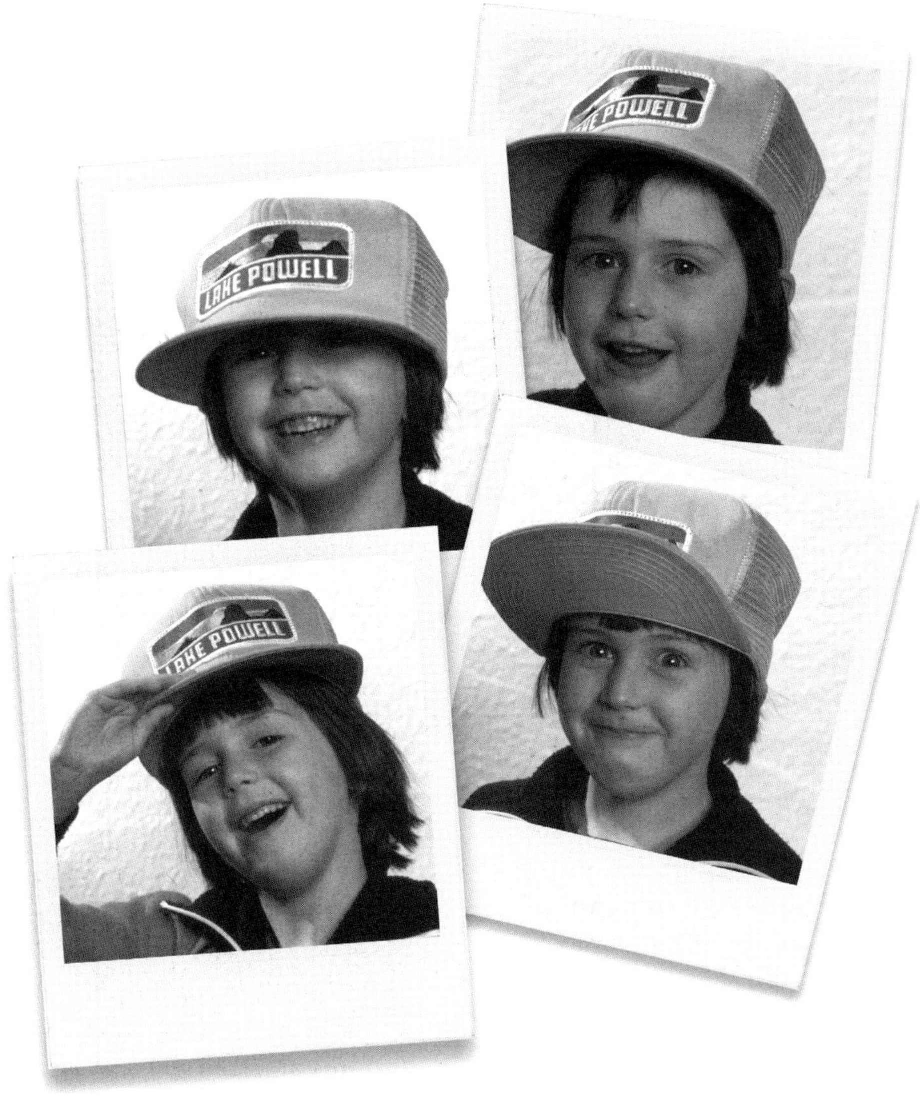

Instant pictures from the 600 Series camera continued the fun element of snapshot photography. (Original pictures in colour.)

for 25 per cent flash against 75 per cent natural light to illuminate the shadowed areas of the picture. Then, as ambient light levels dropped, the percentage changed until, indoors, the flash supplied 100 per cent of the required light.

Aimed more at snapshot-type photographers, these cameras were not single lens reflexes. For those who wanted to graduate to something a little more sophisticated, more experienced photographers turned to the SLR 680, 680SE and 690, which offered through-the-lens reflex viewfinders and programmed exposure with sonic autofocus. Unlike the snapshot cameras, which had solid bodies, these reflex versions of the 600 Series cameras folded flat like the older SX-70 models.

Image/Spectra

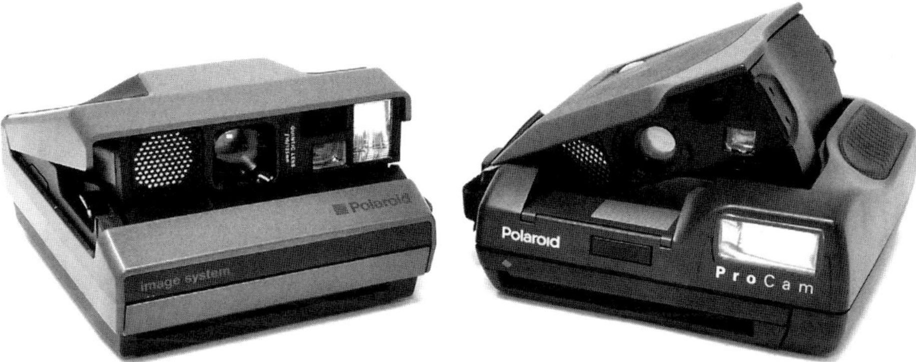

The first Image System camera (left) and a later ProCam.

Known as the Image System in the UK and Spectra in America, this new breed of cameras, first seen in 1986, retained the battery in the film pack and print ejection on exposure, but placed it all into a new design that gave a bigger print than before: 75×90mm pictures in 100×103mm white mounts. It was a non-reflex camera that opened like a clamshell into a wedge shape. Exposure and focus were automatic and the camera had a small, built-in flashgun that fired automatically when light conditions demanded it. Snapshot photographers would have used it in its fully automatic mode, but for the more adventurous, a control panel on the camera back offered manual override of several functions.

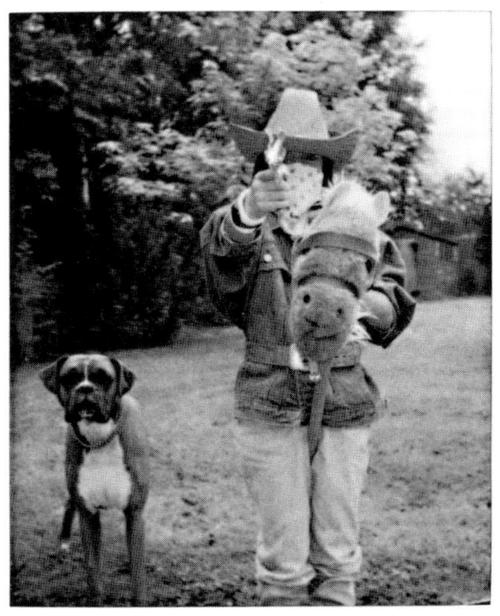

Image System cameras, whose pictures could be taken in a horizontal or vertical format like this one, produced a larger image. (Original picture in colour.)

The launch of Polaroid's Image System cameras also provided easy ways for snapshot photographers to add special effects to their pictures without the need for any technical expertise. What might previously have involved expertise

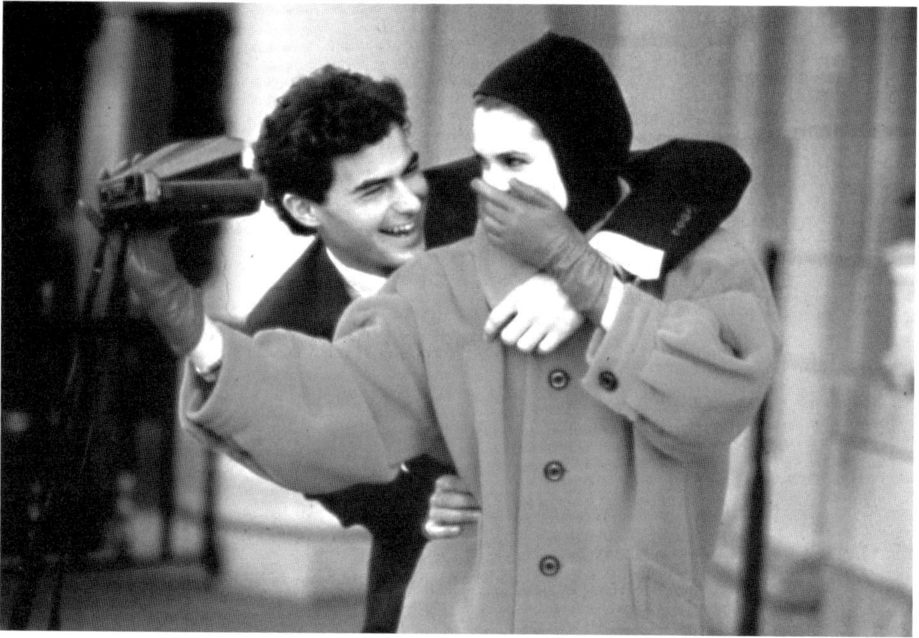

A Polaroid publicity picture for the Image System, issued long before anyone had heard the word 'selfie'.

beyond the scope of the average snapshot photographer was simplified by the use of filters that fitted over the camera lens. With these, the photographer could multiply certain aspects of the subject to appear in the picture up to five times, add soft focus effects, produce the appearance of speed in a static subject and even use double exposures in the camera to allow the same person to appear in two different places in the same picture. And the beauty of instant photography meant photographers could check the special effect immediately and reshoot if it hadn't worked to their satisfaction the first time.

Instant/Spectra models were not made in the abundance enjoyed by SX-70 and 600 Series cameras. Variations included the ProCam, similar to the original Image camera, but designed to unfold in a different way.

Polaroid made a great fuss of introducing the Image/Spectra cameras, with publicity pictures that showed the many ways they could be used, including people holding the camera at arm's length for a self-portrait, many years before the idea would catch on with digital smartphone users and called selfies.

Polaroid's demise

The Image/Spectra system represented Polaroid's last great series of cameras, although those produced in its final years were more likely to have appealed to

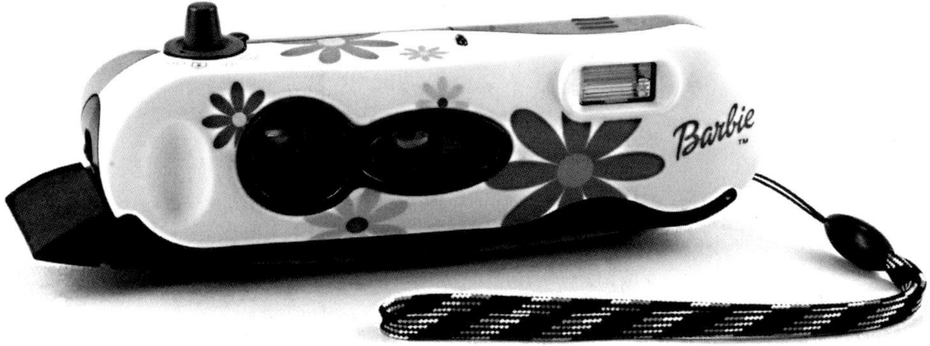

Polaroid i-Zone camera in its Barbie doll version, aimed primarily at children.

snapshot photographers. Weird and wonderful designs proliferated with cameras like the Joycam, the i-Zone and the 1200FF whose lens, viewfinder and flash folded up at 90° to the base, which contained the film.

But by this time, digital photography was beginning to become popular and suddenly Polaroid's unique selling point – the fact that the pictures taken were instantly ready for viewing – was no longer the novelty it had once been. In October 2001, Polaroid filed for bankruptcy. The business was carried on for a while by the holding company, but the glory days of Polaroid instant photography seemed to be over.

Today, instant photography has been revived by a new company that has taken on the Polaroid name and is successfully producing both cameras and film for instant photography in defiance of so many photographers who, wanting to see their pictures the moment they are taken, have switched their allegiance to digital photography.

Other instant camera makers

Although Polaroid dominated the instant picture market, it wasn't alone in producing instant picture cameras. In the mid-1970s, Kodak entered the instant photography market with a camera called the EK2. It was an ugly camera, which worked rather like Polaroid's SX-70 series except that, on exposure, the film had to be wound out of the camera with a handle, rather than being automatically ejected. Later instant cameras from Kodak automated the procedure. The process used was different to Polaroid's but sufficiently similar for Polaroid to go to law over patent infringement. The case battled its way through the courts for more than a decade before Polaroid won in 1986 and Kodak was forced to withdraw all its instant picture cameras and film. Compared to Polaroid, the Kodak instant cameras were ugly and cumbersome to use. Even before

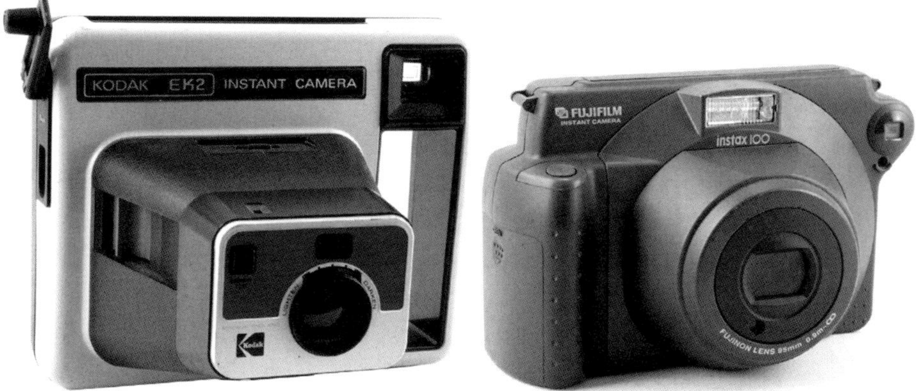

Kodak EK2, the company's first attempt at instant picture photography (left) with Fuji's Instax 100 instant picture camera.

they were forced off the market, they were never as popular as Polaroid cameras.

In 1998, the Japanese Fujifilm company launched the first of what would become a huge range of instant picture cameras. Unlike Polaroid, and to some extent Kodak, Fuji didn't attempt to cover the professional or even the advanced amateur photographer market. Instead, cameras and their marketing were aimed straight at the snapshot photographer, with what would soon become a huge range of different cameras in attractive and sometimes unusual designs. Exposure in almost all the cameras was automatic, which meant snapshot photographers

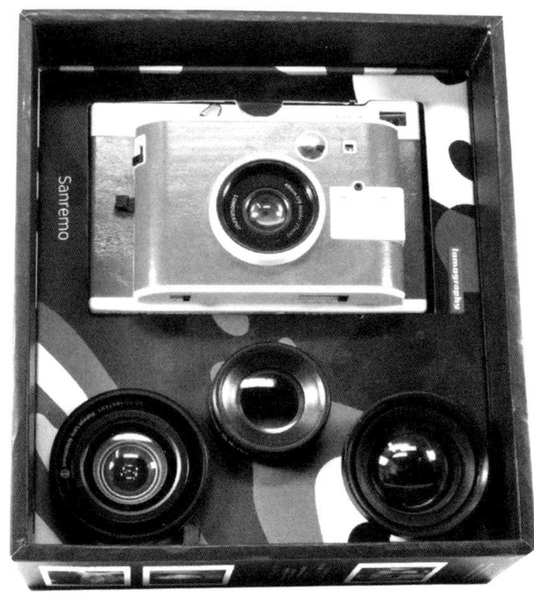

A modern Lomo instant camera outfit, including the camera and its accessory lenses.

didn't have to worry about technicalities and, like Polaroid, prints were ejected from the camera immediately after the picture had been taken. The instant picture sizes varied, according to the model of camera: 46×62mm for the Instax Mini range of cameras, 99×62mm for the Instax Wide range, and 62×62mm for the Instax Square range. Both colour and black and white instant films were available.

Instant picture photography has also been made popular by the Lomo company, which has done so much to resurrect interest in, and the popularity of, film among snapshot photographers. Still available today, the Lomo cameras use Fuji's Instax film.

Despite the popularity of digital photography, which has all but replaced film photography for both serious amateur and professional photographers, Fuji's Instax range of cameras and those carrying the Lomo name remain popular today and have even become something of a cult. Undoubtedly, they will never replace digital cameras, but the novelty of having an actual colour picture in the hand seconds after it has been taken is still attractive to many for whom instant snapshot photography remains alive and well.

Chapter 10

Every Home Should Have One

In the years following the end of the Second World War in 1945, all the way through to the early 1980s, the advent of Bakelite followed by the use of plastic led to sometimes revolutionary new shapes and designs of snapshot cameras. Old names and types of camera took on new shapes. New names and fresh designs began to appear. Old faithfuls that had been around for years finally died and new beginnings led photographers towards the digital age.

Although the early 1950s was a period of austerity, it wasn't long before a new prosperity resulted in people having spare income for the first time. Cameras that appealed to advanced amateur photographers were expensive, but the many and various snapshot models that began to appear on the market were far more reasonably priced. For many, cameras were like lawn mowers, in so far as every home had one, even when no one in the house was a keen gardener. In the same way, every home had a snapshot camera, even though no one in the family would have actually called themselves a photographer.

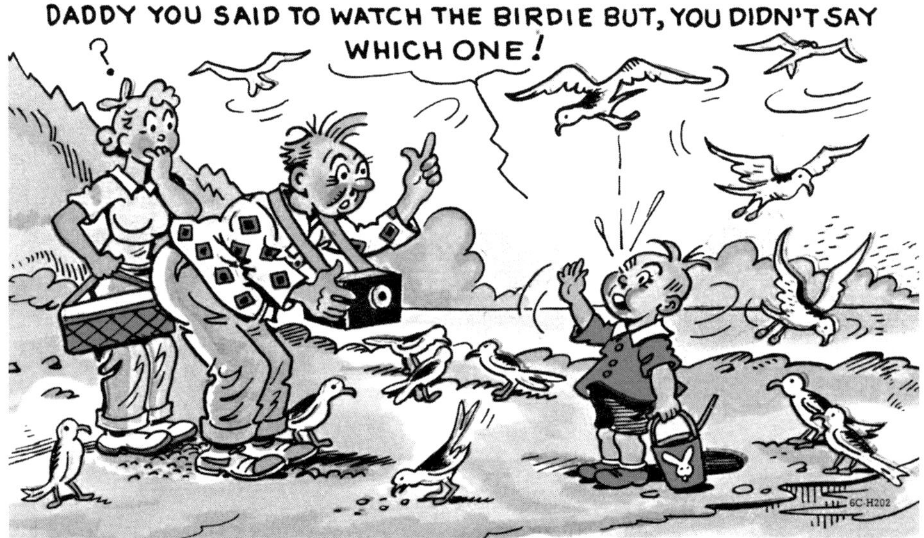

As suggested by a postcard of the time, snapshot photographers took their cameras out once a year for the family holiday.

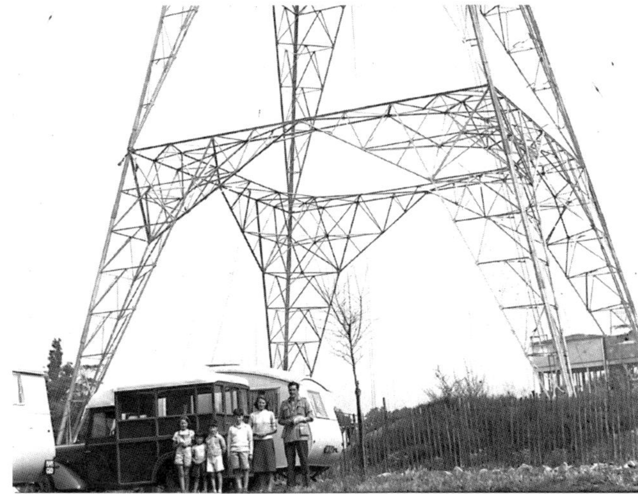

Snapshot cameras were relied on to record the family holiday, even if the caravan site chosen for that year's time away wasn't situated in the most picturesque location.

Snapshot photography had never been easier or more accessible, and yet photography among the snapshot fraternity was for many years reserved only for special occasions. Despite so many people now owning cameras, snapshot pictures were rarely taken for their own sakes or for artistic reasons. They were much more likely to be used to document family occasions like holidays, Christmas, weddings, christenings, children in their first school uniforms, and always with the thought that there were only eight pictures, or sometimes twelve pictures, to a roll of film. As 35mm began to make inroads into the snapshot camera market, bringing with it far more exposures to every roll of film, a joke proliferated among film processors who took in film from snapshot photographers for development: 'We get one roll of film a year and it has a Christmas tree on each end.'

When snapshot photographers took their cameras on holiday, they snapped views of the places they were visiting, but nearly always with a member of the family posed in front of the scene, be it a landscape, a roaring waterfall, a stately home, or whatever. Poses were usually formal, with the subject smiling in an embarrassed way. Snapshots were rarely shot candidly without the subject's knowledge.

Here's a look at the kinds of cameras that this new generation of snapshot photographers was using.

The continual rise of the Brownie

The Brownie story, which had begun in 1900 and, in America, only slowed a little during the war, took up a new pace over the three decades that followed

"OH DEAR! I THINK I'VE GOT SOME SAND IN MY BROWNIE."

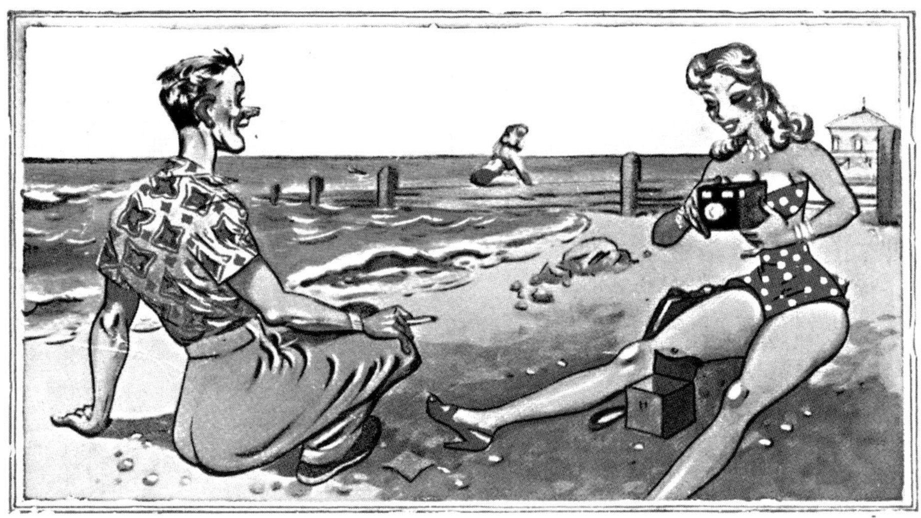

It didn't take much for seaside postcards to find something risqué to say about the ubiquitous Brownie camera.

hostilities. New variations on the camera were launched with never-before-seen designs. All retained the ease of use that had been at the heart of the Brownie ethos from the day the first model appeared.

Brownie Reflex

Starting life in America in 1941 and continuing manufacture until 1960, the Brownie Reflex was typical of the new look snapshot cameras were beginning to take. A true twin lens reflex, used by more professional photographers, used two lenses one above the other, the lower one to shoot the picture and the upper one to reflect its image to a viewfinder screen on top of the camera. Both lenses could be focused in tandem. It was a design that was simplified in

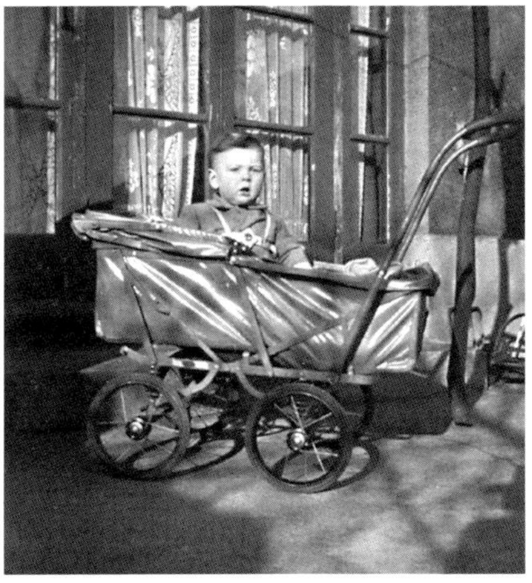

The changing face of the perambulator, better known as a pram, for transporting young sons and daughters. The snapshot was taken around 1948, but it's likely that that pram originated from before the Second World War, which ended only a few years before.

the Brownie Reflex, which had a fixed focus lens, with a fixed aperture and a single shutter speed. It wasn't a true twin lens reflex, but it was a good copy of one and its smart Art Deco design put it a cut above most snapshot cameras of the time.

Brownie Hawkeye
Between 1949 and 1961, the Brownie Hawkeye, made of Bakelite and sporting another shape rarely seen in snapshot cameras, was shaped like a rounded box with echoes of Art Deco and two lenses on the front. The upper one, however, was only to serve the viewfinder. The basic controls were as simple to use as might be expected on a snapshot camera, but it had an added advantage of being able to use a purpose-made flashgun, made for flashbulbs and easy to fit onto the side of the body. The camera was also known as the Brownie Flash and the Brownie Fiesta.

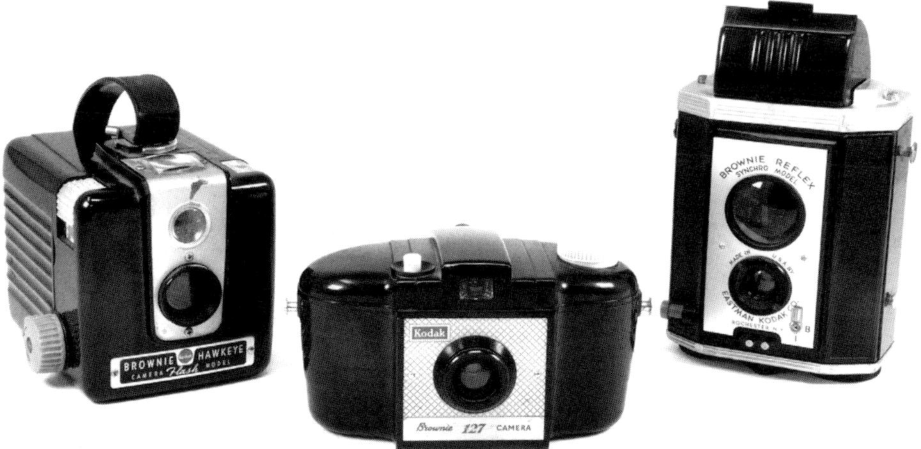

Left to right: Brownie Hawkeye, Brownie 127 and Brownie Reflex.

Brownie 127
In 1952, Kodak launched the Brownie 127, which became one of the most popular cameras ever manufactured by the company. Made of black Bakelite and stylishly finished with a curved ribbed body, there were several models with slightly different styles of faceplate, some striped, others chequered. Its only controls were a white shutter button and film wind knob. The back of the camera, and the subsequent film plane inside, was curved to allow for aberrations inherent in the camera's simple meniscus lens. In 1953, coinciding with the British coronation of Queen Elizabeth II, 5,000 white versions of the Brownie 127 were made. They were test marketed in the Channel Island of Jersey, but never went into full production. The Brownie 127, as its name implied, took eight pictures on 127 size film. In 1955, a larger version of the

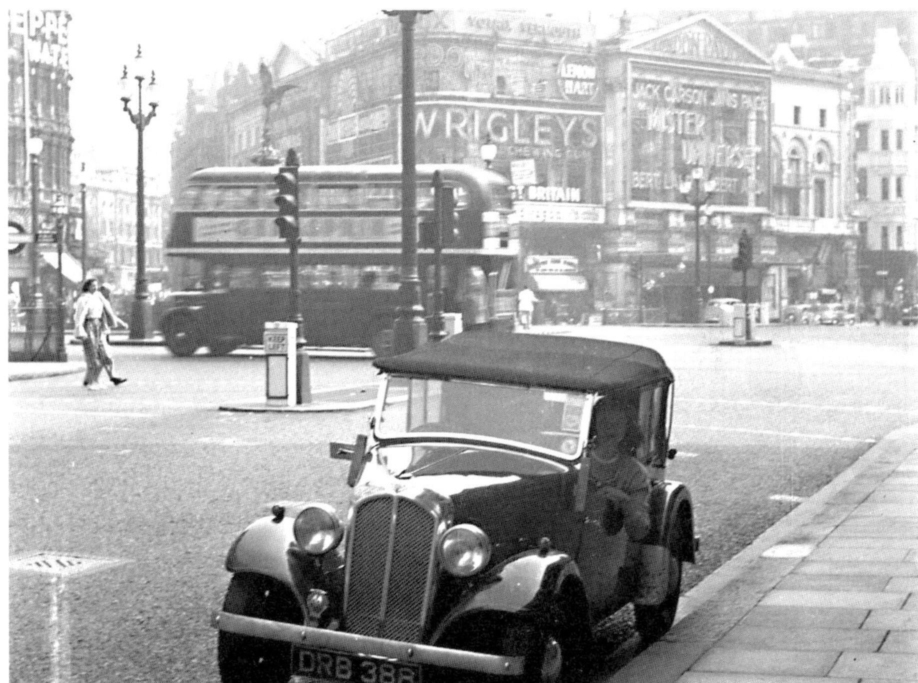

Piccadilly Circus in London. The car is a 1937 Austin 10 Greyhound, but *Mr Universe*, the film seen advertised outside the London Pavilion cinema in the background, was released in 1951. The story behind the snapshot is that the Austin's driver and his wife had driven the car to London from North Wales to attend the Festival Exhibition that opened on the South Bank of the river Thames as part of the Festival of Britain in May that year.

same design, called the Brownie Cresta, was launched to shoot a larger format twelve pictures in 120 size film.

Brownie Bullseye

In production in America from 1954 to 1960, this was a classic example of the way Bakelite could be moulded into new shapes of camera. Vertically styled with a large eye-level viewfinder and shutter button on one side, it shot eight 6×9cm pictures to a roll of film. The camera was first produced in two-tone black and silver and later in gold. It had its own dedicated flashgun that could be attached to one side.

Brownie Flash cameras

Just when it might have been thought the days of the box camera were over, Kodak came back into the market in 1957 with a series of Brownie Flash models, so called because dedicated flashguns could be attached to the sides. Although the first Brownie Flash was little more than a name variant of the aforementioned Brownie Hawkeye, the following cameras were box types, in

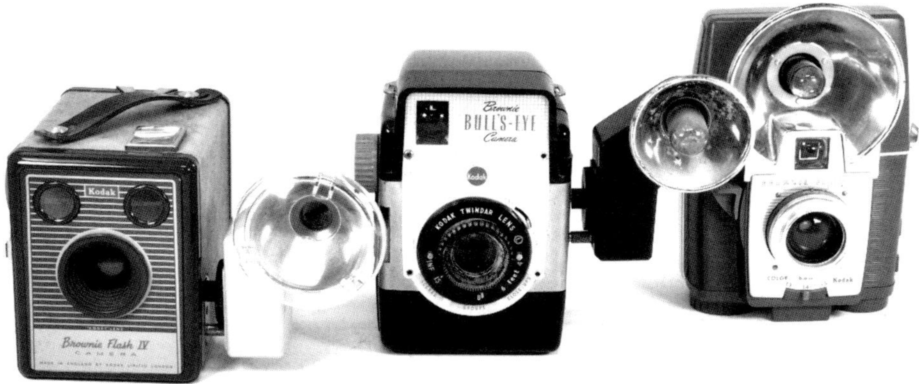

Flash photography comes to the Brownie. Left to right: Brownie Flash IV, Brownie Bullseye and Brownie Flash 20.

new and attractive designs that culminated in the Brownie Flash IV, made in tan leather, with a brown striped faceplate and gold-coloured brass fittings.

Brownie Flash 20

By 1959, it was no longer necessary to attach a separate flashgun to the side of the camera because, with the launch of the Brownie Flash 20, the flashgun became

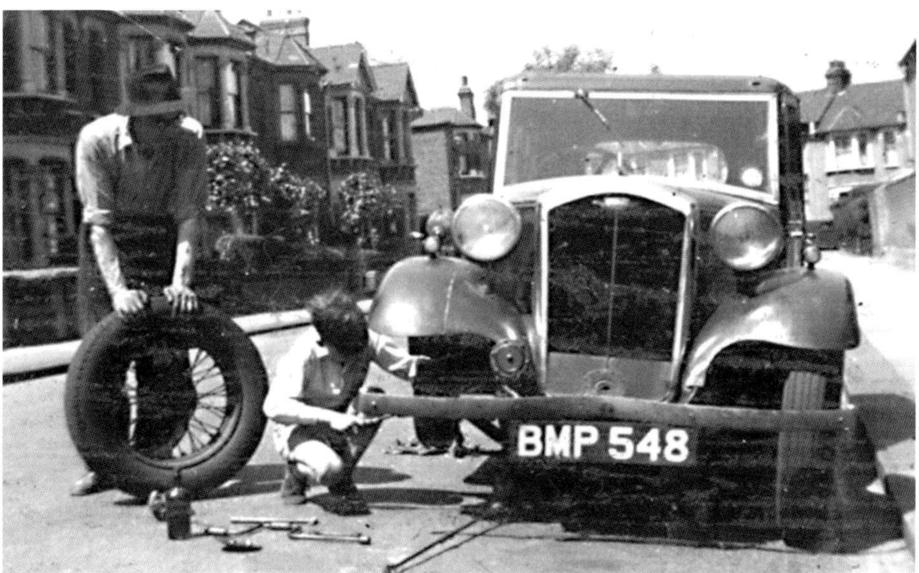

Taken towards the end of the 1950s, here's a snapshot that shows four differences between then and now. First, those lucky enough to actually own a car in the 1950s probably drove one made before the Second World War; this one is actually a 1934 Wolseley 9. Secondly, drivers undertook their own repairs back then. Thirdly, the streets were empty, devoid of passing traffic and with an absence of other parked cars, allowing for said repairs to be safely undertaken at the kerbside. Finally, men wore trilby hats even in summer with their shirtsleeves rolled up.

part of the overall design. This was a camera aimed directly at the snapshot photographer who wanted greater flexibility but still with the Brownie ease of use. The camera was made in blue plastic with a large flashgun integrated into the top of the body, doubling its height. The camera could of course be used without flash in normal daylight. But for shooting indoors, all the photographer needed to do was push a flashbulb into the large reflector on top of the camera and shoot. The bulbs, which were timed to coincide with the shutter opening, could only be used once and had to be ejected after the picture had been taken by pushing a small plunger on the back of the camera. What the photographer never did was attempt to use his or her fingers to pull the bulb out of its holder after the picture had been taken because the bulbs got very hot as they were fired. Many an unwary snapshot photographer, using flash for the first time, ended up with badly burnt fingers.

Brownie 44A

By the end of the 1950s and into the 1960s, Kodak Brownies began to take on more ergonomic designs. The Brownie 44A was beautifully styled in black mounded plastic with a smart grey sculptured top and aluminium back covered with black cloth. Still retaining the Brownie ease of use, it shot twelve pictures in black and white or colour on 127 size film. The first model used a protective flap that covered the lens when not in use. The Brownie 44B that followed was made without the flap,

Brownie Vecta

Brownie camera design reached its peak in 1964 when the Brownie Vecta won a British Design Centre Award. The Vecta was made to take eight pictures on 127 film in a vertical format, based on the idea that it would primarily be used to take people pictures. The camera was finished in an attractive grey colour with a long, white bar across the front in place of the usual shutter button. The theory was that this would assist snapshot photographers in keeping the camera steady during exposure.

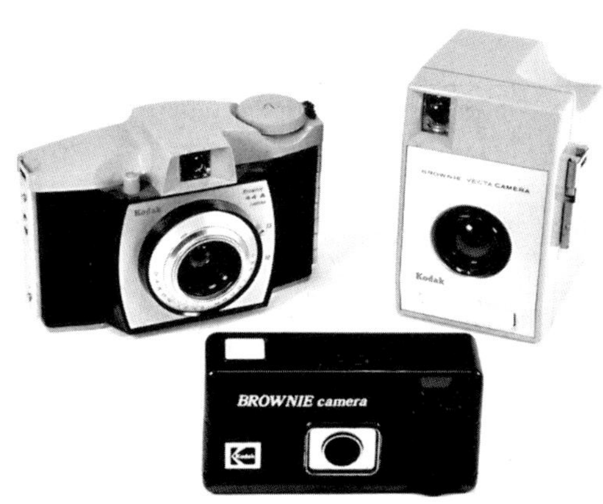

Two of the later and more stylish Brownies, the 44A (left) and Vecta, with one of the last, the Brownie 110.

The last Brownies

What is usually thought of as the last Brownie was made as late as 1980. The Brownie 110 was a name variant of a camera called the Pocket A1, each of which took 110 film, the then most popular film for snapshot photographers. It had a fixed focus, fixed aperture lens and a single shutter speed. Officially, however, the last camera to bear the Brownie name was made in the more traditional style of 110 film camera, with only a brief appearance in 1986.

The cameras mentioned here cover most of the style variations of the Kodak Brownie snapshot cameras, but these only scratch the surface of the huge range of cameras to bear that name. It was a name that remained the popular choice for snapshot photographers from the time of the first Brownie in 1900, and for more than eighty years that followed.

The evolution of box cameras

Although Kodak continued to use the traditional box type of design in many of its snapshot cameras, most notably the Brownie range, changing tastes and new abilities to manipulate raw materials during this era saw the evolution of the old fashioned box cameras. Sometimes it was with little more than small changes to fancy faceplates, though more often the changes involved completely new and unusual designs. The basic specifications of the cameras, however, still restricted their use to pictures taken in daylight, preferably strong sun. They weren't cameras for creative photography, but for snapshot photographers they

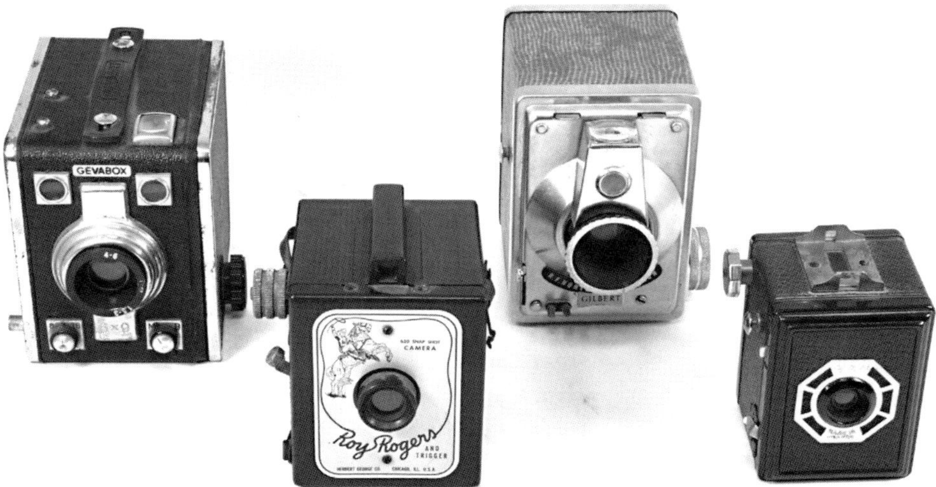

New-look box cameras from around the world. Left to right: the German-made Gevabox, American Roy Rogers, British Gilbert and the French Gap.

represented something a little different for use and to be seen with. Here are just a few of the new developments in box camera design that were made in countries around the world where they were eagerly bought by snapshot photographers.

The Gap

Several things represented a departure from the norm in the Gap camera, produced in 1949. Whereas most box cameras used 120 size film to shoot eight 6×9cm pictures, the Gap switched to 127 film, which meant the body was less than half the size of a normal box camera. Also, by incorporating a system of two red windows to read the film numbers, the Gap doubled the number of pictures that could be taken on a single roll of film to sixteen. It also had a viewfinder on the top of the body for use at eye level and an attractive Art Deco design around the lens, in silver, red, blue or gold. The name of the camera had nothing to do with a gap, as in the space between objects. It was pronounced the French way with a soft 'G' and derived from the name of the manufacturer, George Paris.

Roy Rogers Camera

The Roy Rogers Camera, made by the Herbert George Company in America in 1950, looked at first to be a typical box camera. What set it apart – and what would have attracted snapshot photographers to it – was a front faceplate that showed Roy Rogers, a popular singing cowboy and film character of the time, twirling his lasso while sitting astride his horse Trigger. A similar camera was made by the same company, depicting Davy Crockett.

Gevabox

Unlike most of its contemporaries, the Gevabox, made in 1951, was equipped with a focusing lens that allowed the photographer to focus from 1.5 metres to infinity. Otherwise it was a fairly standard box camera. But later the waist-level viewfinder found on most box cameras was replaced by an eye-level viewfinder that took it away from the box shape of the past. It shot eight exposures 6×9cm on each film.

Gilbert

Made by the English company R.F. Hunter in 1953, the Gilbert differed from its snapshot box-type contemporaries by using a stainless steel body with imitation lizard skin covering. Another break from tradition was its strange viewfinder in a tapered metal box above the lens, which revolved through 90 degrees for taking horizontal pictures. The lens could be focused, but the focusing scale was marked only for 8ft and 20ft. Everything in between relied on guesswork.

Unusual in a camera of this type, the shutter release was linked to the film wind so that, once a picture had been taken, the shutter could not be fired again until the film had been wound. This prevented two or more pictures being taken on the same frame of film – a common mistake among snapshot photographers. The Gilbert shot eight 6×9cm pictures to a roll of film.

Ensign Ful-Vue

This British-made camera began life as a box camera in 1939, but evolved into one of the era's most iconic snapshot cameras. As the original box camera, its principal difference, compared to others of its time, was a larger-than-normal viewfinder whose image was relayed from a second lens above the actual shooting lens on the front of the body. In 1946, an exhibition called *Britain Can Make It* was organised and a request sent out to British manufacturers to exhibit designs for futuristic products. Ensign responded by redesigning the Ful-Vue in a new streamlined shape. The large viewfinder lens on top of the body and its viewing lens on the front were built into a curved dome inset into the body with the viewfinder taking up the whole of its top. In keeping with most cameras, the Ful-Vue was made in black, but that was about to change.

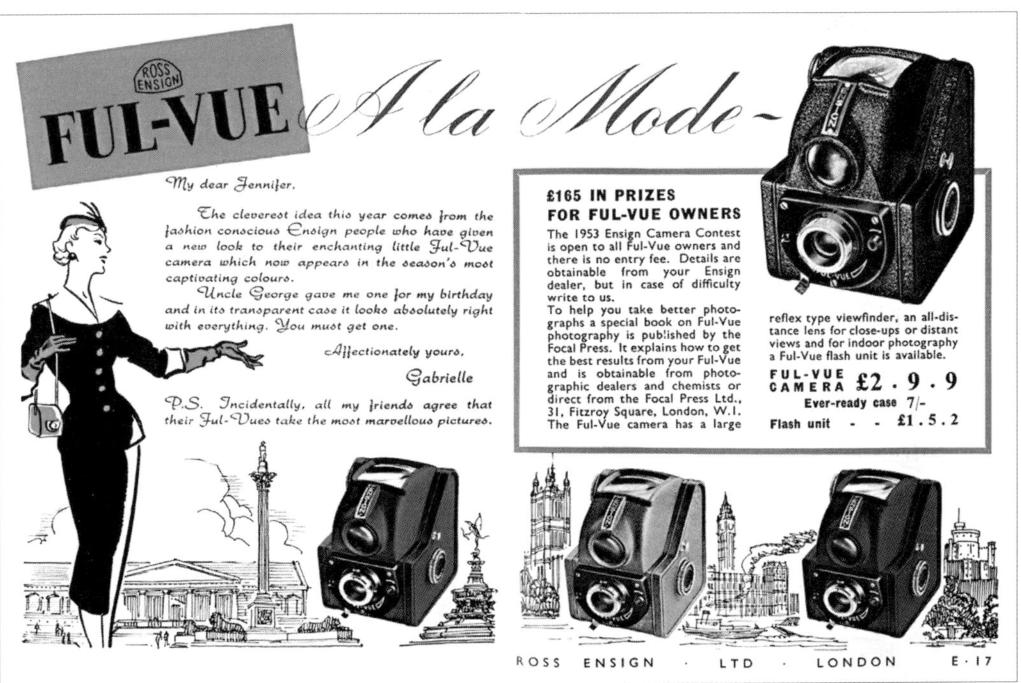

Advertising for the Ful-Vue à la mode cameras.

Tuesday, 2 June 1953 was the day Queen Elizabeth II was crowned. In the months leading up to the coronation the whole country was a riot of red, white and blue: flags in the streets, produce in shop windows, cake and biscuit tins, the wrappers around sliced bread and more. Ensign's contribution to the coronation festivities was to produce the newly shaped Ful-Vue in the three most popular colours of the day – well, almost. It appeared that making a white camera must have proved a little difficult and, instead of red, white and blue, the cameras ended up red, grey and blue. Ensign called the new versions of the camera the Ful-Vue à la mode, and aimed its advertising at the female market in an attempt to encourage more women to buy cameras.

In 1954, by which time various acquisitions and name changes meant the Ensign company was known as Ross-Ensign, a new version of the camera was launched and called the Ful-Vue Super. It retained the streamlined looks, but in a more angular design with a hood that folded up and down over the viewfinder. The camera was made mostly in black, but red, grey and blue versions were also available, although in darker shades than their predecessors.

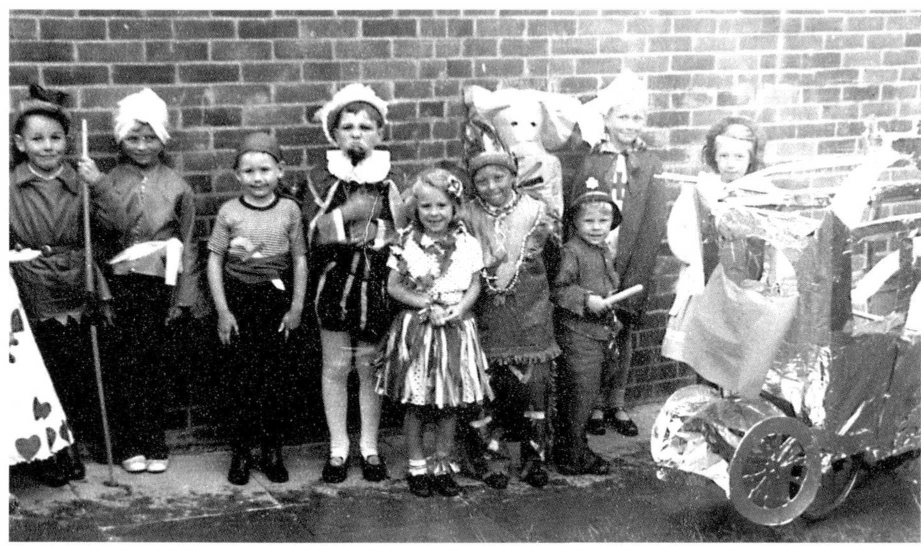

Tuesday, 2 June 1953 was Coronation Day, when Queen Elizabeth II was crowned in Westminster Abbey. It was a day of pomp and ceremony when joyous crowds turned out in their thousands to cheer the procession to and from Buckingham Palace before and after the crowning ceremony. It rained for best part of the day. The next few days were taken up by street parties, mostly for children, as roads were closed, tables were erected along their length, people brought out chairs from their houses either side of the road and a good time was had by all. The children usually attended in fancy dress. This snapshot, taken by the proud parent of one of the children, says it all: a pram converted into the Coronation coach, soldiers, a policeman, foreign dignitaries from overseas, a nurse and, for some strange reason, what appears to be an elephant at the back of the group.

The end of the Ful-Vue line came around 1957, when the Fulvueflex was produced. Although its ancestry could be seen in its design, the manufacture now shifted from a metal to a plastic body, while still retaining the large viewfinder that had epitomised the brand throughout its life. It never gained the popularity enjoyed by the previous cameras.

Although the colours mentioned here were officially made by Ensign, various other colours of the different Ful-Vue versions later came to light, silver being one of the more prevalent. Some of these can be traced back to the Ensign factory while a lot more are known to be definite fakes.

Back in the 1950s, it wasn't unusual for inexperienced snapshot photographers to make a common mistake when using any of the Ful-Vue cameras. Because the viewfinder on the top of the body was made up of a relatively large piece of glass, some photographers mistook this for the lens. With the viewfinder instead of the lens pointed at the subject and the real lens therefore directed upwards, film developers often reported returning rolls of film to customers containing twelve images of out-of-focus noses.

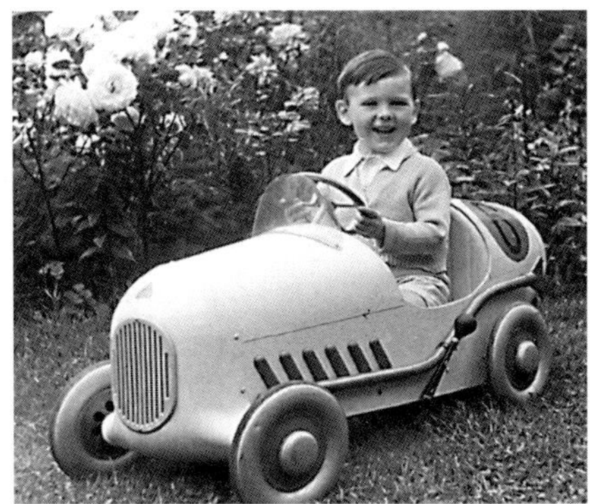

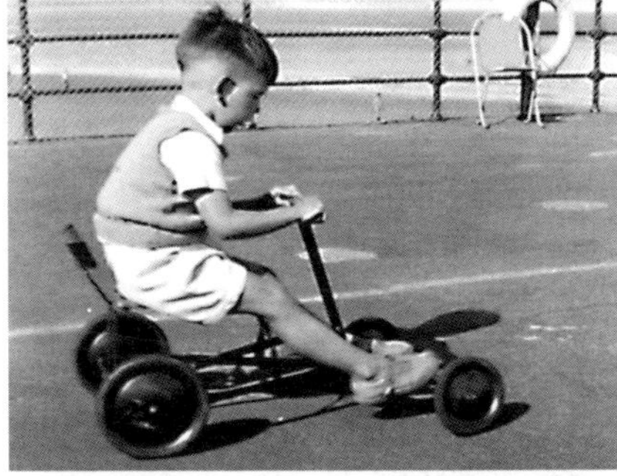

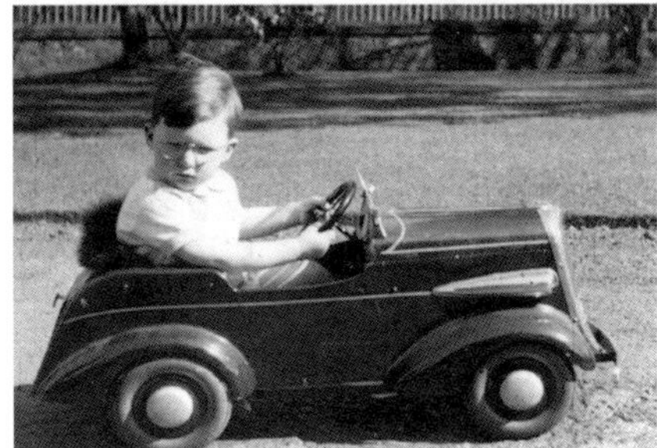

Pedal cars and the little boys (not so much little girls) who drove them have always been keen subjects for parents with snapshot cameras.

Kodak Bantam Colorsnap

By the middle of the 1950s and on into the 1960s, as more families began to own cameras, the demand for something a little more sophisticated than the average snapshot type of model began to spread. Snapshot photographers might have looked at the kinds of cameras used by their more serious photographer friends and thought, 'I'd like a camera like that.' What they meant of course was a camera that looked more professional, but which still retained the snapshot photographer's demand for ease of use. It was this ethos that was likely to have

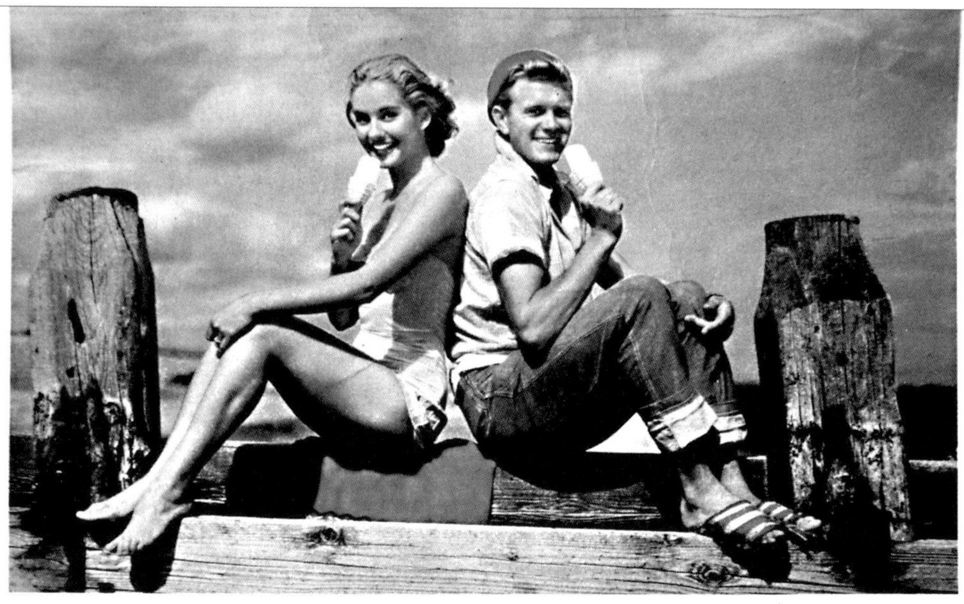

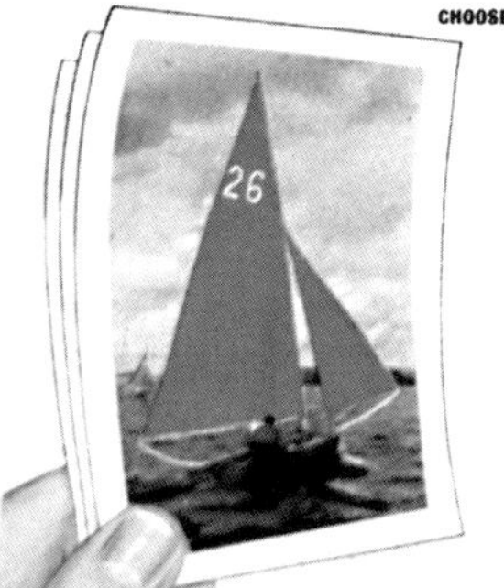

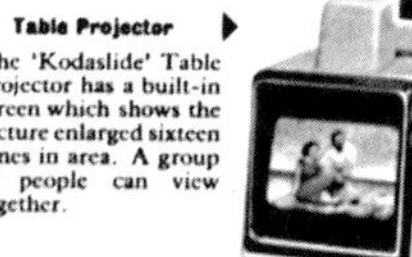

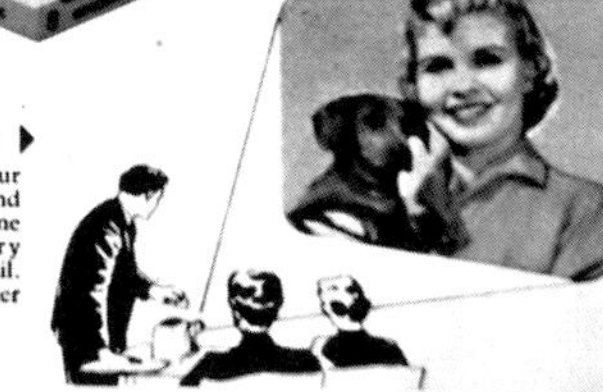

How Kodak advertised the Colorsnap.

led Kodak to produce the Bantam Colorsnap cameras, which true to their name were aimed at snapshot photographers who wanted a simple way of shooting colour pictures for the first time. To quote a Kodak advertisement…

Capture colour with the Kodak Bantam Colorsnap camera. Just press the button. For years, some lucky people have been able to take colour pictures of their holidays and good times. Now you can too. Kodak have designed the Bantam Colorsnap camera to take the technicalities out of colour. There's no need to have used a camera in your life before. Simply load the Colorsnap camera with Kodachrome – the famous colour film – in convenient eight-exposure rolls. Follow the simple instructions built right into the camera back. Then press the button. Your pictures come out with every lovely colour just as you saw them in real life.

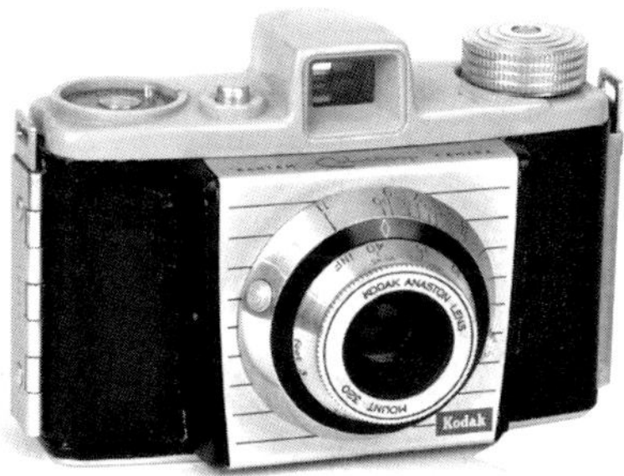

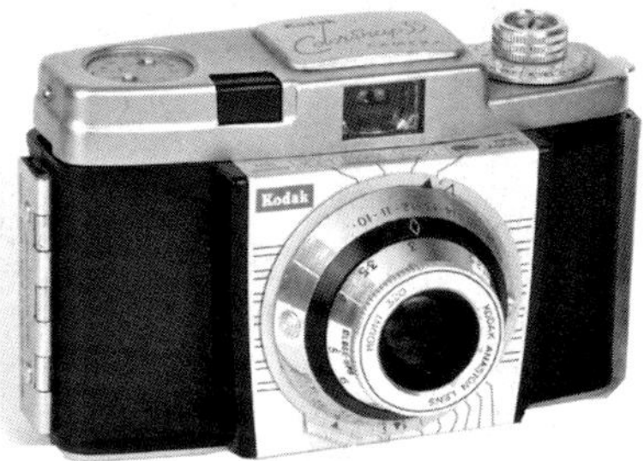

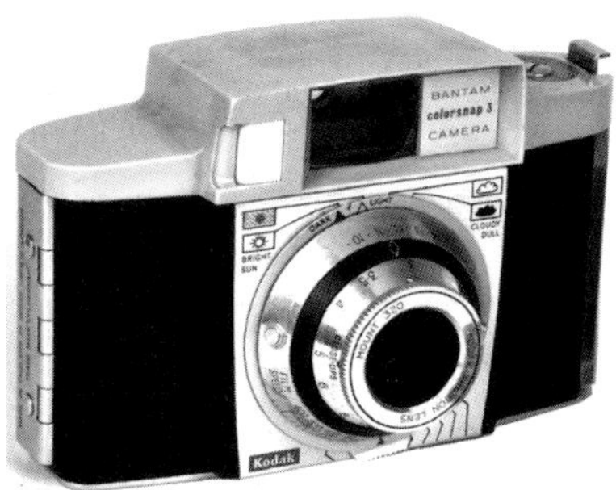

Top to bottom: the original Colorsnap, Colorsnap 35 and Colorsnap 3.

The first Colorsnap camera was launched in 1955 and, despite the Americanisation of the name (no 'U' in 'Color'), it was made by Kodak in England. Its purpose was something that had been dear to the heart of Kodak ever since its first camera, made back in 1888: to simplify the photographic process and bring easy ways of getting good results to people who might not otherwise have thought of buying a camera. In this case, Kodak's aim was to introduce non-technical, inexpert photographers to the wonders of Kodachrome, its famous colour slide film that had been around in 35mm form since 1935, but which was hitherto seen only as the domain of the professional or serious amateur photographer.

The Colorsnap was a metal-bodied camera with a moulded plastic top plate that featured a viewfinder in the centre directly over the lens, a film wind knob at one end and a film type reminder dial at the other, beside the shutter release. When the release was pressed to take a picture, it remained down until the film was wound, thus preventing more than one exposure on the same piece of film, a common mistake among snapshot photographers.

The film was the same size as 35mm, but without the sprocket holes and with backing paper, rolled onto a small spindle. It was known as 828 size, and it shot eight pictures to a roll, each one 30×40mm.

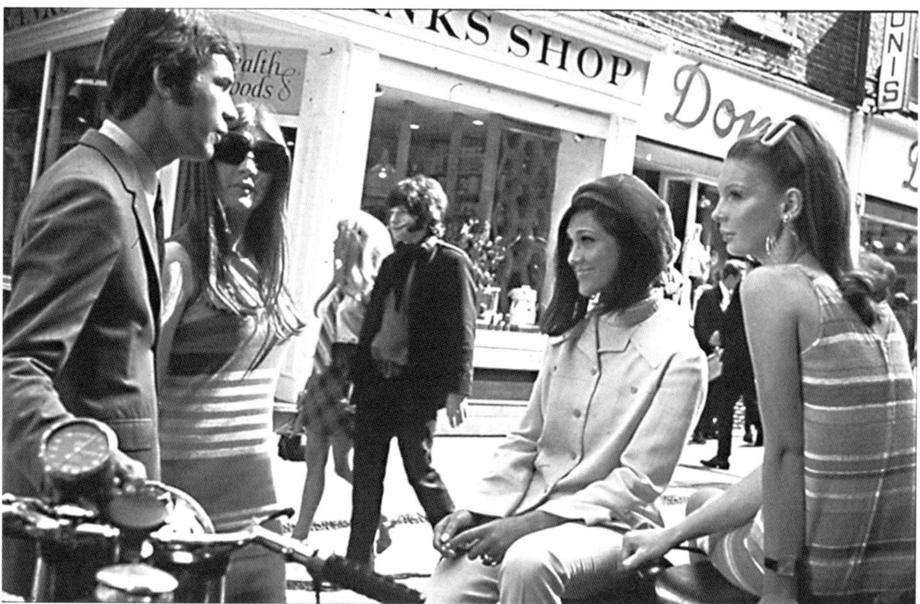

They called it the Swinging Sixties, a time when a youth-driven cultural revolution erupted throughout the land, emanating principally from London for fashion and Liverpool for music. It was symbolised most notably by the emergence of new pop music and, most of all, fashion. This snapshot, unremarkable in itself in merely showing a group of young people talking in the street, actually says a lot about the era. Taken *c.*1966, the location is London's Carnaby Street, the epicentre of the era's fashion industry. The girls' miniskirts, the sharp lines of nearer boy's suit, the perfectly acceptable long hair of the man in the background, all contribute to what was probably a casually taken snapshot, but one that could not have come from any other decade.

The Colorsnap's lens actually had ten different apertures, but in the knowledge that f-stop aperture numbers used in more serious cameras might have confused the snapshot photographer, these were simply designated in what Kodak called light setting numbers. The lowest number indicated when the aperture was at its smallest setting, the highest number indicated a wide-open setting. Although there were only ten apertures, there were actually eleven numbers. This was because the shutter speed was fixed for the vast majority of subjects at 1/50 second. But when light levels were really low and the maximum aperture indicated by light setting 10 wasn't enough, then turning the setting to 11 dropped the shutter speed to 1/25 second, doubling the time it remained open and allowing in just a little more light. The lens needed to be focused, and for this it was rotated in the usual way against distances marked from 3ft to infinity. But engraved alongside the distances, the camera added suggested settings for 'close-ups' at 5ft, 'groups' at 15ft and 'views' at 40ft. So that helped the inexperienced photographer to focus correctly on the subject.

With exposure controlled only by adjustment of the light setting numbers, an exposure calculator on the back of the camera helped the inexperienced photographer get the best pictures. It took the form of a rotating disc on which three subject types – light, average and dark – were set against four weather conditions. These were designated as: Clear Sun (strong shadows), Hazy Sun (soft shadows), Cloudy Bright (little shadows) and Cloudy Dull (no shadows). As the disc was rotated to the appropriate setting, a pointer on the other side indicated the correct light setting number, depending on whether Kodachrome colour film or black and white film was loaded.

So, for the snapshot photographer who knew little about photography, taking his or her first colour picture on Kodachrome amounted to no more than turning the focusing ring to one of three settings, matching the exposure calculator settings against the subject, reading off a number, setting this on the light value ring and pressing the shutter button.

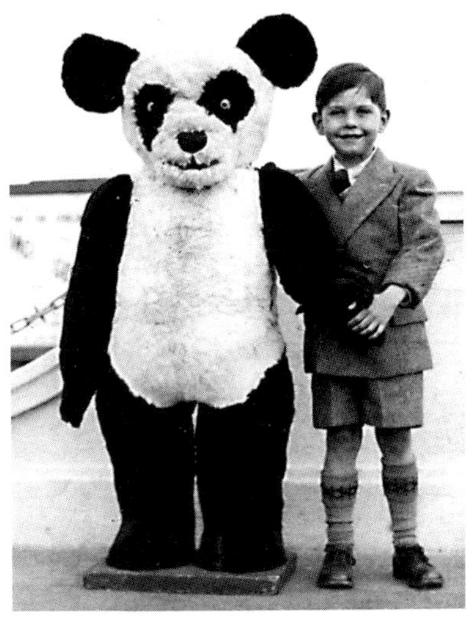

Professional photographers took snapshots too. Roaming seaside resorts, they used their own props to encourage punters, or more likely their children, to be photographed. Although professionally taken, the picture is very much in the spirit of the snapshot.

The first camera was followed in 1959 by the Colorsnap 35, which took 35mm film, and replaced the exposure calculator on the back of the body with a simpler version on a ring around the lens. In 1961, a new improved version called the Colorsnap 3 returned to the use of 828 size film. Colorsnap cameras did a great deal towards introducing snapshot photographers to the wonders of colour photography. The cameras remained in production until 1963 and continued to be used for many years more.

Other snapshot cameras

This era of photography introduced a great many more makes and types of snapshot cameras than space allows to be listed here. What follows, then, is a short overview of some of the more unusual and different types of snapshot camera available from around the world during this period. It proved to be a time when snapshot camera evolution in general began to veer away from roll film and start to use 35mm film to produce far more exposures to a roll.

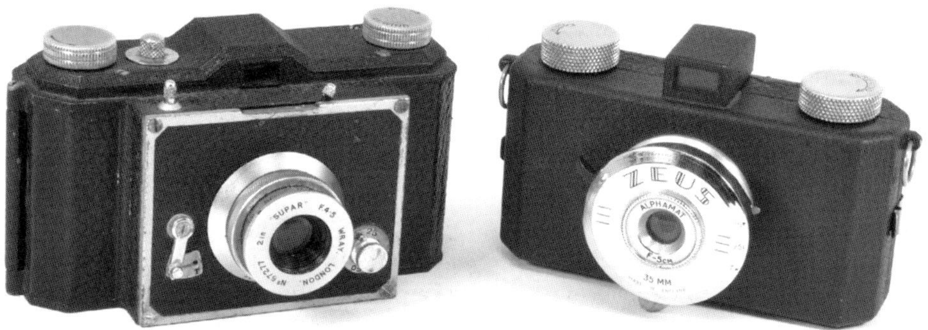

Two British rarities: the Owl (left) and Zeus.

British Owl and Zeus cameras

The Owl is generally thought to have been the first 35mm camera produced in England. It was a solidly built metal camera with a simple viewfinder built into the top of the body and only a few basic controls for snapshot photographers to worry about. Only six cameras were made around 1946 to test the market, but dealers found it too heavy and far too basic, compared to most pre-war German 35mm models, and the camera never went into full production.

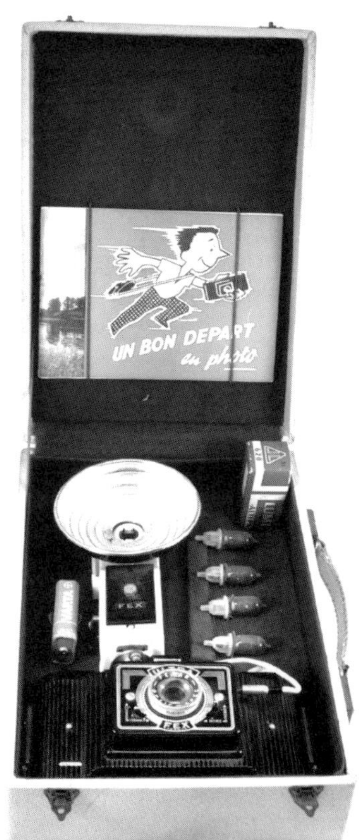

A French Ultra Fex outfit.

Considering Zeus was one of the more powerful Greek mythology gods, in charge of the sky and thunder, the British-made camera named after him was a rather mild affair. Although an attractive design with a brown metal crackle finish, the camera was very basic with only a choice of two shutter speeds to aid exposure setting. Relatively few cameras were made during the 1950s and today the Zeus is considered extremely rare.

French Fex cameras

The French Fex company made simple snapshot type cameras from the 1940s until the early 1980s. Among the best was the Ultra-Fex, introduced in 1946 with a distinctive Art Deco designed Bakelite body. The panel supporting the lens and shutter pulled forward from the body on a shiny metal tube and two small sliding knobs either side of the lens were its only controls. One gave a choice of two shutter speeds, the other offered two apertures related to weather conditions, which it designated as 'normal' and 'intense'. The camera took eight exposures 6×9cm on 120 size film. It was sold in a neat wooden case that had space for the camera, flashgun, battery for the flashgun, flashbulbs, film and a small booklet of instructions. The wording on the front of the booklet summed up the snapshot market at which the camera was aimed: *Un bon depart en photo* (a good start in photography). Other cameras made by the company included the Superfex, Sport-Fex, Élite-Fex and Ultra-Reflex.

Italian Bencini Comet cameras

From 1948 and into the 1950s, the Bencini company in Italy produced a range of very simple, metal-bodied, snapshot cameras that used 127 size film to shoot 3×4cm and 4×4cm pictures. They were made under the name Comet to feature the simple, basic controls favoured by snapshot photographers, and their design was pretty much conventional. Then in 1953, in a complete departure from their normal style, Bencini produced the Comet III with an unusual vertically styled body. Despite appearing to be a 35mm camera – and even looking a little like a small cine camera of the day – it actually produced sixteen exposures 3×4cm on 127 size roll film. A single speed shutter was released by a relatively large, chunky lever at the top of one side of the body. The Comet III was the camera for those who wanted to be seen with something a little different and more stylish than the average snapshot camera.

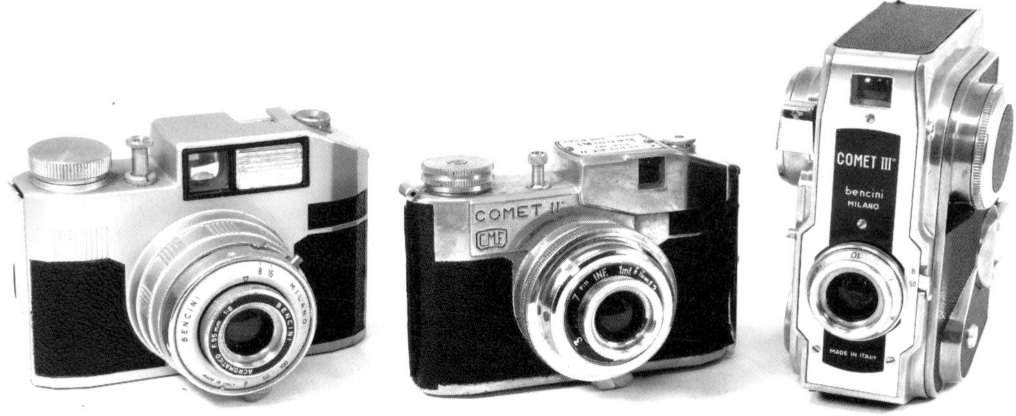

The Italian Bencini Comet III (right) with two more traditionally styled Comet cameras from the same maker.

Duoflex

Between 1949 and 1955, Kodak produced this camera, which shared its viewfinding methods with the then current, and aforementioned, Brownie Reflex and Ensign Ful-Vue: one lens to take the picture and another above it to reflect a brighter-than-normal view into a large magnifying viewfinder on the top of the body. It was a system that attracted snapshot photographers away from the small and difficult-to-use viewfinders more associated with box cameras of the past. Utilising basic snapshot camera controls, it shot twelve square pictures on 620 size film, the same as the more popular 120 size, but wound onto slimmer spindles to allow for more compact camera designs.

Donald Duck Camera

Made in America and available immediately after the Second World War, this was a very basic camera, made of plastic, to take twelve pictures 4×4cm on 127 size film. It took its name from engravings moulded into the plastic on the back of the body, showing Donald Duck photographing his three nephews, Huey, Dewey and Louie. The red window through which film numbers were read was surrounded by rays resembling a child's drawing of the sun. Early models were made in an olive colour; later, the body was changed to black.

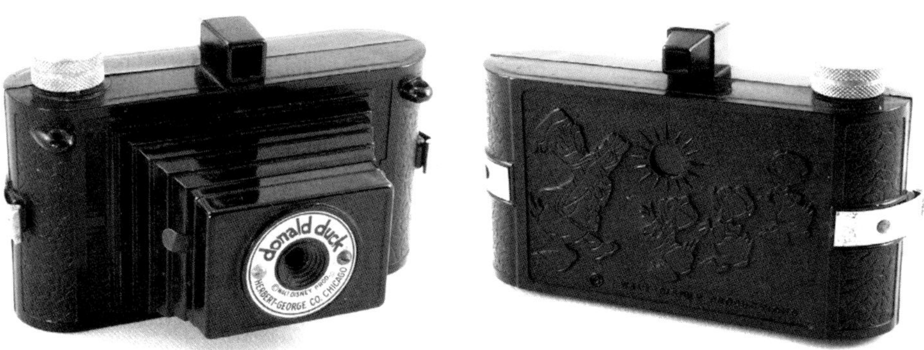

Front and back: the American Donald Duck Camera.

Hit cameras

The original Hit camera was little more than a toy, a remarkably small camera that measured only 5×3×3cm to be easily hidden in the palm of a hand. Aperture, shutter speed and focus were fixed, meaning all the snapshot photographer needed to do was point it, squint through its tiny viewfinder and press a lever on the side. It shot 14×14mm size pictures on miniature rolls of film 17.5mm

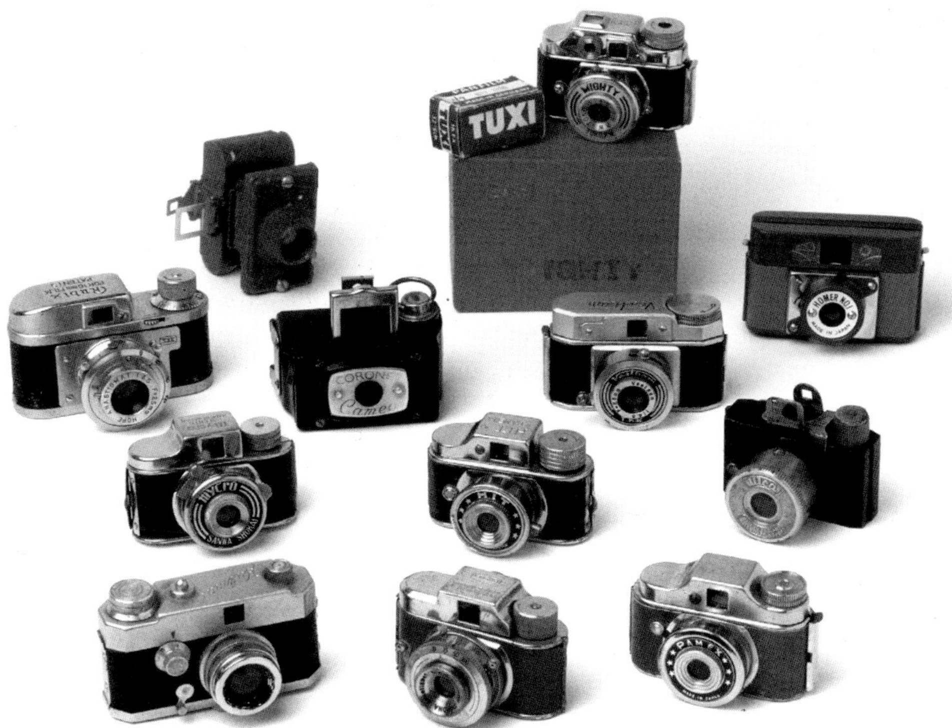

Just some of the many variants of Hit-type cameras.

wide film with backing paper and exposure numbers to be read through a red window on the back of the camera. Made by Tougodo Optical in Japan, it was launched in 1950 and soon became one of the most copied cameras ever, with versions made under a huge variety of names throughout the world. Variants included the Corona, Mighty, Beauty, Peace, Click, Kolt, Midget, Minetta, Sputnik… and many more too numerous to mention. The best of the original and true Hit cameras was one made in gold. Snapshot photographers who bought them soon tired of the low quality images and the difficulty of getting films processed. In the end, Hit-type cameras were treated as little more than an interesting novelty.

Wembley Sports

First made in 1950 by Truvox, whose factory was based at Wembley in North London, the Wembley Sports was one of the era's uglier cameras. It was made of Bakelite and characterised by a huge lens assembly that needed to be screwed out of the front of the body before a picture could be taken. A limited range of shutter speeds and apertures were available and it took eight 6×9cm pictures on 120 size film.

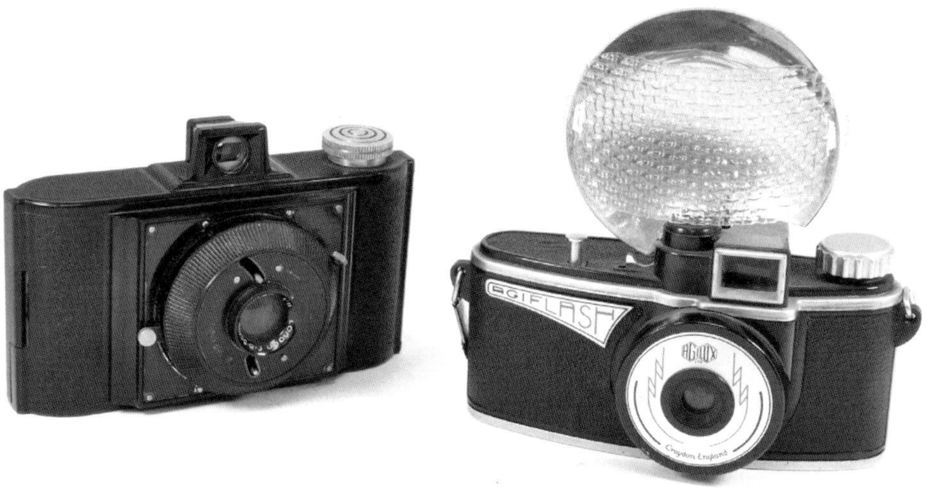

Two unusual English cameras: Wembley Sports (left) and Agiflash.

Agiflash

The Art Deco look of the Agiflash was a little dated by the time the camera was introduced in 1954. Nevertheless, it presented a sleek, smart-looking design that appealed to snapshot photographers who might want to be seen with something a little different. All the usual controls were fixed for simplicity of use and a large flashgun could be attached to the top for pictures taken indoors. It shot eight pictures to a roll of 127 size film.

Alfa

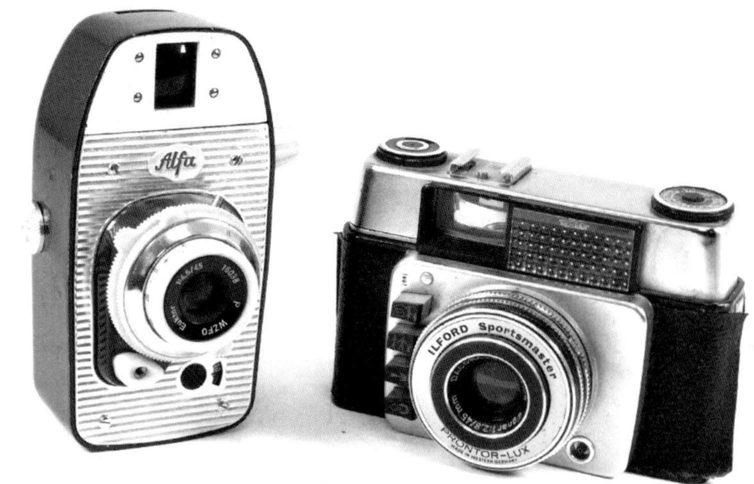

The Polish Alfa (left) with the Ilford Sportsmaster, made in Germany for the British Ilford company.

Not may cameras were made in Poland, and not many cameras looked like the unusual but attractive Alfa. This was a vertically styled 35mm model, made of metal and enamelled in three colours – dark and light blue, plus red – each coupled with a cream trim and with an aluminium faceplate. Within a few years of its launch in 1960, the Alfa-2 was produced, with a different lens, some minor modifications and two extra colours – cream and light green – added to the range.

Sportsmaster

For snapshot photographers who wanted a simple way to focus a lens without having to worry about estimating distance from the camera to the subject, the Sportsmaster, made in Germany for the British Ilford company, had an unusual answer. It featured four shutter buttons, each identified by a symbol and focusing distance. The symbols showed a diagrammatic head and shoulders for 5ft, a full-length person for 8ft, a group of two adults and a child for 13ft and people in front of a house and mountains for infinity. As well as firing the shutter, each button also set the lens to the appropriate focusing distance. By 1961, when the Sportsmaster was released, automation was beginning to appear in snapshot cameras, and this one also incorporated a built-in exposure meter to measure and set the correct exposure.

Novelty cameras

The 1980s and 1990s saw an explosion of highly colourful novelty cameras for snapshot photographers. Some were designed to promote products like Coca-Cola, Kraft cheese or Hershey chocolate bars and might have been used

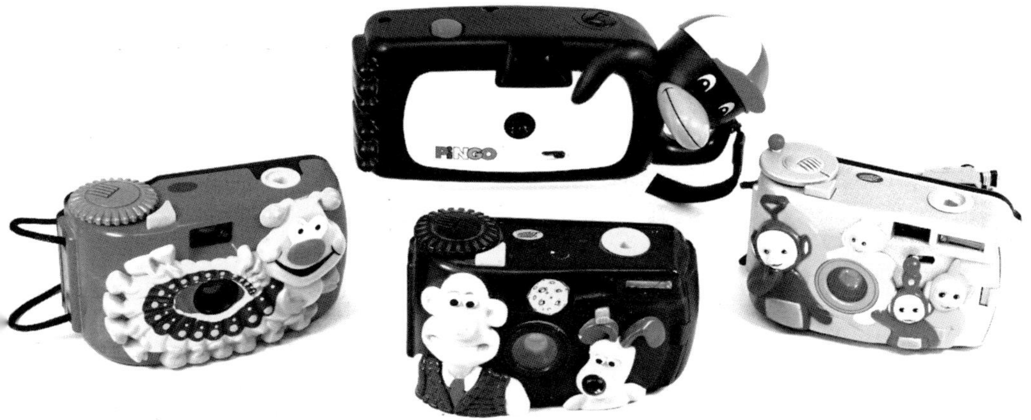

Some of the many novelty cameras aimed principally at children.

by any snapshot photographer who wanted something a little offbeat. The majority, however, were aimed directly at children and decorated with both well-known and lesser-known characters from children's books and cartoons. Thomas the Tank Engine was seen on a talking camera that, at the press of a button, explained, 'Hello, I'm a Thomas talking camera, let's take some pictures,' followed by a train whistle. Cartoon characters that adorned a whole range of basic plastic 35mm cameras included Pingo the Penguin, Wallace and Gromit, the Tellytubbies and much more. Boots, the British chemist chain, was paticularly fond of launching similar cameras covered in lions, tigers, pandas, bears and other animals. The craze for these novelty cameras lasted right up to, and into the early years of, the digital age.

The coming of automation

Snapshot photographers favoured simple cameras for two reasons. First, they didn't consider themselves to be 'real' photographers and had no desire to learn the intricacies of how focusing was affected by apertures, or how apertures needed to be adjusted in conjunction with shutter speeds… and more besides. The second reason was that what might be termed 'real' cameras were very expensive compared to simpler snapshot models. However, by the 1960s, those who could afford a more sophisticated camera but who nonetheless preferred to stick with simplicity of operation began to find their needs catered for by the arrival of automation.

Juggling the combinations of shutter speeds with apertures to set the correct exposure was always a problem for the inexperienced photographer. The simplest snapshot cameras got round that by fixing the settings and then telling users to only use the camera in bright sunlight. In poor light, snapshot photographers would get a poor result, although they were so indoctrinated by the snapshot rule of only shooting when the sun was behind them, it's likely that snapshot photography was rarely attempted without some sign of strong sunlight, and never indoors.

Exposure automation that began to appear in the 1960s went some way to solving this problem. At first cameras provided built-in exposure meters to control a needle that had to be matched to a fixed indicator as apertures and shutter speeds were changed, at which point the required exposure was correct. Then priority automation arrived which meant the photographer could choose an aperture and the camera would select the correct shutter speed, or shutter priority in which the photographer selected a shutter speed and left it to the camera to set the correct aperture. Even this, however, demanded some knowledge of what both apertures and shutter speeds actually did and how best to use the right ones for the subject in hand. Eventually, programmed automation arrived, which meant the camera's inbuilt meter would select and set both shutter speed and aperture. After that, it only remained to automate the process of focusing the lens on the subject, and that eventually arrived in 1977 with the launch of a camera called the Konica C35AF.

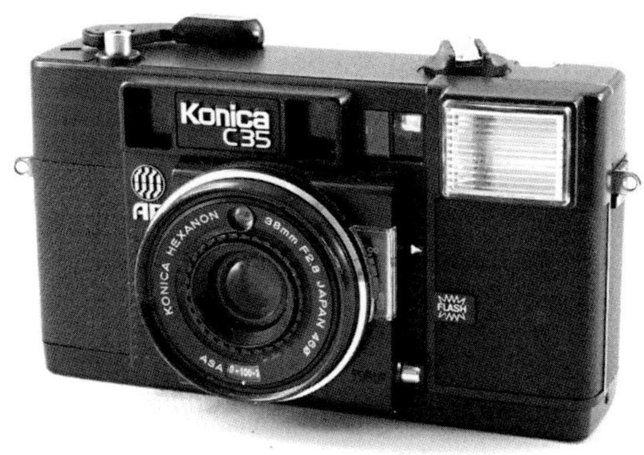

The Konica's automation used two mirrors, one stationary, the other pivoting, together with a prism that reflected twin images from the two mirrors onto a focusing sensor. As the shutter release was pressed, the pivoting

The Konica C35AF, the first camera to offer automatic focusing, on top of what had become the expected automatic exposure control, plus a built-in flash. The internal electronics might have been complicated, but using the camera for even the most inexperienced snapshot photographer was now about as simple as it was possible to get.

mirror began to turn, and the focusing sensor recognised where the images from the two mirrors coincided as the point where image contrast was at its greatest. At the same time, the lens was travelling from infinity to close focusing. When the sensor recognised the point of highest contrast, a solenoid was activated, which stopped the lens at the appropriate focusing distance. All this happened in 80 milliseconds. Apart from the revolutionary autofocus system, the C35AF also featured automatic exposure control and a built-in flashgun for low light conditions or for shooting indoors.

For inexperienced photographers who could afford something more than a simple snapshot camera, who wanted better results in all kinds lighting and didn't want the bother of even having to focus the lens, snapshot photography would never be quite the same again.

Chapter 11

The Instamatic Years

By the start of the 1960s, there were plenty of snapshot cameras around that made pointing and shooting without too much thought simple for even the least experienced photographer. With the advance of electronics and automatic exposure control, simple-to-use cameras also yielded better results than ever before. So getting good results with the minimum of technical knowledge was easy. Loading the camera with film was a different matter. It involved a perceived intricacy that many still found daunting, and photo shop assistants still found themselves faced with customers requesting, 'Please can you unload my camera and reload it with a new film.' In 1963, Kodak solved that problem at a stroke with the introduction of Instamatic cameras.

The first Instamatics

The film for Kodak Instamatic cameras came in plastic Kodapak cartridges. It was 35mm wide, wound with backing paper containing frame numbers to produce 28×28mm images. But the important thing for snapshot photographers was that they had only to open the camera back, drop in the cartridge, snap the back shut and start shooting. The cartridge was made so that it was impossible to insert it in any way other than the correct one. Advertisements of the time were keen to sing the praises of Kodak's new system: 'No more threading or fumbling… you can load the Instamatic in three seconds and in broad daylight.'

The film size was known as 126 and it was a great success, thanks partly to the way Kodak allowed other manufacturers to make their own cameras to take Kodapak cartridges – hence more film sales for Kodak, even though other manufacturers were also allowed to make their own cartridge films. Officially, however, the word 'Instamatic' could only apply to Kodak products. Anyone in those days who referred in print to an Agfa Instamatic was liable to get an angry letter from Kodak.

Kodak Instamatics and the similarly designed, but differently named, versions made by other manufacturers revolutionised snapshot photography as more and more people found they could now load their own cameras and shoot good quality pictures with a newfound ease.

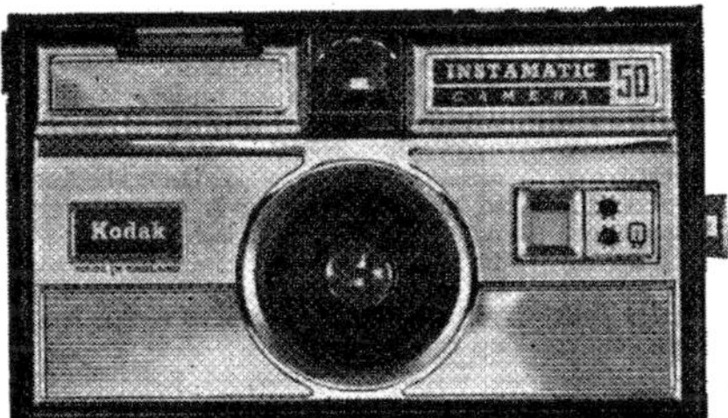
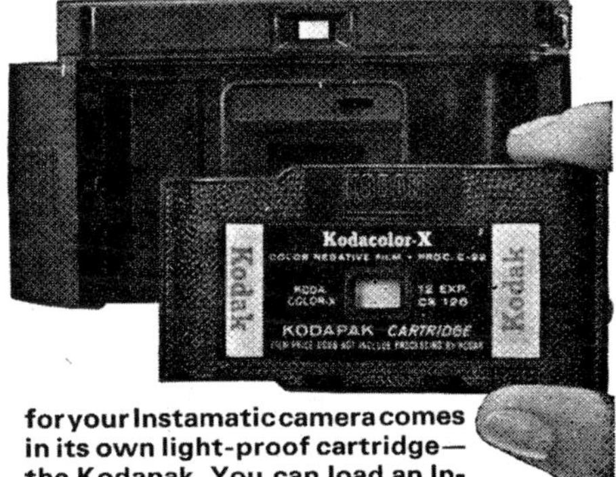

A Kodak advertisement shows how easy and fast it was to load the company's new Instamatic cameras.

Kodak ushered in this new era of snapshot photography with the introduction of four new cameras: the Kodak Instamatic 50, 100, 300 and 400. The Instamatic 50 was the simplest. It featured a fixed focus lens but offered two exposure settings changed by a sliding control beside the lens that indicated the light

How the Kodapak
cartridge of film
dropped into the back
of a Kodak Instamatic
camera.

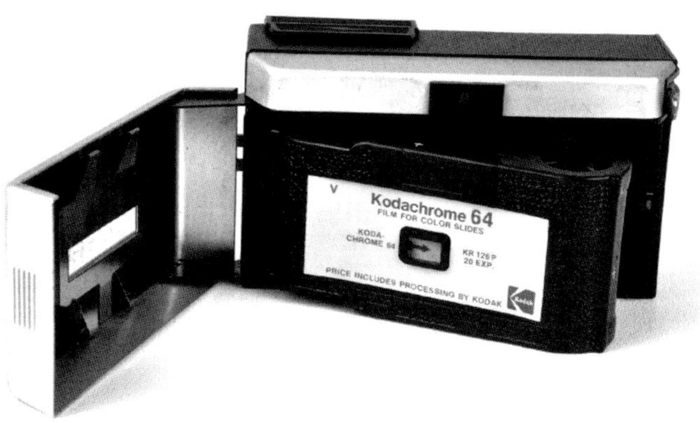

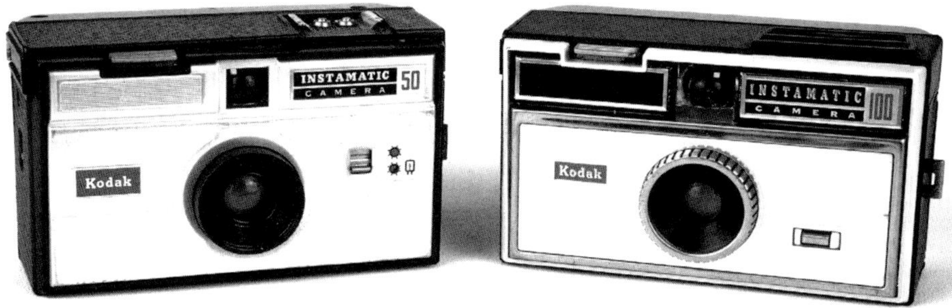

The Kodak Instamatic 50 (left) and 100 were two of the earliest 126 cartridge cameras.

conditions by use of symbols showing a full sun and a partly obscured sun. The latter setting was also used for flash photography, courtesy of a special accessory that took flashcubes and fitted into a slot on the camera that made the necessary electrical connections to the shutter. The shutter release was recessed into the top of the body, and film wind was by a lever. The other three cameras launched along with the Instamatic 50 offered a few extras. The Instamatic 100 had a built-in pop-up flashgun for flashbulbs, the Instamatic 300 added an exposure meter that helped control the correct exposure and the Instamatic

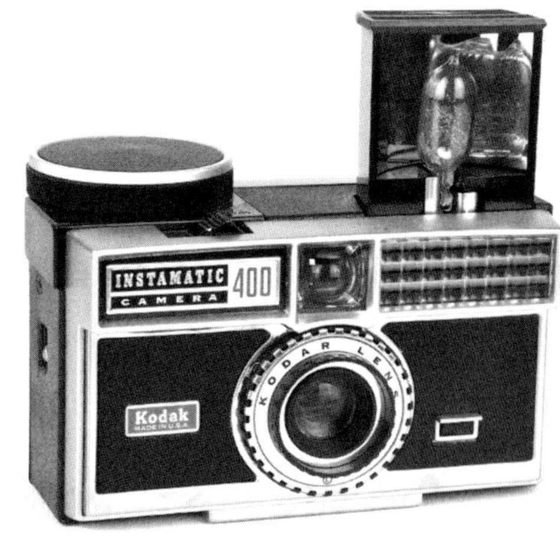

Kodak Instamatic 400, one of the more sophisticated Instamatics, with auto exposure, built-in flashgun and clockwork motor drive.

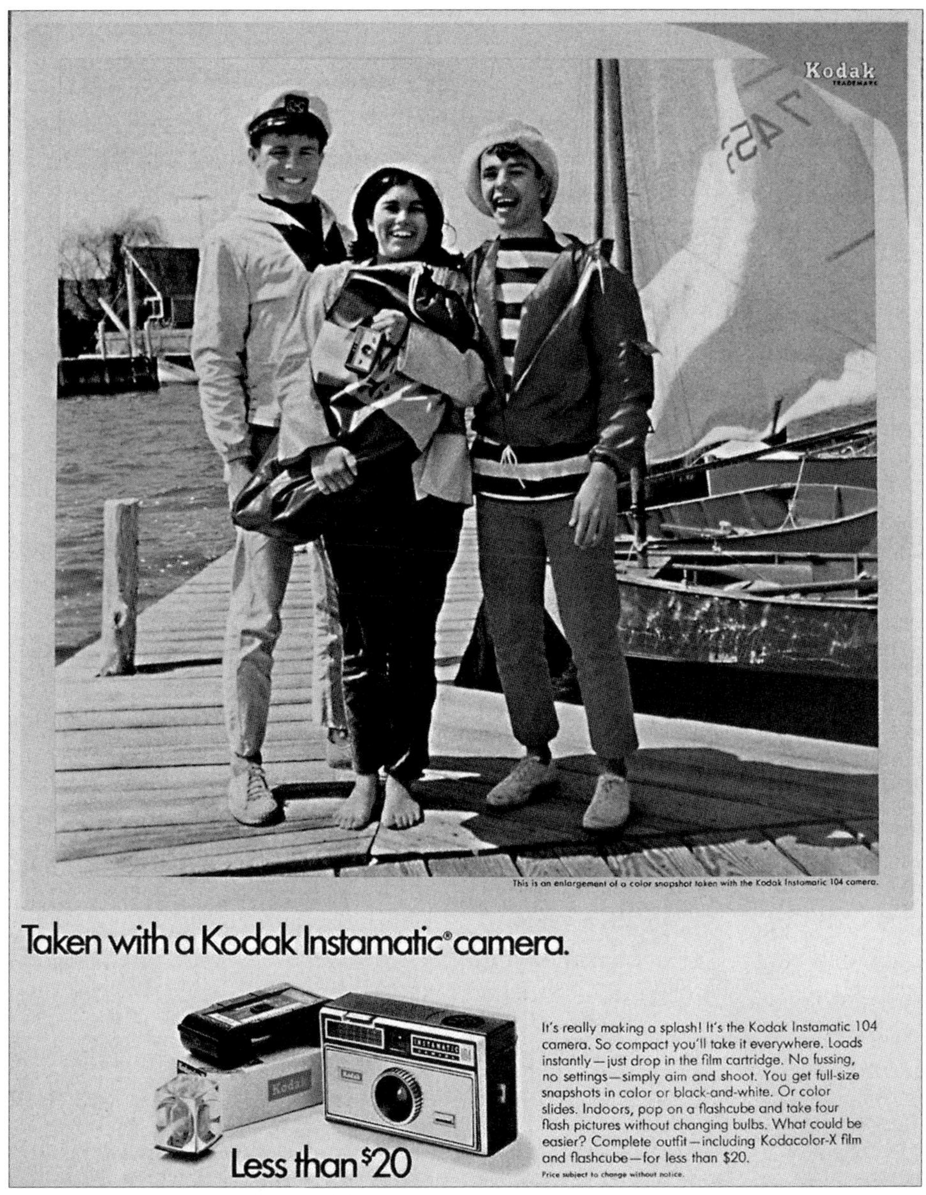

A Kodak Instamatic advertisement for the early cameras illustrates the film's square format.

400 incorporated a clockwork motor that automatically wound the film after each exposure.

For the next ten years, literally hundreds of Instamatic-type cameras flooded onto the market. Kodak alone made more than sixty different models.

ADVERTISEMENT

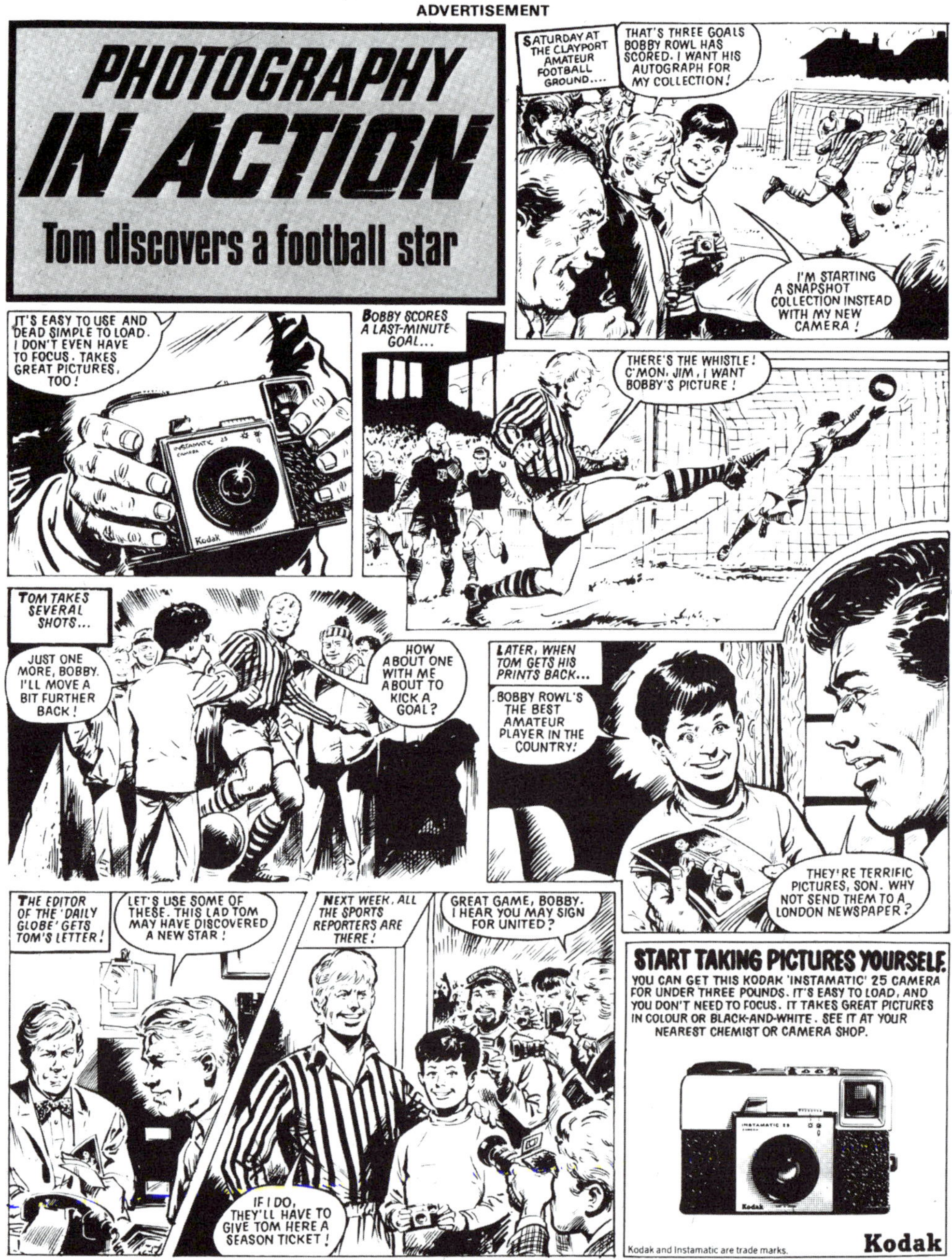

A Kodak advertisement from the days when Instamatic cameras were popular illustrates how easy it was for children to use one.

Other makers

The rise of cameras to take 126 cartridge film, originally introduced by Kodak for its own Instamatic cameras, coincided with the introduction of electronics into cameras, chiefly in the shape of inbuilt exposure meters that measured and set the correct exposure, something that particularly appealed to snapshot photographers. As an example of how the new film revolutionised snapshot camera design, here are just two cameras from non-Kodak manufacturers who took a different look at the concept.

The Minolta Autopak 800 from 1969 was the top of a range of similar Autopak cameras. It featured two shutter speeds for daylight shooting or for flash photography and its apertures were controlled automatically. A flashcube mounted on the top plate could be left in place and only fired when light levels demanded it. Batteries were used for the flash, meter and automatic settings, but the film was wound by a clockwork motor, tensioned by a large knob on the end of the body.

The Ricoh Auto 126, made in 1970, was another 126 film camera with a built-in clockwork motor drive, wound by a knob on the base of the body. Exposure was fully automatic, while focus was adjusted by both a distance scale and pictograms. A flip-up flashgun was built into the top plate.

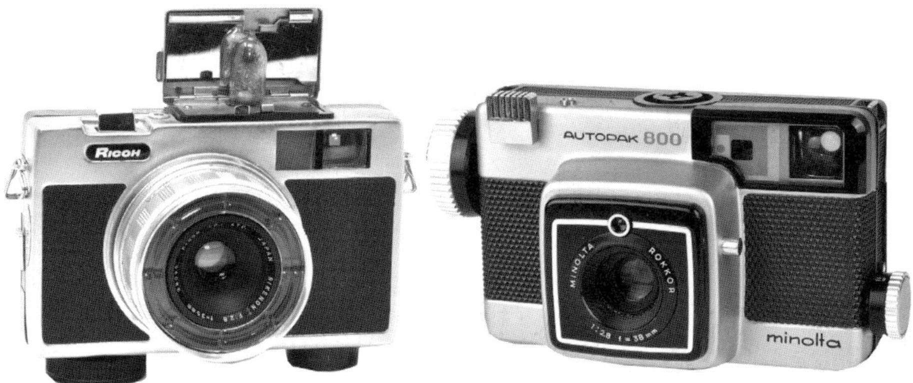

Two of the more unusual 126 cartridge cameras from non-Kodak manufacturers: Ricoh Auto 126 (left) and Minolta Autopak 800.

Mickey and Snoopy

The ease of use that resulted from the introduction of 126 cartridge film cameras opened up a new market for cameras aimed at children, as manufacturers began making cameras in new shapes and styles that would appeal to younger snapshot photographers. Here are two.

The Mick-A-Matic, made in 1971 by Child Guidance Products in America, was in the shape of Mickey Mouse's head with a lens in his nose, a viewfinder in the middle of his forehead and a place for a flashcube on top of his head. In early models, the shutter was released by pulling an ear; later models had a separate lever to the side of the head. A label on the back of Mickey's ear instructed his owner: 'Treat me gently, I'm your pal.'

The Snoopymatic, made in 1980 by the American Helm Toy Corporation, was inspired by Charlie Brown's dog Snoopy in the *Peanuts* comic strip penned by cartoonist Charles Schulz. It was a simple snapshot camera that took the form of Snoopy's dog house with Snoopy himself lying on the roof. The shutter release was on one side of the body, the viewfinder window on the opposite side and the lens was in the door. A flashcube fitted in the chimney.

Pocket Instamatics

The Instamatic design popularised by Kodak was a tremendous success for the best part of a decade. Then, in 1972, Kodak introduced a new range of cameras called Pocket Instamatics. The new 110 size film they took was 16mm wide, enclosed in a long, narrow cartridge and had an image size of 13×17mm. With its introduction, other camera manufacturers began retooling for the latest Kodak film and before long, 110 film cameras ruled the world of snapshot photography.

Kodak produced a vast range of 110 cameras. As an example of this new type of snapshot model, the Pocket Instamatic 300 was just one of a raft of cameras. It used a fixed focus lens and a single fixed shutter

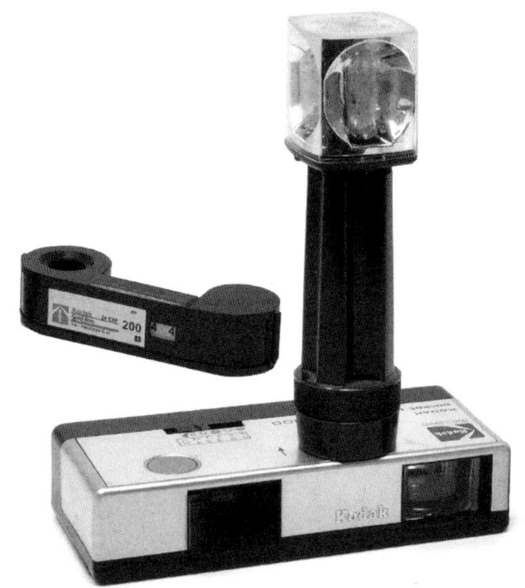

An early Pocket Instamatic 300, pictured with a 110 film cartridge and fitted with its flashcube extender, made to help eliminate redeye when shooting with flash.

speed, but offered a range of apertures controlled by a slider on top of the body, set against weather symbols. This version was made to accept flashcubes, which could be mounted at the top of a special extender that moved the flash away from the lens and so helped to reduce the effect of red eyes often seen in people shot with snapshot cameras using built-in flashguns.

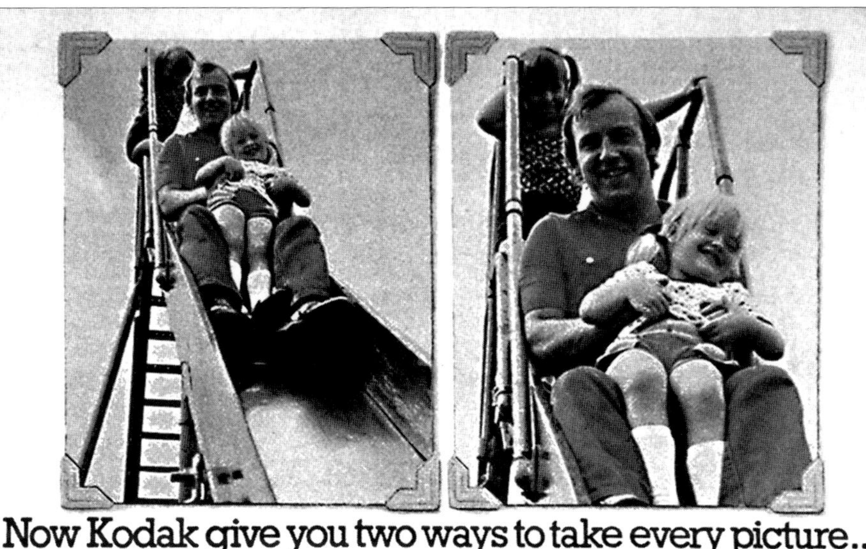

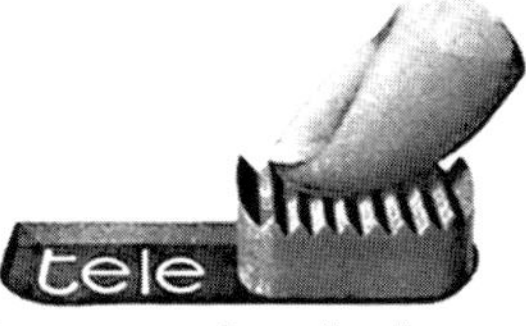

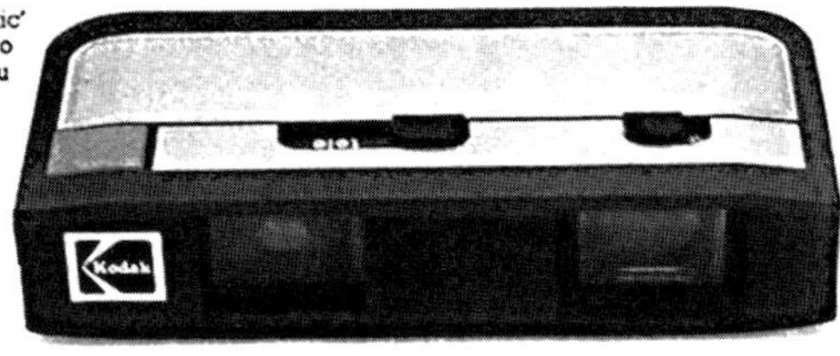

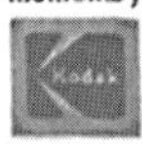

A new format arrived from Kodak with the introduction of the Pocket Instamatic series of cameras, and soon developed into more sophisticated models, as shown in this advertisement for a Kodak 110 camera that incorporated its own telephoto lens.

Other makers

As had been the case previously, the moment Kodak introduced the new snapshot format, other manufactures started tooling up to make their own versions. The cameras they produced were many and various, but here are just three examples that would have been of interest to and easy to use for snapshot photographers.

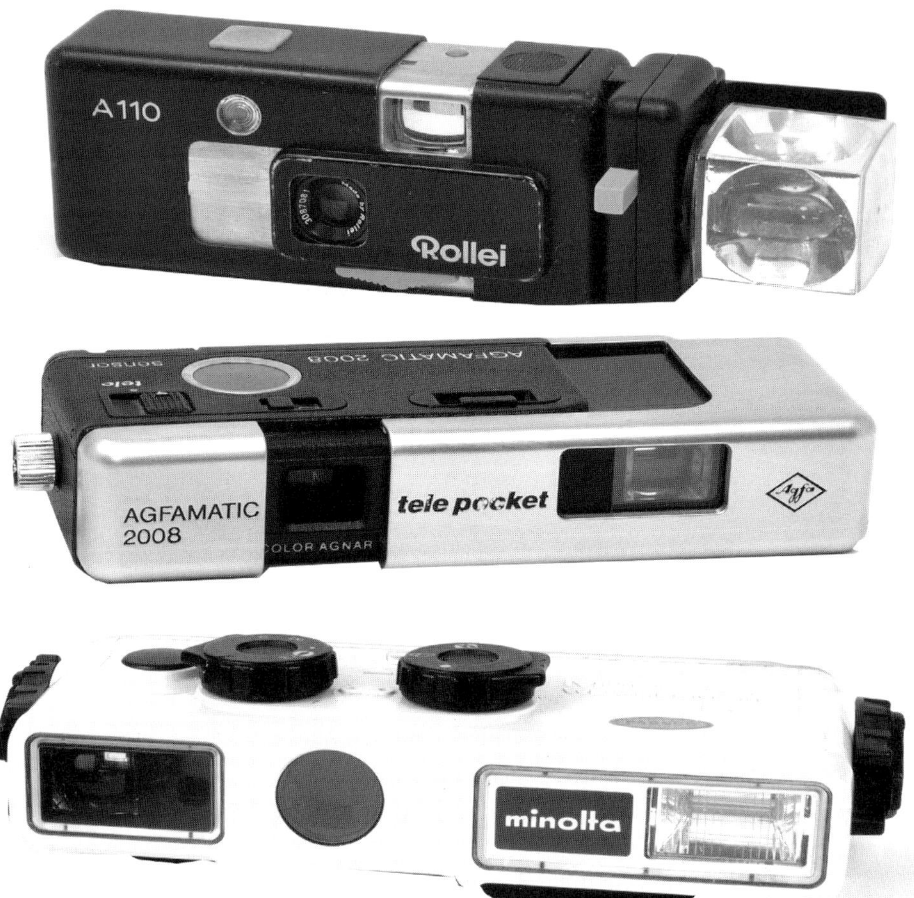

Three cameras made by non-Kodak manufacturers to take the 110 film cartridge. Top to bottom: Rollei A110, Agfamatic 2008 Tele Pocket and Minolta Weathermatic.

The Rollei name was mostly known as a maker of professional cameras, but with the introduction of 110 size film, the company turned to something a little simpler with the Rollei A110, made in 1975. It was one of the smallest and neatest of the well-specified 110 cameras, measuring just 8×4×2.5cm when folded, extending to 10cm for shooting. It was an all-electronic camera that incorporated an exposure meter to control programmed shutter speeds and apertures, while focus was adjusted by a slider beneath the lens. Although a sophisticated camera electronically, it was still very simple to use for snapshot photographers.

While adopting the traditional shape of a typical 110 film camera, the 1976 Agfamatic 2008 Tele Pocket added a few extra tricks. Prime among these was the option to slide in a second lens for telephoto photography.

Dull and bright pictograms on another slider made changing apertures simple. Film wind and shutter tensioning happened as the camera body was push-pulled to open and close it.

Launched in 1980, the bulky and rugged yellow case of the Minolta Weathermatic made it waterproof and capable of underwater use up to a depth of 5 metres for snapshot photographers who enjoyed underwater photography. A knob on the top adjusted focus according to five distance symbols; another beside it adjusted apertures according to three weather symbols; the shutter speed was fixed. The camera even incorporated a built-in flashgun.

Novelty cameras

Like the previous 126 film, the new 110 size lent itself to the novelty camera market with simple models for snapshot photographers that looked like anything but a camera.

The Tanross Supply company was formed in 1954 as a hardware and fishing tackle supplier. The name of the company was changed to Tasco when they diversified into binoculars. In 1980, the company built a pair of binoculars with a camera built in. It was called the Tasco Bino/Cam. The binoculars were used as the viewfinder, and the lens gave a telephoto effect to match the view. Shutter speeds were simplified as being marked '1' and '2'. Early models had fixed focus lenses, but later models allowed the lens to be interchanged for slightly wider and longer angles of view. Another, simpler, binocular camera for 110 film was made by the Japanese ITT company.

Drink cans were one of the favourite novelty disguises for simple 110 film cameras. Paint cans, beer cans and even insect repellent cans were also popular. There were two types. In the first, the lens and viewfinder looked out of one side of the can, with a film wind knob beneath and a shutter release recessed

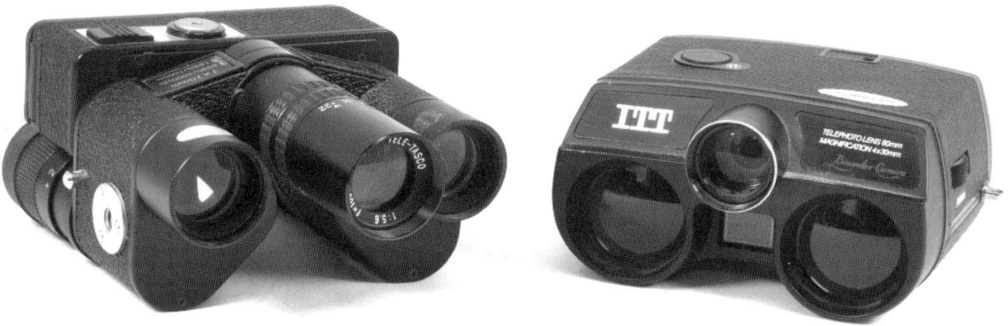

Two binocular-type snapshot cameras for 110 film: Tasco Bino/Cam (left) and ITT Binocular Camera.

further around the circumference. In the second type, part of the can hinged up to reveal the lens and a flashgun.

Other novelty 110 cameras were built into items that included a McDonald's pack of fries, miniature airliners, full-size cigarette packets, small tyres and tiny books. In the same era, Kodak joined forces with Disney to produce two novelty cameras called Mickey-Matics. Although little more than basic snapshot cameras, they were more attractive than most for featuring Mickey Mouse on the top plate and two finishes in pink or blue, aimed at girls or boys.

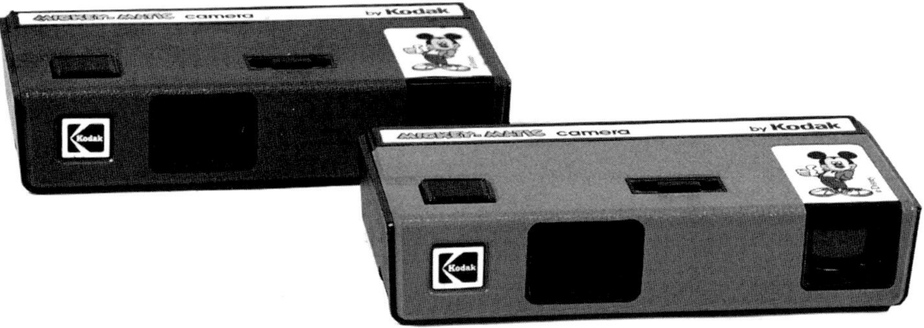

Mickey-Matic 110 cameras in pink and blue.

Disc cameras

In 1981, Kodak revamped the snapshot market yet again with an unusual new type of camera that took a new kind of film. It was called The Disc, and for a while, it was very popular with a new breed of snapshot photographer, even though it didn't have the staying power of the previous Instamatic and Pocket Instamatic cameras.

The Kodak Disc 4000, flagship of the first models to be launched and typifying the shape of Disc cameras from then on, took the form of a small, flat, black and silver box, measuring just 11.5×7.5×2cm. Pulling a lever on the top sprung the back open. It was

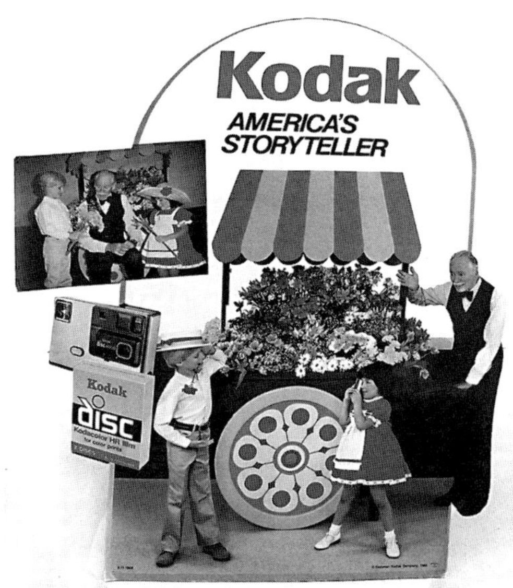

American publicity material that introduced Kodak's Disc cameras.

loaded with a flat cartridge containing a disc, around which fifteen frames of film were arranged, each one offering a 10.6×8.2mm image, less than half the

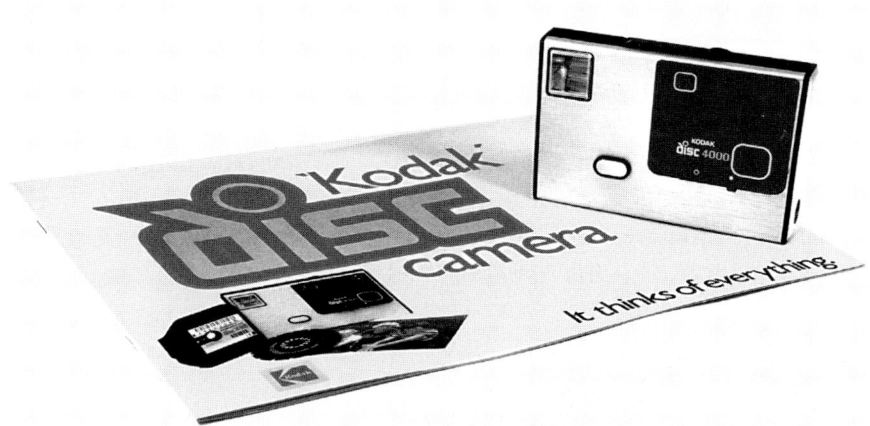

With a publicity brochure from 1982, the Disc 4000, flagship of the early Kodak cameras.

area size of a 110 film image, but still capable of good results on small prints. As the cartridge was loaded into the camera and the back closed, a micro-motor rotated the disc to bring the first frame behind the fixed focus lens.

All the photographer did was flip aside a small catch, which uncapped the lens and viewfinder, then fire the shutter by a button on the front. Exposure was automatic based on two shutter speeds. If the exposure system decided light levels were too low or the light needed balancing, then the flash fired automatically. After each exposure, the disc automatically rotated

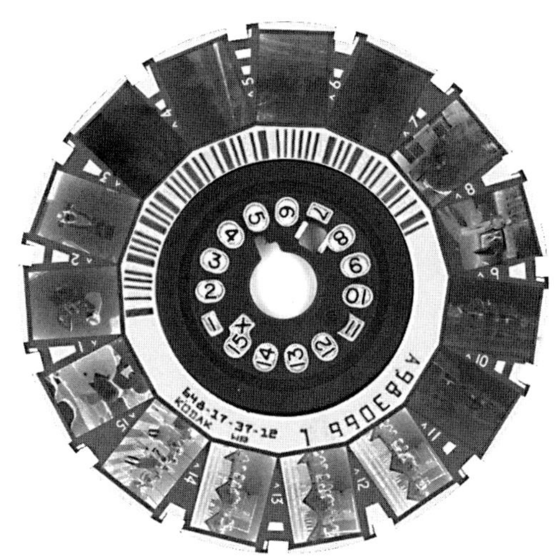

Disc film negatives after processing.

to bring the next frame of film behind the lens until all fifteen frames had been exposed. Frame numbers were read in a small window on the back of the body. Everything was powered by lithium cells, which were originally guaranteed for five years. Each film had its own unique serial number printed on the cartridge and also readable by the purpose-made film processor's computer. After processing, prints were returned with frame numbers and dates printed on the back for easy reference if extra prints were required.

Along with the Disc 4000, Kodak launched the less well-specified Disc 2000 and the slightly better specified Disc 6000. More than twenty more models followed with variations on the original design that included twin-lens cameras for standard and telephoto shooting, and cameras that accepted two AA batteries in place of the lithium cells.

Other makers

Manufacturers other than Kodak didn't jump onto the Disc bandwagon in quite the way they did with the two previous Instamatic cameras. Nevertheless, there were some other makers who took up the idea with enthusiasm and, with the way electronics had begun to appear in cameras by this time, they were all accessible to snapshot photographers without real experience of more traditional cameras. Minolta was one maker, other than Kodak, that really took the Disc concept seriously.

The Minolta Disc-5 was similar in design and specification to the Kodak Disc 4000. The Minolta Disc-7 added a macro mode for close-up photography and a self-timer. This later camera was also sold with a telescopic rod that screwed into a tiltable stand on the side of the camera body and incorporated a button to fire the shutter. In this way, the camera could be extended on the rod to shoot above the heads of crowds, or used to distance the camera from the photographer for a self-portrait, aided by a convex mirror beside the lens for posing purposes. Some years later the idea would re-emerge in the digital age to become known as selfie sticks.

When Minolta teamed up with French fashion designer André Courrèges, Disc cameras became style icons. Known for the way he incorporated modernism and futurism into his designs, Courrèges created new versions of Minolta's cameras. The Disc-5 became the AC 101 with a white body traversed by wavey lines in pastel colours of blue, green, light brown or pink. The

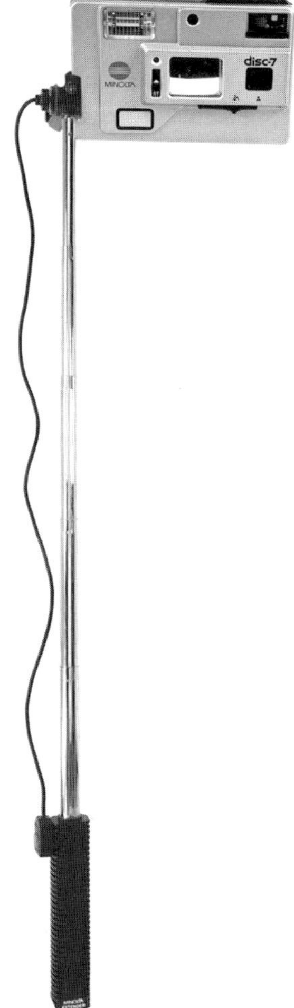
Minolta Disc 7 on its telescopic rod.

Disc-7 became the AC 301, also with a white body, but with gold fittings and tiny gold stylised versions of the designer's initials distributed around the front.

Konishiroku in Japan was another manufacturer that produced its own interpretation of the Disc design with two Konica cameras, one with a fixed focus, the other with an autofocus lens. Unlike most disc cameras, the Konica bodies slid apart to reveal the lens and viewfinder.

Other disc cameras included a collection badged by the photo dealer Dixons. Fujica also made a couple of cameras. Halina sold a neat little mechanical version that omitted the built-in flashgun, while using a single lever to fire the shutter and manually rotate the disc. A series of attractively coloured models were made under the Le Clic name, and a great many cameras were made by some of the more obscure camera manufacturers.

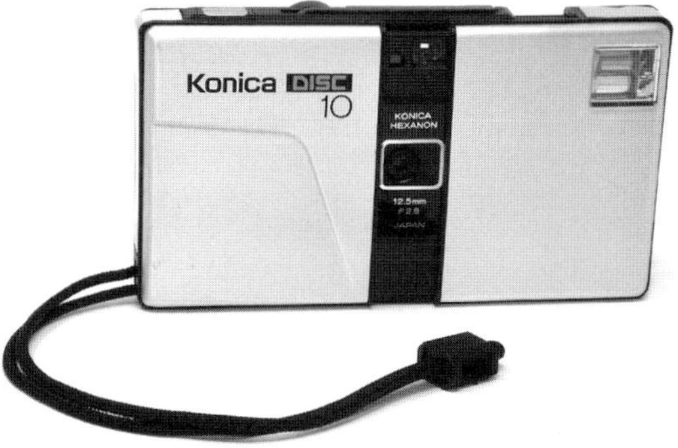

Konica's slightly different take on the disc camera design.

The likes of Nikon, Canon and Pentax kept well away.

Kodak's last disc camera rolled off the production line in 1986, and after that, other manufacturers also began to lose interest. Fujifilm and Konica were among a few other companies that also made disc film. Kodak stopped producing the film in 1999. It was the end of another era in the history of snapshot photography.

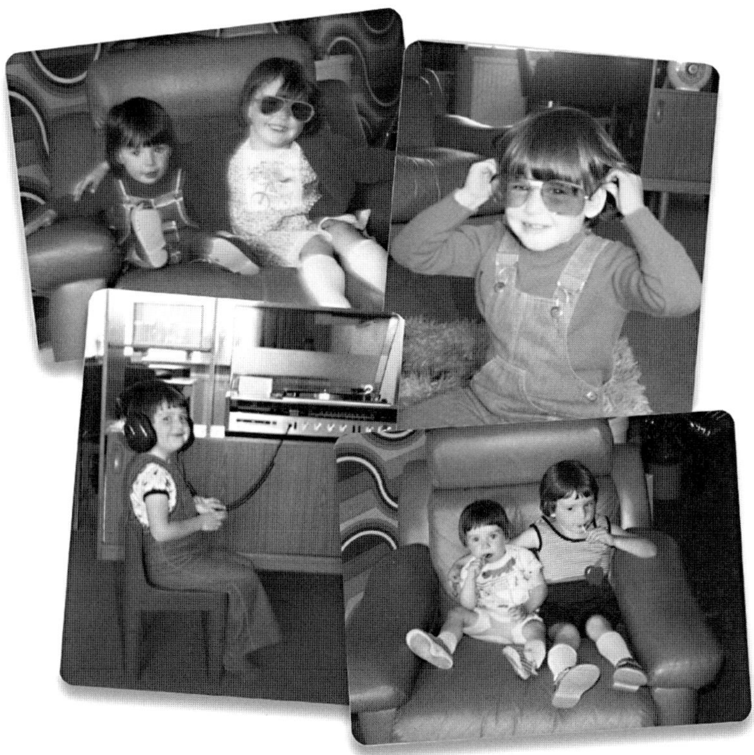

Snapshots from the early 1980s, taken with a Disc 4000 camera using its in-built flashgun.

Chapter 12

Disposable Cameras

If ever a camera typified the whole ethos of snapshot photography, the disposable camera must surely be it. The concept was simple. Each camera came preloaded with enough 35mm film, most often for twenty-four or sometimes twenty-seven exposures. The lens was fixed focus, as were both the shutter speed and aperture, so the only controls to worry about were a button to take the picture and a thumbwheel to advance the film to the next exposure. Some models had built-in flashguns that needed to be turned on when shooting indoors. When the last picture had been taken, the whole camera was taken to a film processor who broke it open, extracted the film for developing and printing, then threw away the rest. Next time more snapshots needed to be taken, the snapshot photographer simply bought another disposable camera.

The craze began in 1987 when Fuji announced this new type of camera, which it called the Fujicolor Quicksnap. The company referred to it, not as a

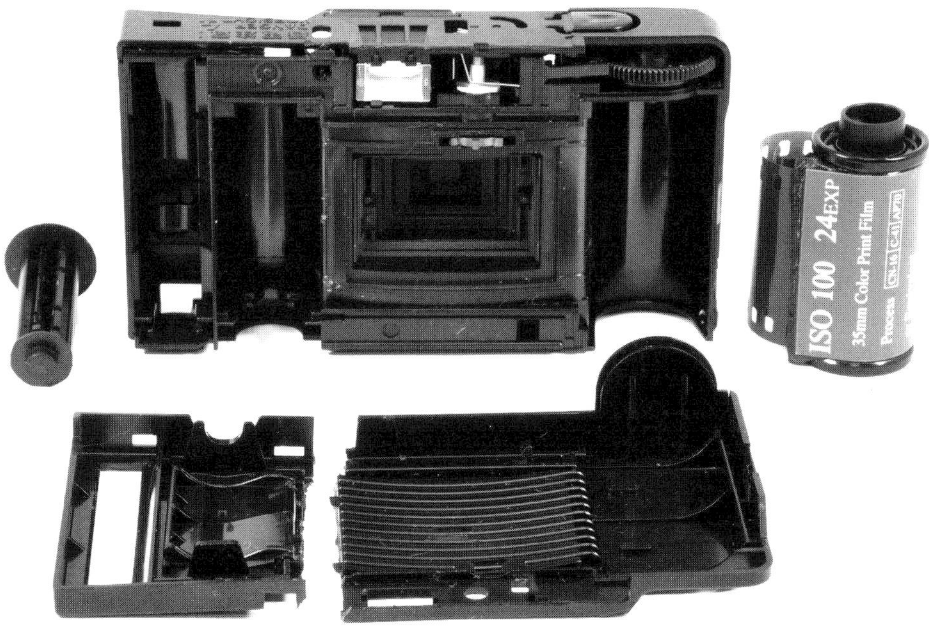

Inside a disposable camera, broken open for the film to be processed.

camera with film, but as a film with lens. It set the style for literally thousands of other disposable cameras initially from Fuji, followed closely by Kodak, then from a profuse number of other manufacturers for several decades to come. The Quicksnap was the first of this new generation of snapshot cameras, but it was by no means the first disposable camera. That honour goes back to a camera launched in America more than 100 years before Fuji entered the market.

The Ready Fotografer

In 1886, the Ready Fotografer Company was formed in San Francisco for the purpose of marketing a camera called the Ready Fotografer. The idea was patented by an ophthalmologist called Alexander Whittell, whose patent stated: 'My invention relates to improvements in apparatus for taking photographs, by which each sensitized plate has its portable folding camera attached and the use of lenses for focusing the picture is obviated.' It was designed to be 'within the understanding of any person of average ability'.

The camera was actually little more than a cardboard box, which unfolded using simple paper bellows. A pinhole aperture at the front projected its image onto a single glass plate at the back. After exposure, the camera was taken to a darkroom, where it was cut open to retrieve the plate, and the body was discarded. Or, if the photographer didn't wish to carry out the development

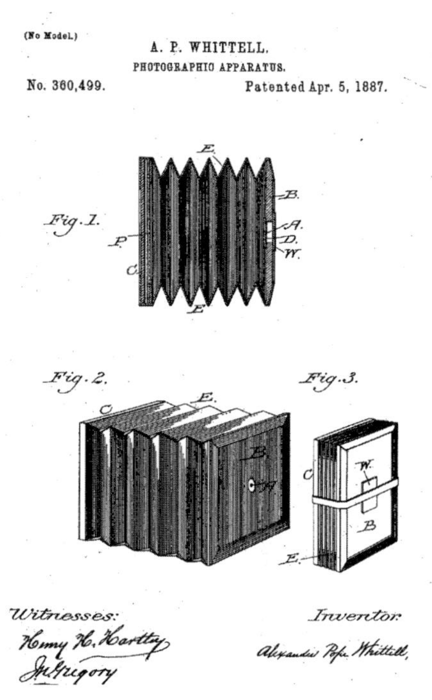

Alexander Whittell's patent for the Ready Fotografer camera.

process himself, the entire camera could be mailed back to the Ready Fotografer Company in San Francisco, where the single plate would be developed and returned to the user, without the camera of course. That was disposable.

The camera was sold with a twenty-four-page manual, explaining how to get the best from the apparatus, including an illustration on the back cover to remind photographers that the camera was so light it might blow away if not tightly secured when the picture was being taken.

The Ready Fotografer can be considered as the first disposable camera, but it was a one-off. It didn't lead to anything else of a similar type or style. In fact,

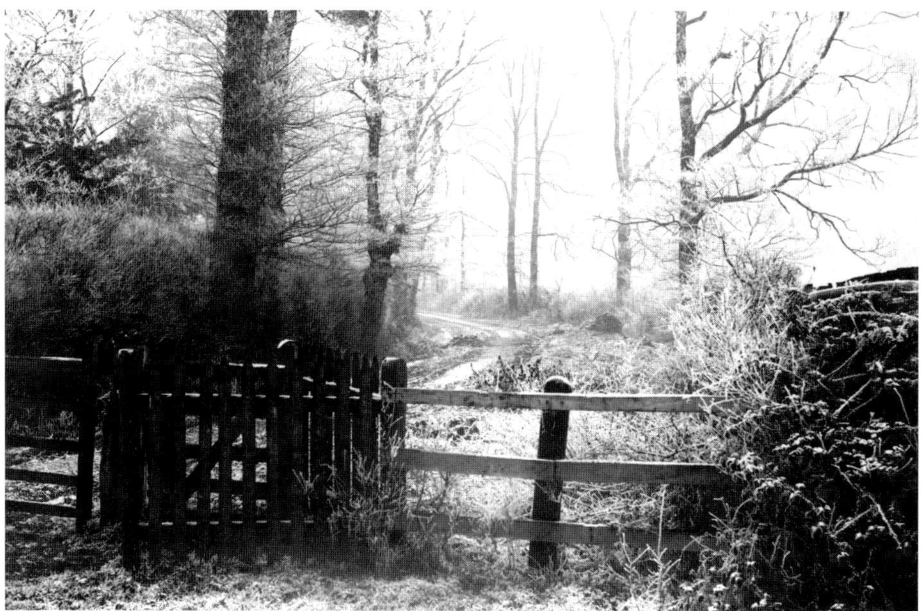

Although this picture was not actually taken with a Ready Fotografer camera, it does demonstrate the kind of subject that camera might have tackled. The picture is known to have been taken in the early 1890s, which is when the Ready Fotographer would have been around. Importantly, though, the picture includes nothing that might involve movement from the likes of people or vehicles. Subjects like these would have been difficult for the Ready Fotografer to handle since its pinhole aperture, in place of a lens, would have necessitated long exposures, leading to blurred movement in the picture it shot.

it really wasn't until the advent of roll film that real disposable cameras began to emerge, and there were two distinct generations, divided by cameras before and after the launch of the Fujicolor Quicksnap in 1987.

The arrival of film

As described in an earlier chapter, in 1888 George Eastman launched the Kodak, the camera that introduced the world to flexible roll film for the first time. It marked the beginnings of snapshot photography for people who knew little about photographic techniques and who might never before have considered owning a camera. In its own way, the Kodak was a little like some of the disposable cameras that were to come later in so far as it was sold preloaded with enough film for 100 exposures and was then returned to the Eastman works for developing and printing the pictures. The difference was that when the film had been removed, the camera was not discarded. Instead, it was loaded again with a new film before being returned to the owner.

In 1916, Canadian inventor Harold Moxon patented what he called a 'film-packed camera'. Inside the body, which contained a lens and a shutter, sheets of film were wound onto a spool. Pulling a tab introduced the first frame of film into its position for exposure and the shutter was released. The film was then drawn into a light-tight chamber where it was stored flat as the next sheet was lined up for the following exposure. Each sheet of film, stacked flat one piece on top of another, remained in the chamber until the camera was broken open, the film sheets removed and developed. The remains of the camera were then discarded. In his patent, Moxon stated: 'Another object is to dispense with the use of spool holders, spools, winding keys and the like, thus permitting the manufacture of the camera loaded with a roll of single films at a low price.'

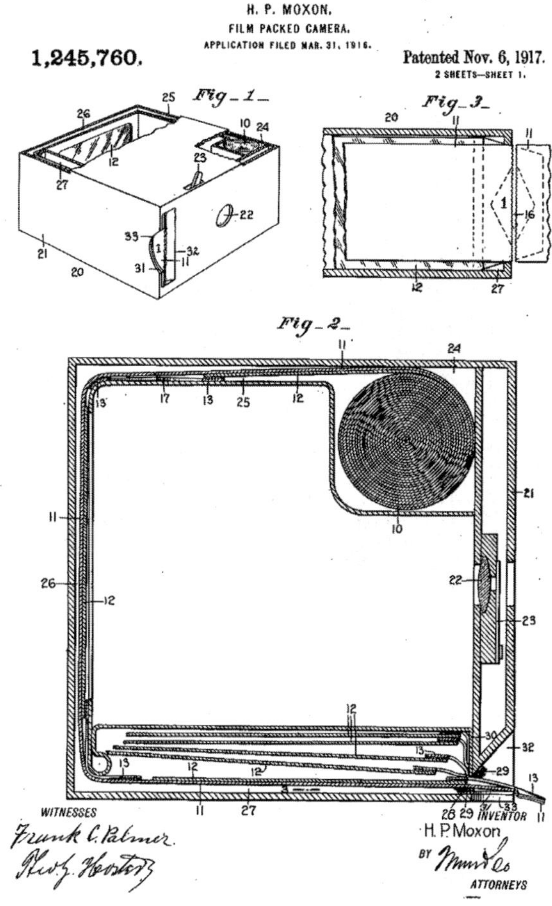

Harold Moxon's patent for his film-packed camera.

There is no evidence to suggest Moxon's camera ever came to market. It was more than thirty years before the next, more successful, disposable camera appeared.

The Picture Box

The first practical disposable camera arrived in 1948. It was the brainchild of American entrepreneur Frederick Bierhorst, who established the Picture Box Manufacturing Company that year to produce a camera called, naturally, the Picture Box. His patent described it as 'a camera which is of simple construction, inexpensive to manufacture and easy to operate, which can be sold fully loaded with film'. Advertising of the day proclaimed it as 'The World's Most Convenient Camera'.

The Picture Box was made of cardboard with brightly coloured outer wrapping paper that contained its name and mailing instructions. Inside, the film was wound on a roll, but advanced by the photographer, who pulled a tab from the back of the body to drop the film into a loose coil at the back. The whole thing was then mailed back to the Picture Box Manufacturing Company, where it was broken open for processing.

There is scant evidence to show that the Picture Box remained on sale for long, or that it attained any great success. The next disposable camera to hit the market was similar in style, but more successful.

The Photo-Pac

American mechanical engineer Alfred Weir was the man behind the Photo-Pac, made by his Photo-Pac Camera Manufacturing Company (early disposable camera makers were apparently not very imaginative when it came to naming their companies). His marketing strategy was described at the time by *Business Week* magazine as being based on two ideas: that people who don't own cameras often wished they did; and that people who do own cameras often forgetfully leave them at home.

The camera was made of plastic rather than cardboard and bought preloaded with enough film to shoot eight exposures. It was launched at the

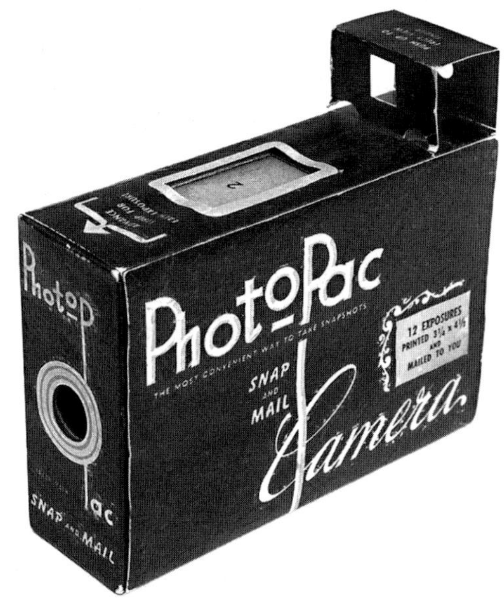

The Photo-Pac, probably the first truly successful disposable camera.

Texas State Fair in 1948, where it sold for ninety-eight cents. According to the marketing, all the user had to do was 'sight, shoot and mail'. Dealer display material for the camera put it another way: 'Snap and mail, that's all you do!'

When all the pictures had been taken, a label on the side of the camera provided space to write the photographer's details, plus the address of the Photo-Pac company at 5403 Greenville Avenue, Dallas, Texas. A seven-cent stamp was added and the whole thing was dropped into a mailbox. On arrival at the Photo-Pac Camera Manufacturing Company, the camera was broken open and the film extracted to be developed and printed. A week later, the photographer received negatives and what the company called jumbo prints,

3¼ × 4¼ inches in size. Also included was a slip of paper analysing the pictures to explain why some might not have been quite as successful as others.

Initially, the Photo-Pac was a great success. Most of the major American department stores stocked the camera, it won an accolade as one of the fifteen winning ideas of the year in a publication called *Fawcett's Inventor's Handbook* and *Mechanix Illustrated* magazine awarded it $50 for its Prize Gadget of the Month in September 1949. In 1950, Weir remodelled the camera to take twelve exposures and the price went up to $1.49. Despite its success, however, the Photo-Pac, and the company that made it doesn't seem to have survived much beyond 1950.

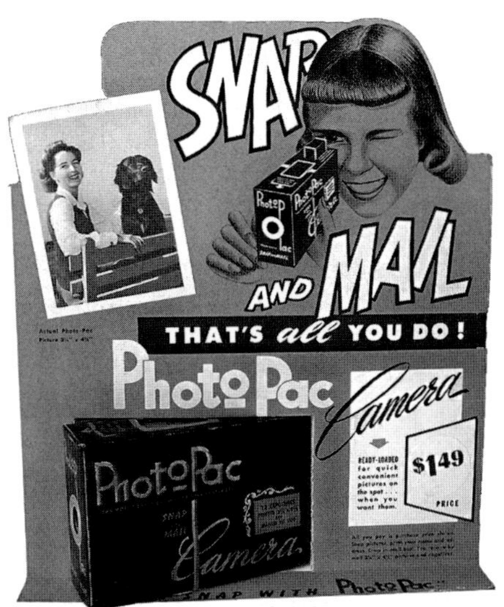

Photo-Pac promotional material explains how the camera was used and shows an actual size example of the pictures it took.

Encore Camera Company

Meanwhile in 1950, a new kind of disposable camera was being launched in California. Until then, disposable cameras, with their colourful designs, had been regarded a lot like novelties. The Encore Camera Company, however, set out to make their cameras look more like traditional box cameras. Although only made of cardboard, the Encore cameras were encased with paper coverings made to look like black leather, snakeskin or lizard skin. The black faux leather camera was called the Encore, the snakeskin model was the Encore De Luxe and the lizard skin version was the Hollywood. The cameras were mostly available as premium gifts, offered to users who saved up enough coupons from cigarette packets. Another variation was badged by, and given away to passengers travelling on, Continental Airlines.

The Hollywood, the most attractive of this new breed of disposables, was preloaded with 127 film and measured 13×9×6.5cm. There was a fixed speed shutter release and film wind knob on the side, a wire-frame viewfinder that pulled up from the front to line up with a pull-up sight at the back and a simple fixed focus, fixed aperture lens. For anyone unfamiliar with the simplicity of using a snapshot camera, full instructions for use were printed on the side.

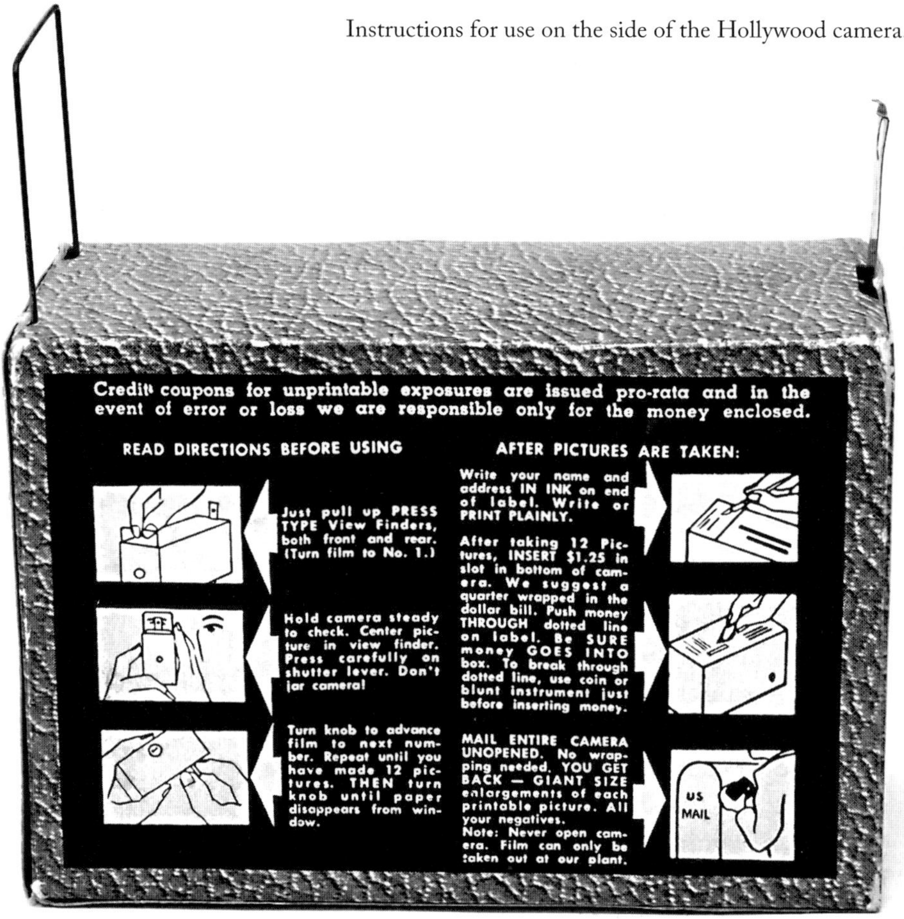

Instructions for use on the side of the Hollywood camera.

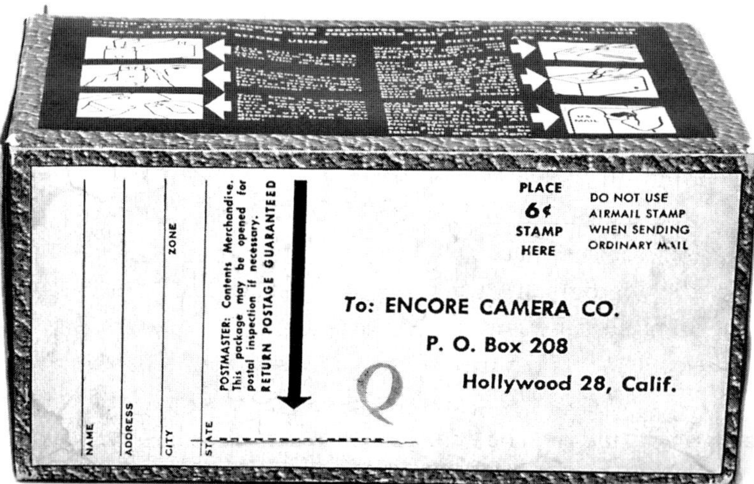

The base of the Hollywood, where the photographer wrote his or her details before mailing.

A label on the base of the camera was preprinted with the name and address of the Encore Camera Company. The label also included a place for the user to write his or her name and address and then the edge of a coin was used to open a perforated slot. Into this the photographer inserted $1.25, suggested to comprise a quarter coin (twenty-five cents) wrapped in a dollar bill. Then all the user had to do was stick a six-cent stamp on the camera and put the whole thing in the mail. Sometime later, a set of pictures would arrive in the post and a new preloaded camera arrived separately. Included with the pictures a small printed sheet gave reasons why some of the negatives might have been unprintable. A coupon on the reverse side offered free reprints of any of the good negatives in compensation for those that hadn't been printed. Apart from any freebies, reprints cost six cents for contact prints, fifty cents for 5×7-inch enlargements and sixty cents for 10×8-inch prints.

The Imp, Pro and Mini-Mate

In 1951, Beaurline Industries in Minnesota introduced a disposable camera made entirely of plastic and called it the Imp (probably in reaction to Kodak's success with the Brownie name). With an upright design, rather like a box camera stood on its end, it cost $1.79 and shot twelve exposures on 35mm film. It was one of the first disposable cameras to incorporate a direct vision viewfinder into the body.

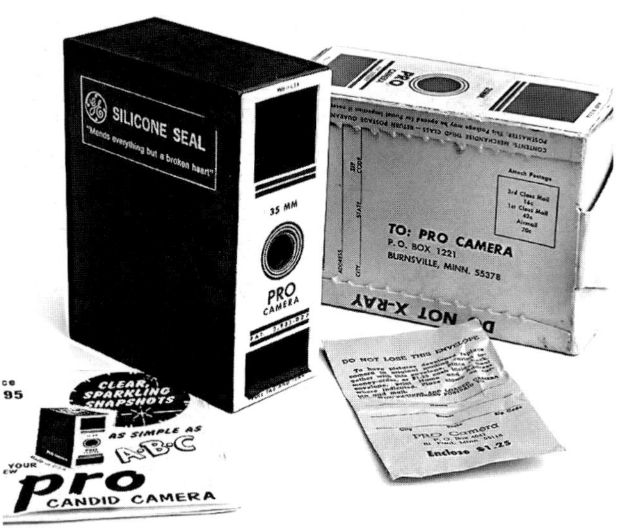

The Pro camera with its box and instructions.

Strictly speaking, the Imp wasn't a disposable camera, although the photographer using it wouldn't have known that. What made it different from the rest was a panel on the back held in place with adhesive tape. When the camera was returned to the factory for film processing, the tape was pulled off, the panel removed and the film extracted without having to destroy the camera. It could then be reloaded, the panel stuck back in place with a new piece of adhesive tape and the recycled camera sent back to the photographer, though not necessarily the one who had sent it to the company for processing.

In the mid-1950s, the Imp's manufacturers consulted a public relations company about the way forward for their business. As a result the Imp was renamed the Pro. With a longer life than most other similar cameras, the Imp/Pro continued to be made into the 1970s, when it was renamed again as the Mini-Mate, offered for the first time with a choice of colour or black and white film.

The Techni-Pak

Technicolor Inc was the company behind the next disposable camera, which was made in Hong Kong. The Techni-Pak was the first disposable camera to offer a choice of two apertures, marked for 'bright' and 'cloudy'. The lens was fixed focus.

The camera, which was available for $2 plus five wrappers from Winston cigarettes, was preloaded with 35mm colour print film. The box in which it was sold doubled as its mailing box. When all the pictures had been taken, it was returned to the Technicolor laboratories, where it was opened to retrieve the film. However, the internal workings used a special and intricate spooling mechanism for the film, which made it impossible to reload by anyone other than a trained Technicolor technician. Processing cost $5.95, which paid for twenty 3½-inch square colour prints.

The Lure Camera Company

In 1972, Kodak introduced 110 film. A year later, the new film size was used to shoot twelve exposures on paper-backed 16mm film in a disposable camera. The makers were the Lure Camera Company, based in Canada. The camera was the size and shape of a traditional 110 model with a mount on top to accept a magicube flashbulb. The mount was rotated to wind the film. The camera was sold under four different names: the Love in America, the Rank in the UK, the Blick in Italy and the Lure X2 in Alaska.

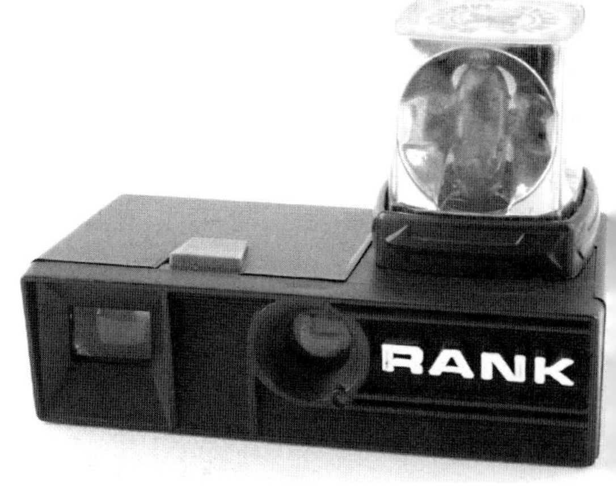

The Rank disposable, also known as the Lure, Blick and Love.

In 1981, a Brazilian company called Sonora bought the Lure company and improved on the design. It looked like the camera was set for a bright future.

But then, along came Fuji, swiftly followed by Kodak, and the manufacture, marketing, sales and use of disposable cameras completely exploded.

Fuji versus Kodak

The second generation of disposable cameras came with the launch, in 1987, of Fuji's Fujicolor Quicksnap. This was the camera that set a style for the way disposable cameras would look and develop in the years ahead. Bodies were made of plastic often completely covered with tight-fitting and colourful cardboard boxes, though some utilised no more than simple slip-on cardboard shells to partially cover and personalise otherwise anonymous-looking black bodies. Most had simple instructions printed on the cardboard wrappers with diagrammatic details of how to shoot in the best light, how and when to use the flashgun built into many models and minimum distances to be adopted between the camera and subject to ensure everything remained in focus.

Although the cameras all looked different outwardly, the majority were much the same internally, with simple lenses and single speed shutters. The film was preloaded wound onto a spool and, as a thumbwheel was turned after each exposure, it advanced back into the cassette ready for the processor to remove and develop in the usual way. Flashguns, where present, were powered by single prefitted AA or sometimes AAA batteries. Most disposables shot twenty-four or twenty-seven exposures, though some specialist cameras only shot twelve. The first disposables were fairly chunky, their size dictated by the dimensions of a standard 35mm cassette. Later cameras were more slender, achieved by use of a slimmer-than-normal cassette.

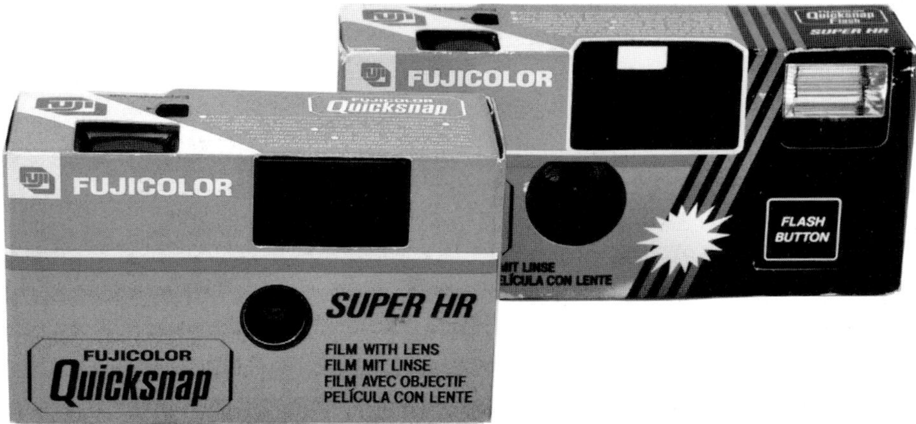

The Fuji cameras that began the second generation craze for disposable cameras: Fujicolor Quicksnap (left) and Quicksnap Flash.

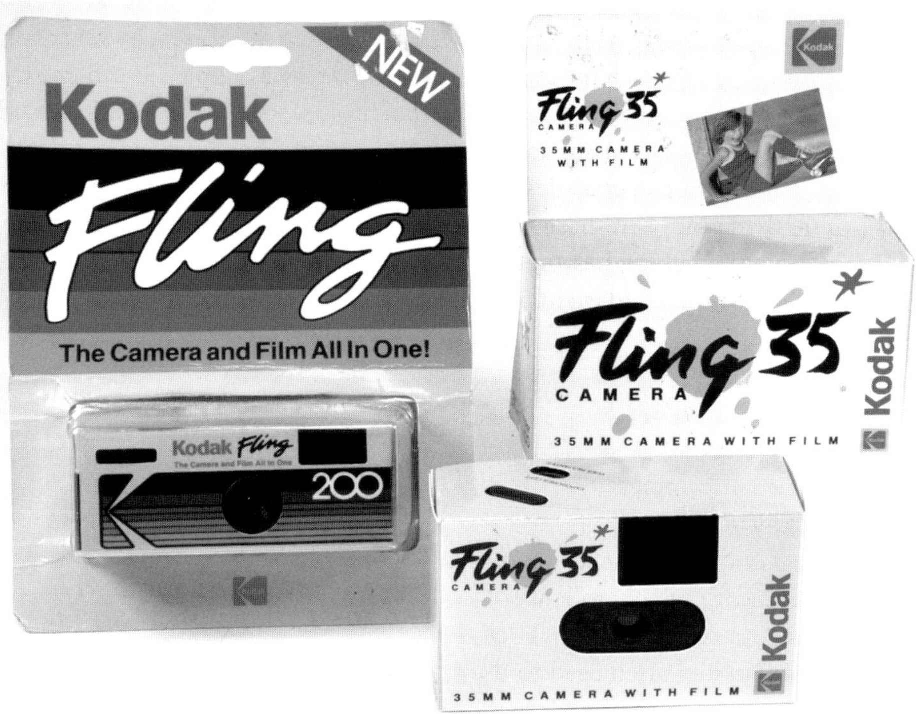

Kodak's answer to Fuji: the Fling, which took 110 film (left), and the Fling 35 for 35mm film.

With the launch of the Quicksnap, Fuji stole a march on Kodak, who were usually out there on top when it came to making snapshot photography easy for the masses. Not to be outdone, Kodak retaliated with a disposable called The Fling, which used 110 film in place of Fujifilm's 35mm, allowing it to sell for a little over half the price of its rival. Despite the lower price, The Fling didn't prove popular, and before long Kodak introduced the Fling 35 for 35mm film – and Fuji retaliated with the Quicksnap Flash, the first disposable with a built-in flashgun. The disposable war was on.

In the years ahead, while the two photo giants battled it out, other manufacturers joined the game. Some disposable cameras came from top brand names like Ilford, Agfa and Konica. Others revealed little about their origins, other than 'Made in Japan' or the ubiquitous 'Made in China' labels.

Many and various

It would be impossible to put a figure on how many disposable cameras were made in the years between the launch of the Quicksnap and the dawn of the digital era. But it was during those days before digital that disposable cameras really made their mark. The vast majority used colour film, although a very few were made for black and white. The film these latter cameras used, however, was called chromogenic, which meant it could be processed in colour film chemistry. So even if the photographer bought a monochrome disposable, the film could still be processed and prints made by any high street film-processing outlet.

Most disposable cameras, despite their fancy bodies and packaging, were little more than point and shoot models easily used by snapshot photographers. Their often garish, though sometimes subtle, designs were used to advertise a multitude of products and events. Intermingled with these were special models that included…

- panoramic cameras
- stereo cameras
- underwater cameras
- twin lens reflexes
- at least one camera specially designed for portraiture
- cameras with telephoto lenses
- cameras to celebrate special occasions
- cameras in kits often used to document details of accidents
- cameras that advertised and promoted a vast range of products and services.

Stereo disposable from ImageTech.

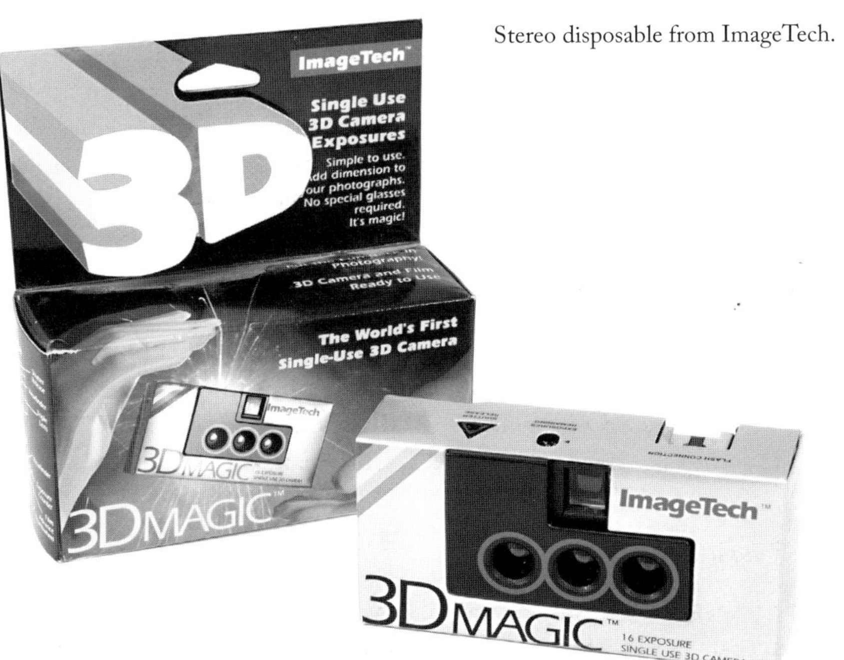

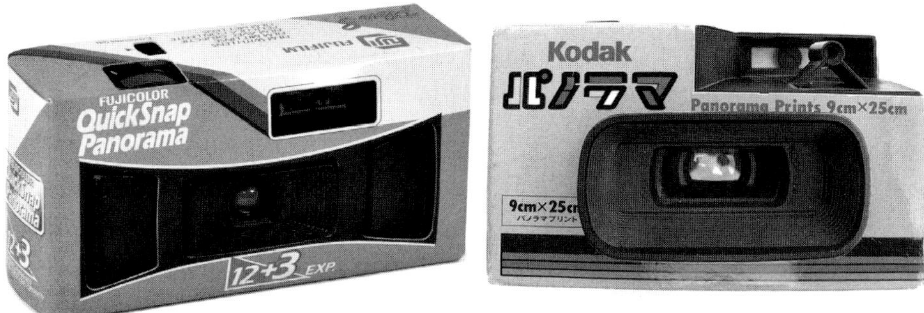

Panoramic disposables from Fuji and Kodak.

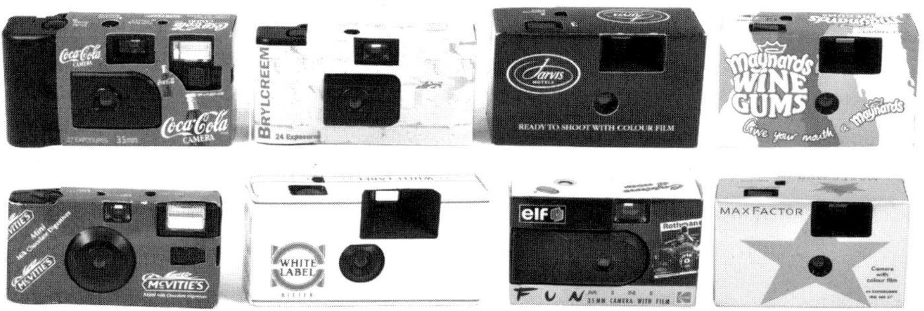

How some companies used disposable cameras to promote their products.

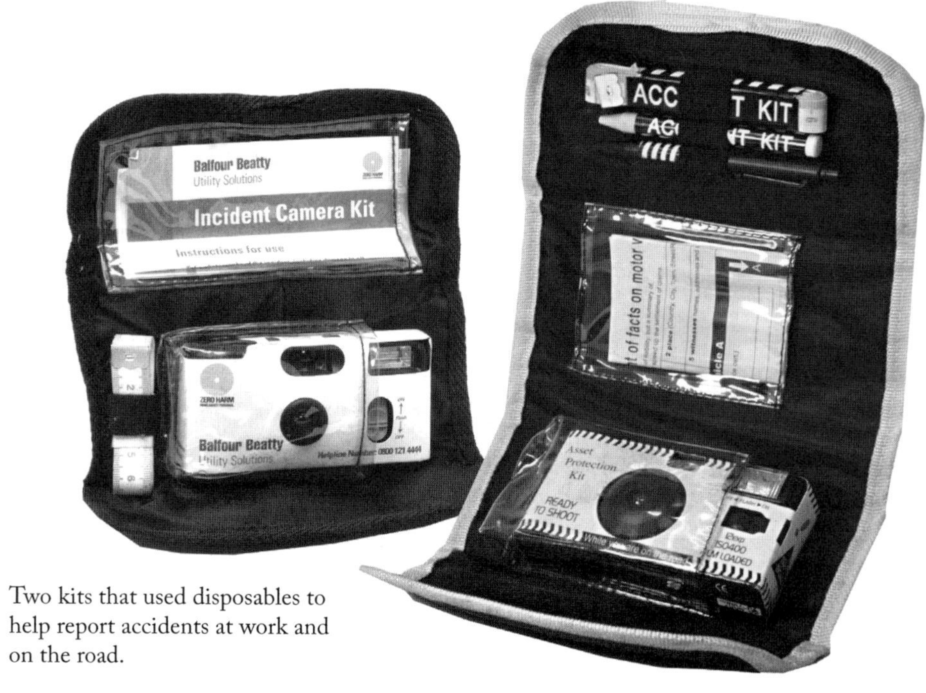

Two kits that used disposables to
help report accidents at work and
on the road.

Stereo disposables such as one made by ImageTech used three lenses to produce three pictures side by side on normal 35mm film. Unlike any other disposable camera, however, the film could not be processed at a normal high street lab. Instead, it was returned to a specialist processor, whose details would be found in the camera's packaging or box, and who used a lenticular printing process to produce a set of prints that gave a three-dimensional impression without the need for special glasses.

Panoramic disposables, including cameras made by Fuji and Kodak, were actually normal 35mm cameras with the picture masked top and bottom to make a panoramic format. Underwater cameras were also sold, recommended for use in clear water when the sun was shining, but only at a depth of up to 3 metres.

Some industries issued disposable cameras in special kits used for recording accident details. They generally came in a cloth rolled-up pouch. One kit, given out at trade shows by construction company Balfour Beatty, was designed to document accidents or damage at work. The complete kit comprised a disposable camera, tape measure, crayon and instructions for use. Another kit issued by insurance companies for drivers to record details of accidents, contained a camera, a form to be filled out by both parties, tape measure, crayon and pen.

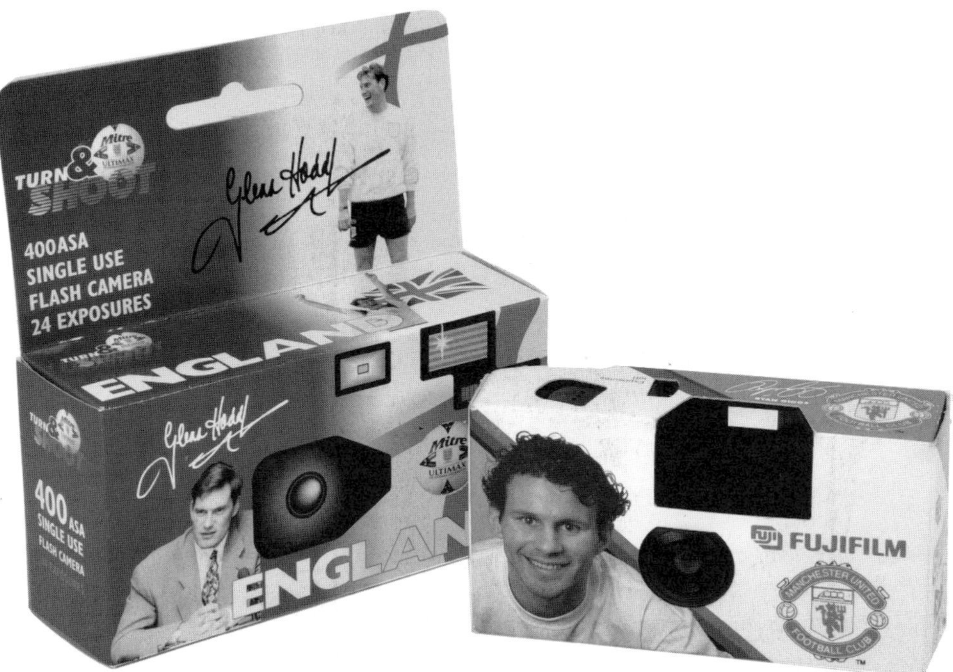

One disposable sold to celebrate England's part in Euro 1996 (left) and another for Manchester United fans.

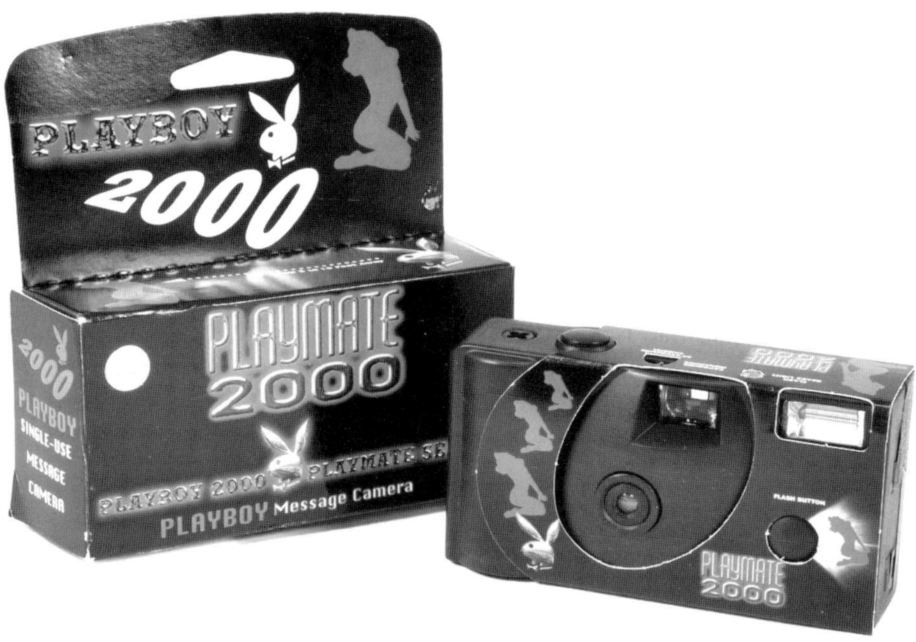

The *Playboy* disposable camera issued to find a Playmate for the millennium.

Then there were cameras issued to illustrate many of the major football tournaments, such as Euro 1996, complete with a picture of then manager Glen Hoddle. (England was knocked out in the semi-finals that year.)

In 1999, *Playboy* magazine in America issued its own range of disposable cameras to encourage aspiring models over the age of 18 to submit their pictures to be considered as the magazine's Playmate of the Month for the January 2000 millennial issue, plus the chance to represent *Playboy* throughout the coming year and a fee of $200,000. The slightly erotic red and black design of the camera and its packaging, which included the silhouette of a *Playboy* type of model, might be considered a little politically incorrect today, as it announced its promotion of the Playboy 2000 Playmate Search, adding instructions for the photographer to keep 3 to 10 feet away from the potential playmate.

Despite the decline of film cameras in favour of digital technology, disposable cameras are one aspect of the film camera market that still remains popular even today.

Chapter 13

Into the Digital Age

By the time the digital age dawned, film camera technology had hit its peak. Electronics had replaced mechanical ways of working; super-accurate built-in exposure meters and controls looked after both aperture and shutter speeds to provide correct exposures; autofocus took care of focusing the lens on the right subject. So digital cameras hit the ground running as far as the technology needed to produce a good quality picture was concerned. It meant that even the least experienced snapshot photographer could buy a camera brim-full of electronic wizardry and, without knowing a thing about the way it all worked, produce decent pictures.

Two factors initially stood in the way of snapshot photographers immediately making the switch to digital. The first was the low quality of the very earliest digital camera images, compared to prints from film, plus the fact that right at the very start, digital pictures could only be viewed on a television screen. The second was the cost. Even the most basic of digital cameras was priced a lot higher than the snapshot film cameras to which photographers like these were more accustomed.

Early history

The first digital camera was the brainchild of American scientist and electrical engineer Steven Sasson, who joined American Eastman Kodak in 1973. A few years earlier, in 1969, the charge-coupled device (CCD) had been conceived by physicists William Boyle and George E. Smith at Bell Labs in America. In 1975, Sasson utilised that technology to build an electronic camera that used a CCD in place of film. With six circuit boards, sixteen nickel cadmium batteries, an analogue/digital converter salvaged from a digital voltmeter, the discarded lens from an old Super-8 movie camera and a portable digital cassette instrumentation recorder, Sasson strung together the first digital camera. It took fifty milliseconds to capture a black and white image, but twenty-three seconds for it to be recorded and stored on magnetic tape. When the tape was placed in a playback device, it took another thirty seconds for the picture to appear on a coupled television. In today's jargon, it was a 0.01 megapixel camera. Those who saw it likened its design to a toaster.

None of this would have had an impact on the average snapshot photographer. In fact, Kodak took the technology no further at that stage, possibly because the film giant saw digital photography as a threat to not only its film sales, but also its film processing division. What was needed was an electronics company with no interest in film to take over the reins. Enter Sony, in 1981, with a camera called the Mavica, short for Magnetic Video Camera. The Mavica was actually a still video camera that incorporated an image sensor and processing hardware similar to those used in analogue video cameras of the time. Each image was stored in its own circle on a rotating magnetic disc. To play back and view the image, the disc was rotated at the same rate as when the image was shot and stored, and the appropriate frame was read repeatedly. The result was a signal that could then be viewed on a television. The camera proved to be only a prototype that never went on sale. Nevertheless, a step had been taken closer to digital snapshot photography even though it was by no means there just yet.

It came a little closer in 1988, when Canon introduced the iON, an acronym for Image Online Network. The iON was designed as a flat body with a lens at one end of the narrow side and a built-in flashgun at the other. Using small spinning discs for storage, it shot fifty pictures, viewed by connecting the camera to a normal television. The camera was used by professional press photographers, but its image quality, good enough for low-resolution newspapers pictures of the time, was not as good as film equivalents for even the least-discerning photographers, plus its price meant that few snapshot photographers would have taken much interest.

In the decade that followed, digital technology raced ahead, image quality improved and gradually prices began to fall until the cameras came within reach of the snapshot photographer. In 1988, Fuji showed the Fujipix DS-1P, with

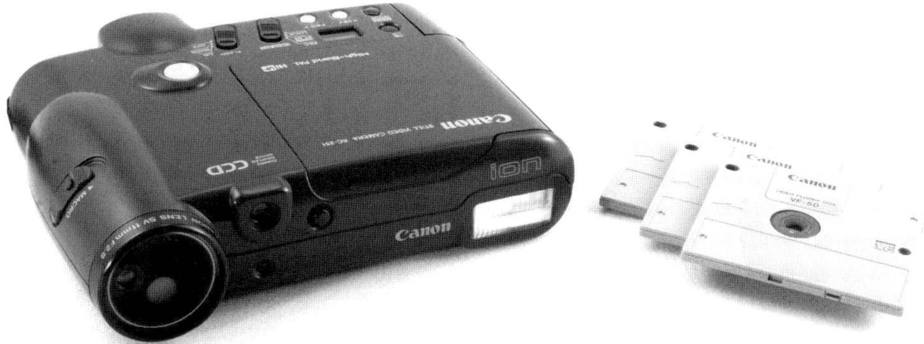

The Canon iON still video camera with the small discs on which it recorded images. It was a very early camera to be made available commercially, but its method of operation was very different from the way digital camera technology was about to proceed.

a removable memory card to replace the rotating disc systems, although the camera never went on sale. In the same year, the QV-1000C still video camera was the first from Nikon with 0.38 megapixels but with a price of more than $20,000. The 1990 Logitech Fotoman, with its 0.08 megapixel black and white images, found favour for a while with estate agents, despite its $600 price. The Apple QuickTake 100, in 1994, was similar in design to the Canon iON. Although badged by Apple, the first two models were made by Kodak and a third model by Fuji. The Casio QV-10 in 1995 was the first with an LCD screen for previewing and viewing pictures. Sony's Mavica name resurfaced in 1997 with the

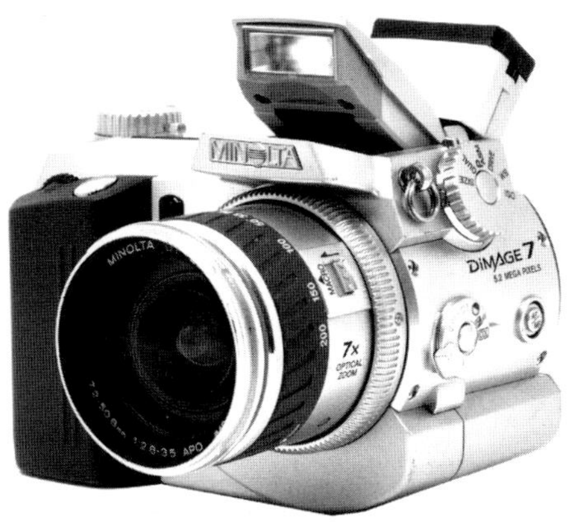

A digital camera like this Minolta Dimage 7 from 2001 looked complicated, but switched to its fully auto functions it could easily have been used by snapshot photographers.

MVC-FD5, featuring a zoom lens, macro function and 2.5-inch LCD screen, recording its images on 3.5-inch floppy computer discs. The Sony MVC-CD500 went one better in 2002 and recorded its images on a CD that slotted into a circular holder on the back of the body. The Spyc@m 100 in 2004 was shaped like a large, chunky pen and shot both still pictures and video clips.

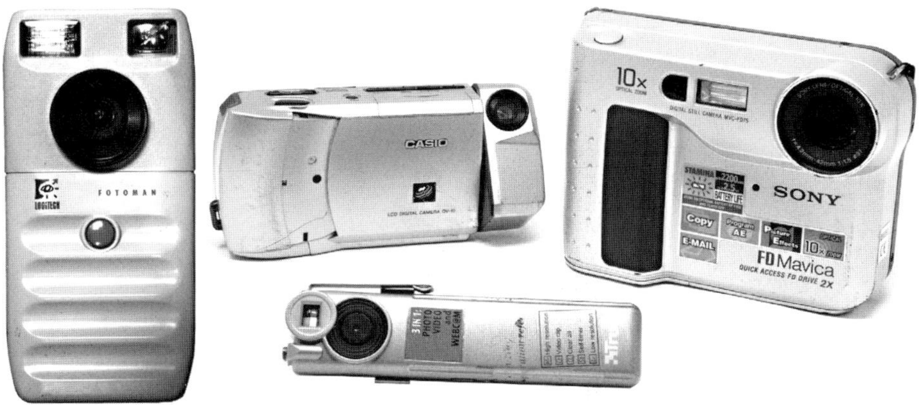

Late twentieth and early twenty-first-century designs. Left to right: Logitech Fotoman, Casio QV-10 and Sony Mavica MVC-FD75, with Spyc@m 100 in front.

Digital snapshots arrive

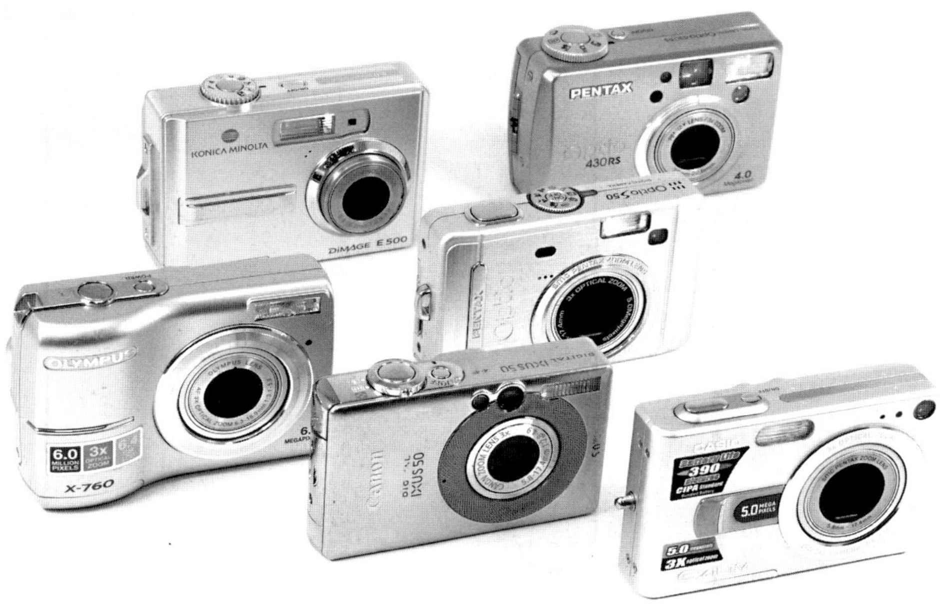

A small selection of the many credit card size cameras that popularised digital snapshot photography.

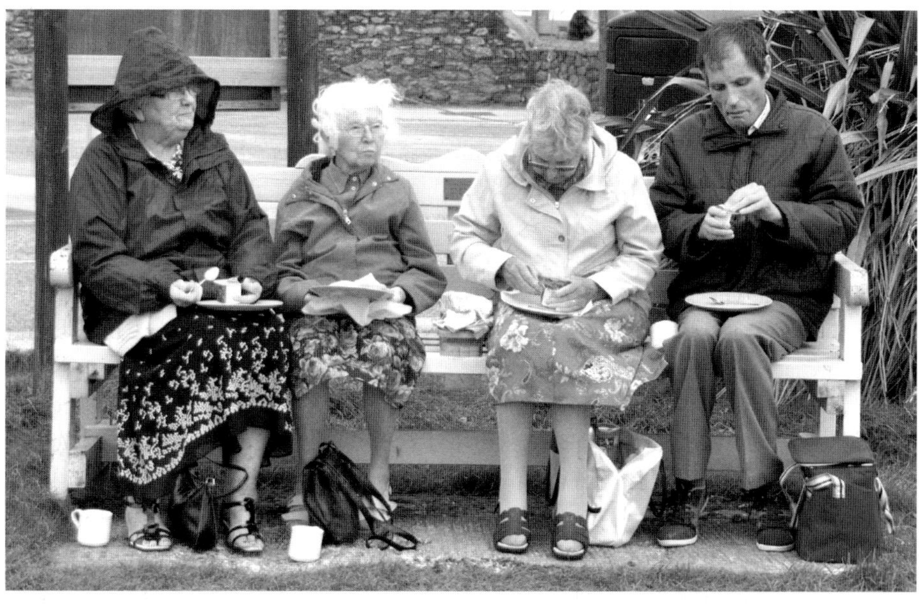

With small digital cameras easy to conceal in the palm of the hand, candid photography became more available to the snapshot photographer. This picture was obviously taken without the knowledge of the subjects, summing up what, for some, could be said to be a typical British holiday.

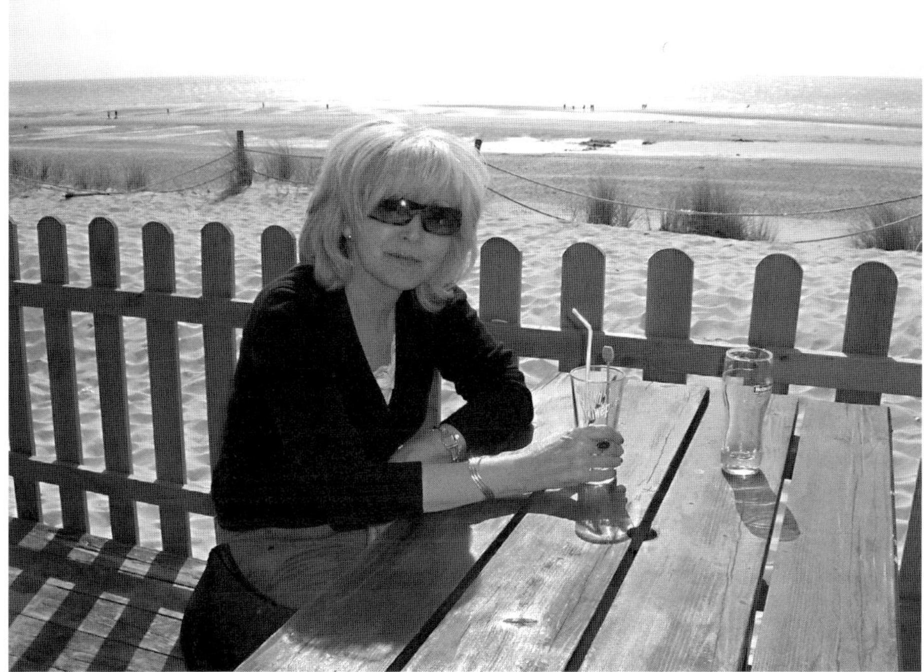

A picture like this, taken casually without too much thought, using one of the early small credit card size cameras, illustrates how an immense amount of technology was condensed into such a small space. The camera has measured and set the correct exposure, adjusted the focus for the main subject, recognised that shooting against the light (as is evidenced by the direction of the shadows) means there is a difference between the level of light in the background and that falling on the subject's face and automatically fired the camera's built-in flash to balance the two. The photographer, taking a straightforward snapshot, would not have needed to know any of this. All that was needed was a quick look through the viewfinder, or a glance at the screen on the back of the camera, and the press of a button. In this way, digital photography brought true image quality to even the most ordinary of snapshots.

As the twenty-first century dawned, and most of the recognised camera makers threw themselves into the digital arena, pixel counts and sensor sensitivity increased, prices fell, LCD screens became the norm on camera backs and rotating discs were replaced by solid-state memory cards to store images. These included memory sticks that comprised thin plastic sheets with embedded chips, then more robust, compact flash cards and finally, much smaller SD cards commonly used today. By then, most of the camera manufacturers, from both the traditional photographic world and the electronics world, were making small cameras about the size of a credit card, with styles, simplicity of operation and price that brought them straight into the snapshot photographer's domain.

While digital cameras for professional and advanced amateur photographers became more and more sophisticated, these small credit card size cameras, with automated technology that made it simple for anyone to use and with prices dropping all the time, became the cameras of choice for every snapshot photographer who for the first time, had the opportunity to carry a digital camera anywhere at any time. It gave rise to a new type of snapshot photography in which pictures could be taken far more casually and, with the size of the cameras making them easy to conceal, for candid photography, in which the subjects were unaware of being photographed as well.

And then something unexpected happened, something that had never been seen before in the history of photography. Cameras began to be incorporated into mobile phones.

Cameras and phones

The first phones with built-in cameras were the Kyocera Visual Phone VP-210 in 1999 and Samsung SCH-V200 in 2000. Unlike those that followed, however, they needed to be plugged into a computer to see the pictures. The first stand-alone phone camera was the Sharp Electronics J-SH04 J-Phone, launched in 2000, although it was available only in Japan.

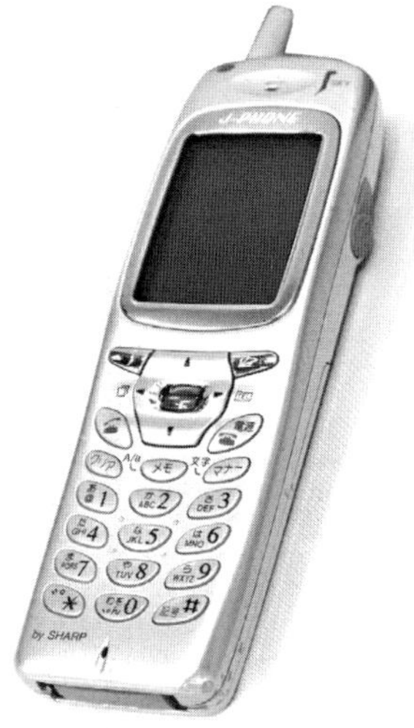

The Sharp J-SH04 J-Phone was the first stand-alone mobile phone with a built-in camera.

The real revolution, however, began in 2007, when Apple launched the iPhone. Very quickly, phone memories grew to allow more pictures to be taken and stored, sensors were improved, 3G, then 4G and 5G technology made it easy to share pictures instantly. And it wasn't long before people realised that the new phone cameras could be used close to, held at arm's length to produce self-portraits anywhere and everywhere. So the selfie was born.

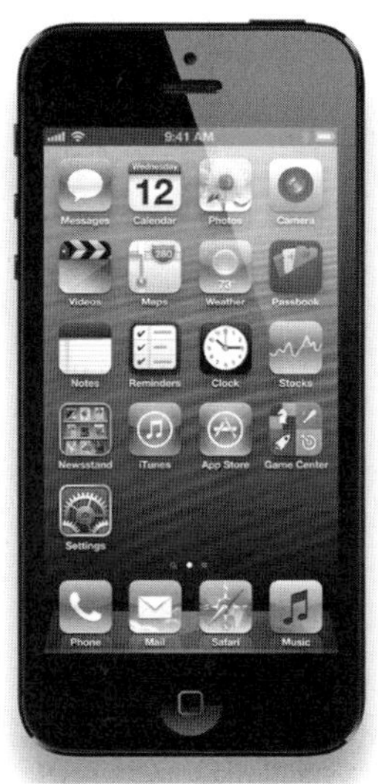

Apple's iPhone led the way towards the phone camera as we know it today.

Today it is reckoned that 92 million selfies are taken worldwide every day. The average age of the selfie-taking snapshot photographer is 24 and more than 95 per cent of young adults have taken a selfie at some time. People smile in 60 per cent of selfies and women take one and half times more selfies than men.

The selfie, and all the other types of pictures taken with any camera phone, are real snapshots in the true sense of the word, in so far as camera phone operators need to know nothing about photography to operate them and can do so at the touch of a button. Thanks to digital innovation and the marriage between cameras and phones, it is probable that snapshot photography, which began as a Victorian craze and survived the test of time though the age of film and into the digital age, has never been more popular than it is today.

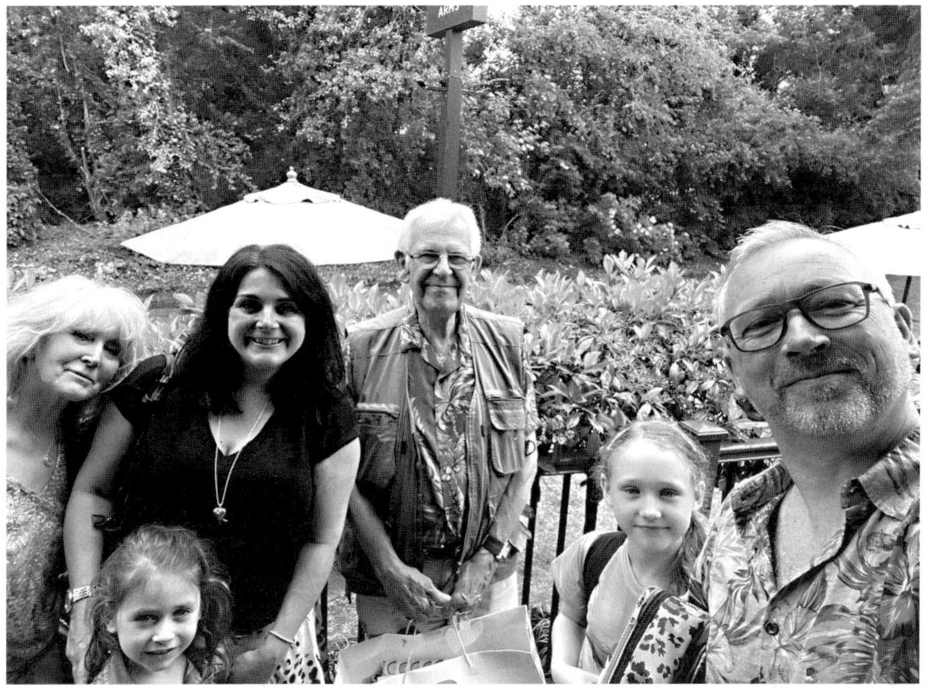

These days any family gathering is not complete without a group selfie shot with a camera phone, taken in this case by the phone operator cum photographer on the right of the picture. Purists would say the composition and the way the people might have been posed could be better. But that's not the point. It's not meant to be a work of art. It's what might be called a selfie today, but at its heart it's a snapshot. The name might have changed, but the ethos is the same today as it ever was.

Picture Credits

<table>
<tr><td>Back cover:</td><td>Public domain, via Wikimedia Commons</td></tr>
<tr><td>Frontispiece:</td><td>Courtesy of John Hannavy</td></tr>
</table>

Book pages:

<table>
<tr><td>1</td><td>Courtesy of George Eastman House</td></tr>
<tr><td>2 (upper)</td><td>Courtesy of George Eastman House</td></tr>
<tr><td>3 (lower)</td><td>By Frederick Church, courtesy of George Eastman House</td></tr>
<tr><td>6</td><td>Part of the Frances Benjamin Johnston Collection at the American Library of Congress, Prints & Photographs Division</td></tr>
<tr><td>13</td><td>Courtesy of Flints Auctioneers</td></tr>
<tr><td>32</td><td>Public domain, via Wikimedia Commons</td></tr>
<tr><td>35 (lower)</td><td>Schlesinger Library, RIAS, Harvard University via Wikimedia Commons</td></tr>
<tr><td>37 (top left)</td><td>Courtesy of eBay seller wish-4-leica, www.VintageCamera.NL</td></tr>
<tr><td>37 (top right)</td><td>Courtesy of Westborn Camera Company</td></tr>
<tr><td>44</td><td>From a 1900 Kodak Trade Circular, courtesy of Charlie Kamerman</td></tr>
<tr><td>46 (upper)</td><td>Courtesy of Charlie Kamerman</td></tr>
<tr><td>55 (upper)</td><td>Courtesy of UK Photo & Social History Archive</td></tr>
<tr><td>55 (lower)</td><td>Public domain via Wikimedia Commons</td></tr>
<tr><td>57</td><td>Courtesy of UK Photo & Social History Archive</td></tr>
<tr><td>59 (upper)</td><td>Courtesy of UK Photo & Social History Archive</td></tr>
<tr><td>59 (lower)</td><td>From the 1915 edition of *Kodakery* magazine, courtesy of John Goddard</td></tr>
<tr><td>62</td><td>Courtesy of UK Photo & Social History Archive</td></tr>
<tr><td>63</td><td>Courtesy of UK Photo & Social History Archive</td></tr>
<tr><td>67 (upper & lower)</td><td>Courtesy of Douglas Thomson</td></tr>
<tr><td>70</td><td>Courtesy of Douglas Thomson</td></tr>
<tr><td>81</td><td>Courtesy of Pat Rowley</td></tr>
<tr><td>82</td><td>Courtesy of David Gardner</td></tr>
<tr><td>85</td><td>Courtesy of Pat Fulford</td></tr>
</table>

86	Library of Congress, Prints & Photographs Division
96	Courtesy of Charlie Kamerman
98	Chalmers Butterfield, CC BY 2.5 via Wikimedia Commons
100	Courtesy of UK Photo And Social History Archive
102	Courtesy of UK Photo And Social History Archive
103	Courtesy of UK Photo And Social History Archive
104	Ministry of Information Photo Division Photographer, Public domain, via Wikimedia Commons
106	Courtesy of UK Photo And Social History Archive
129	Courtesy of Peter Hampson
132	Courtesy of Peter Hampson
138	Courtesy of Phil Bennett
139 (lower)	Courtesy of John Hannavy
142	The National Archives UK, via Wikimedia Commons
162 (lower)	Courtesy of Holger Schult
167	Courtesy of the United States Patent and Trademark Office
169	Courtesy of the United States Patent and Trademark Office
170	Courtesy of Holger Schult
171	Courtesy of Holger Schult
173	Courtesy of Holger Schult
186 (right)	Morio, CC BY-SA 3.0 via Wikimedia Commons
187	Courtesy of Jamie Buckling-Wade

Colour pages:

2 (upper & lower)	Courtesy of Charlie Kamerman
3 (upper)	Courtesy of John Hannavy
9 (lower)	Chalmers Butterfield, CC BY 2.5 via Wikimedia Commons
10 (upper)	Courtesy of Charlie Kamerman
16 (lower)	Courtesy of Byron Sinfield

All other pictures by the author (© John Wade) or from the author's private collection of snapshot images and postcards.

Index

Dear Reader,

We hope you have enjoyed this book, but why not share your views on social media? You can also follow our pages to see more about our other products: facebook.com/penandswordbooks or follow us on Twitter @penswordbooks

You can also view our products at www.pen-and-sword.co.uk (UK and ROW) or www.penandswordbooks.com (North America).

To keep up to date with our latest releases and online catalogues, please sign up to our newsletter at: www.pen-and-sword.co.uk/newsletter

If you would like a printed catalogue with our latest books, then please email: enquiries@pen-and-sword.co.uk or telephone: 01226 734555 (UK and ROW) or email: Uspen-and-sword@casematepublishers.com or telephone: (610) 853-9131 (North America).

We respect your privacy and we will only use personal information to send you information about our products.

Thank you!